Lecture Notes in Information Systems and Organisation

Volume 59

Lecture Notes in Information Systems and Organization—LNISO—is a series of scientific books that explore the current scenario of information systems, in particular IS and organization. The focus on the relationship between IT, IS and organization is the common thread of this collection, which aspires to provide scholars across the world with a point of reference and comparison in the study and research of information systems and organization. LNISO is the publication forum for the community of scholars investigating behavioral and design aspects of IS and organization. The series offers an integrated publication platform for high-quality conferences, symposia and workshops in this field. Materials are published upon a strictly controlled double blind peer review evaluation made by selected reviewers.

LNISO is abstracted/indexed in Scopus

Stefano Za · Robert Winter · Alessandra Lazazzara
Editors

Sustainable Digital Transformation

Paving the Way Towards Smart Organizations and Societies

Springer

Editors
Stefano Za
Department of Management
and Business Administration
University "G. d'Annunzio"
of Chieti-Pescara
Pescara, Italy

Robert Winter
Institute of Information Management
University of St. Gallen
St. Gallen, Switzerland

Alessandra Lazazzara
Department of Social
and Political Sciences
University of Milan
Milan, Italy

ISSN 2195-4968 ISSN 2195-4976 (electronic)
Lecture Notes in Information Systems and Organisation
ISBN 978-3-031-15769-1 ISBN 978-3-031-15770-7 (eBook)
https://doi.org/10.1007/978-3-031-15770-7

This Springer imprint is published by the registered company Springer Nature Switzerland AG
The registered company address is: Gewerbestrasse 11, 6330 Cham, Switzerland

Contents

Digital Transformation and Sustainability: A Means-Ends Perspective

Stefano Za, Robert Winter, and Alessandra Lazazzara

1 Introduction

Digital transformation (DT) and sustainability are disruptive imperatives leading to a paradigm shift in organizations and societies functioning in order to "meet the needs of the present without compromising the ability of future generations to meet their own needs" [1]. Aligning the sustainable development and digitalization goals represents a substantial challenge offering opportunities within and across organizational boundaries in order to paving the way toward pursuing the Sustainable Development Goals (SDGs). However, the emerging of a research interest on the intersection between digital technologies and sustainability is quite recent [2], and little is known about weather and to what extent DT could contribute to SDGs and how to enable a sustainable DT [3, 4].

Sustainability is commonly understood as a multi-dimensional concept that simultaneously refers to economic, ecological and social objectives [2]—an approach which is also known as the "three-pillar model". At the societal level, in order to navigate the sustainability challenges that humanity is facing (e.g., pollution, climate crisis, inequality and social tensions), the 2030 Agenda adopted by all United Nations Member States in 2015 has identified 17 SDGs and 169 targets supported over five pillars (i.e., planet, people, peace, prosperity, partnerships) [5]. This represents an

S. Za (✉)
Department of Management and Business Administration, University "G. d'Annunzio" of Chieti-Pescara, Pescara, Italy
e-mail: stefano.za@unich.it

R. Winter
University of St. Gallen, St. Gallen, Switzerland
e-mail: robert.winter@unisg.ch

A. Lazazzara
University of Milan, Milan, Italy
e-mail: alessandra.lazazzara@unimi.ti

S. Za et al. (eds.), *Sustainable Digital Transformation*, Lecture Notes in Information Systems and Organisation 59, https://doi.org/10.1007/978-3-031-15770-7_1

unprecedented global consensus and governance compass for bridging the so-called "sustainability gap", the divide between country's intentions and actual adoption of sustainable development-oriented policies [3]. Moreover, SDGs adoption has also raised a measurement concern as official data are not sufficient for monitoring them as they are affected by several shortcomings such as technical (e.g., high costs, data gaps) and political (e.g., artificially boosting metrics, lack of contextual details) issues [6]. So, not only the exponential adoption of digital technologies may contribute to create more sustainable patterns of production and consumption [2, 7], but may be considered as a source of more reliable analytic ecosystems (e.g., based on Big Data) or of new ways of collecting data leveraging on citizens' participation, thus generating new approaches to social accountancy and monitoring [8] and speeding up a transition toward sustainability.

Relating to the organizational perspective, sustainability is discussed in Information Systems [e.g., 2, 9] literature as an overarching corporate goal to which IS should contribute. However, a thorough understanding of how DT is a means toward sustainability and the interdependencies among the two is still missing [4]. Applying the "three-pillar model" to the company level, economic sustainability refers to ensuring the enduring reproduction of financial resources such as the capital invested by organizations yields sufficient returns on investment; ecological sustainability refers to the enduring reproduction of natural resources; and social sustainability refers to the enduring human health and well-being [10]. In these three subdomains, sustainability may be intended as the ultimate objective of DT, thus constituting its core objective, or as a guiding principle for designing and implementing DT within organizations. In other words, we may differentiate between two perspectives: sustainability by DT and sustainability in DT [2].

Adopting the first perspective, namely sustainability through DT, scholars focus on how the design of digital artifacts and their adoption may support the achievement of sustainable goals both at the organizational and societal level. For example, digitalization may promote climate protection through smart devices, automated decision-making systems or virtual reality application [11]. Similarly, artificial intelligence (AI) has been adopted in order to develop monitoring technique or warning and forecasting systems for climate change [12]. Moreover, as regards inequality, digital technologies are seen as means to equalize access to opportunities to everyone, such for example advances in digital payments infrastructure and machine learning adoption that are enhancing access to credit for otherwise marginalized subpopulations [13]. In this sense, digital transformation is interpreted as a "problem solver" for improving sustainability. However, it may also be seen as a "fire accelerator" because it is increasing the consumption of natural resources, thereby exacerbating environmental issues and perpetuating or amplifying social injustice and inequality [14]. Thus, a first challenge in IS research is to understand how DT may contribute to the sustainable development and preventing negative effect on economic, ecological and social dimensions.

Adopting the second perspective, namely sustainability in DT, the focus is on how the DT itself can be designed such that the transformation it introduces is sustainable. Traditionally, sustainability in technology has mainly been understood from a techno-centric perspective, according to which the systems' design was aimed at more sustainable patterns of production and consumption and at an increase of the longevity of the digital artifacts [2]. However, DT is an overarching phenomenon which is not only related to technology adoption, but also to a transformative organizational change. Indeed, DT may lead to changing structural (e.g., business models, processes) and human-related (e.g., behaviours, capabilities, mindset) aspects of organizations in order to respond to strategic challenges and alter the value creation paths they have previously relied upon to remain competitive [15]. Therefore, in order to reach a sustainable DT, organizations have to explore the complex social and organizational interactions with technology in order to align the intent behind DT with organizational characteristics and goals. Therefore, the second challenge is to uncover how DT can be designed and implemented more sustainable according to the organizational context and which indicators may measure such fit.

The 17 chapters contained in this volume are revised versions of selected contributions presented at the XVIII Conference of the Italian Chapter of AIS (ItAIS 2021), held at the University of Trento on October 15th–16th, 2021, selected through a double-blind review process. They are grouped in two different sections according to the primary perspective they adopt: *sustainability by DT* and *sustainability in DT,* respectively. These contributions provide a plurality of views that makes this book particularly relevant for scholars but also for practitioners, managers, and policy makers whose concern is to better understand and the complex interrelationships between DT and sustainability, and to consider sustainability issues in DT design and implementation decisions.

2 Sustainability Through Digital Transformation

The first five chapters of this section take into consideration the role of technology for addressing and/or analysing sustainability issues, specifically focusing on the economic ecosystem and financial perspectives. Beretta et al. focus on the disclosure of non-financial information (NFI)—used for reporting sustainability practices—and specifically on the role of the Information Technology (IT) for providing reliable non-financial information. Through a multiple case study analysis, the scholars show that digital accounting information systems have a pivotal role for data collection and for the programming phase, underling also the need to address some security issues in the collection process. Abid et al. investigate the relationship between green orientation and crowdfunding campaign success. The authors used both qualitative and quantitative approaches to build the green orientation index, analysing 210 green campaigns out of 720 crowdfunding campaigns. Based on a cluster analysis, they identify and discuss the characteristics of three clusters of green-oriented crowdfunding campaigns: *social enthusiast*, *green fan*, and *tech-oriented*. In the cluster results discussion, the authors highlight how the *tech-oriented* cluster obtains the highest value and has a positive relationship with the amount raised and crowdfunding's success. Focusing on the business ecosystem, Zoppelletto and Cuel present a case study in which they analyse Gamindo, a multi-sided digital platform that offers gamified services addressing the needs of three different categories of actors: firms, non-profit organizations, and gamers. The analysis explores the interdependencies among the actors/stakeholders, where the Gamindo ecosystem can be seen as a catalyst for purpose-driven complementary actors willing to address the challenges of sustainability, resulting in positive outcomes for the environment and the society. Mansha et al. investigate the role of political connections in the directors' network for enterprise ecosystem in a developing country. The authors used data from a relationship-based economy like Pakistan from 2009 to 2015, creating a network of directors that are connected if they share the same board. The graph describes the direct and indirect interlocking among the firms. Among several analysis, the authors used the eccentricity for investigating the influence of each politician in the network, analysing its decrease across the years in relation to the democratic elections happened after the regime change and so contributing to understanding the role of political sustainability in SMEs development. Finally, Javed and Rapposelli investigate the symmetric and asymmetric effects of oil price, foreign direct investments and economic growth on carbon emissions in Italy. The symmetric results show that economic growth and foreign direct investments intensify carbon emissions both in the long and short-run, while the impact of oil price on emissions is negative in the long-run and positive in the short-run, suggesting that oil price is responsible for environmental degradation only in the short run. The asymmetric results reveal that both in the long and short-run an increase in the oil price produces reductions in carbon emission.

The last four chapters of this section are mainly focused on social aspects. Raucci and Paolini investigate the increasing engagement of doctors in accounting and managerial practices, mainly planning and budgeting, in Italian Public Healthcare Organizations (PHOs). Specifically, the authors analyse doctor-managers' resistance to use budgetary information for decision-making and the role played by the perceived openness in communication (POC) and the perceived utility of budgetary information. Zanutto et al. focus on cardiology telemonitoring exploring the technology adoption in the healthcare system. Through the analysis of the processes performed by two cardiological departments, the authors investigate the main differences and performance concerning the organizational arrangements in adopting similar digital solutions aimed at supporting the same organizational processes. Varriale et al. investigate how digital technologies can make museums 'smart' and 'inclusive' by engaging visitors, especially people with special needs. Adopting a bottom-up approach and a participatory design, this exploratory and qualitative study describes the design and development of a specific App for children with autism syndrome called 'A dip in the Blue' of archaeological museum located in Southern Italy (The Archaeological Museum of Paestum and Velia). Beyond some theoretical and practical implications concerning the design process, the chapter provides some effective best practices for museums to become smarter and more inclusive through digital technologies. Finally, Marchesani et al. provide a systematic literature review examining the relationship between smart cities and the internationalization process. The authors put an emphasis especially on global management strategies for the international development of smart cities.

3 Sustainability in Digital Transformation

The first three chapters of this section discuss some issues that could contribute to promote and sustain a digital transformation process. Abid et al. focus on firms' digitalization process in the Southern Italy. Specifically, the authors investigate the existing relationship between Southern Italian cities' digitalization and firms' financial capabilities and institutional support. The study provides some suggestions, especially targeting policy-makers, in order to make the digital transformation process more sustainable. Mayer et al. focus on the digitalization of the Enterprise performance management (EPM). As transformations towards digital EPM are challenging, the aim of the authors is to develop a forward-looking maturity model to support companies in their EPM digitalization process, making managers more confident in working with data and business analytics tools. De Simone et al. also focus on data issues, such as data value chain and data ecosystem. In order to be able to fully reap the value of data available, firms must delve in big data and Data Value Chain (DVC) discipline. This chapter explores the ecosystem formation as well as the challenges and criticalities encountered by two firms operating in the drones' market. Ecosystems are networks of distributed companies that show multiple links toward their environment to interact via standard and business rules which permit them to be independent but also connected. As a result, the authors found that successful big data integration, accessibility, and standard business rules will allow firms in data-driven sectors, and in particular in computer vision-based data set, to be efficient in the interconnection and to become more agile.

The following two chapters explore issues concerning platform and their ecosystems adopting two different approaches. Schmid develops an agent-based simulation model describing a platform within its surrounding business ecosystem. The simulation model enables a flexible investigation of platform governance decisions and broader environmental conditions. Experimentation results reveal platforms as ineffective at fostering generativity and profitability in low complexity environments, implying platforms to not be uniformly promising or disruptive in all kinds of competitive environments. Thus, the main contribution of this study is an agent-based simulation model to help understand and predict outcomes of platforms as complex phenomena. Staub intends Platform ecosystems as complex ecologies of firms with individual, sometimes conflicting, interests and goals. The aim of the chapter is to explore the role of the platform owners as orchestrator of the ecosystem. He conducted an in-depth study of Salesforce, a thriving B2B platform ecosystem in the enterprise software industry. The study reveals the platform owner made significant resource investments to implement governance mechanisms based on innovative activities. Moreover, the governance mechanisms in B2B platform ecosystems are differently implemented respect to consumer-focused platform ecosystems.

Finally, the last three chapters provide the results of three literature reviews. Mohtar and Badr explore the implication in term of healthcare service sustainability derived by COVID pandemic. Specifically, the authors explore the outcomes associated with the implementation of telehealth technology in healthcare ecosystems. The authors aim to learn from the literature on the impact of Telehealth diffusion on the delivery of quality care. They develop a scoping review and evaluate the outcome through the lens of the six aims of improvement of healthcare quality. Moreover, the authors synthesize the literature around managing the disruption, identifying the risks of unintended consequences and factors affecting adoption. Cipriano and Za discuss Digital Transformation (DT) initiatives focusing on the non-profit organisations (NPOs). Specifically, this study starts from the taxonomy of the literature debating DT in NPOs developed in a previous study. The authors use that classification as dataset for applying some exploratory multivariate techniques performing a cluster analysis. As a result, the authors identify nine clusters recognising some recurrent patterns which would describe DT initiatives in NPOs. Finally, Smit et al. in their literature review, focus on the blockchain. They consider it as an emerging technology with the potential to disrupt and enable collaboration in ecosystem structures, where a proper governance could ensure sustainable growth of a blockchain solution. Through a systematic literature review, the authors compare the empirical approach with the theoretical one by looking at existing dimensions and characteristics that define blockchain governance. Among other contributions, as a practical implication, the taxonomy could support blockchain professionals to design their blockchain governance in a sustainable way.

References

1. World Commission on Environment and Development: Our Common Future. Oxford (1987)
2. Hilty, L.M., Aebischer, B.: Ict for sustainability: an emerging research field. In: Advances in Intelligent Systems and Computing, pp. 3–36. Springer Verlag (2015). https://doi.org/10.1007/978-3-319-09228-7_1
3. del Río Castro, G., González Fernández, M.C., Uruburu Colsa, Á.: Unleashing the convergence amid digitalization and sustainability towards pursuing the Sustainable Development Goals (SDGs): A holistic review (2021). https://doi.org/10.1016/j.jclepro.2020.122204
4. Herberger, T.A., Dötsch Editors, J.J.: Digitalization, digital transformation and sustainability in the global economy risks and opportunities (2021)
5. UN (United Nations): General Assembly Resolution 70/1 (2015)—Transforming our world: the 2030 Agenda for Sustainable Development. (2015)
6. Ballerini, L., Bergh, S.I.: Using citizen science data to monitor the sustainable development goals: a bottom-up analysis. Sustain. Sci. **16**, 1945–1962 (2021). https://doi.org/10.1007/s11625-021-01001-1
7. Ghobakhloo, M., Fathi, M., Iranmanesh, M., Maroufkhani, P., Morales, M.E.: Industry 4.0 ten years on: A bibliometric and systematic review of concepts, sustainability value drivers, and success determinants, (2021). https://doi.org/10.1016/j.jclepro.2021.127052.
8. Cappa, F., Franco, S., Rosso, F.: Citizens and cities: leveraging citizen science and big data for sustainable urban development. Bus. Strateg. Environ. **31**, 648–667 (2022). https://doi.org/10.1002/bse.2942
9. Hanelt, A., Busse, S., Kolbe, L.M.: Driving business transformation toward sustainability: exploring the impact of supporting IS on the performance contribution of eco-innovations. Inf. Syst. J. **27**, 463–502 (2017). https://doi.org/10.1111/isj.12130
10. Strohmeier, S.: Sustainable electronic HRM. In: Encyclopedia of Electronic HRM, pp. 138–143. De Gruyter (2020). https://doi.org/10.1515/9783110633702-021

11. Schieweck, A., Uhde, E., Salthammer, T., Salthammer, L.C., Morawska, L., Mazaheri, M., Kumar, P.: Smart homes and the control of indoor air quality (2018). https://doi.org/10.1016/j.rser.2018.05.057
12. Nishant, R., Kennedy, M., Corbett, J.: Artificial intelligence for sustainability: challenges, opportunities, and a research agenda. Int. J. Inf. Manag. **53**, (2020). https://doi.org/10.1016/j.ijinfomgt.2020.102104
13. Tantri, P.: Fintech for the poor: financial intermediation without discrimination. Rev. Financ. **25**, 561–593 (2021). https://doi.org/10.1093/rof/rfaa039
14. Lenz, S.: Is digitalization a problem solver or a fire accelerator? Situating digital technologies in sustainability discourses. Soc. Sci. Inf. **60**, 188–208 (2021). https://doi.org/10.1177/05390184211012179
15. Vial, G.: Understanding digital transformation: a review and a research agenda. J. Strateg. Inf. Syst. **28**, 118–144 (2019)

Sustainability Through Digital Transformation

Digital Accounting Information System for Non-financial Disclosure: A Case Study Analysis

Valentina Beretta, Maria Chiara Demartini, and Sara Trucco

Abstract The disclosure of non-financial information (NFI) is becoming more and more relevant worldwide, especially after the directive 2014/95/EU. The relevance of the preparation of the non-financial information is increasing even with regard to the role of the Information Technology (IT) system. The review of the prior literature, indeed, shows a gap in the analysis of which are the most effective IT audit tools and procedures that may be used for providing reliable non-financial information. The main aim of this research is to analyze the role of the IT in the preparation ad in supporting the control of the reliability of non-financial data. In order to reach the research aims, we apply a qualitative case study based on interviews and the triangulation of this evidence with a secondary source (such as an annual report or a non-financial disclosure). Therefore, researchers, thought an exploratory approach, carried out semi-structured type interviews. We selected three case studies listed on the Milan Stock Exchange market. The interviewees were actors responsible or substantially involved in the process of the non-financial information. Results of our research show that collecting and reporting data for non-financial disclosure by using a digital accounting information system represents a great challenge for the company. The interviewee stated that the digital accounting information systems are pivotal for the data collection and for the programming phase. Results show that collecting information in a more secure way is needed.

Keywords Digital accounting information · Non-financial information · Case study analysis

V. Beretta · M. C. Demartini
University of Pavia, Pavia, Italy

S. Trucco (✉)
Università degli Studi Internazionali di Roma, Roma, Italy
e-mail: sara.trucco@unint.eu

S. Za et al. (eds.), *Sustainable Digital Transformation*, Lecture Notes in Information Systems and Organisation 59, https://doi.org/10.1007/978-3-031-15770-7_2

1 Introduction

The disclosure of non-financial that is environmental, social and governance-related (ESG) information is becoming more and more important worldwide, especially after the introduction of the directive 2014/95/EU "*disclosure of non-financial and diversity information*" (Bozzolan et al. 2003; Caglio et al. 2020; Merkl-Davies and Brennan 2007). In particular, the mentioned directive may help firms in disclosing high quality, relevant, useful, consistent and more comparable non-financial information in order to be transparent especially with external stakeholders. Hence, starting from the fiscal year 2017, according to the directive 2014/95/EU, larger companies are obliged to disclose some kinds of non-financial information by following a "comply or explain" approach (Hummel et al. 2020). Indeed, scholars agree that disclosing non-financial information is useful to reduce the information asymmetry between external and internal stakeholders, to attract investors and to improve the firm's consensus and reputation among stakeholders (Dhaliwal et al. 2011). Therefore, professional associations and academics agree that an increase of such information should help companies in creating long-lasting value. Moreover, some scholars have pointed out that even financial analysts seem to positively perceive the relevance of the non-financial information and the non-financial indicators (Breton and Taffler 2001; Rogers and Grant 1997).

However, the company's reputation and the value relevance of the information disclosed may increase only if the corporate disclosure is reliable (Anderson 1998). Previous studies stated that external assurance on non-financial disclosure might bring about positive effects on the perceived credibility of such types of information (Brown-Liburd and Zamora 2015; Pflugrath et al. 2011). As since the introduction of the European directive, the non-financial information became mandatory for large companies, some regulations are needed for helping external auditors in carrying out tests and procedures to verify the reliability of data. In the Italian setting, for instance, Consob requires that companies may choose between two different kinds of external assurance on non-financial information, which are are limited assurance and reasonable assurance.

On the other hand, relevant criticisms of the non-financial reporting process are the lack of standardized metrics to assess non-financial performance and a lack of a generally accepted framework (at both national and international level) to guarantee the reliability of the non-financial information. Indeed, formal relationships between the different internal stakeholders in the preparation of the non-financial information are often replaced by informal ones. Since the reporting of sustainability practices is an ongoing process, more informal channels are used to share non-financial information between different teams (Toth 2012).

The relevance of the preparation of the non-financial information is increasing even with regard to the role of the Information Technology (IT) system (Barth et al. 2017; Ergüden et al. 2017; Healy and Palepu 2001). Indeed, the IT system should preserve the property and integrity of data, and should help firms and managers to align IT requirements with business goals, by defining useful IT governance policies (Moeller 2010). A weak IT system may bring about material misstatements in corporate reporting; such risks linked to a weak IT system may negatively affect the integrity, accuracy, completeness, reality and availability of company's reports (Klamm and Watson 2009). The reliability of corporate reports relies mainly on IT system and internal controls, and scholars agree that there is a link between the features of the IT system and a well-designed internal control system (Daneila et al. 2013).

Recent studies highlight an increasing interest on IT audit and on its role in improving the overall quality of information in a firm (Stoel and Havelka 2021). Some scholars focused their research on the role that IT auditors have in helping firms meet compliance requirements and verifying the ability of IT system to create value to the company (Dzuranin and Mălăescu 2016).

However, the review of the prior literature carried out by studying papers in academic journals founded in the major scientific databases (such as ebsco-host and google scholars) shows a gap in the analysis of which are the most effective IT audit tools and procedures that may be used for providing reliable non-financial information. Therefore, the main aim of this research is to analyze, through a qualitative research method based on interviews, the role of the digital accounting information in the preparation of non-financial disclosure and in supporting the control of the reliability of non-financial data. Therefore, the research questions that the paper attempts to answers are: *RQ1: To which extent is IT able to support the data collection into the firm? RQ2: To which extent is IT able to support the predisposition of the NFI? RQ3: To which extent is IT able to support the control of the reliability of data?*

The remainder of the paper is organized as follows: Sect. 2 analyses literature review and presents the research questions; Sect. 3 presents research methodology; Sects. 4 and 5 present results, discussion, limitations and future developments of the research.

2 Theoretical Background

Accounting Information System (AIS) produces knowledge from data and ensures efficiency of the operations and effectiveness of reliability of financial and non-financial data and legal compliance (Toth 2012); therefore, the quality of reporting system is related to the quality of the entire data elaboration process. This process thus supports the decision-making process (Madnick et al. 2009), since one of the main aims of the AIS is to support decisions by providing the right information, in the right time at the right person (Fischer 2012), thereby communicating useful information to both external and internal stakeholders (Teru et al. 2017). Indeed, some studies found that the quality of the decision-making process depends on the quality of data produced by the AIS (Calvasina et al. 2009; Caserio 2011; Fisher et al. 2016) and on the consistency between the architecture of data and structure of the business (Vasile and Mirela 2008). One of the most advanced integrated IT tools used by firms are represented by Enterprise Resource Planning systems (ERP) (Granlund and Malmi 2002). These tools are useful to collect and integrate data by using a common database, and thus they represent the basis for a good information flow inside the firm and for the overall accounting process (Chapman and Kihn 2009).

Literature about advantages related of having an ERP, and more in general a digital accounting information system, is quite abundant; in particular some scholars highlight that the adoption of a new IT system may produce some effects on both financial and non-financial performance indexes (Florescu 2007; Skibniewski and Ghosh 2009; Trucco and Corsi 2014). In general, an IT adoption is useful to integrate business departments and processes, thereby reducing the business process complexity (Broadbent et al. 1999; Karim et al. 2007). Within this context, a stream of literature focuses on the crucial role that a digital accounting information system can have in fostering the relationship between external financial information and internal managerial information. Indeed, the IT system could reduce the gap between financial accounting information and management accounting information and between internal and external stakeholders (Caglio 2003; Innes and Mitchell 1990; Taipaleenmäki and Ikäheimo 2013).

However, other scholars focus their studies on the risks and costs related to the IT system adoption, by highlighting that the most relevant risk related to the strategic investment of having a new IT is that the failure of the IT adoption could even lead to firm's bankruptcy (Davenport 1998; Markus et al. 2000). Furthermore, some scholars found that some IT investments (such as the adoption of a new ERP system) would allow managers to use more discretion in the preparation of accounting information and thus to favor data manipulation (Brazel and Dang 2008). Costs related of having the AIS are both monetary and relative to the human resources required to adopt and manage the IT system within the firm (Granlund and Malmi 2002). Nevertheless, scholars agree the effects of AIS adoption should be analysed through a holistic viewpoint (Gattiker and Goodhue 2005), since the process of AIS adoption deeply affects the entire company and each function (Rose and Kræmmergaard 2006). Several studies investigated the effect of the AIS adoption on corporate performance measured by financial, organizational and social indexes, by highlighting mixed results about it (Nicolaou 2004; Poston and Grabski 2001; Trucco and Corsi 2014).

Therefore, the analysis of the prior literature about this topic shows mixed results about the support of the IT system on the data collection into the firm and, to the best of our knowledge little is known about the support of the IT system to the predisposition of the NFI. On the basis of this theoretical background and with the aim to fill the mentioned gap in the literature, the research questions are expressed as follows:

RQ1: To which extent is IT able to support the data collection into the firm?

RQ2: To which extent is IT able to support the predisposition of the NFI?

The relevance of the role of the IT system within the context of a firm is increasing even with regard to the provision and to the assurance of the non-financial information, since non-reliable data may damage the competitiveness of firms (Barth et al. 2017; Ergüden et al. 2017; Xu 2009). Sajady et al. pointed out that the adoption of AIS may lead to a more effective internal control and a general improvement of the quality of financial disclosure and of the business transactions. We argue that similar considerations may be extended to the side of the quality of the non-financial disclosure. Moreover, some scholars examined the effects of the information system on the level of honesty in managerial reports, by finding that the presence of an IT system increases managerial honesty, even if, according to previous studies, the honesty is lower when the IT system is accurate and vice versa (Hannan et al. 2006).

Despite these considerations, Brazel and Dang found a decrease in the reliability of financial disclosure in the years after the AIS had been adopted; this could happen because of a potential increase in the discretion that managers may use in the predisposition of accounting information (Brazel and Dang 2008). In fact, AIS allow managers greater access and control of financial information (Dillon 1999).

However, the analysis of the prior literature shows a gap regarding the IT audit tools and procedures that may be used for providing reliable non-financial information and for carrying out the assurance of non-financial disclosure; when the AIS is not well designed and built, the system is not able to produce useful information to satisfy stakeholders' needs. Therefore, recent studies show an increasing interest on IT audit and on the consequent overall quality improvement inside the company (Alagic et al. 2018) and some scholars has called for additional research in the area of the IT audit in general area (Curtis et al. 2009; Weidenmier and Ramamoorti 2006). Furthermore, there is little practical guidance for guarantee the reliability of non-financial disclosure from both internal and external viewpoint (Cohen and Simnett 2015).

We grounded our study on the legitimacy theory (Hopwood 2009) and the impression management approach, since the existence of an IT in a firm could represent a signal for external stakeholders, which allows them to make inferences of the quality of the disclosure (Hannan et al. 2006).

On the basis of these considerations, the last research question is expressed as follow:

RQ3: To which extent is IT able to support the control of the reliability of data?

3 Methodology

In order to reach the research aims and to answer the research questions, we apply an interpretive perspective through a qualitative approach. More specifically, the researchers' observations based on their contact with the interviewees have been combined with the triangulation of this evidence with secondary sources (Toth 2012).

In general, this approach allows scholars to improve the quality of the research: indeed, it was possible to understand the experience and perceptions of the participants inside the firms as well as to have insights on the corporate reporting and NFI. Semi-structured interviews have been carried out by the researchers thought an exploratory approach (Yin and Moore 1988). Three different case studies have been selected since they provide rich and insightful descriptions of different perceptions of a phenomenon (Yin and Moore 1988). Five interviewees took part to the study.

Privacy and confidentiality have been ensured by conducting the interviews in a environment and modality that have been jointly chosen by the researcher and the respondents and by adopting an informal and conversational tone. By adopting the Framework Method, the interviews have been recorded using a digital voice-recording device in order to ensure the verbatim transcription of the interview, followed by the familiarization of the researchers with the topic and the interpretation of the results.

We selected three case studies listed on the Milan Stock Exchange market. The interviewees were actors responsible or substantially involved in the process of the non-financial information.

The semi-structured interviews are focused on the investigation of the role of IT in three main areas, which are the data collection phase, the support for the predisposition of NFI and for the control of the reliability of data. The questionnaire was structured as follows:

- Are you obliged to disclose non-financial information according to the directive 2014/95/EU? If so, did you start drafting the NFI only after being subjected to the obligation? If not, who in the company proposed the drafting of the NFS? How long ago did the process start?
- How are the various corporate roles usually mostly engaged in the corporate information flow, such as the Chief Financial Officer, the Investor Relator and the Controller, involved in the process of developing corporate communication with particular reference to NFI?
- Is your non-financial disclosure subject to assurance? If so external/internal? If it is subject to external review, what tests are carried out to verify its reliability? How can company information systems help internal and/or external auditors in carrying out their functions to verify the reliability of the information?
- How can company information systems support the integration process between the area of financial accounting and that of management accounting?

Furthermore, we downloaded the NFI of the selected firms from their websites in order to have a better understanding of the creation process of the corporate reporting.

4 Results

Results of our research show that collecting and reporting data for non-financial disclosure by using a digital accounting information system represents a great challenge for the companies included in the sample. The interviewees stated that the digital accounting information systems are pivotal for the data collection and for the programming phase. Results show that collecting information in a more secure way is needed.

"Alpha" is a big bank (with more than 2,000 employees and more than 200 branches in different Italian regions) which is listed on the Milan Stock Exchange market, subject to the obligation of the non-financial disclosure. The interviewee, represented by the head of financial statements and sustainability, has been actively involved in the preparation of (non)financial disclosures since 2016.

Results show that different actors and data sources are involved in the preparation of non-financial disclosure through an unstructured process. IT plays a fundamental role in collecting data, even if thus fur the collection of financial and non-financial data occurs separately. However, the expectation for the future is to have the same data collection tool/software for both the typologies of data required. In addition, the interviewee stated that IT provides support also in checking the truthfulness of data, not only during the collection phase, but also in the control one.

"Beta" is an information provider mid cap company which is listed on the Milan Stock Exchange market and that employs 2,600 people in 45 Italian operational or commercial branches. The interviewees are the head of investor relations and the CFO.

Results show that there are two different systems, one for accounting and the other for human resources, which are used to collect all the relevant financial and non-financial data. As for the case of "Alpha", the expectation for the future is to have a single system. IT supports the internal control of the truthfulness of data, before the external control of the auditors.

"Gamma" is a service company, which manage different airports, and it represents one of the most important airport systems in Italy. The interview has been conducted with the controller who is also responsible for the non-financial disclosure. As for the previous cases, since Gamma is a listed firm, therefore it is obliged to prepare and disclose the NFD.

Results show that both electronic and in paper format registries are used in data collection phase. Differently from the previous cases, financial accounting and management accounting areas are integrated and, therefore, there is integration also between financial and non-financial information. IT is of a great support in this case for the exploitation of data and databases generated by SAP (the software used by the firm) by auditors, thus in the control phase.

Results related to the role of IT in support of the data collection phase, the predisposition of NFI and the control of the reliability of data are provided in Table 1.

5 Discussion, Limitations and Future Development

The main aim of this paper is to analyze the role of the digital accounting information in the preparation of non-financial disclosure and in supporting the control of the reliability of non-financial data. Indeed, previous studies underlined a gap in the literature with reference to the use of audit tools and procedures that may be adopted in preparing NFI (Alagic et al. 2018; Cohen and Simnett 2015; Curtis et al. 2009; Weidenmier and Ramamoorti 2006). While it is common knowledge that IT could help collecting and systematizing data, little is known about how it could be done.

Table 1 Results description

	IT to support the data collection	*IT to support the predisposition of NFI*	*IT to support the control of the reliability of data*
Alpha	• Different actors and different data sources involved • Unstructured process	• State of the art: not integrated • In the future: the same society for collecting both financial and non-financial information	• Checking of the truthfulness in both data collection and control phases
Beta	• Two systems (accounting and human resources) cover the data collection for all the group • In the future: integration of a sustainability system	• In the process of having a single ERP	• Checking of the truthfulness of data internally, before the auditors' controls
Gamma	• Both electronic and in paper format registries	• Integration between financial accounting management accounting areas and between the financial information and the non-financial one	• Exploitation of data and databases generated by SAP (the software used by the firm) by auditors

The study contributes to the literature in several ways. First, it contributes to the literature of mandatory non-financial disclosure, by highlighting the relevance of having a formal template and a framework in favoring the process of collection and predisposition of information and improving the quality of the non-financial reports (Doni et al. 2019).

Second, the research contributes to the literature on AIS, by highlighting the relevance of AIS in supporting the process of predisposition of the corporate reporting and the control of reliability of financial and non-financial information (Toth 2012).

Third, the research contributes to the stream of literature which consider an AIS/ERP as a facilitator, motivator and even and enabler for the integration between the area of financial accounting and that one of management accounting (Lukka 2007; Trucco 2015). In fact, the non-financial information, more qualitative in nature and future oriented than the financial information push firms to use sophisticated and integrated IT system able to create a common database.

Results of this study provide evidence for the support provided by IT in ensuring reliability of financial and non-financial data (Toth 2012). Thus, adopting IT systems in collecting NFI provides support for the decision making process as well (Fischer 2012; Madnick et al. 2009). According to previous studies, indeed, the quality of the decision-making process is related to the one of the data produced (Calvasina et al. 2009; Caserio 2011; Fisher et al. 2016).

This study provides also evidence that the adoption of an IT system in collecting NFI is useful for the integration of different processes and, also, of the different disclosures of the company (Broadbent et al. 1999; Karim et al. 2007). More specifically, the gap between financial and non-financial information could be reduced

(Caglio 2003; Innes and Mitchell 1990; Taipaleenmäki and Ikäheimo 2013). In addition, more discretion in adopted in the preparation of NFI when investments in IT are made (Brazel and Dang 2008).

To conclude, results of this study largely support the relevance of IT in the control of the reliability of data. As argued by Sajady et al. more effective internal and external control can be exerted when IT is adopted, since it allows managers greater access and control of both financial and non-financial information (Dillon 1999).

The findings of this study should be of interest to national and international practitioners and standard setters, since it increases the awareness and the relevance for firms of having proper AIS able to satisfy different stakeholders' needs. Firms can benefit from the present study in several ways: it can support managers in increasing the awareness of having proper AIS. Firms may also benefit from the study in defining a new managerial profile able to manage information flows among different functions and departments in the firm. Furthermore, it can support managers in choosing the level of integration of the accounting system, taking into account the possibility of exploiting endogenous factors to increase the level of convergence between financial accounting information and management accounting information.

Within this framework, future research may be helpful in order to extend the knowledge with regard to the support of IT in the corporate reporting process and in the assurance of the reliability of financial and non-financial information. In doing so, some research questions arise:

- Do firms need to hire some new skills or to develop training courses in the area of IT?;
- Do standard setters or national/international accounting association need to develop new standards or rules to help firms in using IT system for the NFI creation process?;
- How policy makers can help firms in supporting the process of IT assurance of NFI?

Finally, the present work lays the groundwork for new frontiers of research. Indeed, this research is not without limitations. First of all the research is carried out on three case studies in the Italian context, therefore more case studies could be analyzed and more countries could be selected in the future development in order to do comparison among different setting. Second, the method of the interview is based on the perceptions of interviewees; therefore, caution needs to be used to generalize results to other companies, which belong to different setting and different industrial sector. Furthermore, it could be interesting to extend the context of this analysis to other top managers in order to understand the diversity of perceptions among different cultures and different managerial roles.

References

Alagic, A., Turulja, L., Bajgoric, N.: IT audit quality factors identification in the function of business continuity: a systematic, 9th International Conference of the School of Economics and Business, p. 1. University of Sarajevo, School of Economics and Business Trg oslobodjenja ...(2018)

Anderson, R.H., Regulating corporate annual reports in Australia. Business and economic history (1998)

Barth, M.E., Cahan, S.F., Chen, L., Venter, E.R.: The economic consequences associated with integrated report quality: capital market and real effects. Account., Organ. Soc., Elsevier **62**(2017), 43–64 (2017)

Bozzolan, S., Favotto, F., Ricceri, F.: Italian annual intellectual capital disclosure: an empirical analysis. J. Intellect. Cap., MCB Ltd **4**(4), 543–558 (2003)

Brazel, J.F., Dang, L.: The effect of ERP system implementations on the management of earnings and earnings release dates. J. Inf. Syst. **22**(2), 1–21 (2008)

Breton, G., Taffler, R.J.: Accounting information and analyst stock recommendation decisions: a content analysis approach. Account. Bus. Res., Taylor & Francis **31**(2), 91–101 (2001)

Broadbent, M., Weill, P., St. Clair, D. The implications of information technology infrastructure for business process redesign, MIS Quarterly, pp. 159–182. JSTOR (1999)

Brown-Liburd, H., Zamora, V.L.: "The role of corporate social responsibility (CSR) assurance in investors' judgments when managerial pay is explicitly tied to CSR performance". Audit.: J. Pract. & Theory Am. Account. Assocation **34**(1), 75–96 (2015)

Caglio, A.: Enterprise resource planning systems and accountants: towards hybridization? Eur. Account. Rev., Taylor & Francis **12**(1), 123–153 (2003)

Caglio, A., Melloni, G., Perego, P.: Informational content and assurance of textual disclosures: evidence on integrated reporting. Eur. Account. Rev., Taylor & Francis **29**(1), 55–83 (2020)

Calvasina, R., Calvasina, E., Ramaswamy, M., Calvasina, G., Cedar City, U.T.: Data quality problems in responsibility accounting. Issues Inf. Syst. X **2**, 48–57 (2009)

Caserio, C. Relationships between ERP and business intelligence: an empirical research on two different upgrade approaches, Information Technology and Innovation Trends in Organizations, pp. 363–370. Springer (2011)

Chapman, C.S., Kihn, L.-A.: Information system integration, enabling control and performance. Account., Organ. Soc., Elsevier **34**(2), 151–169 (2009)

Cohen, J.R., Simnett, R.: "CSR and assurance services: A research agenda." Audit.: J. Pract. & Theory, American Accounting Assocation **34**(1), 59–74 (2015)

Curtis, M.B., Jenkins, J.G., Bedard, J.C., Deis, D.R.: Auditors' training and proficiency in information systems: a research synthesis. J. Inf. Syst. **23**(1), 79–96 (2009)

Daneila, M., Vassen, E.H.J., Dameri, R.P.: Accounting information system for decision making. Springer-Verlag, Berlin (2013)

Davenport, T.H. Putting the enterprise into the enterprise system, vol. 76, no. 4, Harvard Business Review (1998)

Dhaliwal, D.S., Li, O.Z., Tsang, A., Yang, Y.G.: Voluntary nonfinancial disclosure and the cost of equity capital: the initiation of corporate social responsibility reporting. Account. Rev. **86**(1), 59–100 (2011)

Dillon, C. Stretching toward enterprise flexibility with ERP, APICS-the performance advantage (1999)

Doni, F., Martini, S.B., Corvino, A., Mazzoni, M.: Voluntary versus mandatory non-financial disclosure: EU Directive 95/2014 and sustainability reporting practices based on empirical evidence from Italy. Emerald Publishing Limited, Meditari Accountancy Research (2019)

Dzuranin, A.C., Mălăescu, I.: The current state and future direction of IT audit: challenges and opportunities. J. Inf. Syst., American Accounting Association **30**(1), 7–20 (2016)

Ergüden, A.E., Kaya, C.T., Sayar, A.R.Z.: Integrated assurance for non-financial reporting. Int. J. Econ., Commer. Manag. **1**, 72–81 (2017)

Fischer, G. (2012) Context-aware systems: the 'right' information, at the 'right' time, in the 'right' place, in the 'right' way, to the 'right' person. Proceedings of the International Working Conference on Advanced Visual Interfaces, pp. 287–294
Fisher, E.S., Shortell, S.M., Savitz, L.A.: Implementation science: a potential catalyst for delivery system reform. Jama, American Medical Association **315**(4), 339–340 (2016)
Florescu, V. TIC et performance de l'entreprise: un modèle général d'analyse, Revue Repères Economique et Informatiques, No. 2 (2007)
Gattiker, T.F., Goodhue, D.L. What happens after ERP implementation: understanding the impact of interdependence and differentiation on plant-level outcomes", MIS Quarterly, pp. 559–585. JSTOR (2005)
Granlund, M., Malmi, T.: Moderate impact of ERPS on management accounting: a lag or permanent outcome? Manag. Account. Res., Elsevier **13**(3), 299–321 (2002)
Hannan, R.L., Rankin, F.W., Towry, K.L.: The effect of information systems on honesty in managerial reporting: a behavioral perspective. Contemp. Account. Res., Wiley Online Library **23**(4), 885–918 (2006)
Healy, P.M., Palepu, K.G.: Information asymmetry, corporate disclosure, and the capital markets: a review of the empirical disclosure literature. J. Account. Econ. **31**(1), 405–440 (2001)
Hopwood, A.G.: Accounting and the environment. Acc. Organ. Soc. **34**(3), 433–439 (2009)
Hummel, K., Mittelbach-Hoermanseder, S., Cho, C.H., Matten, D. Corporate social responsibility disclosure: a topic-based approach. Available at SSRN 3090976 (2020)
Innes, J., Mitchell, F.: The process of change in management accounting: some field study evidence. Manag. Account. Res., Elsevier **1**(1), 3–19 (1990)
Karim, J., Somers, T.M., Bhattacherjee, A.: The impact of ERP implementation on business process outcomes: a factor-based study. J. Manag. Inf. Syst., Taylor & Francis **24**(1), 101–134 (2007)
Klamm, B.K., Watson, M.W.: SOX 404 reported internal control weaknesses: a test of COSO framework components and information technology. J. Inf. Syst. **23**(2), 1–23 (2009)
Lukka, K.: Management accounting change and stability: loosely coupled rules and routines in action. Manag. Account. Res., Elsevier **18**(1), 76–101 (2007)
Madnick, S.E., Wang, R.Y., Lee, Y.W., Zhu, H.: Overview and framework for data and information quality research. J. Data Inf. Qual. (JDIQ) ACM New York, NY, USA **1**(1), 1–22 (2009)
Markus, M.L., Axline, S., Petrie, D., Tanis, S.C.: Learning from adopters' experiences with ERP: problems encountered and success achieved. J. Inf. Technol., Taylor & Francis **15**(4), 245–265 (2000)
Merkl-Davies, D.M., Brennan, N.N.: Discretionary disclosure strategies in corporate narratives: incremental information or impression management? J. Account. Lit. **26**, 116–196 (2007)
Moeller, R.R. IT audit, control, and security, vol. 13. John Wiley & Sons (2010)
Nicolaou, A.I.: Firm performance effects in relation to the implementation and use of enterprise resource planning systems. J. Inf. Syst. **18**(2), 79–105 (2004)
Pflugrath, G., Roebuck, P., Simnett, R.: Impact of assurance and assurer's professional affiliation on financial analysts' assessment of credibility of corporate social responsibility information. Audit.: J. Pract. & Theory, American Accounting Association **30**(3), 239–254 (2011)
Poston, R., Grabski, S.: Financial impacts of enterprise resource planning implementations. Int. J. Account. Inf. Sys-Tems, Elsevier **2**(4), 271–294 (2001)
Rogers, R.K., Grant, J.: Content analysis of information cited in reports of sell-side financial analysts. J. Financ. Statement Anal. **3**, 17–31 (1997)
Rose, J., Kræmmergaard, P.: ERP systems and technological discourse shift: managing the implementation journey. Int. J. Account. Inf. Syst., Elsevier **7**(3), 217–237 (2006)
Skibniewski, M.J., Ghosh, S.: Determination of key performance indicators with enterprise resource planning systems in engineering construction firms. J. Constr. Eng. Manag.-Ment, American Society of Civil Engineers **135**(10), 965–978 (2009)
Stoel, M.D., Havelka, D.: Information technology audit quality: an investigation of the impact of individual and organizational factors. J. Inf. Syst., American Accounting Association **35**(1), 135–154 (2021)

Taipaleenmäki, J., Ikäheimo, S.: On the convergence of management accounting and financial accounting–the role of information technology in accounting change. Int. J. Account. Inf. Sys-Tems, Elsevier **14**(4), 321–348 (2013)
Teru, S.P., Idoku, I., Ndeyati, J.T.: A review of the impact of accounting information system for effective internal control on firm performance. Indian J. Financ. Bank. **1**(2), 52–59 (2017)
Toth, Z.: The current role of accounting information systems. Theory, Methodol., Pract., Univ. Miskolc **8**(1), 91 (2012)
Trucco, S.: Financial accounting. Springer (2015)
Trucco, S., Corsi, K. The influence of ERP systems implementation on accounting, organizational and social improvements: evidence from Italy and the UK. Information systems, management, organization and control, pp. 115–138. Springer (2014)
Vasile, G., Mirela, O. Data quality in business intelligence applications, p. 1359. ANALELE UNIVERSITĂŢII DIN ORADEA (2008)
Weidenmier, M.L., Ramamoorti, S.: Research opportunities in information technology and internal auditing. J. Inf. Syst. **20**(1), 205–219 (2006)
Xu, H.: Data quality issues for accounting information systems' implementation: Systems, stakeholders, and organizational factors. J. Technol. Res., Academic and Business Research Institute (AABRI) **1**, 1 (2009)
Yin, R.K., Moore, G.B.: Lessons on the utilization of research from nine case experiences in the natural hazards field. Knowl. Soc., Springer **1**(3), 25–44 (1988)

Green-Oriented Crowdfunding Campaign: An Explorative Study

Nabila Abid, Federica Ceci, Francesca di Pietro, and Francesca Masciarelli

Abstract The worldwide growing concern for environmental protection compels businesses to incorporate green orientation in their strategies. Crowdfunding has opened new possibilities to attract investors by encompassing green concerns in their agenda. This study investigates the relationship between green orientation and UK crowdfunding campaign success. We have used both qualitative and quantitative approaches to build the green orientation index, for which we have chosen 210 green campaigns out of 720 crowdfunding campaigns. Then we performed a cluster analysis to identify three clusters (social enthusiast, green fan, and tech-oriented) of green-oriented crowdfunding campaign. We performed a predictive validity analysis to identify which cluster is more effective in ensuring the crowdfunding's performance. The results show that tech-oriented obtain the highest value and share a positive relationship with the amount raised and crowdfunding's success. Social enthusiast effectively attracts more crowd through the social platform and thereby successfully raises funds. Green orientation, however, does not affect crowdfunding success or overfunding, which shows that there is a huge difference between the clusters, suggesting that the green orientation itself is not considered so important for the crowdfunding campaigns. It also highlights a crucial point the in the crowdfunding's objectives, the realization of the environmental concern, society, and the long-term sustainability concern is not promising.

Keywords Crowdfunding · Green orientation · Sustainability · Cluster analysis

---

N. Abid (✉) · F. Ceci · F. Masciarelli
Department of Business Administration, University of Gabriele' d Annunzio Chieti-Pescara, Pescara, Italy
e-mail: nabila.abid@unich.it; nabila.abid@studenti.unich.it

F. Ceci
e-mail: federica.ceci@unich.it

F. Masciarelli
e-mail: francesca.masciarelli@unich.it

F. di Pietro
Trinity Business School, The University of Dublin, Dublin, Ireland
e-mail: francesca.dipietro@tcd.ie

S. Za et al. (eds.), *Sustainable Digital Transformation*, Lecture Notes in Information Systems and Organisation 59, https://doi.org/10.1007/978-3-031-15770-7_3

1 Introduction

Crowdfunding is an effort made by an entrepreneurial individual or group to obtain funds for their startups via the internet from a large number of contributors without the support of financial intermediaries [1]. Entrepreneurs seeking financial support need to provide on the crowdfunding platform detailed information about their business. The pitch can be considered a concise version of the business plan but one that offers a persuasive story and provides a solution to a consumer need. The pitch is crucial to secure investors' attention and has a huge impact on the campaign's objective, i.e. to raise the funds required within a set time [2].

The context of green crowdfunding in crowdfunding campaigns has so far been overlooked [3]. There are growing concerns about the climate and environmental crisis globally [4] is bringing people, investors, and policymakers together [5]. Crowdfunding can be the ideal platform to finance green projects or incorporate green orientation in existing campaigns to help the global community reduce harmful emissions, with a series of initiatives to invest in renewable projects or technologies [6]. Crowdfunding campaigns can be seen as a powerful tool to communicate green concerns and influence the process and participation in the energy sector [7]. Green crowdfunding concern can increase the public support, which can help them raise more money for their project [8, 9]. The utilization of green resources and technology can also reduce the production cost and enhance operational efficiency. Therefore, green positioning can help achieve a competitive edge in the market, build a positive public image, and attain sustainability in business, society, and humans [10]. The crowdfunding phenomenon has been analyzed from various perspectives [2, 11, 12], however we miss a comprehensive understanding of how the characteristic of a crowdfunding campaign affects its probability of being successful. Therefore, in order to fill this research gap, we address the following main research question: "How the characteristic of green-oriented crowdfunding campaigns influence its success?" In the present work we develop a novel taxonomy of green-oriented crowdfunding campaign, analyzing their characteristics as well has their probability of superior performance.

We consider the most popular equity-crowdfunding platforms in the UK, Seedrs and Crowdcube. We identified three clusters, namely social enthusiast, green, and tech oriented. Our results suggest that social enthusiast effectively attracts more crowd through the social platform and thereby manage to raise funds for their campaigns. Crowdfunding campaigns should stress more to develop interaction networks as explained by the campaign extracts reported in the paper. Second, results also suggested that tech-orientated campaigns effectively achieve success and over-funds for the crowdfunding campaigns. For such campaigns, being innovative is less risky, and more customers are attracted to the tech-oriented campaigns. Such campaigns help achieve the environmental protection goal and increase the efficiency to attain the targeted goals. Third, our results also suggest that incorporating green concern in the crowdfunding campaigns is not enough for achieving superior performance. Raising public awareness towards the surrounding environment can attract them more toward the green-oriented campaigns, which can be the possible long-run success determinant for the crowdfunding campaign. In most UK crowdfunding funding campaigns, this concern is not apparent and thereby is not related to the success and overfunding of the campaigns.

We contribute to this stream of work by emphasizing the role of communicators to appeal to an audience of potential investors. In addition, we propose a new taxonomy that help both investors and entrepreneurs to classify the crowdfunding campaigns and we shed light of how green orientation, innovation and social enthusiasm might favor firm access to credit.

The paper is organized as follows. The next section provides a brief literature review, explaining also the theoretical framework adopted in this study; then we explain our research methodology, which we follow by discussing our results and their significance. In the final section we offer the conclusions of the study, discuss its limitations, and the directions for future research.

2 Literature Review

2.1 Crowdfunding for Sustainable Businesses

Crowdfunding is a collective effort by the network of people to raise funds for various business or nonprofit initiatives [13, 14]. The crowdfunding industry has emerged as an effective financing solution which has managed to acquire 16.2$ billion in 2017 compared to 1.5$ in 2011 [15, 16]. Although, initially crowdfunding acted as a platform to raise funds in social sectors in exchange for non-financial rewards [17], but with time the connection between crowdfunding campaigns and sustainability has started capturing attention from the relevant stakeholders [8, 9, 18].

The crowdfunding literature to date, has extensively investigated entrepreneurial fundraising efforts and the determinants of success of crowdfunding campaigns (see [19], for a comprehensive review), frequently relying on signaling theory [20], which is concerned with reducing information asymmetry in the investor-investee relationship, as a preferred theoretical lens to understand investment transactions between investors and entrepreneurs [16, 17]. Among the signals influencing external equity fundraising, research shows the importance of product certifications from stakeholders [2, 19, 21], the participation of expert investors [22], information about the borrowers or founding team [23, 24], early investors' engagement [25], third-party endorsements [26], as well as company's past achievements and future developments [27].

More recently a study from [28] raised the issue that green entrepreneurial initiatives, may face significant challenges in accessing financial resources, especially in countries with a limited environmental sustainability orientation.

Pertaining the role of innovation, anecdotal evidence suggests that crowdfunding can often help entrepreneurs finance innovative ideas [29], a claim that has been overlooked so far by scholars. Many crowdfunding studies have instead focused on the effects of informational cues on crowdfunding outcomes [2, 5]. These assume that when investors choose which ventures to support, they rely on analytical processing to identify and interpret informational cues related to project quality [2, 6]. Some scholars have found that project quality cues such as a pitch video, the human and social capital of entrepreneurs, and the location of the venture can affect funding outcomes [2, 7, 13], but have not examined how sheer innovativeness can affect successful funding.

Since crowdfunding bears the potential to help green-oriented companies and in general companies more prone to embrace sustainable business practices [30], in this study we explore how company's sustainable orientation may influence the attraction of external capital via crowdfunding.

2.2 *Sustainability and Green Orientation*

Sustainability is a complex concept beyond the comprehension of one single definition, and different academicians, policymakers, and researchers provide different views on what sustainability is [31, 32]. The literal meaning of sustainable is to sustain what you have now for present and for future times. The environment is a core determinant of sustainability which ensures the protection of the environment and humans living in it [33]. Maude [34] further stated that sustainability is all about a balance between social, economic, environmental, and cultural setup. According to Birdsall [37] sustainability encompasses social well-being with economic growth in it. Bocken et al. [34] and Raine et al. [32] argued that sustainability has several dimensions, but all revolve around three concepts, people, profit, and the plant, and humans and nature are primary stakeholders in the global system.

In the business world, sustainability refers to the expansion of the financial resource hierarchy from one to three levels, including environmental and social aspects of the business strategy [35]. The dynamic work is imposing huge challenges on businesses to stay competitive in changing marketing. Businesses realize the importance of involving sustainability in their vision and positioning themselves to balance the financial, social, and environmental interests [36]. Soppe [37] emphasized that sustainability is not just about creating the balance between the business, society, and environment, but the connection must be made for the present and future generations.

There are growing concerns about the climate and environmental crisis globally [4] and to sustain life, the protection of the environment is bringing people, investors, and policymakers together [5]. Crowdfunding can be the ideal platform to finance green projects or incorporate green orientation in existing campaigns to help the global community reduce harmful emissions, with a series of initiatives to invest in renewable projects or technologies [6]. Kunze and Becker [7] stressed the role of crowdfunding campaigns as a powerful tool to communicate green concerns and influence the process and participation in the energy sector. This situation, in turn, can increase the public support for the campaigns, which can help them raise more money for their project, which also addresses the climate issues [8, 9].

Calic and Mosakowski [38] reveal that green sustainability-oriented projects are more likely to increase the money than non-sustainable projects. However, the study of Hörisch [39] find that green orientation of crowdfunding does not share any significant correlation with the success of the campaigns. Green businesses can serve as the means to produce eco-friendly products and services. Incorporating green in the business does not only serve the sustainability goals, but the use of green resources and technology can also reduce the production cost and enhance operational efficiency. Therefore, green positioning can help achieve a competitive edge in the market, build a positive public image, and attain sustainability in business, society, and humans [10].

Most traditional businesses and companies avoid financing green projects or incorporating green concerns in their strategy due to the high risk and uncertainty involved in it [40, 41]. Despite the enormous gap and scientific relevance of the matter, the literature on green crowdfunding is still minimal [3], and the existing research result is also mix.

3 Methods

3.1 Sample Description

We analyzed 210 crowdfunding campaigns from the most popular equity crowdfunding platforms in the UK. The UK accounted for 73% of the entire European equity crowdfunding market in 2017 [42]. Crowdcube and Seedrs were the first online investment platforms launched in the UK, in 2011 and 2012 respectively. Both have grown significantly over time and have attracted start-ups as well as early- and growth-stage businesses from a broad range of sectors, including fintech, education, food and drink, real estate, and many others. Both platforms are authorized and regulated by the UK Financial Conduct Authority and are ranked respectively first and second in the UK equity crowdfunding market in terms of transaction volumes and number of start-ups funded. Seedrs and Crowdcube work according to a transaction fee business model involving a charge based on the amount transacted and operate on an all-or-nothing funding basis—that is, the entrepreneur receives funding only if the campaign achieves the preset target amount [13, 43, 44]. In the present study, we focused on green-oriented camping, i.e. campaign that present some reference to sustainability, green growth, circular economy and similar [45].

We collected data on closed crowdfunding campaigns on these platforms in the period that goes from April 2017 to March 2019. Closed campaigns refer to campaigns that either reached the funding target within the allotted time period (i.e., successful campaigns) or where the campaign time had expired (i.e., unsuccessful campaigns). The average age of the ventures in our sample was 3.7 years: 24% of

Table 1 Green orientation index

Word	Word count	Word	Word count
Environment	96	Pollution	8
Sustainable	179	Protection	44
Sustainability	54	CSR	20
Carbon/CO2	53	Cleaner	14
Emissions	8	GHG	11

firms were less than one year old, 53% were between one and five years old, and 23% were more than five years old. Approximately 30% of the sample ventures had achieved the target funding.

3.2 Operationalization of Variables

To form the clusters, we used 5 taxonomic variables. We operationalized the taxonomic variables as follows.

3.2.1 Green Orientation Index

Green orientation index measures the number of Green-related words used in the description of the campaign. We constructed the variable applying a content analysis. In the past, different researchers [46–51] identify green orientation as a business commitment to protect the environment by incorporating environmental goals and objective in their strategic plans. To determine the sustainable green orientation indicators in crowdfunding campaigns, we followed [52], who identified a series of keywords. We have used content analysis to do the word count of green words in 720 crowdfunding campaigns. The output of word count is then further utilized to develop a green orientation index. The word count matrix is used to identify the series of green words used in crowdfunding campaigns which depict the campaign commitment towards the environment and sustainability. The green orientation words and index are displayed in Table 1.

3.2.2 Science-Based

Science-based crowdfunding campaigns accelerate innovation and have excellent potential to gain success in the global market [53, 54]. Science-based crowdfunding campaigns can equally be important for social scientists and potential entrepreneurs looking to start their campaigns [54]. The innovation lies a core element of the science-based crowdfunding campaigns [53].

3.2.3 Innovativeness

Innovativeness is measured by conducting manual content analysis of each campaign. Two research assistants analyzed the campaign texts, and the researchers manually checked the entire text to understand how innovation was described in the crowdfunding campaign. We referred to the [55] matrix, which classifies innovation based on its alignment to the customer base and technology developments. We consider four quadrants of the Leonard-Barton matrix: user-driven enhancement, which refers to the search for an improved solution/technology to meet already known customer needs; developers-driven development, which refers to the search for a new solution to an existing customer need; new application of technology, which refers to the search for a new target customer for an existing solution identified through a process of market matching; and technology-market coevolution, which refers to the development of a new technology and simultaneous identification or development of a new customer base [55]. The Leonard-Barton matrix provides two distinct measures of venture innovativeness based on the dummy variables Incremental innovation and Radical innovation. For further clarification, please refer to [56].

3.2.4 Facebook (FB) Like

Facebook (FB) like is a continuous variable that proxies for company activity on social media. We also used three variables to validate the cluster. In order to test the predictive validity of the cluster configuration, we used three indicators of performances, described as follows,

Success is a dummy variable taking value 1 if the company reaches the fundraising target amount; 0 otherwise.

Amount raised is a continuous variable calculated as the total amount of funding (in GB£) raised by the entrepreneur when the campaign expired.

Overfunding is a dummy variable taking value 1 if the company raised more funds than the target amount (target amount- funds raised >0); 0 otherwise.

3.3 Analytical Approach

To identify possible different orientation within the sample, we applied a clustering algorithm to the 200 crowdfunding campaign, using the five variables above described. The technique of cluster analysis is useful to summarize the data and, in an explorative way, to group the different categories of firms into 'clusters' according to their similarities or dissimilarities Following the recommendations provided in [57, 58], we standardized the taxonomic variables to limit the spurious influence of different scales and we employed the Ward's minimum variance method to form clusters.

We used a two-stage clustering procedure to determine a final solution and to minimize the impact of outliers [59]. In the first stage, we conducted a hierarchical clustering analysis using Ward's method and eliminated from the sample the 10% of the observations that had the largest multivariate distance from the others (i.e., potential outliers). Dendrogram is reported in Fig. 1. Then, to identify the number of clusters, we looked for pronounced increases in the tightness of clusters as measured by the R2 and the pseudo-F statistic [60], and for managerial interpretability of the clusters [58, 61]. The initial Ward's solution was used to identify the initial seeds for the second-stage analysis, in which we used an iterative K-means approach to search for improved solutions. The analysis, conducted with the CLUSTER procedures in STATA, generated a three-cluster solution containing 109, 62 and 22 observations. The three clusters were named social enthusiast ($n = 62$), green fan ($n = 109$) and tech oriented ($n = 22$).

We used several tests to assess the robustness and the validity of the solution. An overall multi-variate test of significance using the Wilks' lambda criterion and the associated F statistic indicated that the null hypothesis that the four clusters were equal across all defining variables could be rejected with $p < 0.0001$ [62, 63]. To test the statistical power of the configurations, we performed a series of one-way comparisons and Kruskal–Wallis equality-of-populations rank test among the three clusters using the discriminating variables. Finally, to assess the external validity of the proposed configurations [58], we compared clusters against two performance indicators, the success of the campaign and the amount of overfunding received. Results are reported in Table 2.

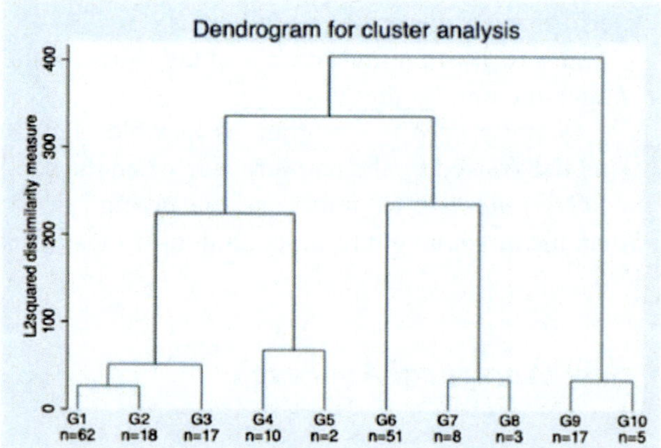

Fig. 1 Dendrogram for the cluster analysis

Table 2 Characteristics of the clusters

	Social enthusiast (n = 62)	Green fan (n = 109)	Tech oriented (n = 22)	F-value *or* chi-squared[b] (probability)
Taxonomic variables				
Green orientation index				
Cluster mean[a]	−0.3256	0.1847	−0.0047	5.25
St. deviation	*0.2737*	*1.2382*	*0.8710*	*(0.006)*
Science based				
Cluster mean	−1.2728	0.6661	0.2470	101.788
St. deviation	*0.4539*	*0.3448*	*0.90005*	*(0.0001)*
Innovativeness				
Cluster mean	−0.35068	−0.3506	2.8373	58.175
St. deviation	*0*	*0*	*0*	*(0.0001)*
FB likes				
Cluster mean	0.35149	−0.1286	-0.3483	6.34
St. deviation	*1.5292*	*0.5921*	*0.2357*	*(0.002)*
Predictive variables				
Success				
Cluster mean	−0.2579	−0.0235	0.6273	7.979
St. deviation	*0.8476*	*0.9917*	*1.0931*	*(0.018)*
Amount raised				
Cluster mean	−0.1421	0.0061	0.0061	0.39
St. deviation	*0.3686*	*1.0666*	*1.0811*	*(0.679)*
Overfunding				
Cluster mean	0.3007	−0.1281	−0.1639	3.99
St. deviation	*1.2950*	*0.8764*	*0.4783*	*(0.020)*

[a] Cluster means represent the average values of the taxonomic variables (standardized) for the clusters

[b] F-values are reported for continuous variables, chi-squared values are reported for categorical variables

4 Discussion of Results

4.1 Descriptive Validity: Characteristics of the Clusters

Before analyzing performance differences among the clusters, it is worth examining the characteristics of the clusters identified through the analysis. The three configurations can be characterized with respect to their respective group centroids (means) of the 4 taxonomic variables (Table 1). The results show that the variables included in the model strongly discriminate among clusters.

Social Enthusiast is composed of 62 firms that present a strong presence on the social network Facebook. This cluster represents the second-largest centroid among our group. The centroid of the variable "Facebook likes" is higher in the sample, followed by "Overfunding." The social aspect of crowdfunding is meaningful in creating the impact by connecting more with the masses on the campaign's mission. People are drawn to such campaigns over social platforms and connect to the vision of the movements, which is meaningful for them. Thereby, such campaigns managed to get more funding, and the centroid shows the significant rise of money for social enthusiast campaigns. "It's Not Easy Being Green" to elaborate this statement, [64] argued that adopting the green approach does not cost the business but instead helps it adapt to more innovative measures to capture new market opportunities and raise more money. Therefore, if socially engaged crowdfunding involves more green orientation in their campaigns, they would be able to draw more funding.

Green Fan is composed of 109 firms that present a strong presence on the social network Facebook. The centroid of the variable "Green orientation index" is higher in the sample. This cluster represents the firms that successfully managed to raise the amount, are involved in science-based activities, and have a higher green orientation index value than the other clusters. Adhami et al. [45] further argued that people assume that the green approach yields minimal business benefits and avoids investing energy in it. Bonzanini et al. [65] stressed the importance of the green approach in crowdfunding, as it will determine the success (amount raised) and environmental protection. According to Kunze and Becker [7] crowdfunding is a powerful tool of communication. Our study suggests that the green approach shares a positive association with the amount raised and the science-based practice of the campaigns, which impose directions for the other campaigns to identify the benefits of the green approach for both the movement and the surroundings as a whole.

Tech Oriented is composed of 22 firms that present a strong presence on the social network Facebook. The centroid of the variable "Innovativeness" is higher in the sample. Moreover, also the variable "Science-based" is positive in the sample. Those two variables are interpreted together to understand a cluster of campaigns oriented toward innovativeness and new technologies. The positive values of the amount raised, and success imply that the tech orientation approach is practical to draw more money and success for the crowdfunding, focusing on innovative and science-orientated strategies and activities of the campaigns. According to Ordanini et al. [66], crowdfunding with an innovative and tech-orientated approach can attract more consumers and successfully create a good-will impact. However, little stress has been given to the elements that can accelerate the green path in crowdfunding platforms [28]. Green orientation is more legitimate and fosters the resources needed to survive and expand the activities in the early and later stages of the profit and nonprofit entities [67]. Although tech orientation campaigns successfully get more money with science-based and innovative measures, the number of the campaigns is very small compared to other clusters. Therefore, the crowdfunding platforms must realize the importance of technology, science, and innovative green measures to the campaign's success and the well-being of the surroundings.

4.2 Predictive Validity: Performance Differences

The study targeted UK crowdfunding campaigns, and Table 2 explicitly describes three clusters: social enthusiast, green-oriented, and the variables success, and amount raised to determine which cluster has more potential to channel the performance of the campaigns. Table 2 sheds light also on the impact that the positioning of the campaign have on their performance. The results provide evidence of predictive validity, as we found significance differences among the three configurations with respect to most of the variables used to validate clusters. Whilst the three groups display significant differences in the success of the campaign (Chi-squared = 7.979, with $p < 0.05$) and in the access to overfunding ($F = 3.99$, with $p < 0.05$), they do not display equally large differences in the ability to raise money with the campaign ($F = 0.39$, with $p > 0.1$).

This leads us to formulate three possible suggestions. First, social enthusiasts can go viral and successfully manage to raise funds for their campaigns. Colombo et al. [12] also suggested that it's straightforward to reach more customers or potential investors if crowdfunding campaigns utilize different social media platforms. Crowdfunding campaigns should stress more to develop interaction networks as explained by the storii care and fobo campaigns in Table 3. Social enthusiast campaigns leverage on network externalities, which will help crowdfunding campaigns reach the masses and increase the amount raised obtaining overfunding.

Second, positive coefficient values of success (0.6273) and amount raised (0.0061) suggested that tech-orientated campaigns effectively achieve success and overfunds for the crowdfunding campaigns. For the campaigns, being innovative is less risky, and more customers are attracted to the tech-oriented campaigns. Such campaigns help achieve the environmental protection goal and increase the efficiency to attain the targeted goals (Table 3 e.g., Fresh rang and recycling technologies).

Third, a positive value of the amount raised by 0.0061 implies that green-oriented campaigns can increase the amount. Still, the negative results of crowdfunding success and (−0.0235, −1281 respectively) show that incorporating green concern in the crowdfunding campaigns is not enough. Kubo et al. [68] argued that could achieve the success of the campaigns without including the environmental concern in the company code. Still, in the dynamic competitive environment, just social and tech concerns will no longer be compelling. Raising public awareness towards the surrounding environment can attract them more toward the green-oriented campaigns, which can be the possible long-run success determinant for the crowdfunding campaign. In most UK crowdfunding funding campaigns, this concern is not apparent and thereby is not related to the success and overfunding of the campaigns [69–74].

Table 3 Excerpts from the text

Cluster name	Example of campaigns
Social enthusiast	"Being the world's first proactive hybrid dating business, we have successfully created a business platform where we have merged social media, online dating, and offline events. Hence, people have an opportunity to expand their network both online and offline. By providing a "favorable offline" option to connect with people, our business has bridged the gap to re-empower interpersonal relationships. After successfully testing groups in Manchester, Liverpool, Chester, and maid stone, we launched our social groups and gained 2600 members in the first five months of the launch. Today we have 240 groups on Facebook and groups in Canada, Australia, and the USA". (Fobo) S"torri care is established with a vision to set person-centered care goals worldwide. In the health care sector, we have embraced digital technology than simply relying on paper-based manual systems. storii care is determined to provide care management systems to the people and encouraging more person-centered changes in the health care industry. Staff in care sectors use our platform on cell phones or desktop devices to evidence the care. Staff can also provide access to the user profiles, share memories, pictures, videos, and life stories that help relatives connect to them from anywhere in the world and helps inspiring others facing similar issues. We thereby created a community where staff uses this content for person-centered therapy. On social platforms, we describe our clients as "the Facebook for care." (Storri care)
Green fan	"In the UK alone, there are around 50 million tyres that are discarded, every year. These are a huge potential hazard to both the environment and human health. Our specially designed "Mishergas Process" will aim to eventually clean up at least 10% of the waste tyres in this country. Not only that, we plan to convert them into saleable commodities; these will be oil, recycled carbon black and steel. By recycling the oil from the tyres, we believe this will reduce the need for fracking and by refining the carbon black and collecting the steel, it also will cut down on the necessity for minin." (Mishergas Energy) "The world has been facing dire energy challenges and the consequences of carbon discharge. To meet the challenges of climate change, we are striving to build "Green," eco-friendly sustainable buildings for housing, schools, and businesses and effectively addressing the climate challenge. The growth rate is 18% for green buildings, which is expected to rise to 50% in Europe by 2050. The sustainable modular is designed to enhance energy-saving with minimal carbon output, green roofs, enhanced security systems with smart technology features. The development of these building specifically focuses on using resource efficiently with less waste and more labor productivity with just 2–3 days installation time" (Green unit)

(continued)

5 Conclusions, Limitations, and Future Research

The study intended to explore how green-oriented crowdfunding campaigns position themselves in the market and what their expected outcomes. We have applied both qualitative and quantitative approaches to identify, develop and analyze the

Table 3 (continued)

Cluster name	Example of campaigns
Tech oriented	"There is 200£ billion food industry working in the UK; still millions of people are facing diet-illness and shortened life span. On the one hand, farmers are paid less, and there are fewer retail platforms for consumers and producers; on the other hand, a handful of retailers and food companies are generating billions of pounds. We provide a secure technology platform connecting small or massive producers with suppliers on short or fast supply chains. This technology infrastructure performs multi-functions, from emphasizing the sourcing diet to connecting with local farmers, makers, fisherman, and bakers, enabling retailing and catering customers from both public and private sectors. This technology channel helps small producers earn adequate and help customers eat healthy, affordable, fresher food with provenance". (Fresh range) "Plastic footprints impact all types of life on this planet; among the whole plastic waste, only 12% is subject to recycling, the member, so f UK plastic pact represents 80% of the plastic packaging, and they intend to use 100% recyclable packaging by 2025. Intending to provide recycling solutions to the world, we have established recycling technologies and signed the new plastics economy global commitment to eliminate plastic waste. We have developed a machine "RT7000" which recycle plastic in more economy and commercially attractive way. This machine turns plastic into a product called PLAXX, which is used to make wax and new plastic products. In Swindon, the RT7000 is deployed to "recycle the unrecyclable" to explain films, plastics, trays, and caps. Laminated packaged etc." (recycling technologies)

constructs. In the first part of the study, we developed an exclusive green orientation index and we used it to perform a cluster analysis over UK crowdfunding campaigns. We divided the 210 campaigns identifying three clusters: social enthusiast, green fan, and tech-oriented campaigns. The three cluster has been tested to validate their predictive validity to determine which clusters have better performance. The results suggested that tech-oriented is most compelling to achieve crowdfunding success among the three clusters, followed by the social enthusiast. People tend to attract more toward the tech-oriented campaigns as they think of them as less risky, and social enthusiast campaigns can draw sufficient attention by utilizing various social media platforms. Moreover, result shows that green-orientated campaigns do not cause crowdfunding success and overfunding. The reason could be the restricted number of the campaigns, which focuses more on the success of the campaign, which they could achieve without incorporating the green orientation in their mission.

Our study offers the following managerial and policy implications. First, crowdfunding managerial lines tend to lean more toward success and growth and are not focusing much on the green orientational aspect in their business strategies. It's an ethical and moral duty of crowdfunding campaigns to consider the environmental aspect. Second, investors are attracted toward less risky campaigns or campaigns that attract sufficient public attention using social media platforms. Thereby, it's the duty of the legal legislators and policymakers to raise awareness in the public and potential investors regarding environmental concerns and at the same time, devise and implement environmental policies on crowdfunding campaigns and evaluate the results to avoid deviation and ignorance.

Our research has some limitations. First, we focus on green oriented campaigns while future studies could enrich our analysis using a larger dataset. Second, our analysis is confined to the context of equity crowdfunding and does consider venture capitalist, rewards-based crowdfunding, business angels, and could provide important insight to test our proposed taxonomy. In addition, we focus on one single country (UK) and we are therefore unable to catch cultural differences in crowdfunding campaigns. Finally, as with most research on crowdfunding, we adopt a cross-sectional perspective that might limits our insights pertaining the longer-term effects of costly and costless signals on successfully obtaining equity crowdfunding.

Despite of these limitations which open up new directions for future studies, we do believe that this research presents important findings that will be useful to both practitioners and scholars interested on new form of entrepreneurial finance, i.e. equity crowdfunding in the context of sustainability and green orientation. The future research can consider venture capitalist and reward-based crowdfunding with green orientation variables in a larger context. In future, the green orientation phenomenon could be explored in different business models to explore what type of model support the deployment and promotion of green orientation. Our analysis provides investors and entrepreneurs with useful guidelines, that explore the specific characteristics and the peculiar features of each campaign.

References

1. Schwienbacher, A., Larralde, B.: Crowdfunding of small entrepreneurial ventures. SSRN Electron. J. (2010, 2012). https://doi.org/10.2139/ssrn.1699183
2. Mollick, E.: The dynamics of crowdfunding: an exploratory study. J. Bus. Ventur. **29**(1), 1–16 (2014). https://doi.org/10.1016/j.jbusvent.2013.06.005
3. Nielsen, L.A., Reisch, K.R.: Crowdfunding for sustainability—the role of value orientation frames in guiding individual investment behavior (2016)
4. Pernick, C., Wilder, R..: The Clean Tech Revolution : The Next Big Growth and Investment Opportunity, 6th edn. Collins, New York (2007)
5. Giudici, G., Guerini, M., Rossi-Lamastra, C.: The creation of cleantech startups at the local level: the role of knowledge availability and environmental awareness. Small Bus. Econ. **52**(4), 815–830 (2019). https://doi.org/10.1007/s11187-017-9936-9
6. Nigam, N., Mbarek, S., Benetti, C.: Crowdfunding to finance eco-innovation: case studies from leading renewable energy platforms. J. Innov. Econ. **26**(2), 195 (2018). https://doi.org/10.3917/jie.pr1.0033
7. Kunze, S., Becker, C.: Energy Democracy in Europe: A Survey and Outlook. (2014) [Online]. https://www.google.com/search?q=Energy+Democracy+in+Europe%3A+a+survey+and+outlook+2014+pdf&rlz=1C1CHWL_enUS846US846&sxsrf=ALeKk02xHnxXqGT_5nBHGDNxr22Rq1wK6w%3A1621441286369&ei=BjulYMfsFYuckwX5nbioDw&oq=Energy+Democracy+in+Europe%3A+a+survey+and+outlook+2
8. Agrawal, A., Catalini, C., Goldfarb, A.: Crowdfunding: geography, social networks, and the timing of investment decisions. J. Econ. Manag. Strateg. **24**(2), 253–274 (2015). https://doi.org/10.1111/jems.12093

9. Belleflamme, P., Lambert, T., Schwienbacher, A.: Crowdfunding: tapping the right crowd. SSRN Electron. J. (2012). https://doi.org/10.2139/ssrn.1578175
10. Queensland government: The benefits of an environmentally friendly business. The environment and your business (2020). https://www.business.qld.gov.au/running-business/environment/environment-business/benefits. Accessed 19 May 2021
11. Ajay, K.A., Catalini, C., Goldfarb, A.: The geography of crowdfunding. (2011). https://doi.org/10.4324/9780429319785-5
12. Colombo, M.G., Franzoni, C., Rossi-Lamastra, C.: Internal social capital and the attraction of early contributions in crowdfunding. Entrep. Theory Pract. **39**(1), 75–100 (2015). https://doi.org/10.1111/etap.12118
13. Bento, N., Gianfrate, G., Thoni, M.H.: Crowdfunding for sustainability ventures. J. Clean. Prod. **237**, 117751 (2019). https://doi.org/10.1016/j.jclepro.2019.117751
14. Vasileiadou, E., Huijben, J.C.C.M., Raven, R.P.J.M.: Three is a crowd? Exploring the potential of crowdfunding for renewable energy in the Netherlands. J. Clean. Prod. **128**, 142–155 (2016). https://doi.org/10.1016/j.jclepro.2015.06.028
15. Massolution, C.L.: Crowdfunding industry report: market trends, composition and crowdfunding platforms. Newyork (2012). [Online] https://www.crowdfunding.nl/wp-content/uploads/2012/05/92834651-Massolution-abridged-Crowd-Funding-Industry-Report1.pdf
16. Hogue, J.: 10 Crowdfunding Statistics to Raise More Money (2017). https://www.crowd101.com/crowdfunding-success-statistics-raise-money-online/. Accessed 19 May 2021
17. Hemer, J.: A snapshot on crowdfunding. Enconstor 39 (2011)
18. Gafni, H., Marom, D., Sade, O.: Are the life and death of an early-stage venture indeed in the power of the tongue? Lessons from online crowdfunding pitches. Strateg. Entrep. J. **13**(1), 3–23 (2019). https://doi.org/10.1002/sej.1293
19. Di, P.F.: Crowdfunding for Entrepreneurs: Developing Strategic Advantage through Entrepreneurial Finance, 1st edn. Routledge (2020)
20. Michael, S.: Job market signaling. Q. J. Econ. **87**(3), 355–374 (1973). https://doi.org/10.2307/1882010
21. Cordova, A., Dolci, J., Gianfrate, G.: The determinants of crowdfunding success: evidence from technology projects. Procedia Soc. Behav. Sci. **181**, 115–124 (2015). https://doi.org/10.1016/j.sbspro.2015.04.872
22. Kim, K., Viswanathan, S.: The 'Experts' in the crowd: the role of experienced investors in a crowdfunding market. MIS Q. **53**(9) (2018)
23. Connelly, B.L., Certo, S.T., Ireland, R.D., Reutzel, C.R.: Signaling theory: a review and assessment. J. Manage. **37**(1), 39–67 (2011). https://doi.org/10.1177/0149206310388419
24. Spence, M.: Signaling in retrospect and the informational structure of markets. Am. Econ. Rev. **92**(3), 434–459 (2002). https://doi.org/10.1257/00028280260136200
25. Vismara, S.: Information Cascades Among Investors in Equity Crowdfunding. SSRN Electron. J. 1–49 (2015). https://doi.org/10.2139/ssrn.2589619
26. Courtney, C., Dutta, S., Li, Y.: Resolving information asymmetry: signaling, endorsement, and crowdfunding success. Entrep. Theory Pract. **41**(2), 265–290 (2017). https://doi.org/10.1111/etap.12267
27. Di Pietro, F., Grilli, L., Masciarelli, F.: Talking about a revolution? Costly and costless signals and the role of innovativeness in equity crowdfunding. J. Small Bus. Manag. **00**(00), 1–32 (2020). https://doi.org/10.1080/00472778.2020.1816435
28. Butticè, V., Colombo, M.G., Fumagalli, E., Orsenigo, C.: Green oriented crowdfunding campaigns: their characteristics and diffusion in different institutional settings. Technol. Forecast. Soc. Change **141**, 85–97 (2019). https://doi.org/10.1016/j.techfore.2018.07.047
29. John, R.: Crowdfunding technology innovation. IEEE **46**(3), 100–103 (2013). https://doi.org/10.1109/MC.2013.89
30. Short, J.C., Ketchen, D.J., McKenny, A.F., Allison, T.H., Ireland, R.D.: Research on crowdfunding: reviewing the (very recent) past and celebrating the present. Entrep. Theory Pract. **41**(2), 149–160 (2017). https://doi.org/10.1111/etap.12270

31. Birdsall, S.: Measuring student teachers' understandings and self-awareness of sustainability. Environ. Educ. Res. **20**(6), 814–835 (2014). https://doi.org/10.1080/13504622.2013.833594
32. Isaksson, R.B., Garvare, R., Johnson, M.: The crippled bottom line – measuring and managing sustainability. Eletronic Libr. **34**(1), 1–5 (2017)
33. Maude, A.: A sustainable view of sustainability?. Geography **99**(1) (2014). https://doi.org/10.1080/00167487.2014.12094391
34. Bocken, N.M.P., Short, S.W., Rana, P., Evans, S.: A literature and practice review to develop sustainable business model archetypes. J. Clean. Prod. **65**, 42–56 (2014). https://doi.org/10.1016/j.jclepro.2013.11.039
35. Peng, R.: Does environmental management improve financial performance? a meta-analytical review. Soc. Environ. Account. J. **34**(3), 189–190 (2014). https://doi.org/10.1080/0969160x.2014.967958
36. Dixon-Fowler, A.M.R.H.R., Slater, D.J., Johnson, J.L., Ellstrand, A.E.: Beyond '"does it pay to be green?"' a meta-analysis of moderators of the CEP–CFP relationship. J. Bus. Ethics **122**(2), 179–191 (2017). https://doi.org/10.1007/s10551
37. Soppe, A.: Sustainable corporate finance. J. Bus. Ethics **53**(1), 213–224 (2004). 10.1023/B.
38. Calic, G., Mosakowski, E.: Kicking off social entrepreneurship: how a sustainability orientation influences crowdfunding success. J. Manag. Stud. **53**(5), 738–767 (2016). https://doi.org/10.1111/joms.12201
39. Hörisch, J.: Crowdfunding for environmental ventures: an empirical analysis of the influence of environmental orientation on the success of crowdfunding initiatives. J. Clean. Prod. **107**, 636–645 (2015). https://doi.org/10.1016/j.jclepro.2015.05.046
40. Dilger, M.G., Jovanović, T., Voigt, K.I.: Upcrowding energy co-operatives—evaluating the potential of crowdfunding for business model innovation of energy co-operatives. J. Environ. Manage. **198**, 50–62 (2017). https://doi.org/10.1016/j.jenvman.2017.04.025
41. Hart, M.B., Milstein, S.L.: global sustainability and the creative destruction of industries. Loan Manag. Rev. **41**(1), 23 (1999)
42. Ziegler, B., Shneor, T., Garvey, R., Wenzlaff, K., Yerolemou, K., Hao, N., Zhang, R.: The 3rd European Alternative Finance Industry Report. (2018). [Online]. https://www.jbs.cam.ac.uk/faculty-research/centres/alternative-finance/publications/expanding-horizons
43. Cumming, D.J., Leboeuf, G., Schwienbacher, A.: Crowdfunding models: keep-it-all vs. all-or-nothing. Financ. Manag. **49**(2), 331–360 (2020). https://doi.org/10.1111/fima.12262
44. Haas, P., Blohm, I., Leimeister, J.M.: An empirical taxonomy of crowdfunding intermediaries. In: 35th International Conference on Information System Building a Better World Through Information System (ICIS), pp. 1–18. (2014)
45. Adhami, S., Giudici, G., Pham, H., Anh, N.: Crowdfunding for green projects in Europe : success factors and effects on the local environmental performance and wellbeing. Glob. Sustain. Invest. Rev. 1–34. (2016)
46. Ajay, B.J.J., Kohli, K.: Market orientation: the construct, research propositions, and managerial implications. J. Mark. **54**(2) (1990). https://doi.org/10.1177/002224299005400201
47. Christmann, P., Taylor, G.: Globalization and the environment: strategies for international voluntary environmental initiatives. Corp. Environ. Responsib. **16**(3), 563–577 (2017). https://doi.org/10.4324/9781315259277-30
48. Day, G.S.: The capabilities of market-driven organizations. J. Mark. **58**(4), 37–52 (1994). https://doi.org/10.1177/002224299405800404
49. Gungor, A., Gupta, S.M.: Issues in environmentally conscious manufacturing and product recovery: a survey. Comput. Ind. Eng. **36**(4), 811–853 (1999). https://doi.org/10.1016/S0360-8352(99)00167-9
50. Hitt, M.A., Dacin, M.T., Levitas, E., Arregle, J.L., Borza, A.: Partner selection in emerging and developed market contexts: resource-based and organizational learning perspectives. Acad. Manag. J. **43**(3), 449–467 (2000). https://doi.org/10.2307/1556404
51. Sinkovics, R.R., Roath, A.S.: Strategic orientation, capabilities, and performance in manufacturer—3Pl relationships. J. Bus. Logist. **25**(2), 43–64 (2004). https://doi.org/10.1002/j.2158-1592.2006.tb00220.x

52. Wiese, A., Kellner, J., Lietke, B., Toporowski, W., Zielke, S.: Sustainability in retailing—a summative content analysis. Int. J. Retail Distrib. Manag. **40**(4), 318–335 (2012). https://doi.org/10.1108/09590551211211792
53. Song, C., Luo, J., Holtta-Otto, K., Seering, W., Otto, K.: Crowdfunding for design innovation: prediction model with critical factors. IEEE Trans. Eng. Manag. 1–12 (2020). https://doi.org/10.1109/tem.2020.3001764
54. Vachelard, J., Gambarra-Soares, T., Augustini, G., Riul, P., Maracaja-Coutinho, V.: A guide to scientific crowdfunding. PLoS Biol. **14**(2) (2016). https://doi.org/10.1371/journal.pbio.1002373
55. Dorothy Leonard, B.: Wellsprings of knowledge: building and sustaining the sources of innovation. Harvard Business School Press, Boston, Massachusetts (1995)
56. Di Pietro, F., Buttiè, V.: Institutional characteristics and the development of crowdfunding across countries. Int. Rev. Financ. Anal. (2020). https://doi.org/10.1016/j.irfa.2020.101543
57. Punj, G., Stewart, D.: Cluster analysis in marketing research: review and suggestions for application. J. Mark. Res. **20**, 134–148 (1983)
58. Ketchen, D., Shook, C.: The application of cluster analysis in strategic management research: an analysis and critique. Strateg. Manag. J. **17**(6), 441–459 (1996)
59. Menor, L., Roth, A., Manson, C.: Agility in retail banking: a numerical taxonomy of strategic service groups. Manuf. Serv. Oper. Manag. **3**(4), 273–292 (2001)
60. Milligan, G., Cooper, M.: An examination of procedures for determining the number of clusters in a data set. Psychometrika **50**(22), 159–179 (1985)
61. Hair, J., Tatham, R., Anderson, R., Black, W.: Multivariate data analysis. Prentice Hall (1998)
62. Miller, J., Roth, A.: A taxonomy of manufacturing strategies. Manage. Sci. **40**(3), 285–304 (1994)
63. Ceci, F., Masini, A.: Balancing specialized and generic capabilities in the provision of integrated solutions: empirical evidence from the IT sector. Ind. Corp. Chang. **20**(1), 91–132 (2011). https://doi.org/10.1093/icc/dtq069
64. Richard, J.S., Clarke, A., Stavins, R.N. Greeno, J.L., Bavaria, J.L., Cairncross, F., Esty, D.C., Clarke, B.R.A., Stavins, R.N., Greeno, J.L., Bavaria, J.L., Cairncross, F., Esty, D.C., Smart, B., Piet, J., Richard P.W: The Challenge of Going Green. Sustainability (1994). https://hbr.org/1994/07/the-challenge-of-going-green. Accessed 21 May 2021.
65. Bonzanini, D., Giudici, G., Patrucco, A.: The crowdfunding of renewable energy projects. December 2016
66. Ordanini, A., Miceli, L., Pizzetti, M., Parasuraman, A.: Crowd-funding: transforming customers into investors through innovative service platforms. J. Serv. Manag. **22**(4), 443–470 (2011). https://doi.org/10.1108/09564231111155079
67. Zimmerman, M.A., Zeitz, G.J.: Beyond survival: achieving new venture growth by building legitimac. Acad. Manag. Rev. **27**(3), 414–431 (2002). https://doi.org/10.2307/4134387
68. Kubo, T., Veríssimo, D., Uryu, S., Mieno, T., MacMillan, D.: What determines the success and failure of environmental crowdfunding?. Ambio (2018, 2021). https://doi.org/10.1007/s13280-021-01522-0
69. Moss, T.W., Neubaum, D.O., Meyskens, M.: The effect of virtuous and entrepreneurial orientations on microfinance lending and repayment: a signaling theory perspective. Entrep. Theory Pract. **39**(1), 27–52 (2015). https://doi.org/10.1111/etap.12110
70. Di, P.F.: Deciphering Crowdfunding. In: Disrupting Finance; Palgrave Studies in Digital Business and Enabling Technologies, pp. 1–14 (2018)
71. Signaling in equity crowdfunding. Entrep. Theory Pract. **39**(4), 955–980 (2015). https://doi.org/10.1111/etap.12157.
72. Bapnaa, S.: Complementarity of signals in early-stage equity investment decisions: evidence from a randomized field experiment. Manage. Sci. **65**(2), 933–952 (2019). https://doi.org/10.1287/mnsc.2017.2833

73. Bernstein, S., Korteweg, A., Laws, K.: Attracting early-stage investors: evidence from a randomized field experiment. J. Financ. **72**(2), 509–538 (2017). https://doi.org/10.1111/jofi.12470
74. Kgoroeadira, R., Burke, A., van Stel, A.: Small business online loan crowdfunding: who gets funded and what determines the rate of interest? Small Bus. Econ. **52**(1), 67–87 (2019). https://doi.org/10.1007/s11187-017-9986-z

Playing (with) Sustainability: A Multi-purpose Gamification Case

Alessia Zoppelletto and Roberta Cuel

Abstract The paper analyzes the Gamindo case study, a multi-sided digital platform that offers gamified services to answer the needs of three different categories of actors: firms, non-profit organizations, and gamers. The analysis focuses on the interdependencies between actors/stakeholders on an intermediary digital platform which acts as a focal firm in the digital business ecosystem. The paper adopts a qualitative methodology to analyze a four-year longitudinal case study of an Italian startup. Together with direct observation and participation in the development of the startup ecosystem in its early stages, the authors collected secondary data, interviews and organized several focus groups. In the rapidly evolving context represented by the game industry, the selected case study highlights the growth of a highly innovative digital platform ecosystem combining new mutual relationships between actors in a market. The Gamindo ecosystem can be seen as a catalyst for purpose-driven complementary actors willing to address the challenges of sustainability resulting in positive externalities for the environment and society as a whole. The paper theoretically contributes to the rapidly growing body of literature investigating both gamification for business and business ecosystems. It also contributes to existing CSR literature by providing new insights on how intermediary platforms may play a role in the spread of the innovative practices connected with sustainability outcomes. The practical implications of the paper demonstrate how purposed-advergames can be used by firms to develop CSR activities; how non-profit organizations might raise money from networking externalities and the involvement of gamers/donators; and how Gamindo orchestrates a multi-purposed game ecosystem.

Keywords Casual game · Advergames · Digital business ecosystem · Intermediary platform · Sustainability

A. Zoppelletto · R. Cuel (✉)
Department of Economics and Management, University of Trento, Via Inama, 5, 38123 Trento, Italy
e-mail: roberta.cuel@unitn.it

A. Zoppelletto
e-mail: alessia.zoppelletto@unitn.it

S. Za et al. (eds.), *Sustainable Digital Transformation*, Lecture Notes in Information Systems and Organisation 59, https://doi.org/10.1007/978-3-031-15770-7_4

1 Introduction

In 2021, 1 billion online gamers worldwide (China, South Korea, and Japan included) are estimated to have added $21.1 billion to global revenues. The Covid-19 pandemic emergency increased these numbers by 22% and in 2025, online gaming audiences are estimated to surpass 1.3 billion [7]. Game markets, serious games, purpose games, and gamification have received increased attention by marketing firms and CSR departments in both public and non-profit organizations. Intermediaries have thus met this market by providing game solutions for companies that need to offer different services for inhouse training, consumer advertising, and brand awareness to name but a few.

The scenario described above calls attention to the fact that gaming platforms are becoming collaborative environments that support the co-creation of value, similar to what happens in any inter-organizational business network [24].

Marchand and Hennig-Thurau [20] point out that the phenomenon of technological platforms within the digital game industry sector is increasing as a result of the disruptive transformations which occurred within its value chain [22]. These gaming platforms can be analyzed using the digital business ecosystem framework because digital platform ecosystems comprise a "*platform owner that implements governance mechanisms to facilitate value-creating mechanisms on a digital platform between the platform owner and an ecosystem of autonomous complementors and consumers*" [16, p. 90].

The paper provides empirical studies within the framework of business ecosystems by investigating "*longitudinal, within-industry or cross-industry research linking changes in modularization with the emergence and growth of ecosystems*" as suggested by Jacobides et al. [18, p. 2267]. A four-year longitudinal case study is proposed: Gamindo, a multi-sided platform, acts as an intermediary digital platform providing gamified services to three different types of actors. The paper focuses on the interdependencies between the different stakeholders involved in the platform.

This case study aims to provide insight into the emergence of the phenomena of multi-purpose gamification ecosystems. In particular, the study focuses on how intermediary platforms may play a role in the spread of new practices connected with sustainability outcomes.

In the next section, the literature review is sketched out, and the methodology is described in Sect. 3. The case study is presented and analyzed in Sects. 4 and 5, followed by the discussion and conclusions.

2 Literature Review

2.1 Business Ecosystems

The term digital business ecosystem was initially referred to as a *"...collaborative environment made up of different entities that co-create value through information and communication technologies* [21, 25].

In the last decade, however, ecosystem literature has drawn attention to the concept of "ecosystem" as a new category to describe the environment [14, 18]. For example, the bibliometric analysis in [27] shows a citation network of over 300 selected papers on this topic, and the academic debate has made significant steps towards a systematic analysis of this concept.

A useful definition of the ecosystem concept was given by Adner [1, p. 2] as *"the alignment structure of the multilateral set of partners that need to interact in order for a focal value proposition to materialize"*.

Furthermore, a recent study [18] gave an important contribution to a theory of ecosystems by drawing a crystal-clear distinction between ecosystems and entities like markets, alliances, or hierarchically managed supply chains. According to this study, ecosystems are typically formed by a set of actors experiencing (different degrees of) complementarities in production and consumption. Hou and Shi [17] suggest that a coevolution view helps in understanding the complementarities between actors, and how affiliation in ecosystems occur and allow the focal firm to continuously innovate. Jacobides et al. [18] also differentiated between business ecosystems (focused on a particular innovation or value proposition), innovation ecosystems (explicit innovation), and platform ecosystems (how actors organize around a specific platform).

Studies on platform-based ecosystems have attempted to define different categories of platform ecosystems, such as industry platforms, digital platforms, multi-sided platforms, etc. [12, 15, 19, 28]. Indeed, by analyzing a wide range of industry platforms Gawer and Cusumano [12] identified internal or company-specific platforms and external or industry-wide platforms as the two predominant types of platforms. However, we can find other distinctions in literature such as the one proposed by Hein et al. [15] regarding digital platforms which *"combine and deploy technologies in new ways to incubate and coordinate an ecosystem of supply and demand"* [15, p. 88].

Most studies regarding digital platforms also consider the role of the leading firm or orchestrator [8, 13] since ecosystem platforms are centered around a technology platform comprising a core and a periphery [4–6, 12, 23, 26, 29].

2.2 Gamification and Sustainability

As pointed out in the extensive review [20], the game industry sector has undergone great transformation over the last decade and game mechanics have been applied to ethical cause-related initiatives [11] by developing serious games, or games on purpose. On the one hand, games on purpose develop new attractive methods of learning, developing knowledge or skills in an engaging and motivating way [3]. On the other, serious games employ game mechanics or gamification to educate and change patterns of experience and/or behaviors [9].

The diffusion of mobile technology represents a remarkable opportunity to leverage sustainability action into taking advantage of the resulting new channels of communication. Through games companies can capture the full attention of players by engaging them in stories, activities, actions, advertising banners, brands, etc. As underlined by Alilnikula et. al. [2, p. 247], *"mobile technology offers great opportunities for renewing corporations' sustainability agenda"* since they can engage with gamers who are potential customers.

An increasing number of intermediary platforms that combine gaming with sustainability issues are springing up across Europe: the authors identified six innovative digital intermediary platforms and summarized a number of their most significant features in Table 1.

The first intermediary presented is *GreenAPES,* a platform that provides services to three different stakeholders: the public actor, enterprises and individuals. On the platform any public administration can develop virtual and real games to encourage citizens to change their conduct into more sustainable attitudes, and to measure and reward their sustainable behaviors. The public actor can decide which actions to reward (mobility, waste management, participation and volunteering, energy savings, local consumption, etc.), by developing a game and a scheme of incentives and rewards. Enterprises can benefit from the platform to attract consumers who are attentive to sustainability issues, and involve citizens in loyalty programs by using the platform to develop corporate social responsibility projects and strategies (CSR). GreenAPES also offers tailor-made solutions to involve company employees in CSR projects. Finally, even single individuals can benefit from the platform by participating in and developing a community which shares good practices and promotes the adoption of new eco-innovative processes and habits.

The second intermediary is *Gamindo* which involves enterprises, non-profit organizations and users. With Gamindo the user/gamer can donate to specific social projects by playing video games. The economic resources donated to the campaign receivers do not come directly from the users, but from CSR investments undertaken by enterprises that have the opportunity to customize the games transforming them into an advergame. This will be used to sponsor products, services, and brands in the games available on the platform. Receivers, usually non-profit organizations, obtain donations through the platform simply and transparently.

DonaApp is the third intermediary platform proposed and involves companies, non-profit organizations and users. Users can transform their purchases made in

Table 1 Intermediary platforms: stakeholders involved

	Stakeholders involved by the intermediary platform					
Intermediary	For profit	Users	Non profit	Public sector	Intermediary payoff	Intermediary founded in
GreenAPES	✓	✓		✓	"The social network for environmental sustainability"	2014
Gamindo	✓	✓	✓		"Donate by playing video games"	2018
Donapp	✓	✓	✓		"Put together companies and non-profit organizations, allowing consumers to donate "at zero cost" by buying goods and services online or physically in the shops that join the circuit"	2013
Charity miles		✓	✓		"Walk, Run, Bike for a Cause"	2012
Treedom	✓	✓			"Let's green the planet"	2010
WeGiveIt	✓		✓		"Digital for Brands with Purpose"	2015

different shops into donations through the platform. Companies can develop a campaign of cause-related marketing through Donapp and at the end of the campaign, the company can convert its budget into a specific donation after considering the preferences expressed by its customers.

Charity Miles is an intermediary for users and non-profit organizations that enables people to earn money for charity whenever they walk, run or bike. On this platform, a community of people sharing the same interests (sport) is created by building a scheme of incentives, prizes and rewards. Many people raise money by doing activities like marathons and taking part in running events. The more money users earn for their selected charity, the more chances they will have to win *cool* prizes from the platform's sponsors.

The fifth intermediary is *Treedom* which involves enterprises and users. Through the donation of users or firms, Treedom finances rural/farm enterprises that want to plant trees in Asia, Africa, South America and Italy. The platform supports their work in the early years when the trees are still not productive. Farmers receive know-how and technical support for planting and tree management, and the trees are photographed, geographically localized, and monitored by Treedom over time. Through its planting activities, Treedom contributes to the achievement of ten United Nations Objectives to ensure a sustainable future.

The last intermediary presented is *WeGiveIt* and involves enterprises and non-profit organizations. The platform works with ethical businesses and charities by helping to optimize their digital brand presence and develop their cause marketing strategy. The platform mediates the needs of charities, that ask for help in navigating a digital transformation, and enterprises that need advice on incorporating their sustainable activities/side into their overall marketing and business strategy.

The study recognizes the need to provide extensive insights into the field of purpose gaming and to answer the research question by investigating the case of an Italian startup that represents an intermediary in the purpose-driven gamification market.

3 Methodology

To provide a more in-depth understanding of the business model, the processes, the interdependencies among actors of a digital ecosystem platform, the paper investigates one of the above-mentioned intermediary solutions, namely Gamindo. It is an innovative startup that connects different actors (for-profit, non-profit and gamers). Gamindo can be considered as a digital platform ecosystem which produces innovation for the single participant: (i) the contributors (usually profit firms that invest in Corporate Social Responsibility—CSR); (ii) non-profit organizations that require funding for social projects; (iii) the users or gamers that desire to play and spend their time fruitfully donating to non-profit organizations. The authors also selected Gamindo because one of the authors was actively involved in the startup's strategy definition from 2018 to 2021 as well as in the preparation of the business plan.

In line with [10, 30], an explorative case study was conducted to analyze the phenomena of a purpose-driven ecosystem, taking into consideration multi-purpose gamification. Data was collected during the whole process, at several points of time, and a blueprint was developed (see Fig. 1) to better understand how the purpose-driven ecosystem was created. The evolution of the intermediary involved the following phases: (1) foundation and beta testing, (2) incubation period in a startup accelerator, and (3) systematic growth.

Nicolò Santini developed the original idea for Gamindo in 2018 during his master's thesis project. Soon a second founding member, Matteo Albrizio, decided to join the project and several game developers were onboarded. During this first stage of the Gamindo evolution, the business plan was written, and partnerships with enterprises and non-profit organizations were developed. Thanks to these activities, the initial funds were raised, and the first beta test of the platform took place. After having

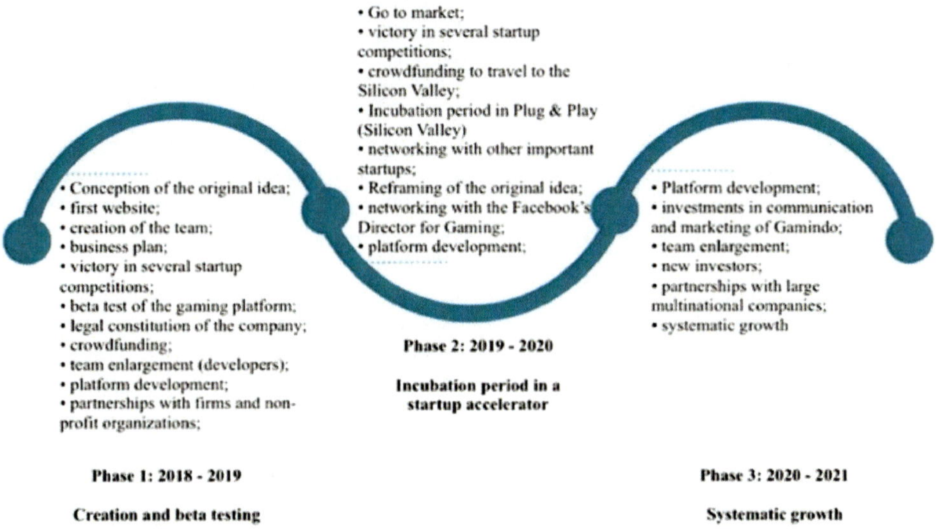

Fig. 1 Gamindo blueprint. *Source* Author's elaboration

analyzed the collected data, the authors called the first year of Gamindo "*foundation and beta testing*".

Not long after, the well-known startup accelerator, Plug&Play, incubated Gamindo allowing them to develop the beta version of the platform and, thanks to the competencies acquired during the incubation period, the project was refined, in particular concerning its blueprint and hardware investments. This second phase, which lasted another year, was entitled the "*incubation period in a startup accelerator*".

From 2020 onwards the startup platform experienced a phase of "*systematic growth*"; the team has and is still expanding with six new job offers now available on the Gamindo website. Moreover, several important partnerships have been established both with large companies (e.g., Nespresso, Coca-Cola) and non-profit organizations (e.g., WWF, Emergency) and the number of gamers all over the world is still increasing. Additionally, from the financial standpoint, in August 2021 the Gamindo founders ask for a capital injection of €450,000 and, thanks to new investors, the Gamindo shareholder composition changed.

For the case study, data was collected from participant observation, personal interviews, and by collecting written material both online and offline; for example, published official documents, internal documents, articles, and company brochures: see Table 2.

By using the theoretical framework of digital business ecosystems and a qualitative narrative approach, in the following section we analyze the multi-purpose gamification ecosystem where the Gamindo intermediary operates. Each stakeholder involved in the ecosystem will be analyzed utilizing the narrative of the Gamindo founders by directly quoting their words during interviews.

Table 2 Data collection. *Source* Author's elaboration

Collected data	Number	Note
Phase 1: Creation and beta testing		
Focus Group	5	At the beginning (May 2018), five different focus groups led to the definition of the business plan. The protagonists were the two founders, and two business angels: a research fellow in the University of Verona and an accountant
Direct observation	2	On two different days, one before the creation and one after the definition of the business plan, the startup pitched the business idea to investors
Internal Document	1	A business plan was shared by the startup with investors and business angels in order to participate in a national contest on research and innovation, the so-called *PNI*, *Premio Nazionale per l'Innovazione* - National Prize for Innovation
Direct participation	3	Three days of activities for beta testing the platform
Phase 2: Incubation period in a startup accelerator		
Online published Internal document	1	A document on the crowdfunding campaign was published by the startup to benefit from the opportunity to participate in an accelerator phase at Plug & Play (San Francisco incubator—USA)
Interviews	3	During phase 2, three informal interviews took place with the two startup founders to understand the development of the incubation phase
Direct observation	4	During direct observations, researchers participated in meetings to discuss the strengths and weaknesses of the digital platform, and the business process analysis of any inefficiencies. Researchers also participated in the repetitive testing of the new advergames in this phase
Phase 3: Systematic growth		
Interviews	1	During Phase 3, one structured interview was conducted by the intermediary on the topic of the future of the platform and the stakeholders involved
Notes from direct observations	20 pages	Notes were taken during all the phases of the project. Official documents, internal documents, articles, and company brochures were consulted

4 Case Presentation

The Gamindo digital platform provides branded video games aimed at both promoting company products/services and involving gamers to play. This enables the company to donate to non-profit organizations.

In practice, the platform contains a list of advergames, each one a branded casual game designed by Gamindo for a specific company. Casual games are very simple video games targeted at a wide, mass-market audience with a very simple set of rules, and shorter sessions and less learned skills than hardcore games. The advantage of these games is that they can be played anywhere and at any time by everyone. The casual games can be customized according to the specific needs of a firm or chosen from a list—a game catalogue—and then branded by the Gamindo team. The cost to the company depends on two factors: the development of the advergame/related advertising campaign, and the investment in CSR in the form of a donation to the third party.

This number of games allows players to collect coins (or stars) and then choose where to allocate them among the non-profit social projects available in a specific Gamindo catalogue. The virtual coins are transformed into a real economic value and given to third parties, usually specific social projects undertaken by non-profit organizations, via company CSR campaigns. As a result, gamers donate just by spending time on the platform and playing, companies improve their CSR campaigns, and non-profit organizations get their project funded. To ensure maximum transparency on how funds are allocated, the gamers themselves allocate the coins and choose the specific social project. Moreover, once a social project is completely funded, the gamer will receive feedback informing them on how the money has been donated and has been used by the institution. The founders call Gamindo a "*win–win-win platform*" on which users have fun and donate without spending money, companies promote their brand in an engaging CSR game, and non-profit organizations raise funds. Everything is done in a transparent manner raising the trustworthiness of the platform.

5 Case Analysis

Gamindo represents the orchestrator platform of an emergent business ecosystem based on a digital platform that develops a technological standard and creates and maintains *ties* between three groups of stakeholders: profit firms, non-profit organizations and gamers. Gamindo is an intermediary providing disruptive innovation because: (1) firms draw on advergames and implement CSR activities, (2) users/gamers become involved in donation, and (3) non-profit organizations gain increased economic sustainability for their social projects.

As schematized in Fig. 2, Gamindo has changed the relationship between firms, clients, and non-profit organizations by mediating their bond and gathering the different needs of stakeholders. Moreover, Gamindo adds value to the whole network as well as enabling trustworthiness and transparency. In this multi-purpose gamification ecosystem, the intermediary manages a *technological standard* represented by the development of advergames customized to the specific needs of single stakeholder: each game can be considered a digital envelope in which data utilization is collected and managed by the orchestrator.

As shared by one of the Gamindo founders:

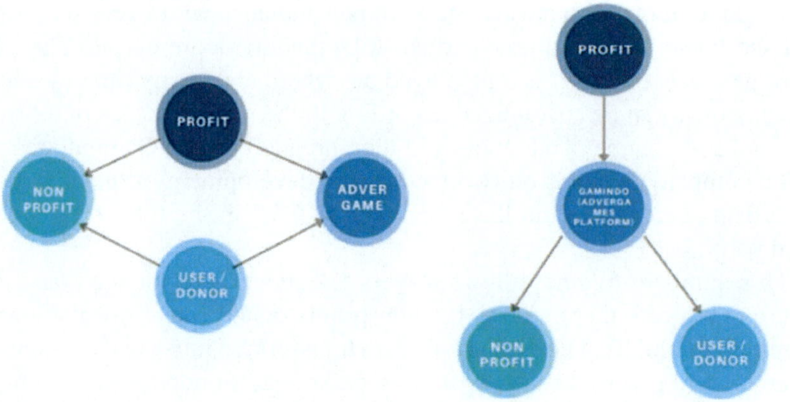

Fig. 2 CSR enterprise strategy with and without the Gamindo digital platform

> A multinational corporation for whom we will make a game in September [2021] contacted us saying that we are the only ones in the world offering this particular service.

In the following subsections each stakeholder contribution, needs and peculiarities will be discussed in detail, and if and how the intermediary induces stakeholders to adopt new behaviors.

5.1 Enterprises

Enterprises are one important actor involved in the ecosystem. Their contribution concerns the investments in CSR made and converted by the platform into donations as well as their requirement to engage with potential customers through sustainability-oriented advergames. In these advergames, the online promotion of the brand is perfectly integrated into the videogame.

> Our bet is that the interaction of the videogame creates an engagement with the potential customer that is stronger than the one provided by an image or a video. These traditional ways of promoting a business do not guarantee a high level of attention from the audience that looks at your content. Therefore, one euro invested in Gamindo has more value than one euro invested in traditional forms of advertisement (e.g., television or radio). Moreover, firms also obtain benefits in terms of reputation by using a form of socially responsible advertising that allows the linking of advertising with CSR (Founder of Gamindo).

Gamindo represents an innovative way to conduct CSR. The platform allows the creation of new languages to engage potential consumers, and to increase a company's impact from a social and environmental perspective as well as the brand reputation of companies investing in CSR.

It is interesting to note that the Gamindo solution might induce changes in the internal organizational coordination processes of profit firms. One of the founders pointed out that often Marketing and CSR departments do not interact, but in using

Gamindo, they need to cooperate since the advertising campaign has a strong social impact. In other words, the sustainability strategy of the firm needs to be combined with the marketing one. *"To exploit the platform benefits is not always easy because in large companies the Marketing Department that deals with the advertising and the CSR Department that deals with social responsibility do not speak to each other. If we simply want to deal with Marketing Departments and not care about the social impact, we would probably put in 70% less effort because the hardest part is connecting these two worlds inside the company that, in most cases, do not communicate"*. (Founder of Gamindo).

5.2 *Individual Users or Gamers*

Individual users choosing Gamindo to play casual video games answer their need to donate without spending or asking for transparent financing of social projects. At the same time, they effectively contribute to the platform ecosystem by impartially allocating economic resources (the collected coins).

What is peculiar to this gaming ecosystem is that the target users are mixed:

"The gamer that plays this kind of advergame isn't the "typical nerd" that comes into the mind of all of us when we think of video game players" (Founder of Gamindo). Gamindo addresses the *"casual gamers"*, people who play video games in their free time and enjoy simple games. These people instead of choosing games that have a lot of annoying advertisements during the game experience (such as banners) use the intermediary platform that does not have invasive advertising and where they can also have the social benefit of converting their time into donations.

The Gamindo platform also has positive externalities since by giving users rewards (coins) or incentives (e.g., best player ranking), the platform motivates people to play in order to see the results of their positive actions.

In this way, the platform sets the conditions to achieve the economic sustainability of social projects over time: in the future, Gamindo will also allow users to directly donate their private resources inside the platform.

5.3 *Non-profit Organizations*

Non-profit organizations are the beneficiaries of the platform and can be divided essentially into two classes: the international non-profit organizations, which are well structured and operate in various countries, and the smaller and less articulated local organizations.

Gamindo offers non-profit organizations the possibility to collect resources through engaging in fundraising activities. Non-profit organizations present valuable social projects that can be included in the platform and selected by users. Their objective is to collect economic resources (or donations) to finance social projects and sensitize the population to those important causes.

> For the Third Sector, the value of the platform is represented by its ability to raise public awareness about social causes, increase confidence in nonprofit organizations by incrementing transparency and, above all, raise funds to help in guaranteeing their economic stability in the long term (Founder of Gamindo).

Through its innovative services, Gamindo induces non-profit firms to be proactive in presenting their projects to the platform, thus helping these organizations to communicate the value and the importance of their work.

5.4 The Future of the Multi-purpose Gamification Ecosystem

To conclude, this new ecosystem has substantial growth potential. In the words of one of the Gamindo founders:

> In the future, many new players are going to increase in number and join the ecosystem. For instance, nowadays the eSports industry is growing, and the visors industry is developing its technology. Additionally, new dimensions are going to be part of the world of video games, let's think for example about the potential of the music industry. Just to give an example of the magnitude that the following developments can have in this market, let's think of Travis Scott's concert that took place inside the Fortnite game in April 2020, which was followed by 27.7 million players. Moreover, Burger King's case was interesting too, because it put together the world of enterprises with the real world through a game: if you won something in the game, then you received a free coupon to have a food product in real life. (Founder of Gamindo).

Moreover, regarding new potential competitors, the point of view of Gamindo is very clear:

> Currently there are no direct competitors that use video games like Gamindo does but there are still competitors who use gamification to give people the opportunity to donate, such as Charity Miles. We hope that new players will increase in this sector (also companies that will do similar things to us) because this means that there is a market, that this market attracts collective attention and that there is demand. This is a very positive thing that happened to other innovative startups in the past. For example, Just Eat started in 2000 and in 2011 other competitors entered the market (for example Deliveroo, Foodora). Since then, Just Eat has not declined, on the contrary, it has grown even more (Founder of Gamindo).

6 Discussion and Conclusion

This paper focuses on the impact of multi-purpose gamification ecosystems by presenting the case of Gamindo, an intermediary that developed an innovative digital platform based on purpose gaming. As stated by Gawer and Cusumano [12], digital platforms have enabled significant industry transformation and created new foundations for ecosystem innovation.

In the last ten years, the game market has seen the growth of new digital gaming platforms, with a particular orientation to sustainability issues, founded by intermediaries that have started to mediate the relationship between different actors (enterprises, users, non-profit and public actors) in order to address a sustainable challenge. These multi-sided platforms offer gamification services to encounter the needs of very different actors, highlighting the emergence of the phenomena of multi-purpose gamification.

In this new scenario, Gamindo emerged as a frontrunner in sustainability-oriented digital gaming platforms: the intermediary was able to exploit not only the benefits connected to network externalities, but it also represents the first mover and the orchestrator in this particular ecosystem.

In this study case, the ecosystem itself does not produce innovation only for the end-user but does so for every single participant in the ecosystem, namely both contributor and user.

Because sustainability is a global issue and requires to be addressed in a collaborative manner from different stakeholder perspectives, this case study highlights the potential of a multi-purpose gamification ecosystem to represent an innovative way in guaranteeing the economic sustainability of social projects in the long term. The Gamindo ecosystem can be seen as a catalyst for purpose-driven actors—for-profit firms engaging in CSR, non-profit organizations attempting to raise resources for social projects, and gamers wishing to donate—that are complementary in addressing the challenges of sustainability, resulting in positive externalities for the environment and society as a whole.

6.1 Practical Implications

Our results have several important implications. First, through the use of purposed-advergames, firms can incorporate a sustainability strategy into their overall marketing and business strategy, thus strengthening the engagement with their stakeholders. Various studies have demonstrated that sustainability-oriented firms are more likely to benefit from the support of loyal customers in difficult times and such firms can improve their financial resilience.

Secondly, non-profit organizations can benefit from the development of this type of gaming platform to sensitize people to social causes, and to guarantee the availability of social services and social projects in the long term. By exploiting these solutions, charities that need help in navigating the digital transformation can improve the communication strategy of their social projects and increase awareness on global and local issues.

Thirdly, the development of multi-purposed game ecosystems can also have an effect at the individual level: previous studies have found that purpose and cause-related games (often called prosocial games) increase mutual helping behavior.

Finally, sustainability-oriented policymakers can benefit from the existence of these ecosystems that, together with public resources, help in guaranteeing the economic sustainability of social projects carried out by non-profit organizations.

6.2 Theoretical Implications

The authors contribute to the existing CSR literature by providing new insights on how intermediary platforms may play a role in the spread of innovative practices connected to sustainability outcomes.

The authors also propose an interesting case study in which the digital business ecosystem theory is used to identify actor interdependencies. Moreover, the specific characteristics of the case study demonstrate that the theoretical model can be used to analyze small-medium size networks, thus underlying the role of digital platform intermediaries as focal players in the digital business ecosystems.

Finally, the study contributes to the rapidly growing body of literature investigating both gamification for business, and business ecosystems.

6.3 Limitations and Future Research

The following limitations should be considered when interpreting our results. First, since this is a case study, the generalizability of the outcomes is possible only to a limited extent. It would be interesting to investigate sustainable gamification cases in different socioeconomic contexts as well as in different industry settings. Additionally, this paper focuses on the case of market sustainability-oriented advergames: other ecosystems employing gamification elements might demonstrate different peculiarities from those in the present case study. However, these limitations can be considered avenues for future research. For instance, studies can be developed in different social or economic contexts, and investigation and comparison of the present case with other intermediary platforms and ecosystems employing gamification mechanisms could be undertaken.

References

1. Adner, R.: Ecosystem as structure: an actionable construct for strategy. J. Manag. **43**(1), 39–58 (2017). https://doi.org/10.1177/0149206316678451
2. Alinikula, P., Latikka, J.L., Paanajärvi, J.: Gaming for good changing the game for corporate sustainability. ICT for Sustainability 2014, ICT4S 2014, No. Ict4s, pp. 245–247 (2014)
3. Argenton, L., Pallavicini, F., Barone, G., Zini, A., Garcea, G., Zanacchi, A., Mantovani, F.: Hacking well-being: can serious games fit positive technology framework?". In: Integrating Technology in Positive Psychology Practice, pp. 230–246 (2016)

4. Beirão, G., Patrício, L., Fisk, R.P.: Value co-creation in service ecosystems: investigating health care at the micro, meso, and macro levels. J. Serv. Manag. **28**, 227–249 (2017)
5. Ceccagnoli, M., Forman, C., Huang, P., Wu, D.J.:Cocreation of value in a platform ecosystem! The case of enterprise software. MIS Q. 263–290 (2012)
6. Cennamo, C., Santaló, J.: Generativity tension and value creation in platform ecosystems. Organ. Sci. **30**, 617–641 (2019)
7. Clement, J.: Online Gaming—Statistics & Facts, Published on May 7, 2021. Retrieved from https://www.statista.com/topics/1551/online-gaming/, 1 June 2021
8. De Reuver, M., Sørensen, C., Basole, R.C.: The digital platform: a research agenda. J. Inf. Technol. **33**, 124–135 (2018)
9. Deterding, S., Dixon, D., Khaled, R., Nacke, L.: From game design elements to gamefulness: defining" gamification. In Proceedings of the 15th International Academic MindTrek Conference: Envisioning Future Media Environments, pp. 9–15. (2011)
10. Eisenhardt, K.M.: Building theories from case study research. Acad. Manag. Rev. **14**(4), 548 (1989)
11. Fleming, T.M., Bavin, L., Stasiak, K., Hermansson-Webb, E., Merry, S.N., Cheek, C., Hetrick, S.: Serious games and gamification for mental health: current status and promising directions. Front. Psych. **7**, 215 (2017)
12. Gawer, A., Cusumano, M.A.: Industry platforms and ecosystem innovation. J. Product Innov. Manag. **31**(3), 417–433 (2014)
13. Gawer, A.: Digital platforms' boundaries: the interplay of firm scope, platform sides, and digital interfaces. Long Range Plan. **54**(5), 102045 (2021)
14. Gupta, R., Mejia, C., Kajikawa, Y.: Business, innovation and digital ecosystems landscape survey and knowledge cross sharing. Technol. Forecast. Soc. Chang. **147**, 100–109 (2019)
15. Hein, A., Schreieck, M., Wiesche, M., Böhm, M., Krcmar, H.: The emergence of native multi-sided platforms and their influence on incumbents. Electron. Mark. 1–17 (2019)
16. Hein, A., Schreieck, M., Riasanow, T., Setzke, D.S., Wiesche, M., Böhm, M., Krcmar, H.: Digital platform ecosystems. Electron. Mark. Electron. Mark. **30**(1), 87–98 (2020)
17. Hou, H., Shi, Y.: Ecosystem-as-structure and ecosystem-as-coevolution: a constructive examination. Technovation **100**, 102193 (2021)
18. Jacobides, M.G., Cennamo, C., Gawer, A.: Towards a theory of ecosystems. Strateg. Manag. J. **39**(8), 2255–2276 (2018)
19. Kopalle, P.K., Kumar, V., Subramaniam, M.: How legacy firms can embrace the digital ecosystem via digital customer orientation. J. Acad. Mark. Sci. **48**(1), 114–131 (2020)
20. Marchand, A., Hennig-Thurau, T.: Value creation in the video game industry: industry economics, consumer benefits, and research opportunities. J. Interact. Mark. **27**, 141–157 (2013)
21. Nachira, F., Dini, P., Nicolai, A.: A network of digital business ecosystems for Europe: roots, processes and perspectives. Introductory Paper 106, European Commission, Bruxelles (2007)
22. Nucciarelli, A., Li, F., Fernandes, K.J., Goumagias, N., Cabras, I., Devlin, S., Cowling, P.: From value chains to technological platforms: the effects of crowdfunding in the digital game industry. J. Bus. Res. **78**, 341–352 (2017)
23. Pera, R., Occhiocupo, N., Clarke, J.: Motives and resources for value co-creation in a multi-stakeholder ecosystem: a managerial perspective. J. Bus. Res. **69**, 4033–4041 (2016)
24. Schoenberger, E.: From Fordism to flexible accumulation: technology, competitive strategies, and international location. Environ. Plan. D Soc. Space **6**, 245–262 (1988)
25. Senyo, P.K., Liu, K., Effah, J.: Digital business ecosystem: literature review and a framework for future research. Int. J. Inf. Manage. **47**, 52–64 (2019)
26. Subramaniam, M., Iyer, B., Venkatraman, V.: Competing in digital ecosystems. Bus. Horiz. **62**(1), 83–94 (2019)
27. Suominen, A., Seppänen, M., Dedehayir, O.: A bibliometric review on innovation systems and ecosystems: a research agenda. Eur. J. Innov. Manag. **22**, 335–360 (2019)
28. Vargo, S.L., Wieland, H., Akaka, M.A.: Innovation through institutionalization: a service ecosystems perspective. Ind. Mark. Manage. **44**, 63–72 (2015)

29. Wareham, J., Fox, P.B., Cano Giner, J.L.: Technology ecosystem governance. Organ. Sci. **25**, 1195–1215 (2014)
30. Yin, R.K.: Case Study Research: Design and Methods B2—Case Study Research: Design and Methods. Sage Publications, California, CA (1984)

How to Measure Political Connection in the Directors' Network

Sohail Mansha, Stefano Za, and Gianluca Antonucci

Abstract Informal social contract such as political connection plays a significant role for directors' network but difficult to explore their role through traditional measures. Different social network measures labelled as "centralities" have previously been used in the network analysis community to find influential nodes in a network. It is debatable how valid these centrality measures for the political connection are. This paper aims not only to identify the political connection through social network analysis but to analyze the different levels of political connection through different centrality measures according to the country's institutional environment. For this purpose, we used data from a relationship-based economy like Pakistan from 2009 to 2015. We analyze the five different levels of political connection and examine their role through five social network measures: degree, closeness centrality, betweenness centrality, eigenvector, and eccentricity. Our finding demonstrates that degree, betweenness centrality, and eigenvector are not suitable measures for political connection role and control in the directors' network. Closeness centrality gives a better understanding of how other directors are closed to politically connected directors and which level of political connection attracts the other directors but couldn't explain how far a political director can access. We found eccentricity as the most suitable measure for the political connection and their different role. We also found the federal and provincial level political connections become more central and important through the eccentricity measure after the regime's shift from autocratic to democratic.

Keywords Political connection · Director network · Graph theory · Social network analysis · Eccentricity

S. Mansha (✉) · S. Za · G. Antonucci
DEA—Department of management and Business Economics, G.d'Annuzio University of Cheiti-Pescara, Viale Pindaro, n. 65127, Pescara, Italy
e-mail: sohail.mansha@unich.it

S. Za et al. (eds.), *Sustainable Digital Transformation*, Lecture Notes in Information Systems and Organisation 59, https://doi.org/10.1007/978-3-031-15770-7_5

1 Introduction

Over the recent years, a growing body of literature is extensively employing graph theory and networking measures to explore the importance of informal ties, which consists of multilayer of networks and challenging to find out through the traditional measures [1–3]. Previously, the scholars pointed out the networking theories and analysis based on the social capital and social structures in the western countries [4–6]. At the same time, a recent body of the literature links the networking assumption to investigate the informal social contracts and their role in the corporate sector [7, 8]. Specifically, in the relationship-based economies, studies found that several informal social contracts have a significant influence on the corporate sectors, such as Wasta in Arab, Blat in Russia, Yongo in South Korea, and Guanxi in China [9, 10]. Similarly, some researchers identify also the political connection as an important informal social contract for corporate firms across different countries [11]. Due to the significant presence and control, the findings emphasize the beneficial role and structural control of political connection in both emerging and developed economies [12]. But the benefits arising from the political connections are highly associated with their type, according to the country institutional environment [13] and the position into the corporate network. These insights are difficult to be identified through the conventional quantitative approach.

In the corporate networks, firms share their directors with other firms, leading to directors' networks. Under the resource-based view, literature accentuates that a directors' network provides assistance to access the external and internal resources [14]. Highly connected directors provide legitimacy, skills, information, and relations with the other stakeholder. Moreover, better-connected directors increase social capital and reduce the external environmental uncertainties [15]. Furthermore, directors with different attributes are more beneficial for the corporate outcomes, such as financial and legal experts are highly connected in the Indian corporate network [2].

It is therefore imperative to analyze how informal social contracts such as political connections assist the director network formation over the period. In this regard, network measures more suitable for investigating the different actors are based on "centrality", which helps to identify position, knowledge transformation, and ties among the other nodes of the network. Financial studies mainly focused on centrality measures, such as degree, closeness, betweenness, and eigenvalues [16–18]. However, eccentricity might be the most appropriate measure to identify how far a node can reach, in the network, when it comes to the distance-based relationship [5]. Thus, it remains a critical unexplored question *which network measure is more suitable to identify the informal social contract as the political connection in the director networks.*

To address this question, the study deploys the different social network analysis measures to identify the important political connection position and their influence in the director network. Additionally, the study compares the different network measure outcomes to look for the most suitable network measure for the political connection understanding. In order to reach its aim, the study used data from 2009 to 2015 from an emerging country like Pakistan. For achieving the study goal, Pakistan is a more suitable market due to several reasons. First, several researchers reveal the extensive existence of political connections in Pakistani corporate firms. An immature financial system and weak legal environment help political connections to take the benefits for the corporate decisions [19, 20]. Secondly, Pakistan faced three autocratic regimes after the independence in 1947, and the last autocratic regime ended in 2008 after ten years. Nevertheless it provided the opportunity for civil and military personals to penetrate the corporate world.

Moreover, after 2008, the democratic government flourishes the ground for the elected members. In 2013, for the first time since the independence a democratic government completed its tenure and shifted the power to another elected government. This unique institutional setting allows us to investigate the directors with a different political background, their position, and influence in the directors' network over the period. Thirdly, different types of political connections help to better understand the different network measures according to the country institutional setting over the time period.

The paper is structured as follows. The following paragraph describes the importance of social network measures. The third one presents the methodology. The fourth one presents social network analysis findings and discussion. The last one shows the conclusion.

2 Traditional Approach to Measure Political Connections and Board Interlocking Importance

To understand the phenomenon of political connection, researchers have used different definitions and quantitative approaches for politically connected firms according to the legal system and authorities of every investigated country. Researchers have constructed binary variables for political connections through corporate lobbying activities for the USA [39], executive and supervisory board members close to the ruling party in Germany [36], board members as politicians with respect to being provincial or federal assembly members in Pakistan [40], CEO politicians, government officers or military personnel in China [35], board members from government committee members [38], industry regulators [37], top appointed bureaucrats [33], and chiefs of state or those closely related to the top politicians [12]. Similarly, Wong and Hooy [13] exploited different levels of political connection in Malaysia on the basis of government ownership, boards of directors, family members and through business owners' personal relations.

However, Tsai et al. [41] highlighted the importance of social networks and assembled political connections, for which the vertices were the board members and the edges represented the co-attendance of a firm's participants at the same government institutions. Findings indicated that the benefits of political connections highly depend on the type of politicians on the board and their respective power. Similarly, other studies have revealed that direct connections with the government and the appointment of political members on boards are costly for firms [34]. In this regard, board interlocking provides an important channel to build relationships with the political connection by sharing their directors rather than directly appointing them to the board. In corporate networks, firms share their directors with other firms, leading to directors' networks.

From a resource-based view, the literature accentuates that a directors' network provides assistance to access both external and internal resources [14]. Highly connected directors provide legitimacy, skills, information and relations with the other stakeholders. Moreover, better-connected directors increase social capital and reduce the external environmental uncertainties [15]. Directors with different attributes are more beneficial for the corporate outcomes; for example, financial and legal experts are highly connected in the Indian corporate network [2]. It is necessary to enhance our understanding of how political connections matter for the directors' network with different power and authorities and which measure can better capture the presence of political members for the network formation under institutional environmental change.

3 Social Network Measures

Apart from the traditional approach, graph theory and social network analysis techniques have become, over the recent years, more popular to explore the social interactions among the different actors of corporate networks. Various studies utilize social network analysis techniques for the potential corporate outcomes [11, 21]. Different measures are employed to identify important node in the network, and the outcomes are highly associated with the properties and position of the node in the network [22]. The importance can be interpreted in different ways and motivations, leading to the different measure of "centralities" for identifying the central node. Previous studies focused on the centrality measures such as degree, closeness, betweenness, and eigenvalues for the corporate networks [2, 11]. Each measure gives different information about the nodes and their ties, which can be described as.

3.1 Degree

Degree is defined as the number of links incident upon a node [4]. For an undirected network, the degree of a node in the network can be written as:

$$C_D = \sum_{i=1}^{n} a(V_i, T_j) \tag{1}$$

where $a(V_i, T_j) = 1$ if and only if V_i and T_j are connected by a line in the network. It is the simplest and widely used measure. The degree of each director explains the number of direct ties with the other directors in the directors' network. High degree values indicate the more connected directors in the network.

3.2 Closeness Centrality

Closeness centrality takes into account the shortest distance of each node to every other node in the network. If the length of a node v has the shortest path to all the other nodes in the network, then node v has a greater value and closeness centrality is defined as the inverse of the shortest distance of node v to all the other nodes, which can be written as:

$$C_C(v) = \frac{n-1}{\sum_t^n dist(v,t)} \tag{2}$$

where v *and* t are nodes of a network. For the information diffusion process, a director with high closeness centrality values received quicker information than the other directors in the network.

3.3 Betweenness Centrality

Betweenness centrality estimates the proportion of times a node falls along the shortest path between pairs of nodes in the network. It indicates the ability of a node to control the flow of information through it. Betweenness centrality of a node can be expressed as:

$$C_B(v) = \sum_{s \neq v \neq t} \frac{\sigma_{st}(v)}{\sigma_{st}} \tag{3}$$

where σ_{st} is the shortest path from node s to node t and $\sigma_{st}(v)$ are the shortest paths that intersect node v. For the director networks, high betweenness centrality directors may have the ability to change or hinder the flow of information through them.

3.4 Eigenvector Centrality

Eigenvector centrality measures the node importance by giving importance to the nodes' neighbours [23]. Essentially it is a measure of how well connected are the nodes to which a given node is connected. It is the measure of the influence of a node in the network and can be written as:

$$\lambda v = Av \tag{4}$$

where A is the adjacency matrix of the graph, λ is a constant and v is the eigenvector of a node. Eigenvector centrality counts the number of connected nodes to a node and considers how many well-connected nodes are attached to that node. In the directors' network, the eigenvector helps to identify the influential directors in the networks.

As mentioned above, each measure gives information related to the close ties for each node and explains how they control and access the information. But when it comes to exploring the distance-based influence of political connections and their reach in the network, all the four measures do not fully explain the characteristics of the politically connected directors in the network. For this purpose, eccentricity is a simple notion.

3.5 Eccentricity

The eccentricity of a node is the value of the maximum distance from any other node in the connected network. It gives us information on how a node can access any other node in the network [24]. It allows measuring the wideness of a node within the network. The eccentricity of a node v in the connected network G is the maximum distance to any node u within the network [5]. However, for a disconnected network, the eccentricity of a node is infinite [24]. Formally eccentricity can be presented as in Eq. 5:

$$e_G(v) = \max\{distance_G(v, u) : u \in v_G\} \in N \cup \{\infty\} \tag{5}$$

Eccentricity provides helpful insights to overlook director's access to the other directors in the network. Especially for the political connection perspective, eccentricity can tell how political directors take benefits from the external environment and how they access the resources in the connected network. Eccentricity is also valuable to understand how other directors in the network try to build a relationship with the politically connected directors and change their positions in the network according to the political change.

4 Data Collection and Methodology

To achieve the research objective, we selected the listed firms at the Pakistan stock exchange for 2009–2015 as per coverage of democratic regimes, as explained in §1. After excluding the financial sector, due to different corporate governance codes, 415 firms were found for the analysis. For what regards data collection and methodology

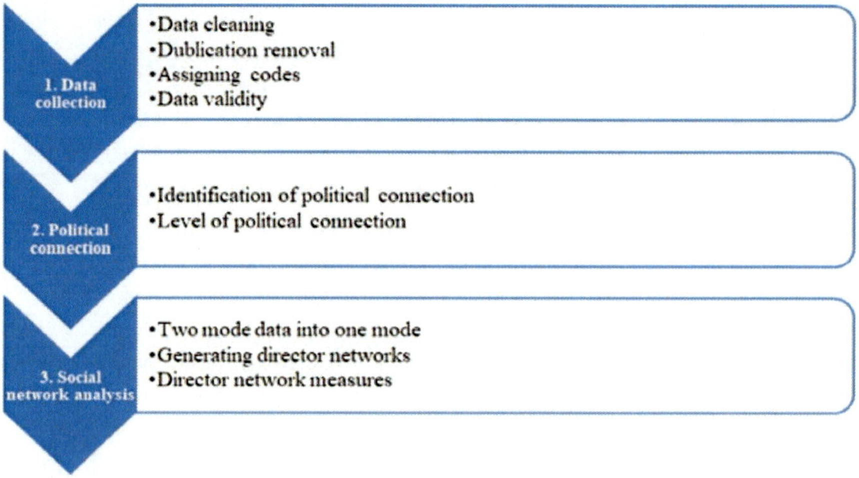

Fig. 1 Steps for the data collection and methodology

process, Fig. 1 represents the step by step procedure we adopted for this study and it can be described as in the following sub-paragraphs.

4.1 Data Collection

In the first step, directors' bibliographies were detected manually from the specific sections made available by companies in their annual reports and from other reliable sources such as Osiris, national newspapers, and companies' websites. The study excluded the firms whose data were not available for a consecutive three-year period for the network formation under the regime change. To rectify data duplications and repetitions, we assigned a code to each director with the help of a unique contact identifier given on the Osiris site. Some director codes were not available in Osiris data. The study also confirmed those directors' "identity" searching reliable information from their bibliography and company site information, to avoid replicating through the respective years.

4.2 Political Connection Measurement

In the second step, we constructed a second database for the political connection purpose, collecting all electoral data of general and senate elections obtained from the Election Commission of Pakistan website. After that, the study matched both databases to find the elected or contested politically connected directors. In addition to the matching process, each director's profile has been checked through the annual

Table 1 Summary statistics directors, directorships, and levels of directors' political connection

Level of political connection	Rank
Federal connection (FLC)	5
Provincial connection (PLC)	4
Current or retire Civil officer connections (CLC)	3
Current or retired military officer (MLC)	2
Government committee members (GCM)	1
Non-political connected directors	0

reports and company sites for civil, military, and government committee members.[1] By following this procedure, the study constructed political connection (PC), like a dummy variable with 1 if director $\boldsymbol{i}$ was a political personnel in the board in year $\boldsymbol{t}$, otherwise 0. To identify the types of political connections, based on their current and past experiences, the study constructed the different levels of politicians according to their affiliation by following the definition of Cao et al. [25] and assigning different values to the directors, based on their political level. Table 1 indicates the different levels of political connection in which federal connection is the highest level because, in a democratic regime, federal parliament controlled all policies and regulations. Government committee members were ranked as lowest because they are neither elected nor civil-military officers, finally for all non-political directors the value is zero.

4.3 *Social Network Analysis*

After the data collection and politically connected director identification, we performed, in the third step, the social network analysis. Social network analysis has become a powerful instrument to analyze the social structure apart from the quantitative methods of statistics. Extensive development in graph theory and the SNA technique allow researchers to explore the hidden social relationship of directors at a different level [26–29]. Corporate networks are consisting of directors, organizations, and ties arising due to the interlock of directors. These types of networks are called two-mode networks or affiliation networks bipartite graphs [30]. Two-mode networks can be converted into one mode by suitable folding of graphs. We converted the two-mode graph into one mode director network, in which each node represents the director, and the edges between the nodes represent the same board at the time t. Table 2 presents the summary statics of directors' networks for each year. In Pakistani directors' network, political connected directors hold relative more

[1] Mr. Arif Habib is the chairman of various firms listed on Pakistan stock exchange. He has served on various government committees such as privatization commission, board of investment, tariff reforms commission and security and exchange ordinance review committee during autocratic as well as democratic regimes.

Table 2 Summary statistics directors, directorships, and political connections

Years	2009	2010	2011	2012	2013	2014	2015
Number of board seats	1917	2063	2180	2207	2244	2212	1859
Number of directors	1467	1571	1651	1662	1695	1686	1480
Avg seat held by director	1.31	1.31	1.32	1.33	1.32	1.31	1.26
Number of PC directors	103	106	109	111	111	127	107
Seats held by PC directors	170	179	187	190	190	200	154
Avg seat held by PC director	1.65	1.69	1.72	1.71	1.71	1.57	1.44
Seats held by FLC directors	20	24	23	25	24	23	19
Seats held by PLC directors	25	26	24	25	25	25	24
Seats held by CLC directors	26	25	27	27	27	26	23
Seats held by MLC directors	60	62	65	62	64	73	52
Seats held by GCM directors	39	42	48	51	50	53	36

average directorship as compared to the average directorship held by the other directors in the networks. Similarly the significance of the presence of each political level connected directors provide sufficient data to analyze the further exploration and network formation through different measures of social network analysis techniques.

5 Results and Discussion

After creating the one-mode director network, we measured the various centralities to identify the suitable position, influence, and control on information flow for the politically connected directors. In the next sub-sections, we discuss our results based on a centrality-based comparison of the network data sets under study.

5.1 Degree

The degree centrality has been calculated via Eq. 2, as reported above, for each year. Figures 2a presents the graphical representation of the directors' network for the year 2009. The size of the node means the different levels of political connection (i.e. larger the node, greater the number of connections), and the color of the node represents the degree of each director in the network. We constructed these graphs for each year, respectively and measured the degree. Figure 2b depicts the distribution of degree values for the different levels of political connections. We found that in each year directors change their connections in the network and all the central nodes, calculated through the degree measure, change. Similarly, for the politically connected directors, we found that in 2009, after one year of autocratic regime end,

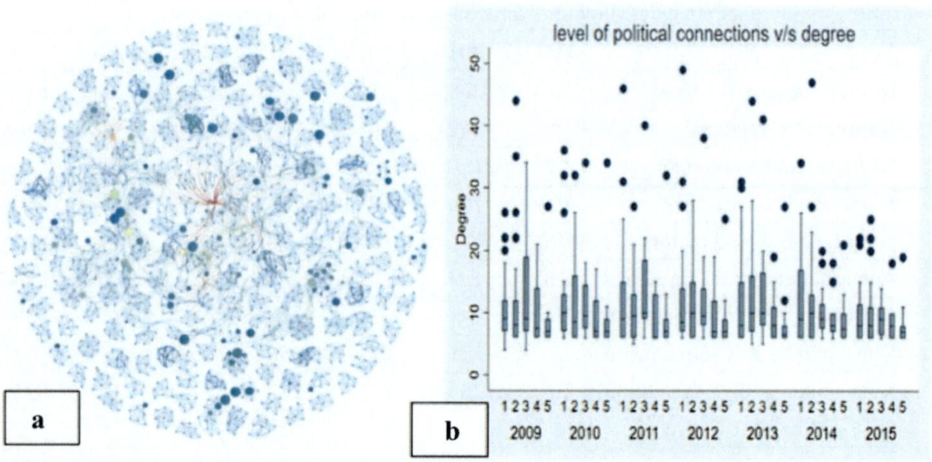

Fig. 2 Graphical representation of directors' degree for year 2009 (**a**). **b** represents the relationship between degree and levels of political connections

retired civil-military officers and government committee political connected directors had higher degrees compared to the parliamentarian connections. While over the time, elected politically connected directors became more central than the other levels of political connection. These findings support our argument that, in corporate networks, political connections attract according to the country's institutional environment and give information about each director's direct ties. But, a degree was found not able to explain the information flow, control, and how far a director can access the network.

5.2 *Closeness Centrality*

We measured the closeness centrality by using Eq. 2 for each year. Figure 3a is a graphical representation of closeness centrality for the year 2009, in which the node size indicates the political level for each director (i.e. greater the size, higher the political level) and the red colour portrays a higher closeness value of directors. Figure 3b shows the distribution of closeness centrality of a director according to their political level across the period. Findings indicate that the retired civil and provincial level political connected directors are more central through the closeness centrality than other political connections. After the autocratic regime, corporate members changed their position, and elected members became more central in the directors' network than the retired civil-military officers and government committee members. As the closeness centrality gives the information related to the nearest path, it is still unclear which political member can reach as far in the director network that can be more beneficial for the corporate firm to enhance human and social capital.

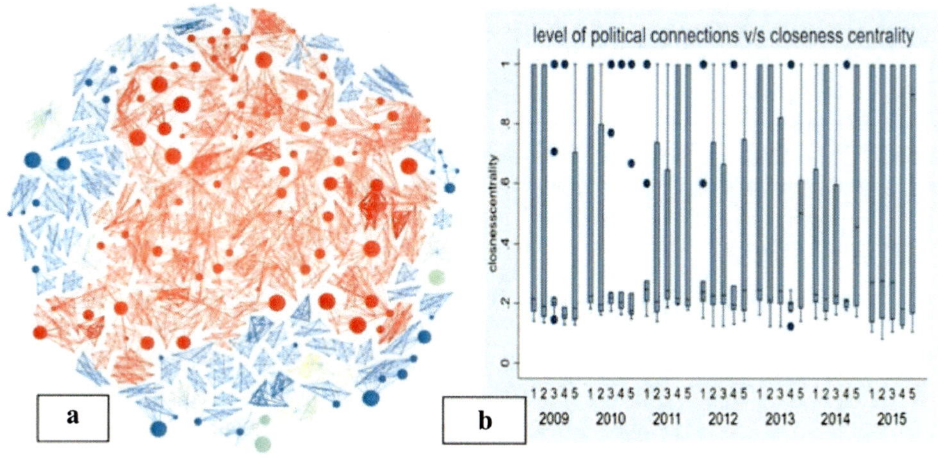

Fig. 3 Graphical representation of directors' closeness centrality for year 2009 (**a**). **b** represents the relationship between closeness centrality and levels of political connections

5.3 *Betweenness Centrality*

To enhance further analysis, we measured the betweenness centrality for each year by using Eq. 3. Figure 4a shows the graphical representation of directors' network for the year 2009, in which node size indicates the level of political connections (i.e. greater the size, higher the political level) while the node colour represents each director betweenness value. Figure 3b is the distribution of betweenness values for each level of political connection for the selected period. We found that the civil and military level connected directors had a high value compared to the other political levels.

5.4 *Eigenvector Centrality*

To analyze the influence of each director, we measured the eigenvector distribution, through Eq. 4, for each year. Figure 5a is the graphical representation of eigenvector distribution for the year 2009. Similar to the previous graph, node size indicates the political connection level, and colour represents the eigenvector values. Overall results remain the same across the period for each level of politically connected directors, and we could not identify the central politically connected director through the eigenvector.

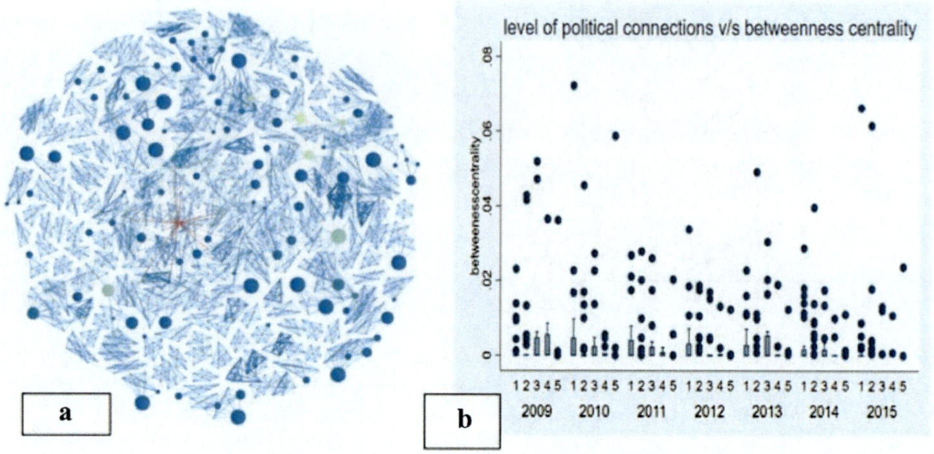

Fig. 4 Graphical representation of directors' betweenness centrality for year 2009 (**a**). **b** represents the relationship between betweenness centrality and levels of political connections

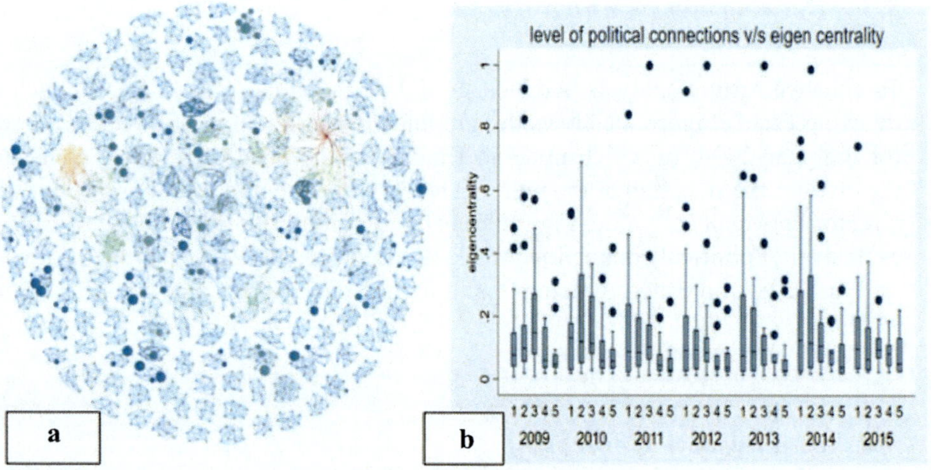

Fig. 5 Graphical representation of directors' eigenvector for year 2009 (**a**). **b** represents the relationship between eigenvector and levels of political connections

5.5 Eccentricity

We measured the eccentricity through Eq. 5 for each year. Eccentricity plays a vital role to analyze the benefits of politically connected directors in the networks. It allows us to understand how political members of a network can reach any director in the network, according to the change in a country's institutional environment. In Fig. 6a, the red colour represents the high value of directors' eccentricity for the year 2009. Comparatively, all politically connected directors have a high eccentricity value compared to the other directors in the giant component. Figure 6b indicates the relationship between eccentricity values and levels of political connection for all the years. In-depth analysis suggests that, in 2009, retired civil and military officer had a higher value level of political connection compared to the other political directors; while in 2015, they decreased their eccentricity value. This finding indicates the importance of the different types of political connections in which directors of networks change their position, to benefit from the political connection, according to their institutional environment. The result shows the decrease of the mean value of eccentricity for federal level connections across the given years. A significant reduction in eccentricity was also found in the election year of 2013. It indicates that the government's change also encouraged the corporate firms to change their board members.

Furthermore, a legislative change in 2012, in which the federal government transfers much of authority power to the provinces, also decreased the importance of federal-level political connections in the corporate networks. It also indicates that the transfer of authority from federal to provincial level, and political stability, raised the matter of provincial-level political connections in the corporate network. All the members in the network built their direct and indirect relationships with the provincial level political connected board members. Moreover, results show that the mean values of current or retired civil, military, and government committee members gradually decreased over time. Change in regime shift from autocratic to democratic, transfer of authority from the federal government to provincial governments and political stability decreased the importance of all bureaucratic connected personnels for the other members in the corporate networks.

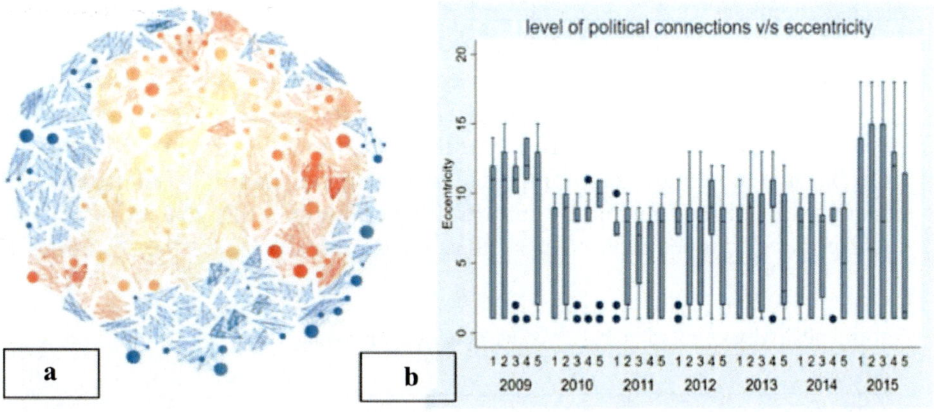

Fig. 6 Graphical representation of directors' eccentricity for year 2009 (**a**). **b** represents the relationship between eccentricity and levels of political connections

5.6 Summary of the Discussion

The overall analysis shows that each centrality measure has unique information to analyze each director in the network. We did not find the degree, betweenness, and eigenvector as a suitable measure for the politically connected directors. Contrary, both closeness and eccentricity indicate the reachability of politically connected directors in the network. Closeness centrality utilizes the minimum distance from a target node to all the other nodes in the network. In contrast, eccentricity centrality gives the maximum geodesic distance from the target node to all the other nodes. These findings are consistent with Batool and Niazi [31], who found closeness and eccentricity a more suitable measure to identify the key nodes in the networks. Table 3 represents the correlation matrix between all the measures of the networks. Our findings are also consistent with the literature affirming that closeness and eccentricity have a significant negative relationship [5]. For the political connection, it is necessary to utilize a measure to give information about how far a politically-connected director can access the network. For this purpose, we found eccentricity as the most suitable centrality measure to identify the political connection and its type's in the directors' network. High eccentricity values provide related information and help a corporate firm to access external resources.

Similarly, eccentricity is also important to analyze the changes into an institutional setting. We noticed that, with the change of regime, a director changes his/her position and the eccentricity values change for the different level of politically connected directors. As soon after the end of the autocratic regime, the civil-military officers and government committee members had high eccentricity values, due to inherited power within the autocratic regime, but during the stability of the democratic regimes, elected members such as federal and provincial level connections became more important, and directors shared their position according to the institutional change. We observed a significant rise in their eccentricity values after the stabilization of the democratic regime. Moreover, in 2012, when the federal government shifted the power to the provincial authorities after the legislation, the provincial-level connections became more important for the network formation and significantly raised their eccentricity values. This finding confirms that corporate firms give more value to the local political connections because they have more access to the resources [32].

Table 3 Pairwise correlation matrix between network measures

Variables	(1)	(2)	(3)	(4)	(5)
(1) Degree	1	–	–	–	–
(2) Closeness centrality	−0.27*	1	–	–	–
(3) Betweenness centrality	0.72*	−0.14*	1	–	–
(4) Eigenvector	0.79*	−0.43*	0.52*	1	–
(5) Eccentricity	0.22*	−0.93*	0.12*	0.39*	1

*** $p < 0.01$, ** $p < 0.05$, * $p < 0.1$

Other centrality measures could not depict these changes according to the institutional setting. Comparatively, eccentricity is the more suitable and valuable measure that can give information about power, influence, and reachability of the politically connected directors according to his/her type of political connection.

6 Conclusion

This study investigated the different measures of SNA to analyse informal contracts, such as political connections, in relationship-based economies like Pakistan. The data consisted of the 287 non-financial listed companies of the Pakistan Stock Exchange for 2009–2015. The directors' network encompassed a maximum of 1695 directors sitting on various corporate boards and the five different levels of politically connected directors. The position of a director in the network had a significant impact on their access to market resources, such as capital, status, prestige and legitimacy within the corporate environment. Still, in analysing the specific social contract, it is important to compare the outcome of different social network measures. This study contributes that degree, betweenness and eigenvector could not better explain the politically connected director characteristics in the network. In comparison, closeness and eccentricity proved more suitable. In-depth analysis indicates that eccentricity is a much more important measure to observe the political director's reachability, influence and access to other directors in the network. It allows examining the institutional change effects on corporate directors' networks. We found that politically connected directors had more central positions after the stability of democratic regimes and the legislation regarding authority transformation, based on their eccentricity values.

This study gives new directions to practitioners and researchers to study directors' political connection effects on corporate outcomes. Apart from the comparison of the different measures, there are some limitations to this study. We did not include financial firms due to different corporate governance requirements. We also did not analyse the difference between winning and losing politically connected directors. Future studies could address these concerns.

References

1. Helmers, C., Patnam, M., Rau, P.R.: Do board interlocks increase innovation? Evidence from a corporate governance reform in India. J Bank Financ **80**, 51–70 (2017). https://doi.org/10.1016/j.jbankfin.2017.04.001
2. Prem Sankar, C., Asokan, K., Satheesh Kumar, K.: Exploratory social network analysis of affiliation networks of Indian listed companies. Soc Netw. **43**, 113–120 (2015). https://doi.org/10.1016/j.socnet.2015.03.008
3. Chuluun, T., Prevost, A., Puthenpurackal, J.: Board ties and the cost of corporate debt. Financ Manag **43**, 533–568 (2014). https://doi.org/10.1111/fima.12047
4. Freeman, L.C.: Centrality in social networks. Soc Netw **1**, 215–239 (1979). https://doi.org/10.1016/0378-8733(78)90021-7
5. Hage, P., Harary, F.: Eccentricity and centrality in networks. Soc Netw **17**, 57–63 (1995). https://doi.org/10.1016/0378-8733(94)00248-9
6. Davis, G.F., Yoo, M., Baker, W.E.: The small world of the American Corporate elite, 1982–2001. Strateg Organ **1**, 301–326 (2003). https://doi.org/10.1177/14761270030013002
7. Li, X., Fung, A., Fung, H.-G., Qiao, P.: Directorate interlocks and corporate cash holdings in emerging economies: evidence from China. Int Rev Econ Financ **66**, 244–260 (2020). https://doi.org/10.1016/j.iref.2019.12.002
8. Harjoto, M.A., Wang, Y.: Board of directors network centrality and environmental, social and governance (ESG) performance. Corp Gov **20**, 965–985 (2020). https://doi.org/10.1108/CG-10-2019-0306
9. Xia, C., Zhang, X., Cao, C., Xu, N.: Independent director connectedness in China: an examination of the trade credit financing hypothesis. Int Rev Econ Financ **63**, 209–225 (2019). https://doi.org/10.1016/j.iref.2018.09.010
10. Horak, S., Afiouni, F., Bian, Y., et al.: Informal networks: dark sides, bright sides, and unexplored dimensions. Manag Organ Rev **16**, 511–542 (2020). https://doi.org/10.1017/mor.2020.28
11. Abdul Wahab, E.A., Jamaludin, M.F., Agustia, D., Harymawan, I.: Director networks, political connections, and earnings quality in Malaysia. Manag Organ Rev **16**, 687–724 (2020). https://doi.org/10.1017/mor.2020.26
12. Faccio, M., Masulis, R.W., Mcconnell, J.J.: Political connections and corporate bailouts. J Financ **61**, 2597–2635 (2006). https://doi.org/10.1111/j.1540-6261.2006.01000.x
13. Wong, W.Y., Hooy, C.W.: Do types of political connection affect firm performance differently? Pacific Basin Financ J **51**, 297–317 (2018). https://doi.org/10.1016/j.pacfin.2018.08.009
14. Sapinski, J.P., Carroll, W.K.: Interlocking directorates and corporate networks. Handb. Int. Polit. Econ. Corp. 45–60 (2018). https://doi.org/10.4337/9781785362538.00009
15. Coleman, J.: Social capital in the creation of human development. Am. J. Sociol. **94**, 95–120 (1988)
16. Wong, L.H.H., Gygax, A.F., Wang, P.: Board interlocking network and the design of executive compensation packages. Soc Netw **41**, 85–100 (2015). https://doi.org/10.1016/j.socnet.2014.12.002
17. Bajo, E., Croci, E., Marinelli, N.: Institutional investor networks and firm value. J Bus Res **112**, 65–80 (2020). https://doi.org/10.1016/j.jbusres.2020.02.041
18. Mazzola, E., Perrone, G., Kamuriwo, D.S.: The interaction between inter-firm and interlocking directorate networks on firm's new product development outcomes. J Bus Res **69**, 672–682 (2016). https://doi.org/10.1016/j.jbusres.2015.08.033
19. Khwaja, A.I., Mian, A.: Do lenders favor politically connected. Q J Econ **120**, 1371–1411 (2005)
20. Saeed, A., Belghitar, Y., Clark, E.: Theoretical motives of corporate cash holdings and political connections: firms level evidence from a developing economy. Int Rev Appl Econ **28**, 813–831 (2014). https://doi.org/10.1080/02692171.2014.923387
21. Cheng, S., Felix, R., Zhao, Y.: Board interlock networks and informed short sales. J Bank Financ **98**, 198–211 (2019). https://doi.org/10.1016/j.jbankfin.2018.11.002

22. Samkin, G., Allen, B., Munday, D.: The social network of New Zealand directors: an exploratory study. Corp Board Role, Duties Compos, 6, pp. 19–38 (2010). https://doi.org/10.22495/cbv6i1art2
23. Bonacich, P.: Factoring and weighting approaches to status scores and clique identification. J Math Sociol **2**, 113–120 (1972). https://doi.org/10.1080/0022250X.1972.9989806
24. Krnc, M., Sereni, J., Skrekovski, R., et al.: Eccentricity of networks with structural constraints to cite this version: HAL Id : hal-01385481 Eccentricity of networks with structural constraints ∗. 0–18 (2018)
25. Cao, X., Pan, X., Qian, M., Tian, G.G.: Political capital and CEO entrenchment: evidence from CEO turnover in Chinese non-SOEs. J Corp Financ **42**, 1–14 (2017). https://doi.org/10.1016/j.jcorpfin.2016.11.003
26. Mizruchi, M.S.: What do interlocks do? An analysis, critique, and assessment of research on interlocking directorates. Annu Rev Sociol **22**, 271–298 (1996). https://doi.org/10.1146/annurev.soc.22.1.271
27. Newman, M.E.J.: The structure and function of complex networks (2003)
28. Wasserman, S., Galaskiewicz, J.: Advances in social network analysis: research in the social and behavioral sciences (2012)
29. Scott, J.: Networks of corporate power: a comparative assessment. Annu Rev Sociol **17**, 181–203 (1991). https://doi.org/10.1146/annurev.soc.17.1.181
30. Faust, K.: Centrality in affiliation networks. Soc Netw **19**, 157–191 (1997). https://doi.org/10.1016/S0378-8733(96)00300-0
31. Batool, K., Niazi, M.A.: Towards a methodology for validation of centrality measures in complex networks. PLoS One 9 (2014). https://doi.org/10.1371/journal.pone.0090283
32. Piotroski, J.D., Zhang, T.: Politicians and the IPO decision: the impact of impending political promotions on IPO activity in China. J Financ Econ **111**, 111–136 (2014). https://doi.org/10.1016/j.jfineco.2013.10.012
33. Boubakri, N., Cosset, J. C., Saffar, W.: Political connections of newly privatized firms. J Corp Finan **14**(5), 654–673. (2018). https://doi.org/10.1016/j.jcorpfin.2008.08.003
34. Du, J., Bai, T., Chen, S.: Integrating corporate social and corporate political strategies: performance implications and institutional contingencies in China. J Bus Res **98** (February), 299–316. (2019). https://doi.org/10.1016/j.jbusres.2019.02.014
35. Fan, J. P. H., Wong, T. J., Zhang, T.: Politically connected CEOs, corporate governance, and Post-IPO performance of China's newly partially privatized firms. J Finance Econ **84**(2), 330–357. (2007). https://doi.org/10.1016/j.jfineco.2006.03.008
36. Ferguson, T., Voth, H. J.: Betting on Hitler - The value of political connections in Nazi Germany. Q J Econ **123**(1), 101–137. (2008). https://doi.org/10.1162/qjec.2008.123.1.101
37. Gao, W., Huang, Z., & Yang, P.: Political connections, corporate governance and M&A performance: evidence from Chinese family firms. Res Int Bus Finance **50**(April), 38–53. (2019). https://doi.org/10.1016/j.ribaf.2019.04.007
38. Han, J., Zhang, G.: Politically connected boards, value or cost: evidence from a natural experiment in China. Account Finance **58**(1), 149–169. (2018). https://doi.org/10.1111/acfi.12215
39. Hill, M. D., Fuller, K. P., Kelly, G. W., Washam, J. O.: Corporate cash holdings and political connections. Rev Quant Finance Account **42**(1), 123–142. (2014). https://doi.org/10.1007/s11156-012-0336-6
40. Khwaja, A. I., Mian, A.: Do lenders favor politically connected firms? Rent provision in an emerging financial market. Q J Econ **120**(4). (2005). https://doi.org/10.1162/003355305775097524
41. Tsai, L. C., Zhang, R., & Zhao, C. F.: Revisiting Corporate Political Connections Using Social Networks and Prediction of Post-IPO Performance. Emerg Mark Financ Trade **0938**, 1–18. (2018). https://doi.org/10.1080/1540496X.2019.1646125

Examining Environmental Sustainability in Italy: Evidence from ARDL and Non-linear ARDL Approaches

Aamir Javed and Agnese Rapposelli

Abstract One of the reasons behind environmental degradation and climate change is greenhouse gases that are mainly consisted of carbon dioxide (CO_2) emissions. Besides, CO_2 emissions negatively affect human health. Consequently, national institutions should understand which factors are affecting carbon emissions in order to achieve sustainable (environmental, social and economic) development. The main objective of this paper is to examine the symmetric and asymmetric effects of oil price, foreign direct investments and economic growth on carbon emissions in Italy. To this purpose, the long and short-run impact of these variables on carbon emissions have been investigated by applying the autoregressive distributed lag (ARDL) and non-linear ARDL methodologies to Italian data for the period 1970–2019. The symmetric results show that economic growth and foreign direct investments intensify carbon emissions both in the long and short-run, while the impact of oil price on emissions is negative in the long-run and positive in the short-run, suggesting that oil price is responsible for environmental degradation only in the short run. The asymmetric results reveal that both in the long and short-run an increase in the oil price imply reductions in carbon emission.

Keywords Sustainable development · Carbon dioxide emissions · ARDL model · Non-linear ARDL model

1 Introduction

Environmental degradation and climate change have become eminent risk factors around the world. Global warming shows no signs of slowing. One of the reasons behind those risk factors is greenhouse gases (GHGs) that are mainly consisted of

A. Javed (✉)
"G.d'Annunzio, Department of Management and Business Administration, University of Chieti-Pescara, Viale Pindaro 42, 65127 Pescara, Italy
e-mail: aamir.javed@studenti.unich.it

A. Rapposelli
"G.d'Annunzio, Department of Economic Studies, University of Chieti-Pescara, Viale Pindaro 42, 65127 Pescara, Italy

S. Za et al. (eds.), *Sustainable Digital Transformation*, Lecture Notes in Information Systems and Organisation 59, https://doi.org/10.1007/978-3-031-15770-7_6

carbon dioxide (CO_2) emissions. Besides, CO_2 emissions also have harmful effects on human health, by contributing to respiratory and cardiovascular disease from smog and air pollution.

It has been demonstrated that if we continue as usual, we will emit 65 billion tonnes of GHGs in 2030. According to the Circularity Gap Report published by Circle Economy (2021), however, a circular economy could be the key to reduce greenhouse gases emissions and meet climate targets. In Europe, switching to a circular economy could reduce greenhouse gas emissions by 39%. If those principles were applied, 22.8 billion tonnes of carbon emissions could be saved and help avoid climate breakdown, according to the above study. Consequently, nowadays it is very important for national institutions to investigate which factors are affecting carbon emissions in order to minimize environmental disamenities and achieve sustainable (environmental, social and economic) development, as suggested also by sustainable development goals of Agenda ONU 2030. For example, the 2020 EU Circular Economy Strategy Action Plan developed a policy framework to attain a cleaner and competitive economy (Gastaldi et al. 2020; Lombardi et al. 2021).

In this context, the aim of this article is to examine the symmetric and asymmetric effects of oil price, foreign direct investments and economic growth on carbon emissions in Italy. To this purpose, the impact of these variables on CO_2 emissions will be assessed both in the long-run and in the short-run by using the autoregressive distributed lag (ARDL) and non-linear autoregressive distributed lag (NARDL) models. In particular, the analysis focuses on Italian data for the period 1970–2019, by also investigating the existing nexus between economic growth and environmental degradation in the form of Environmental Kuznets Curve (EKC).

The article is organized as follows. Section 2 reviews the literature, Sect. 3 presents the data used and reviews the methodology used, Sect. 4 describes the results obtained and Sect. 5 gives the conclusions.

2 Literature Review

2.1 Economic Growth and Carbon Emission

Many researchers have examined the relationship between economic growth and carbon emissions to test the EKC hypothesis. However, the results of these studies are inconclusive: some studies support the existence of EKC hypothesis (Grossman and Krueger 1995; Schmalensee et al. 1998; Selden and Song 1994; Lee and Oh 2015; Baek 2016; Alpher and Onur 2016; Zambrano-Monserrate et al. 2018: Usman et al. 2019), whereas other studies do not support the EKC hypothesis (Bartlett 1994; Coondoo and Dinda 2002; Galeotti et al. 2006).

By employing ARDL and VECM, Ahmad et al. (2017) investigated the long-run and causal relationship between economic growth and carbon emission in Croatia for the period 1992–2011. The results demonstrated a long-run relationship and confirmed the existence of EKC. Bölük and Mert (2015) examined the short and long-run association between carbon emissions, GDP and electricity produced from renewable resources from 1961 to 2010. The findings of this study support the existence of EKC hypothesis by using ARDL cointegration approach. Farhani and Shahbaz (2014) explored the causal relationship between electricity consumption, output and carbon emissions in 10 MENA countries for the period 1980–2009, confirming the existence of EKC hypothesis in all these countries. Using time series data from 1995 to 2014, Fan and Lei (2017) investigated the relationship between environmental deterioration, transportation, and economic development in Beijing. According to the estimated results, transportation and CO_2 emissions show a positive impact on economic growth. Using the ARDL model, Sulaiman and Abdul-Rahim (2017) evaluated the relationship between CO_2 emissions, energy consumption, and economic growth in Malaysia from 1975 to 2015. The findings revealed that energy consumption and CO_2 emissions had no effect on economic growth, but that energy consumption and economic growth had a positive impact on CO_2 emissions. Finally, Saboori et al. (2017) used the Johansen cointegration test to investigate the link between the research variables and oil consumption, economic growth, and environmental deterioration in three Asian nations from 1980 to 2013. The results revealed a one-way correlation between oil consumption and economic growth in China and Japan, and oil consumption and CO_2 emissions in South Korea.

Hence, in order to check the long run economic growth in Italy, we aim to investigate the hypothesis that economic growth has a positive association with carbon emissions.

2.2 *Foreign Direct Investment and Carbon Emission*

Foreign direct investment (FDI) benefits countries in a variety of ways, including enhancing production capacity and employment (Oxelheim and Ghauri 2008), increasing innovation (Ito et al. 2012) and upgrading managerial abilities (Lin et al. 2009). However, as a result of global warming, the environmental impact of FDI is also picking up steam. Evidence of a connection between carbon emissions and FDI is complicated, as some researchers have demonstrated that this association is positive (Haug and Ucal 2019), while some others have proved that the relationship is negative (Jiang et al. 2018; Tang and Tan 2015).

With regard to the direct impact of FDI on environment, the relationship between FDI and pollutant emissions involves two challenging scenarios: the pollution haven and halo hypotheses (Antweiler et al. 2001; Zhang and Zhou 2016; Sarkodie and Strezov 2019). According to the pollution haven theory, due to improved environmental restrictions in developed economies, some businesses with high pollution and high energy consumption are relocated to developing and transition nations via FDI, thus resulting in significant contamination discharge. On the other hand, the pollution halo hypothesis claims that the emergence of foreign enterprises will result in positive environmental overflows in the host country because multinational corporations have more cutting-edge technologies than their domestic counterparts and are more likely to spread clean and environmentally friendly technologies (Birdsall and Wheeler 1993). Zhang and Zhou (2016) used a linear panel data model to confirm the presence of the pollution halo hypothesis, arguing that inflows of FDI with advanced technology result in a decrease in pollutant emissions rather than environmental degradation. Koçak and Şarkgüneşi (2018) evaluated the influence of FDI on CO_2 emissions in Turkey, using a variety of cointegration approaches to analyse data from 1974 to 2013. The findings suggest that FDI has a positive impact on CO_2 emissions.

Conversely, some studies suggest that FDI inflows have a negative impact on CO_2 emissions (Al-Mulali and Tang 2013; Sung et al. 2018; Jiang et al. 2018), thus backing up the pollution halo hypothesis. Other researchers, on the other hand, claim that FDI flows are not harmful to the environment (Lee 2013; Chandran and Tang 2013; Hakimi and Hamdi 2016). In addition, several studies do not support either the good or negative effects of FDI and have found inconsequential outcomes, such as the study by Kivyiro and Arminen (2014) on various Sub-Saharan African nations. Surprisingly, research on BRICS countries also show contradictory results (Dong et al. 2017; Azevedo et al. 2018; Danish and Wang 2019). These studies, however, do not consider the crucial elements of financial development and growth, which can yield more accurate results when combined with FDI.

Hence, based on the above literature, in this study we aim to demonstrate the hypothesis that in Italy FDI has a positive association with carbon emissions.

2.3 *Oil Price and Carbon Emission*

The impact of oil prices on energy use and carbon dioxide emissions has been studied in a few empirical works. Suliman and Abid (2020) claimed that there is a causal relationship between oil price and energy consumption in Tunisia. Agbanike et al. (2019) investigated the causal relationship between oil price and carbon emissions by using the ARDL model. According to their results, there is a positive relationship between oil prices and carbon emissions in Venezuela. Apergis and Payne (2015) applied a panel data model to show that there was a positive and statistically significant relationship between oil price and carbon emissions per capita in 11 South American countries in the period 1980–2010. Simsek and Yigit (2017) applied the vector autoregression model to examine the relationship between carbon emissions and oil prices in Brazil, Russia, India, China, and Turkey. The results revealed that oil prices have a significant impact on carbon emissions in all the countries examined. The ARDL model was also used by Malik et al. (2020) to explore the impact of oil price on the carbon emissions level in Pakistan. The results of this study revealed that oil price increases carbon emissions in the short term while reduces them in the long term. Finally, Katircioglu (2017) examined the impact of oil prices on carbon emissions in Turkey by using the ARDL methodology, showing that there is an inverse relationship between oil prices and carbon emissions levels, while Zou

(2018) concluded that there are no significant interactions between oil price and carbon emissions in China.

Based on the above studies, we expect a negative impact of oil price on environmental quality in Italy. Hence, in this study our hypothesis is that in Italy oil price has a negative association with carbon emissions.

3 Methodology and Data

3.1 Model Specification

The empirical model we used in this study is specified as follows:

$$LnCO2_t = \beta_0 + \beta_1 LnGDP_t + \beta_2 LnGDP_t^2 + \beta_3 LnFDI_t + \beta_4 LnOP_t + \delta_5 Control_t + \varepsilon_t \quad (1)$$

where $LnCO2_t$ is the logarithm of per capita carbon emissions in Italy at time t, $LnGDP_t$ is the logarithm of per capita GDP, $LnGDP_t^2$ is the logarithm of the square term of per capita GDP, $LnFDI_t$ is the logarithm of per capita foreign direct investment, $LnOP_t$ is the logarithm of oil prices, *Control* means control variables included in the model, and ε_t is the error term.

According to the EKC hypothesis, the relationship between the square term of per capita GDP and environmental quality is represented by an inverted U-shape curve. Hence, if the sign of β_1 is positive and the sign of β_2 is negative, the EKC hypothesis is proved to be true for Italy.

Autoregressive distributed lag model. In order to examine the long-run cointegration relationship among variables, literature provides several techniques (Engle and Granger 1987; Johansen and Juselius 1990; Saikkon 1991; Stock and Watson 1993; Johansen 1996). In this study we use a new cointegration approach developed by Pesaran and Smith (1995) and Pesaran et al. (2001), the autoregressive distributed lag (ARDL) model, also known as the bounds testing approach. This methodology has several econometric advantages in comparison with other multivariate cointegration techniques: first of all, it overcomes the problem of the same order of integration of regressors, as it could be applied with regressors integrated of order I(0) or I(1) or combination of both; second, it avoids the problem of endogeneity and serial correlation among variables; finally, it estimates long and short-run parameters of the model simultaneously and it provides better results even with small sample.

Hence, in this work we apply the ARDL methodology to investigate the existence of a long-run relationship between per capita income, FDI, oil price, and carbon emissions. The Unrestricted Error Correction Model (UECM) corresponding to the ARDL bounds test is specified as follows:

$$\Delta lnCO2_t = \beta_0 + \sum_{i=1}^{p} \beta_1 \Delta lnC02_{t-1} + \sum_{i=1}^{p} \beta_2 \Delta lnGDP_{t-1} + \sum_{i=1}^{p} \beta_3 lnGDP^2_{t-1} + \sum_{i=1}^{p} \beta_4 \Delta lnFDI_{t-1} + \sum_{i=1}^{p} \beta_5 \Delta lnOP_{t-1} + \lambda_1 \Delta lnC02_{t-1} + \lambda_2 \Delta lnGDP_{t-1} + \lambda_3 lnGDP^2_{t-1} + \lambda_4 \Delta lnFDI_{t-1} + \lambda_5 \Delta lnOP_{t-1} + \varepsilon_t \quad (2)$$

where Δ is the difference operator; p defines the lagged value of both the dependent variable and each independent variable; $\beta_1, \ldots, \beta_5$ denotes the short-run coefficients; $\lambda_1, \ldots, \lambda_5$ denotes the long-run coefficients; ε_t is the error term.

In order to examine the existence of a long-run relationship between a dependent variable and a set of regressors, Pesaran et al. (2001) proposed a test based on the F-statistic for the joint significance of the estimated coefficients of the lagged level of variables. The null hypothesis $H_o : \lambda_1 = \lambda_2 = \lambda_3 = \lambda_4 = \lambda_5 = 0$ implies that there is no cointegration between variables. If the F-statistic value is lower than the lower bound critical value I(0), the null hypothesis of no long-run relationship cannot be rejected; if the F-statistic value is higher than the upper bound critical value I(1), the null hypothesis is rejected: this implies that cointegration exists between variables. However, if the F-statistic value falls between the lower I(0) and upper I(1) bound critical value, the results are inconclusive. For this reason, an alternative way to test for the existence of long-run cointegration is to consider the lagged value of the error correction term ECT_{t-1}. If the value of ECT_{t-1} is significant and holds the negative sign, it confirms the existence of a long-run relationship between variables. Moreover, we use the critical bounds suggested by Narayan (2005), which are more appropriate for small sample size ($30 \leq n \leq 80$).

If the long-run relationship exists, we examine the short-run relationship between the variables considered by means of the following error correction model associated with the long-run estimates:

$$\Delta lnCO2_t = \beta_0 + \sum_{i=1}^{p} \beta_1 \Delta lnC02_{t-1} + \sum_{i=1}^{p} \beta_2 \Delta lnGDP_{t-1} + \sum_{i=1}^{p} \beta_3 lnGDP^2_{t-1} + \sum_{i=1}^{p} \beta_4 \Delta lnFDI_{t-1} + \sum_{i=1}^{p} \beta_5 \Delta lnOP_{t-1} + \theta_i ECT_{t-1} + \varepsilon_t \quad (3)$$

where θ_{i} is the coefficient of the error correction term; it represents the speed of the adjustment required for long-run equilibrium after a shock in the short-run.

Non-linear autoregressive distributed lag model. In order to investigate the asymmetric relationship among the variables considered both in the short and long-run, in this work we apply the non-linear ARDL methodology developed by Shin et al. (2014). Similar to ARDL model, NARDL model also overcomes the variables requirement to be integrated at the same order.

Hence, we extended the model given in Eq. (1) as follows:

$$LnCO2_t = \beta_0 + \beta_1 LnGDP_t + \beta_2 LnGDP_t^2 + \beta_3 LnFDI_t^+ + \beta_4 LnFDI_t^- + \beta_5 LnOP_t^+ + \beta_6 LnOP_t^- + \varepsilon_t \tag{4}$$

where $\boldsymbol{LnFDI_t^+}$ and $\boldsymbol{LnFDI_t^-}$, $\boldsymbol{LnOP_t^+}$ and $\boldsymbol{LnOP_t^-}$ represent the partial sum of positive and negative changes in FDI and OP at time t, respectively.

The NARDL model is specified for this study as follows:

$$\begin{aligned}\Delta lnCO2_t = {} & \delta_0 + \sum_{i=1}^{p} \delta_1 \Delta lnC02_{t-1} + \sum_{i=1}^{p} \delta_2 \Delta lnGDP_{t-1} + \sum_{i=1}^{p} \delta_3 lnGDP_{t-1}^2 \\ & + \sum_{i=1}^{p} (\delta_4^+ \Delta lnFDI_{t-1}^+ + \delta_5^- \Delta lnFDI_{t-1}^-) \\ & + \sum_{i=1}^{p} (\delta_6^+ \Delta lnOP_{t-1}^+ + \delta_7^- \Delta lnOP_{t-1}^-) \\ & + \lambda_1 \Delta lnC02_{t-1} + \lambda_2 \Delta lnGDP_{t-1} \\ & + \lambda_3 lnGDP_{t-1}^2 + \lambda_4^+ lnFDI_{t-1}^+ + \lambda_5^- lnFDI_{t-1}^- \\ & + \lambda_6^+ lnOP_{t-1}^+ + \lambda_7^- lnOP_{t-1}^- + \varepsilon_t \end{aligned} \tag{5}$$

where $\sum_i^p (\delta_i^+ \Delta lnFDI_{t-1}^+ + \delta_i^- \Delta lnFDI_{t-1}^-)$ and $\sum_i^p (\delta_i^+ \Delta lnOP_{t-1}^+ + \delta_i^- \Delta lnOP_{t-1}^-)$ captures the short-run positive and negative asymmetric effects of FDI and OP on carbon emissions, while $\lambda_4^+ \Delta lnFDI_{t-1}^+, \lambda_5^- \Delta lnFDI_{t-1}^-, \lambda_6^+ \Delta lnOP_{t-1}^+, \lambda_7^+ \Delta lnOP_{t-1}^+$ captures the long-run positive and negative asymmetric effects.

The error correction model for Eq. (5) is specified as follows:

$$\begin{aligned}\Delta lnCO2_t = {} & \delta_0 + \sum_{i=1}^{p} \delta_1 \Delta lnC02_{t-1} + \sum_{i=1}^{p} \delta_2 \Delta lnGDP_{t-1} + \sum_{i=1}^{p} \delta_3 lnGDP_{t-1}^2 \\ & + \sum_{i=1}^{p} (\delta_4^+ \Delta lnFDI_{t-1}^+ + \delta_5^- \Delta lnFDI_{t-1}^-) \\ & + \sum_{i=1}^{p} (\delta_6^+ \Delta lnOP_{t-1}^+ + \delta_7^- \Delta lnOP_{t-1}^-) + \theta_i ECT_{t-1} + \varepsilon_t \end{aligned} \tag{6}$$

where θ_{i} is the coefficient of the error correction term; it represents the long-run equilibrium speed of adjustment after the shock in the short-run.

In order to test the existence of a long-run cointegration between variables, also in this case we perform the F-test for the joint significance of the coefficients of the lagged level of variables. Furthermore, we conduct the Wald test to check long-run (H_0: $\lambda^+ = \lambda^-$) and short-run (H_0: $\delta^+ = \delta^-$) asymmetries of FDI and OP on CO_2 emissions.

3.2 *Data*

This study uses annual data for the period 1970–2019. The dependent variable is carbon emissions (CO_2, metric tons per capita), while the independent variables are gross domestic product per capita (GDP), inflow of foreign direct investment per capita (FDI) and cured oil price per barrel (OP). Besides, the following control variables are included in the model: human capital index, based on years of schooling and returns to education (HC), inflation per capita (INF), exports of goods and services per capita (EXP), financial development (domestic credit to the private sector, FD) and urban population as percentage of total population per capita (UP). All the variables are transformed in logarithm form. Our principal source of information regarding these data was World Bank, while data regarding HC, FDI and OP were extracted from Peen World Table, UNCTAD and Statista database, respectively.

Table 1 provides the descriptive statistics of the variables for the examined years.

Unit root tests. Before running the ARDL cointegration procedure, we tested our variables for stationarity by implementing different unit root tests (Agovino et al. 2019). In particular, we applied the augmented Dickey-Fuller (ADF) test and the Phillips-Perron (PP) test to check for the stationarity of the data. Both tests indicate that the variables under analysis are stationary at first difference (Table 2). Furthermore, we performed the Zivot-Andrews unit root test with structural breaks to accommodate any structural break in the data (Table 3). The results confirm that variables are not stationary in level, but they become stationary at the first difference.

Table 1 Descriptive statistics

	CO_2	GDP	FDI	OP	HC	INF	EXP	FD	UP
Mean	1.920	10.296	4.212	3.171	0.961	1.425	3.108	4.165	4.208
Median	1.915	10.386	4.308	3.245	0.975	1.416	3.108	4.135	4.203
Max	2.106	10.552	6.615	4.695	1.153	3.036	3.450	4.544	4.259
Min	1.662	9.780	0.435	0.191	0.725	−0.829	2.719	3.852	4.163
Std. dev	0.116	0.230	1.646	1.026	0.129	0.957	0.195	0.214	0.021

Table 2 ADF and PP unit root tests—results

	ADF test		PP test	
Variables	At level	At first difference	At level	At first difference
CO_2	0.1481	−5.8794***	0.1066	−5.8670
GDP	2.3821	−3.7979***	2.9138	−3.7073***
GDP-SQ	2.2929	−3.7920***	2.8065	−3.7008***
FDI	3.9720	−3.5118***	0.1135	−18.4218***
OP	0.7283	−6.1052***	0.6429	−6.1053***
HC	0.3276	−2.512**	9.0281	−2.133**
INF	−1.3528	−7.9504***	−1.3923	−8.2641***
EXP	1.5635	−6.4932***	1.7027	−6.4919***
FD	−0.2269	−3.2537***	0.1771	−3.2480***
UP	0.9385		3.830	−2.456**

Note ***, ** and * show significance at 1, 5 and 10% level respectively

Table 3 Zivot-Andrews unit root test—results

Variables	At level		At first difference	
	Test statistic	Break year	Test statistic	Break year
CO_2	0.319	2007	−5.145***	2007
GDP	−3.506	1999	−5.881***	1980
GDP-SQ	−3.596	1999	−5.145***	1991
FDI	−0.655	1983	−21.817***	2012
OP	−1.437	1981	−6.933***	1980
HC	1.91	1990	−5.439***	1990
INF	−2.814	1991	−6.842***	1980
EXP	−2.807	1978	−7.675***	2009
FD	−0.696	2009	−4.493*	2008
UP	−0.374	2013	−10.150***	1981

Note ***, ** and * show significance at 1, 5 and 10% level respectively

4 Results and Discussion

4.1 ARDL Model

This paragraph presents the results of the ARDL model estimation. Before proceeding with the ARDL bound test, we first tested for the stationarity status of the variables under analysis, in order to ensure that none of the variables is integrated of order two (this procedure is not valid in the presence of I(2) series). As reported in paragraph 3.2, unit root tests applied show that all variables are integrated of order one. Then,

Table 4 ARDL bound test

F-bounds test statistic		Null hypothesis: no levels relationship		
		Significance (%)	I(0)	I(1)
F-statistic	3.591**	10	2.2	3.09
K	4	5	2.56	3.49
		2.50	2.88	3.87
		1	3.29	4.37

Note *** *, ***, ** and * show significance at 1, 2.5, 5 and 10% level respectively

we focused on lag order selection. The lag-length criteria used (LR, FPF, AIC, SC, HQ) indicate lag-length equal to 4 for conducting the cointegration.

In order to investigate the long-run relationship between the variables considered, we performed the F-statistic joint significance test against the bound critical values provided by Pesaran et al. (2001). The computed F-statistic value confirms the existence of la long-run association between the variables considered, as shown in Table 4. F-statistic value is also higher than the upper bound values suggested by Narayan (2005), and found to be statistically significant at 1% level, thus confirming the existence of long-run cointegration among per capita income, FDI, oil price, and carbon emission. This is confirmed also by the coefficient of error correction term ECT_{t-1}, which is negative and statistically significant.

Tables 5 and 6 list the long-run and short-run results of ARDL bounds testing approach. The results show that both in long and short-run the relationship between per capita income and carbon emission is positive and statistically significant. In Italy economic growth, both in the short and in the long-run, has the largest influence on carbon dioxide emissions, thus increasing environmental degradation. These results are expected and in line with previous literature (Behera and Dash 2017; Zhang and Zhang 2018; Naz et al. 2019; Malik et al. 2020). Furthermore, we can observe that the relationship between the square term of per capita GDP and environmental quality (measured by CO_2 emissions) is negative and statistically significant. Hence, we confirm for Italy the EKC hypothesis, given that the coefficients of GDP and GDP^2 are statistically significant with positive and negative signs, respectively. These findings are also in line with the literature (Nasir and Ur Rehman 2011; Shujaj ur et al. 2019).

With regard to FDI, both the long and short-run results indicate that in Italy FDI has a positive and significant impact on carbon emission. These results are consistent with the findings of Danish et al. (2018) and Zhang and Zhang (2018). Besides, the ARDL results show that in the long-run oil price negatively affects carbon emission, as its estimated coefficient is statistically significant and equal to −0.044. This implies that in the long-run any increase in oil price could imply reductions in carbon emissions. On the contrary, oil price tends to increase environmental degradation in the short-run. In the case of exports our results show significant and positive relationship with carbon emission both in the short and long-run, suggesting that higher exports enhance the demand and use of energy consumption and other resources and, as

Table 5 ARDL long-run estimates with diagnostic tests

Variables	Model 1	Model 2	Model 4	Model 6
ARDL long-run estimates				
GDP	16.950*	21.289***	14.577**	30.031***
GDP-SQ	−0.831*	−1.010***	−0.718**	−1.455***
FDI	0.058**	0.055***	0.047***	0.063**
OP	−0.044**	−0.079***	−0.052***	−0.098***
HC	–	−0.575	–	–
EXP	–	–	0.134**	–
UP	–	–	–	−0.388
Constant	−86.525*	−110.994***	−74.428**	152.787***
ARDL bound test				
F-statistic	3.591**	18.868***	11.105**	4.513**
Sel. model	(4,4,3,4,4)	(1,4,3,4,4,4)	(2,3,3,2,4,2)	(1,4,4,4,4,4)
Model statistics				
R-squared	0.995	0.998	–	–
Adj. R-sq	0.982	0.995	–	–
F-statistic	76.738***	250.427***		
Diagnostic tests				
Normality	0.213	1.490	2.562	–
Serial-Corr	0.282		2.523	–
Hetero	1.349	0.468	0.489	–
ARCH	0.547	0.976	0.401	–
CUSUM	Stable	Stable	Stable	Stable
CUSUM-Sq	Stable	Stable	Stable	Stable

Note *** *, ***, ** and * show significance at 1, 2.5, 5 and 10% level respectively

Table 6 ARDL short-run estimates

Variables	Model 1	Model 2	Model 4	Model 6
GDP	37.169***	77.692***	40.393***	100.532***
GDP-SQ	−1.726***	−3.724***	−1.922***	−4.822***
FDI	0.044***	0.042***	0.007*	0.050***
OP	0.039**	0.059***	0.019*	0.083***
HC	–	16.872***	–	–
EXP	–	–	0.014	–
UP	–	–	–	26.146**
Coint. Eq. (-1)	−0.102***	−0.391***	−0.006***	−0.267***

Note *** *, ***, ** and * show significance at 1, 2.5, 5 and 10% level respectively a result, carbon emission increases (Tables 5 and 6, Model 4). Finally, we do not find any statistically significant findings for the relationships between human capital and carbon emission and urbanization and carbon emission in the long-run (Table 5, Models 2 and 6), while both of them are positive and statistically significant in the short-run, with the estimated coefficients equal to 16.872 and 26.146, respectively (Table 6, Models 2 and 6). Finally, by focusing on the short-run results (Table 6), we can observe that the coefficient value of the error correction term (negative and statistically significant) indicates that any deviation from long-run equilibrium is adjusted at the speed of 10% yearly.

We performed several diagnostic tests, such as Jarque-Bera test for normality, Breusch-Pagan-Godfrey heteroscedasticity test, LM-ARCH heteroscedasticity test, Breusch-Godfrey serial correlation test. We also tested for the dynamic stability of the model by applying the cumulative sum of recursive residuals (CUSUM) and cumulative sum of recursive residuals square (CUSUM-Sq) stability test. The results of these tests show that there is no problem of normality, heteroscedasticity and serial correlation (Table 5).

4.2 *NARDL Model*

This section presents the results of the NARDL model estimation. Table 7 presents the results of F-statistic in the case of NARDL methodology. The results show that the F-statistic value is higher than the upper bound critical values suggested by Narayan (2005). Hence, we can reject the null hypothesis of no cointegration against the alternative hypothesis of cointegration. Furthermore, the value of the coefficient of the lagged error correction term confirms the existence of long-run cointegration among per capita income, FDI positive, FDI negative, OP positive, OP negative, and carbon emissions.

After confirming the long-run cointegration relationship between the variables considered, we determined the long and short-run asymmetric results. Tables 8 and 9 present the results for long and short-run models, respectively. The results show that the relationship between economic growth and carbon emission is positive and statistically significant both in the short and in the long-run, in line with the results of

Table 7 NARDL bound test

F-bounds test statistic		Null hypothesis: no levels relationship		
		Significance (%)	I(0) bound	I(1) bound
F-statistic	6.825***	10	2.12	3.23
		5	2.45	3.61
		2.50	2.75	3.99
		1	3.15	4.43

Note *** *, ***, ** and * show significance at 1, 2.5, 5 and 10% level respectively

ARDL model. Moreover, the negative and statistically significant value of the square term of per capita income (GDP^2) confirms the presence of EKC hypothesis also in this case.

Table 8 NARDL long-run estimates with diagnostic tests

Variables	Coefficient	Std. error	t-statistic	Probability
GDP	9.056*	5.059	1.789	0.091
GDP-SQ	−0.4289*	0.250	−1.709	0.056
FDI-Positive	0.054***	0.016	3.255	0.007
FDI-Negative	0.048***	0.013	3.578	0.002
Oil-Positive	−0.088***	0.020	−4.277	0.000
Oil-Negative	−0.038	0.023	−1.614	0.124
Constant	−47.203*	25.693	−1.837	0.083
Model statistics				
R-squared	0.996			
Adjusted R-sq	0.989			
F-statistic	152.352***			
Probability	(0.000)			
Diagnostic tests				
			χ^2	Probability
Normality			1.964	(0.375)
Serial-Corr			2.641	(0.901)
Hetero			1.435	(0.221)
ARCH			0.607	(0.440)
CUSUM			Stable	
CUSUM-Sq			Stable	

Note ***, ** and * show significance at 1, 5 and 10% level respectively

Table 9 NARDL short-run estimates

Variables	Coefficient	Std. error	t-statistic	Probability
D(GDP)	12.890***	4.187	3.078	0.006
D(GDP-SQ)	−0.573**	0.205	−2.796	0.012
D(FDI-Positive)	0.057***	0.009	6.536	0.000
D(FDI-Negative)	−0.020***	0.003	−5.805	0.000
D(Oil-Positive)	−0.025*	0.0122	−2.011	0.060
D(Oil-Negative)	0.048***	0.013	3.699	0.001
Coint. Eq(-1)	−0.192***	0.024	−8.039	0.000

Note ***, ** and * show significance at 1, 5 and 10% level respectively

Table 10 NARDL Wald test

Variables	Short-run		Long-run	
	F-statistic	Probability	F-statistic	Probability
FDI	23.330***	(0.000)	26.719***	(0.000)
OP	1.266	(0.276)	5.610**	(0.030)

Note ***, ** and * show significance at 1, 5 and 10% level respectively

In the case of the long-run asymmetric relationship between FDI and carbon emission we can note that increases in FDI (positive changes in the partial sum of FDI) enhance carbon emissions. The short-run results are also statistically significant and explain that any positive shock in FDI increases carbon emissions, while negative shocks in FDI reduce carbon emissions. With regard to oil price, the results for the long-run relationship between oil price and carbon emission show that any increase in the oil price (positive variations in the partial sum of OP) imply reductions in carbon emission, whereas a decline in the oil price (negative shocks in the OP) does not show any significant impact on carbon emissions. The results of short-run asymmetric relationship between oil price and carbon emission are statistically significant. In particular, an increase in the oil price imply reduces CO_2, while a decrease in the oil price increases CO_2 in the short run. Finally, the coefficient value of the error correction term indicates that any disequilibrium in past years is adjusted at the speed of 19% yearly.

The results of the Wald Test for assessing the equality of short-run and long-run positive and negative shocks of FDI and OP on carbon emissions are presented in Table 10. With regard to FDI, the Wald Test value is statistically significant both in short and in long-run: it means that we can reject the null hypothesis of symmetry against the alternative hypothesis and we can conclude that the impact of FDI on carbon emission is asymmetric. In the case of OP, the results confirm the asymmetric effect of OP on carbon emission only in the long-run.

The results of the diagnostic tests provide no evidence of serial correlation, heteroscedasticity, normality, and stability issues (Table 8).

Causality analysis and robustness analysis. We also checked the direction of causality among the variables considered. For the causality analysis, we performed the block exogeneity Wald test, which gives the causality results for both short and long-run. The results show an unidirectional causality running from per capita income (economic growth), the square term of per capita income, FDI, oil price, human capital, exports, urban population, inflation, and financial development towards carbon emission (Table 11).

In order to check for the robustness of the long-run results obtained from the ARDL methodology, we applied another univariate cointegration technique, the dynamic ordinary least square (DOLS). The DOLS results are in line with the results of the long-run ARDL model (Table 12). These results also confirm the existence of EKC hypothesis in Italy under all methodologies used.

Table 11 Causality test

Independent variable	Dependent variables									
	CO2	GDP	GDP-SQ	FDI	OP	HC	INF	EXP	FD	UP
CO2	–	3.194	3.221	1.795	6.047	2.636	5.631	12.631***	0.935	6.812*
GDP	7.762*	–	0.789	0.305	1.147	4.794	0.496	2.746	0.283	2.945
GDP-SQ	8.379**	0.829	–	0.327	1.170	4.599	0.667	2.704	0.238	3.170
FDI	39.162***	3.560	3.627	–	2.059	2.838	0.433	5.467	1.153	2.058
OP	14.024***	3.402	3.383	1.362	–	2.828	1.203	7.245*	0.310	3.227
HC	15.905***	5.570	5.596	3.282	0.997	–	9.760**	8.477**	4.214	8.951*
INF	14.537***	5.381	5.378	14.273***	2.425	2.307	–	3.590	0.695	11.139**
EXP	4.733	0.792	0.818	0.756	1.918	2.206	2.311	–	0.637	5.101
FD	9.624**	2.341	2.292	1.227	0.221	6.735*	4.085	5.412	–	4.750
UP	6.319*	3.961	3.929	4.289	2.603	2.896	2.615	10.810**	1.557	–

Note ***, ** and * show significance at 1, 5 and 10% level respectively

Table 12 Dynamic OLS results

Variables	Coefficient	Std. error	t-statistic	Probability
GDP	5.665***	0.798	7.096	0.005
GDP-SQ	−0.250**	0.045	−5.572	0.011
FDI	0.038**	0.009	4.394	0.021
OP	−0.006	0.010	−0.557	0.615
HC	0.232	0.479	0.485	0.660
INF	0.106**	0.027	3.952	0.028
EXP	0.340***	0.057	5.965	0.009
FD	−0.151**	0.058	−2.605	0.080
UP	−7.328***	0.898	−8.163	0.003
R-squared	0.999			
Adjusted R-sq	0.996			

Note ***, ** and * show significance at 1, 5 and 10% level respectively

5 Conclusion

In this work we have examined the symmetric and asymmetric effects of oil price, foreign direct investments and economic growth on carbon emissions in Italy. To this purpose, the long and short-run impact of these variables on carbon emissions have been investigated by applying the ARDL and non-linear ARDL methods to Italian data for the period 1970–2019. Lastly, we have investigated the combined direction of causality between carbon emissions and its determinants.

The results of the study confirm the presence of cointegration between carbon emissions and the set of regressors considered, as well as the presence of the EKC hypothesis for Italy. In particular, the results provided by ARDL model show that economic growth and FDI intensify carbon emissions both in the long and short-run, while the impact of oil price on emissions is negative in the long-run and positive in the short-run, suggesting that OP is responsible for environmental degradation only in the short run. The results obtained from NARDL model reveal that both in the long and in the short-run an increase in the oil price imply reductions in carbon emissions.

Hence, the present study represents an additional source of useful information to policy makers for future environmental protection policies in order to take care of environmental quality.

References

Agbanike, T.F., Nwani, C., Uwazie, U.I., Anochiwa, L.I., Onoja, T.G.C., Ogbonnaya, I.O.: Oil price, energy consumption and carbon dioxide (CO2) emissions: insight into sustainability challenges in Venezuela. Latin American Economic Review **28**(1), 1–26 (2019)

Agovino, M., Bartoletto, S., Garofalo, A.: Modelling the relationship between energy intensity and GDP for European countries: an historical perspective (1800–2000). Energy Economics **82**, 114–134 (2019)

Ahmad, N., Du, L., Lu, J., Wang, J., Li, H.Z., Hashmi, M.Z.: Modelling the CO2 emissions and economic growth in Croatia: is there any environmental Kuznets curve? Energy **123**, 164–172 (2017)

Al-Mulali, U., Tang, C.F.: Investigating the validity of pollution haven hypothesis in the gulf cooperation council (GCC) countries. Energy Policy **60**, 813–819 (2013)

Alper, A., Onur, G.: Environmental Kuznets curve hypothesis for sub-elements of the carbon emissions in China. Nat. Hazards **82**(2), 1327–1340 (2016)

Antweiler, W., Copeland, B.R., Taylor, M.S.: Is free trade good for the environment? American economic review **91**(4), 877–908 (2001)

Apergis, N., Payne, J.E.: Renewable energy, output, carbon dioxide emissions, and oil prices: evidence from South America. Energy Sources Part B **10**(3), 281–287 (2015)

Azevedo, V.G., Sartori, S., Campos, L.M.: CO2 emissions: a quantitative analysis among the BRICS nations. Renew. Sustain. Energy Rev. **81**, 107–115 (2018)

Baek, J.: Do nuclear and renewable energy improve the environment? Empirical evidence from the United States. Ecol. Ind. **66**, 352–356 (2016)

Bartlett, A.A.: Reflections on sustainability, population growth, and the environment. Popul. Environ. **16**(1), 5–35 (1994)

Behera, S.R., Dash, D.P.: The effect of urbanization, energy consumption, and foreign direct investment on the carbon dioxide emission in the SSEA (South and Southeast Asian) region. Renew. Sustain. Energy Rev. **70**, 96–106 (2017)

Birdsall, N., Wheeler, D.: Trade policy and industrial pollution in Latin America: where are the pollution havens? J Environ Dev **2**(1), 137–149 (1993)

Bölük, G., Mert, M.: The renewable energy, growth and environmental Kuznets curve in Turkey: an ARDL approach. Renew. Sustain. Energy Rev. **52**, 587–595 (2015)

Chandran, V.G.R., Tang, C.F.: The impacts of transport energy consumption, foreign direct investment and income on CO2 emissions in ASEAN-5 economies. Renew. Sustain. Energy Rev. **24**, 445–453 (2013)

Circle Economy: Circularity Gap Report (2021)

Coondoo, D., Dinda, S.: Causality between income and emission: a country group-specific econometric analysis. Ecol. Econ. **40**(3), 351–367 (2002)

Danish, T.H., Baloch, M.A., Suad, S.: Modeling the impact of transport energy consumption on CO2 emission in Pakistan: evidence from ARDL approach. Environ. Sci. Pollut. Res. **25**(10), 9461–9473 (2018)

Dong, K., Sun, R., Hochman, G., Zeng, X., Li, H., Jiang, H.: Impact of natural gas consumption on CO2 emissions: panel data evidence from China's provinces. J. Clean. Prod. **162**, 400–410 (2017)

Engle, R.F., Granger, C.W.: Co-integration and error correction: representation, estimation, and testing. Econ. J. Econ. Soc. 251–276, (1987)

Fan, F., Lei, Y.: Responsive relationship between energy-related carbon dioxide emissions from the transportation sector and economic growth in Beijing—Based on decoupling theory. Int. J. Sustain. Transp. **11**(10), 764–775 (2017)

Farhani, S., Shahbaz, M.: What role of renewable and non-renewable electricity consumption and output is needed to initially mitigate CO2 emissions in MENA region? Renew. Sustain. Energy Rev. **40**, 80–90 (2014)

Galeotti, M., Lanza, A., Pauli, F.: Reassessing the environmental Kuznets curve for CO2 emissions: a robustness exercise. Ecol. Econ. **57**(1), 152–163 (2006)
Gastaldi, M., Lombardi, G.V., Rapposelli, A., Romano, G.: The efficiency of waste sector in Italy: an application by data envelopment analysis. Environ. Clim. Technol. **24**(3), 225–238 (2020)
Grossman, G.M., Krueger, A.B.: Economic growth and the environment. Q. J. Econ. **110**(2), 353–377 (1995)
Hakimi, A., Hamdi, H.: Trade liberalization, FDI inflows, environmental quality and economic growth: a comparative analysis between Tunisia and Morocco. Renew. Sustain. Energy Rev. **58**, 1445–1456 (2016)
Haug, A.A., Ucal, M.: The role of trade and FDI for CO2 emissions in Turkey: nonlinear relationships. Energy Econ **81**, 297–307 (2019)
Ito, B., Yashiro, N., Xu, Z., Chen, X., Wakasugi, R.: How do Chinese industries benefit from FDI spillovers? China Econ. Rev. **23**(2), 342–356 (2012)
Jiang, L., Zhou, H.F., Bai, L., Zhou, P.: Does foreign direct investment drive environmental degradation in China? An empirical study based on air quality index from a spatial perspective. J. Clean. Prod. **176**, 864–872 (2018)
Johansen, S., Juselius, K.: Maximum likelihood estimation and inference on cointegration—with applications to the demand for money. Oxford Bull. Econ. Stat. **52**(2), 169–210 (1990)
Johansen, S.: Likelihood-Based Inference in Cointegrated Vector Autoregressive Models. Oxford University Press, Oxford (1996)
Katircioglu, S.: Investigating the role of oil prices in the conventional EKC model: evidence from Turkey. Asian Econ Financ Rev **7**(5), 498–508 (2017)
Kivyiro, P., Arminen, H.: Carbon dioxide emissions, energy consumption, economic growth, and foreign direct investment: causality analysis for Sub-Saharan Africa. Energy **74**, 595–606 (2014)
Koçak, E., Şarkgüneşi, A.: The impact of foreign direct investment on CO2 emissions in Turkey: new evidence from cointegration and bootstrap causality analysis. Environ. Sci. Pollut. Res. **25**(1), 790–804 (2018)
Lee, J.W.: The contribution of foreign direct investment to clean energy use, carbon emissions and economic growth. Energy Policy **55**, 483–489 (2013)
Lee, S., Oh, D.W.: Economic growth and the environment in China: empirical evidence using prefecture level data. China Econ. Rev. **36**, 73–85 (2015)
Lin, P., Liu, Z., Zhang, Y.: Do Chinese domestic firms benefit from FDI inflow?: Evidence of horizontal and vertical spillovers. China Econ. Rev. **20**(4), 677–691 (2009)
Lombardi, G.V., Gastaldi, M., Rapposelli, A., Romano, G.: Assessing efficiency of urban waste services and the role of tariff in a circular economy perspective: empirical application for Italian municipalities. Working Paper (2021)
Malik, M.Y., Latif, K., Khan, Z., Butt, H.D., Hussain, M., Nadeem, M.A.: Symmetric and asymmetric impact of oil price, FDI and economic growth on carbon emission in Pakistan: evidence from ARDL and non-linear ARDL approach. Sci. Total Environ. **726**, 138421 (2020)
Mohammed Suliman, T.H., Abid, M.: The impacts of oil price on exchange rates: evidence from Saudi Arabia. Energy Explor. Exploit. **38**(5), 2037–2058 (2020)
Narayan, P.K.: The saving and investment nexus for China: evidence from cointegration tests. Appl. Econ. **37**(17), 1979–1990 (2005)
Nasir, M., Rehman, F.U.: Environmental Kuznets curve for carbon emissions in Pakistan: an empirical investigation. Energy Policy **39**(3), 1857–1864 (2011)
Naz, S., Sultan, R., Zaman, K., Aldakhil, A.M., Nassani, A.A., Abro, M.M.Q.: Moderating and mediating role of renewable energy consumption, FDI inflows, and economic growth on carbon dioxide emissions: evidence from robust least square estimator. Environ. Sci. Pollut. Res. **26**(3), 2806–2819 (2019)
Oxelheim, L., Ghauri, P.: EU–China and the non-transparent race for inward FDI. J. Asian Econ. **19**(4), 358–370 (2008)
Pesaran, M.H., Smith, R.: Estimating long-run relationships from dynamic heterogeneous panels. J. Econ. **68**(1), 79–113 (1995)

Pesaran, M.H., Shin, Y., Smith, R.J.: Bounds testing approaches to the analysis of level relationships. J. Appl. Economet. **16**(3), 289–326 (2001)

Saboori, B., Rasoulinezhad, E., Sung, J.: The nexus of oil consumption, CO2 emissions and economic growth in China, Japan and South Korea. Environ. Sci. Pollut. Res. **24**(8), 7436–7455 (2017)

Saikkonen, P.: Asymptotically efficient estimation of cointegration regressions. Econ. Theory 1–21 (1991)

Sarkodie, S.A., Strezov, V.: Effect of foreign direct investments, economic development and energy consumption on greenhouse gas emissions in developing countries. Sci. Total Environ. **646**, 862–871 (2019)

Schmalensee, R., Stoker, T.M., Judson, R.A.: World carbon dioxide emissions: 1950–2050. Rev. Econ. Stat. **80**(1), 15–27 (1998)

Selden, T.M., Song, D.: Environmental quality and development: is there a Kuznets curve for air pollution emissions? J. Environ. Econ. Manag. **27**(2), 147–162 (1994)

Shin, Y., Yu, B., Greenwood-Nimmo, M.: Modelling asymmetric cointegration and dynamic multipliers in a nonlinear ARDL framework. In: Festschrift in Honor of Peter Schmidt, pp. 281–314. Springer, New York, NY (2014)

Shujah ur, R., Chen, S., Saleem, N., Bari, M.W.: Financial development and its moderating role in environmental Kuznets curve: evidence from Pakistan. Environ. Sci. Pollut. Res. **26**(19), 19305–19319 (2019)

Simsek, T., Yigit, E.: Causality Analysis of BRICT Countries on Renewable Energy Consumption, Oil Prices, CO2 Emissions, Urbanization and Economic Growth (2017)

Stock, J.H., Watson, M.W. A simple estimator of cointegrating vectors in higher order integrated systems. Econ. J. Econ. Soc. 783–820 (1993)

Sulaiman, C., Abdul-Rahim, A.S.: The relationship between CO 2 emission, energy consumption and economic growth in Malaysia: a three-way linkage approach. Environ. Sci. Pollut. Res. **24**(32), 25204–25220 (2017)

Sung, B., Song, W.Y., Park, S.D.: How foreign direct investment affects CO2 emission levels in the Chinese manufacturing industry: evidence from panel data. Econ. Syst. **42**(2), 320–331 (2018)

Tang, C.F., Tan, B.W.: The impact of energy consumption, income and foreign direct investment on carbon dioxide emissions in Vietnam. Energy **79**, 447–454 (2015)

Usman, O., Iorember, P.T., Olanipekun, I.O.: Revisiting the environmental Kuznets curve (EKC) hypothesis in India: the effects of energy consumption and democracy. Environ. Sci. Pollut. Res. **26**(13), 13390–13400 (2019)

Wang, Z.: Does biomass energy consumption help to control environmental pollution? Evidence from BRICS countries. Sci. Total Environ. **670**, 1075–1083 (2019)

Zambrano-Monserrate, M.A., Silva-Zambrano, C.A., Davalos-Penafiel, J.L., Zambrano-Monserrate, A., Ruano, M.A.: Testing environmental Kuznets curve hypothesis in Peru: the role of renewable electricity, petroleum and dry natural gas. Renew. Sustain. Energy Rev. **82**, 4170–4178 (2018)

Zhang, C., Zhou, X.: Does foreign direct investment lead to lower CO2 emissions? Evidence from a regional analysis in China. Renew. Sustain. Energy Rev. **58**, 943–951 (2016)

Zhang, Y., Zhang, S.: The impacts of GDP, trade structure, exchange rate and FDI inflows on China's carbon emissions. Energy Policy **120**, 347–353 (2018)

Zou, X.: VECM model analysis of carbon emissions, GDP, and international crude oil prices. Discret. Dyn. Nat. Soc. **2018**, 1–11 (2018)

Openness in Communication and Budgetary Information in the Participative Budgeting Research. The Case of Italian Public Healthcare Organizations

Domenico Raucci and Manuela Paolini

Abstract In the last decades, the diffusion in Italian Public Healthcare Organizations (PHOs) of accounting and managerial practices, centered on planning and budgeting, have increased doctors' presence into management roles. Clinical heads of units, becoming budget holders, have to face new accountability purposes. However, PHOs still struggle in implementing effectively hybrid professionalism, due to doctor-managers' resistance to use budgetary information for decision-making. To overcome these criticalities, doctor-managers' involvement in PHOs' budgeting process may be beneficial, as highlighted by Behavioral Management Accounting research on budgetary participation. Nevertheless, without the support of openness in communication with top management, doctor-managers' hybrid nature might lead them to develop a cognitive distance that may do not fit their predisposition to participate. A strengthening of their involvement in the budgetary information features design might mitigate these risks. In the BMA perspective, this paper explores the role of perceptions of openness in communication in improving the predisposition of doctor-managers to participate in the budgeting process, via the indirect effect of perceived utility of budgetary information. Data were collected administering a questionnaire to 332 doctor-managers of Italian PHOs. The response rate was of 37.95%. Hypotheses were tested through a regression analysis. Our study contributes to the interpretative research on the organizational factors affecting the involvement of doctor-managers in PHOs' management, offering new insights into the psychological antecedents of budgetary participation. Results show that: perceptions of openness in communication have a positive effect on perceived utility of budgetary information; this latter has a positive effect on budgetary participation of doctor-managers.

Keywords Budgetary participation in Italian PHOs · Value-expectancy theory · Perception of openness in communication · Perceived utility of budgetary information

D. Raucci · M. Paolini (✉)
Department of Economic Studies, University G. d'Annunzio of Chieti-Pescara, Pescara, Italy
e-mail: manuela.paolini@unich.it

D. Raucci
e-mail: domenico.raucci@unich.it

S. Za et al. (eds.), *Sustainable Digital Transformation*, Lecture Notes in Information Systems and Organisation 59, https://doi.org/10.1007/978-3-031-15770-7_7

1 Introduction

As in other countries, the Italian Public Healthcare Organizations (PHOs) have faced the evolutions produced by NPM-inspired reforms [4, 5]. These have promoted the regionalization of the National Health Service (NHS), the diffusion of a quasi-market culture, increased levels of autonomy and responsibilities of PHOs for their economic results, as well as the orientation towards performance measurement and management control approaches from the private sector [60, 75, 92]. This orientation has recently intensified, due to the need to manage the impacts of the pandemic crisis caused by Covid-19 [7, 69, 70].

In the accounting information systems of Italian PHOs, these reforms, coupled with the adoption of more advanced ITC tools [71, 98], have led to the diffusion of accounting techniques and managerial practices, based on planning and budgeting, to maximize the objectives of efficiency while preserving the quality and the appropriateness of the health services provided [72, 81].

Furthermore, the links with medical management reforms and the organizational orientation of PHOs towards departmental models have increased the involvement of clinicians in managerial roles and management control practices [53, 87, 97]. Clinicians heading of Operational Units (OUs), in particular, have become budget holders and, as such, more directly involved in the pursuit of the economic objectives of these organizations.

Thus, budgetary responsibilities have overlapped traditional clinical-professional responsibilities, making these clinicians accountable for the management of the overall performance of their OUs in terms of efficiency, costs and clinical outputs [17, 39, 89]. Literature has highlighted how this "hybrid" nature of doctor-managers might generate risks of role ambiguity [31, 80, 94], due to the potential misalignment between the professional values of autonomy and patient-centricity, traditionally inspiring the actions of clinicians, and the pursuit of the budgetary objectives imposed by the new managerial roles [1, 57].

In this sense, management accounting studies have investigated the contribution of budgetary information in reducing these risks and the possible negative effects on managerial performance [21, 56, 65]. Empirical evidence, however, revealed the limited use of this information to support the decision-making of doctors-managers and the scarce effectiveness of budgetary information alone in encouraging greater commitment in pursuing economic objectives [38, 75, 78].

To overcome these criticalities, the research fields focused on the role of organizational factors in increasing the usefulness of such information suggest the advantages deriving from a greater involvement of doctor-managers in the definition of the features associated with the information in the budgeting process of PHOs [2, 50, 81, 105]. Higher levels of involvement in this process can constitute a means of effective implementation of hybrid professionalism [3, 53, 80] and, in particular, a useful factor of increasing the levels of acceptance of economic responsibilities by these middle managers [62, 78].

Interpretative research perspectives have investigated these models of collaboration mostly in the relations between clinicians and controllers, to improve the design of the features of the accounting information systems in PHOs [3, 85].

Some studies emphasized how the individual and cultural differences, enhanced by collaboration, can constitute important organizational drivers for influencing the interpretative mental schemes of these professionals regarding their managerial role and behavioral approaches to the budgeting practices [57, 78, 81, 87].

In this theoretical framework, some studies on organizational identification perspectives, mostly building on Social Identity Theory [108], highlighted the potential of managers' sense of association and identification with the organization in allowing their internalization of organizational values [20, 93] and motivating their Organizational Citizenship Behavior (OCB), which benefits the organizational functioning [68, 82, 83]. These aspects can also be influenced by managerial personality traits and how they impact individual choices about which activities to engage in and how much effort to exert on them [77].

Acting on such organizational drivers might influence the perceptions of doctors-managers on the usefulness of budgetary information provided by PHOs, inducing greater levels of participation in the budgeting process. These dynamics can be usefully explored in the research fields of Behavioral Management Accounting (BMA) [9, 90, 95], and, in particular, in those fields underlining the influences exerted by mental states and individual perceptions in the cognitive-behavioral schemes linked to participation in the budgeting process [18, 33, 111].

In fact, some of these studies have underlined how the practices of budgetary participation alone cannot assure that their benefits in aligning behaviors with the expected economic objectives will be effectively materialize. A fruitful participation process does not arise only from the predisposition of the superior to allow it, but also from the substantial predisposition to participate of the other actors involved, which can be influenced by various intervening factors [19, 22, 33, 65]. Studies on budgetary participation based on the agency theory have highlighted that when subordinates are involved in the budgeting process, their cooperative effort within organization is often plagued by self-interest or opportunistic behavior [18, 25, 113]. In this perspective, the individual differences and the divergent interpretations of context, values and objectives by doctor-managers might arise perceptions of cognitive distance from top management [86, 102, 103], which are likely to increase the typical behaviors deriving from information asymmetry and the risks of creating budgetary slacks [67, 99] that, instead, budgetary participation should reduce. Further, these perceptions might discourage the motivation and the commitment of doctor-managers to participate in the budgeting process and reduce their contribution in designing budgetary information deemed satisfactory and more useful for their decision-making [16, 45].

To reduce these effects of the cognitive distance and induce the participation of doctors-managers in the budgeting process, a significant contribution could derive from the effectiveness of the organizational support provided to their managerial role in the hierarchical relation with top management of PHOs. Consistently with the generalist literature on the functions of communication and influence of participative budgeting [24, 34, 42, 66, 96], we assume that this effectiveness can be linked, in particular, to the perceptions that these middle managers have of the openness in communication, within PHOs' practices of budgetary participation, through which the support is provided to them by top management, with the assistance from the controllers.

In fact, doctor-managers' perceptions of the levels of openness in communication in PHO's budgetary system, the mental schemes with which they interpret the information exchange and the communication transparency in the participation process, the shared definition of job-relevant information, and, above all, the perceptions of listening of their voice on the operational criticalities and the needs of UOs [35, 47, 73, 102] might influence the psychological processes underlined by the Value Expectancy-Theory (VET) [109].

According to this theory, higher levels of perceived openness in communication by doctors-managers might address their motivation towards a greater predisposition to participate in the budgeting process through the strengthening of their individual expectancy of influencing the budgetary objectives as well as of their perceptions of the value that may arise from their participation. In fact, these value-expectancy perceptions might reduce the dysfunctional behaviors linked to the information asymmetry and to the creation of budgetary slacks and mitigate the resistance to accept the budgetary responsibilities, with positive effects on role ambiguity [46, 48, 67, 74, 79]. Further, the links value-expectations, positively influencing perceptions of cognitive distance, might address the efforts allocation of these budget holders by increasing their predisposition and commitment to participate in the budgeting process of PHOs.

The cognitive-motivational dynamics activated by these Perceptions of Openness in Communication (POC), integrating the behavioral aspects of collaboration based on the agency model, should allow to improve the agency relation between middle and top management of PHOs, by leveraging trust and perceptions of others, which are essential dimensions in trust-based settings such as those of the budgetary participation process [24, 48, 115].

In this perspective, we can provide a richer psychological representation of how POC in PHOs might encourage the predisposition of doctor-managers to a substantial involvement in the budgetary participation process and, on this way, their commitment to accept the economic responsibilities linked to their managerial role.

Even if there's a consolidated generalist literature recognizing that budgetary participation plays a key role in influencing managerial performance, through its beneficial effects on mental states, attitudes and behaviors [66, 100], the drivers of the predisposition to participate in the budgeting process have still remained relatively unexplored [22, 65, 99]. In particular, there are few studies focusing on the role played by subordinate's perceptions of superiors or contextual factors [19, 30, 113], especially in BMA research in the context of PHOs based on budgetary participation approaches [3, 62, 88, 95, 110]. In the Italian context [11, 55, 107], the main contributions have explored its beneficial effects on influencing doctor-managers' attitudes, motivation, and subsequent behavior and performance within different theoretical frameworks [13, 61, 63]. In this perspective, some studies have deepened the role of doctor-managers' budgetary participation in influencing performance though the perceived features of budgetary information [58, 59]. However, the causalities antecedent of an effective budgetary participation of doctor-managers are still largely overlooked. In particular, there are still no studies on the role of their perceptions of the openness in communication by top management of PHOs in arising their predisposition to budgetary participation.

Adopting a BMA approach in budgeting research, this paper aimed at analyzing, in the framework of VET, the impact of POC on budgetary participation of doctor-managers via the indirect effect of the perceived utility of budgetary information.

The study attempts to contribute to the healthcare management accounting research on the organizational factors of the empowerment of doctor-managers' commitment to and use of budgetary information for decision-making, based on their involvement in PHOs' budgeting process.

To test our model, a survey was conducted among doctor-managers working in Italian PHOs, before the Covid-19 pandemic period.

The paper is structured as follows: Sect. 2 provides the theoretical background on VET; Sect. 3 provides a literature background on budgetary participation, deepening studies in Italian PHOs and showing the research design; Sect. 4 describes the sample and the research methodology; Sect. 5 shows the results and Sect. 6 presents the discussions, drawing policy conclusions and managerial implications.

2 The Value-Expectancy Theory

According to the Value-Expectancy Theory (VET) [109], individual behaviors are the result of rational decision-making, aimed at maximizing the benefits and the related satisfaction that the agents can derive from their own courses of action. In particular, this theory assumes that the motivation to behave in a certain manner depends on the strength of two subjective dimensions, namely the expectancy and the value characterizing the course of action in the individual's ex ante perception.

VET has been used in management control studies to investigate the relation between motivation and individual performance [27, 59]. In our work, the same theoretical framework is applied to investigate the cognitive-motivational dynamics, antecedents to budgetary participation, which are activated by the POC within the budgeting process.

Prior research has documented the benefits of adopting such communication, such as enhancing subordinates' loyalty and trust in the organization [41, 43, 91], favoring greater cooperation and flexibility at all managerial levels [26, 112], reducing subordinates' misconduct and increasing subordinates' engagement, job satisfaction [32, 101] and overall performance [12, 32].

In the relation between communication and managerial performance, we analyze the cognitive dynamics starting from the POC that motivates doctor-managers to participate in the budgeting process.

Based on VET, the support received and the availability of information useful for carrying out a specific action are among the factors considered capable of influencing the degree of subjective expectancy on the same action. On this basis, we assume that the extent to which the organization effectively supports the managerial role of doctor-managers can be expressed by doctor-managers' POC in the budgeting process. In fact, openness in communication means open information policy in PHO's budgetary system, making decision observable to doctor-managers, shared definition of job-relevant information, giving the opportunity to have a voice on the budgetary information system's design, that, as a result, takes into account the criticisms and the operational problems of their OUs, rather than solely the cost-containment regulations [47, 81, 87, 102]. The related POC allows not only to increase the perception of the amount of budgetary information available, but also to enhance the perceived quality of budgetary information, which positively affects the perceived utility of budgetary information to make the decision-making process [44, 45, 107]. This latter perception might address the psychological processes theorized by VET, on the one hand, by influencing the expectancy of doctors-managers with respect to participation in the definition of budgetary objectives, on the other, by influencing their perceptions of the value that may arise from their participation, which stimulate a greater countervalue motivating them to budgetary participation.

3 Literature Background on Budgetary Participation

Budgetary participation is a process whereby middle managers have the opportunity to get involved in and have influence on the definition of the budgetary objectives of their UOs [15, 34, 79]. The BMA research on budgeting have unleashed the potential of this budgeting practice in increasing the effectiveness of the budgeting system, addressing middle managers towards higher levels of motivation in the pursuit of economic objectives with consequent improvements in the managerial performance [9, 22, 30].

Given the key role of budgetary participation, the BMA research on the causal antecedents of an effective managerial involvement in the budgeting process is particularly relevant. In fact, even if top management allows budgetary participation of middle management, as highlighted by some studies based on the agency theory, subordinates' cooperative effort in the budgeting process is often plagued by self-interest or opportunistic behavior [1, 18, 113].

Nevertheless, while there has been a strong research focus on how this budgeting practice influences positively managerial performance through the mediating role of mental states, attitudes and behaviors [66, 100], the antecedents of budgetary participation have still remained relatively unexplored [22, 65, 99]. Further, in this latter stream of research, most of the existing studies have adopted a superior-centric approach, aimed at explaining why organizations allows budgetary participation [14, 18, 52]. On the other hand, literature have largely recognized that incentive is a crucial variable to assure an effective involvement in the budgeting process, suggesting to organizations the identification of budgetary mechanisms that can create conditions for greater interaction between superiors and subordinates, through which these latter might be encouraged to participate in the budgeting process, so that the result of this participation can positively influence the performance [1, 2]. In this perspective, Kyj and Parker [45] stated that subordinates may be encouraged to participate in the budgeting process as part of superior's leadership approach of fostering trust and open and meaningful communication with subordinates [28]. However, few studies have investigated subordinate's perceptions of superiors or contextual factors, such as the accessibility and predictability of information, and their links with middle managers' motivation to participate in the budgeting process [19, 113]. A study of da Silva Zonatto et al. [19] demonstrated that leaders with a friendly, accessible leadership style, who treat subordinates equally, care about subordinate well-being and explain actions to be developed clearly, are likely to encourage managers to participate in the budgetary processes of the organizations. Lau et al. [49] showed that perceptions of organizational politics are an important dimension of how subordinates perceive their work environment, which affect their motivation, and, thus, their extent of involvement and influence in the budgetary process.

As noted by Mahlendorf et al. [65], such research has not only stalled, but also only very few variables have been identified and studied so far, calling for further studies to develop propositions about the underlying causalities of budgetary participation not previously addressed as well as theories regarding the interaction between contextual factors and psychological variables.

Thus, our research attempts to address the call of Mahlendorf et al. [65] within the context of PHOs, in order to seek potential antecedents of an effective involvement of doctor-managers in the budgeting process.

3.1 Budgetary Participation in Italian PHOs

BMA research on budgetary participation within the context of PHOs suggests that it can be an important driver for addressing doctor-managers' behaviors towards the achievement of budgetary objectives [3, 57]. In particular, doctor-managers' involvement in the budgeting process can help them to increase their levels of acceptance of the economic responsibility and their commitment towards budgetary goals as well as to overcome the limited use and the partial effectiveness of budgetary information in the management control, as underlined by larger studies on performance measurement systems [21, 51, 75, 86]. However, the BMA studies on budgetary participation in PHOs are still scarce. Further, they have strictly focused on the role of mental states and behaviors in the link budgetary participation—performance [2, 110].

Focusing on the Italian health care sector, there are few studies investigating the cognitive-behavioral dynamics in PHOs' budgeting practices [55, 57]. These contributions are mainly focused on the effects of budgetary participation of doctor-managers within different theoretical frameworks. For example, in the theoretical framework of Goal setting, Rizzo [95] have explored the mediating role of job satisfaction and commitment to budgetary objectives in the relation of budgetary participation with doctor-managers' performance. Subsequent studies, adopting the lenses of Psychological Ownership theory [61], Engagement Theory and Social Cognitive Theory [62, 63], have explored the impact of several variables, such as role clarity, affective commitment and engagement, in the link between budgetary participation and managerial performance. Cattaneo and Bassani [13], applying the Self-Determination Theory, have highlighted how mechanisms of involvement and integration in the budgeting process represent useful tools for internalizing organizational values and aligning the individual performance with the organizational objectives. In the framework of Organizational Support Theory, Raucci and Paolini [88] have analyzed the role of job satisfaction and work engagement in addressing budgetary participation towards higher levels of doctor-managers' managerial performance. In the same perspective, less studies have deepened the effects of budgetary participation on the features of budgetary information, as perceived by doctor-managers. In the Goal Setting Theory, it has been investigated the role of budgetary participation in enhancing doctor-managers' satisfaction on budgetary information [58] as well as its influence on the use of budgetary information, further investigating the links of these variables with performance [59]. Another study of Macinati and Rizzo (59), in the light of the Expectancy Theory, have deepened the beneficial effects of budgetary participation in improving doctor-managers' perceptions of the characteristics of budgetary information, namely accuracy and utility, which move them towards better performance.

The study of budgetary participation's antecedents in PHOs remain still largely overlooked, even if these causal dynamics play a crucial role mostly in the healthcare sector, because the predisposition of doctor-managers to participate in the budgeting process can be negatively influenced by the individual differences and the interpretations of context, values and objectives that, diverging from those of top management, may prevent that the expected benefits of participation will be effectively materialize. In particular, these differences might arise perceptions of cognitive distance from top management [84, 103], which are likely to increase the typical behaviors deriving from information asymmetry and the risks of creating budgetary slacks [67, 99] that, instead, budgetary participation should reduce. Further, these perceptions might discourage the motivation and the commitment of doctor-managers to participate in the budgeting process and reduce their contribution in designing budgetary information deemed satisfactory and more useful for their decision-making [2, 16, 45].

Within these conceptual perspectives, the research fields on organizational behavior, based on the assumptions of Social Identity Theory [106], have highlighted the role played by managers' sense of association and identification with the organization in allowing their internalization of the organizational values [6] and motivating them to expend effort towards the organizational objectives [20, 108]. In particular, some Authors have highlighted how an organizational culture that gives greater importance to cooperative approaches, more attention to managerial extra-role behaviors, impacting on OCB, might enhance the organizational functioning [68, 82]. Further, these aspects can also be driven by other managers' characteristics, such as how their personality traits influence the vocational interests and the choices individuals make about which activities to engage in and how much effort to exert on them [77, 83], leading to different levels of OCB [8, 36, 82].

However, in this research on the possible organizational drivers of cognitive-behavioral schemes, there are still no studies on Italian PHOs investigating the causal role of POC in influencing the predisposition of doctor-managers to participate in the budgeting process.

3.2 Research Design and Hypotheses Development

The present study hypothesizes that a higher perception of doctor-managers of the openness in communication by top managers of PHOs increases their perceived utility of budgetary information, which, in turn, leads them to a greater budgetary participation (Fig. 1).

Openness in communication between top managers and doctor-managers means that these latter are allowed to be involved in the design of the features of budgetary information system [30, 44, 66, 81, 87]. Literature has showed how POC plays a cognitive role, allowing doctors-managers to formalize their information needs in the process output [47]. Thus, the related POC initiates the clarification of role ambiguity, both mitigating doctor-managers' information asymmetry and reducing the need to create budgetary slacks [67, 99]. In fact, it influences not only the amount of information available to doctor-managers, but also how this information is perceived by them [2, 75]. In particular, a budgetary information system responding to their needs enhances the perceived quality of budgetary information [44, 45, 107, 115] in terms of adequacy, accuracy and timeliness features [34, 49, 59], increasing consequently their perceptions on the utility of the related contents, i.e. the extent to which users believe that the information meets their needs for the decision-making process [34, 37], since it increases the possibility of directly intervening on their content [58, 64]. On this basis, we assume that the perceptions of doctor-managers of the openness in communication, by top management of PHOs, leads them to enhance their perception of utility of budgetary information. Thus, the following hypothesis is tested:

Hp 1. POC of doctor-managers positively influences their perceived utility of budgetary information.

Previous budgetary literature has showed that budgetary participation, as job condition, enhances the perceived utility of budgetary information [15, 59]. However, perceived utility of budgetary information, as derived by POC, may also acts as a

Fig. 1 The research design

driver, offering doctor-managers a greater motivating countervalue [10] to move towards a greater attention to the pursuit of economic objectives [11, 74]. In fact, such perception means having an adequate informational support to conduct the decision-making process. In this perspective, a higher level of perceived utility of budgetary information, addressing the psychological processes underlined by VET, might motivates doctor-managers to a better predisposition to participate in the budgeting process [2]. Therefore, the following hypothesis is tested:

Hp 2. Perceived utility of budgetary information positively influences budgetary participation of doctor-managers.

4 Research Sample and Methodology

Empirical analyses were carried out in four PHOs of the Italian NHS located in the Region Abruzzo. Based on the strategic plan and the organizational chart of each PHO, we identified 332 heads of unit, which constituted our initial study sample.

Data were collected, before the Covid-19 pandemic period, through a questionnaire [29], which encompassed four sections. The first section collected data on the attributive characteristics of respondents. This area aims to collecting general data on the sampled units, to describe them in terms of age, gender, education, work. Each of the following areas collected data on the observed variables through close-ended questions, to which the respondent has to express the degree of agreement or disagreement using a 7-point Likert-type scale. POC was measured reproducing the three-item scale developed by Locke and Latham [54] according to the informational perspective adopted in this study. In particular, items related to POC aim at understanding the extent to which doctor-managers' perceive that the organization support their managerial role by budgetary information policies and resources. Perceived utility of budgetary information was measured by a three-items scale derived from Doll and Torkzadeh [23] and modified on the basis of Abernethy and Vagnoni [2]. Through these items, we investigate the degree to which doctor-managers perceive budgetary information as accurate, appropriate, and timely. The three-item Milani [76] scale was used to measure budgetary participation. In this last area of the questionnaire, we explore the extent to which doctor-managers are involved in the budgeting process.

After a pilot-test verified its effectiveness, we collected all the institutional e-mail addresses by online search on the websites of PHOs, but also keeping in contact with doctor-managers by phone calls and during academic courses in-person on site; then, the questionnaire was administered to heads of unit by sending it to their institutional e-mail address [114]. The overall response rate was of 37.95%, corresponding to a total of 126 questionnaire, fully completed, which constituted our final study sample.

Preliminary descriptive and correlation analyses were conducted. Then, a regression analysis was performed using software STATA to test our research hypotheses.

5 Results

5.1 Descriptive Statistics and Correlations

Data collected in the first area of the questionnaire gave us some preliminary information on the attributive characteristics of respondents.

With reference to the demographic characteristics, results show that doctor-managers:

- are predominantly male (87%);
- have, on average, 59 years old.

Regarding the characteristics of their work, it emerges that they:

- have been employed, on average, 31 years in the NHS;
- have been heads of units for 10 years;
- held the current managerial position for 8 years;
- are responsible for Complex Operational Units in the 74% of the cases;
- were previously ward unit head in the 36% of the cases;
- held other management positions in departments and/or institutes in the 19% of the cases.

Managerial education of doctor-managers shows that:

- almost half of the sample (47.6%) had undergone at least one training or continuing education related to management and organization of health care services in the last three years.

Table 1 reports the descriptive statistics of variables and pairwise correlations.

The average value of the POC (perc_open_comm) is equal to 3.28, with a standard deviation near to 1.50. Given the extension of the measurement scale (1–7), results show that sampled doctor-managers have a moderate perception of the openness in communication by top management. The mean of perceived utility of budgetary information (utility_budginfo) is slightly lower than 4, presenting a standard deviation of 1.39. Based on the measurement scale, which moves from a minimum

Table 1 Descriptive statistics and correlations

Variable	Mean	Stand. dev	Min	Max	1st quart	Median	3rd quart	1	2	3
1. perc_open_comm	3.28	1.47	1	7	2	3	4.34	1		
2. utility_budginfo	3.83	1.39	1	7	2.8	4	4.8	0.493*	1	
3. budget_particip	3.3	1.76	1	7	1.67	3.34	4.91	0.68*	0.723*	1

*p-value ≤ 0.05

of 1 to a maximum of 7, the perception of the utility of budgetary information by survey respondents is in a median position. Given the same extension of the measurement scale (1–7), the average value of budgetary participation (budget_particip), which is close to the neutrality threshold (3.3), suggests a moderate involvement of doctor-managers in the budgeting process.

Results of Spearman correlation analysis give some preliminary evidence on the association between variables, showing that POC correlated positively with perceived utility of budgetary information ($r = 0.493$, $p \leq 0.05$), which, in turn, correlated positively with budgetary participation ($r = 0.723$, $p \leq 0.05$).

5.2 *Inferential Analysis*

Factor Analysis. Preliminary to regression analysis, Exploratory Factor Analysis (EFA) [40] was performed, in order to determine a small number of unrelated latent factors. Table 2 shows the extracted factors and the explained cumulative variance.

The factorial values of variables' items, all above the threshold of 0.50, confirmed the convergent validity of the measures, while the absence of major cross-loadings between factors confirmed the discriminant validity of the scales. The explained cumulative variance greater than 60% for all the variables highlights a good factorial structure (Table 2).

To complete the test on the psychometric properties of the variables, the Kaiser–Meyer–Olkin (KMO) sample adequacy test was conducted; values obtained for each variable are above the cut-off of 0.60, confirming that data were appropriate (Table 3). Cronbach's Alpha values higher than the threshold of 0.70 [104] confirmed the reliability of all the scales.

Table 2 EFA

Variable	Item	1	2	3	% explained cumulative variance
POC	perc_open_comm 1	0.889			73.91
	perc_open_comm 2	0.879			
	perc_open_comm 3	0.808			
Perceived utility of budgetary information	utility_budginfo 1		0.917		68.16
	utility_budginfo 2		0.873		
	utility_budginfo 3		0.749		
Budgetary participation	budget_particip 1			0.918	70
	budget_particip 2			0.957	
	budget_particip 3			0.918	

Table 3 Kaiser–Meyer–Olkin and Cronbach's Alpha tests

Test	POC	Perceived utility of budgetary information	Budgetary participation
Kaiser–Meyer–Olkin	0.696	0.79	0.725
Cronbach's Alpha	0.822	0.88	0.923

Table 4 Regression results

Dependent variable	Independent variable		R^2	Associated hypothesis
	perc_open_comm	utility_budginfo		
utility_budginfo	0.698** (0.079)		0.413	H1
budget_particip		0.711** (0.062)	0.528	H2

Standard error in brackets

** p-value ≤ 0.01

Regression Analysis. A linear regression analysis was performed to test the relations between the observed variables. Regression results are reported in the following table.

Table 4 highlights that POC (perc_open_comm) is a significant determinant of perceived utility of budgetary information (utility_budginfo) ($\beta = 0.698$, $p \leq 0.01$), confirming hypothesis H1. Regression analysis also confirmed the research hypothesis H2, revealing that perceived utility of budgetary information is significantly and positively related to doctor-managers' budgetary participation (budget_particip) ($\beta = 0.711$, $p \leq 0.01$).

6 Discussion and Conclusions

In the framework of VET, our paper aimed at investigating the role of doctor-managers' perception of openness in communication by top management of PHOs in addressing heads of UOs towards higher levels of budgetary participation, via the indirect effect of perceived utility of budgetary information.

Results of regression analysis confirmed both the research hypotheses, highlighting how the effectiveness of budgetary participation in PHOs depends on doctor-managers POC, which acts as a cognitive-behavioral driver reducing the risks of dysfunctional behavior related to role ambiguity. In particular, results confirmed Hp 1, according to which doctor managers' POC, enhancing the perceived quality of budgetary information highlighted by some studies [44, 45, 107] plays a cognitive role in increasing their perceived utility of budgetary information [34, 37]. They also showed that perceived utility of budgetary information, in turn, strengthening the perception of informational support to their decision-making process, has a positive effect on doctor-managers' budgetary participation [10, 59], confirming Hp 2.

In the light of VET, the study highlights how the extent to which doctor-managers perceive that top management supports their managerial role by openness in communication in the budgeting process [26, 66, 115], which gives them the opportunity both to reduce the information asymmetry and have a voice on the budgetary information system's design [47, 81], increasing the perceived utility of budgetary information to make their decision-making process, both influence the expectancy of doctors-managers on the participation in the definition of budgetary objectives and the perceptions of the value arising from it, stimulating a greater countervalue motivating them to participate in the budgeting process.

Seeking to overcome doctor-managers' resistance to the use of budgetary information, the study contributes to the healthcare management accounting research on the organizational approaches to the empowerment of doctor-managers' commitment to and use of budgetary information for decision-making based on their involvement in PHOs' budgeting process [57, 74, 87]. To this end, the study also responds to the call for further research on the antecedents of budgetary participation of Mahlendorf et al. [65], within the lines of BMA budgeting research on the psychological antecedents of an effective involvement in the budgeting process in the context of PHOs [46, 96, 109]. On this way, the study validates the causal model described by VET, providing a richer psychological representation of how to unleash the potential of the agency relation of doctor-managers with top managers.

Results suggest to top management and policy makers that similar managerial approaches as well as policies aimed at favoring an openness in communication, affecting the managerial culture and the behavior of doctor-managers, would allow PHOs to give greater effectiveness to the budgetary information systems, contributing to increase the overall efficiency of budgeting process. Further, these approaches, increasing the predisposition of doctor-managers to support budgetary objectives, would also lead to implement effectively hybrid professionalism and enhance the accountability of healthcare middle management, especially within the complex hierarchical system of responsibility characterizing the NHS.

However, this study has some limitations. Firstly, it should be noted that all the variables, included budgetary participation, are based on the individual perceptions of the respondents, who are influenced by their organizational context, setting limits to generalizations. Further, the causal model follows the assumptions of VET. Therefore, subsequent studies adopting different theoretical models could reach different conclusions. Finally, the study focused on the Italian context.

On this basis, future research using more objective measurements of the variables, as alternative to self-measurement scales, would allow to mitigate the effects of common method bias. Other contribution could adopt other research methodologies, such as interviews with doctor-managers, as well as extend the sample of analysis at the international level, in order to make comparison of our results with those collected in PHOs of other countries. In these perspectives, it could be also interesting integrating the theoretical model adopted in this study. In particular, as we observed in the literature background, the links with the studies based on Social Identity Theory and Organizational Identification Theory, would allow us to extend the analysis, deepening the role played by doctor-managers' characteristics, such as their OCB factors, in moderating or mediating the relations among the variables of our research model, as well as the role played by personality traits of doctor-managers in predicting OCB and interpreting the degree of budgetary participation and POC. Regarding this latter variable, it could be also investigated the effectiveness of new ICT tools in driving greater perception of openness in communication, as well as deepen our study, verifying the relevance of organizational factors that we explored following the Covid-pandemic period.

References

1. Abernethy, M.A., Brownell, P.: The role of budgets in organizations facing strategic change: an exploratory study. Account. Organ. Soc. **24**(3), 189–204 (1999). https://doi.org/10.1016/s0361-3682(98)00059-2
2. Abernethy, M.A., Vagnoni, E.: Power, organization design and managerial behaviour. Account. Organ. Soc. **29**(3–4), 207–225 (2004). https://doi.org/10.1016/s0361-3682(03)00049-7
3. Abernethy, M.A., Chua, W.F., Grafton, J., Mahama, H.: Accounting and control in health care: behavioural, organisational, sociological and critical perspectives. In: Chapman, C.S., Hopwood, A.G., Shields, M.D. (eds.) Handbooks of Management Accounting Research, vol. 2, pp. 805–829. Elsevier, Oxford, UK (2006). https://doi.org/10.1016/S1751-3243(06)02014-1
4. Andrews, R., Beynon, M.J., McDermott, A.: Configurations of new public management reforms and the efficiency, effectiveness and equity of public healthcare systems: a fuzzy-set qualitative comparative analysis. Public Manag. Rev. **21**(8), 1236–1260 (2019). https://doi.org/10.1080/14719037.2018.1561927
5. Anessi-Pessina, E., Cantù, E.: Multiple logics and accounting mutations in the italian national health service'. Account. Forum **40**, 265–284 (2016). https://doi.org/10.1016/j.accfor.2016.08.001
6. Ashforth, B.E., Mael, F.: Social identity theory and the organization. Acad. Manag. Rev. **14**(1), 20–39 (1989). https://doi.org/10.5465/amr.1989.4278999
7. Benvenuto, M., Viola, C., Rosa, A.: Analisi prospettica per il design di un nuovo dominio di pianificazione, programmazione e controllo sociotecnico nel settore della salute. Mecosan **113**(1), 259–269 (2020). https://doi.org/10.3280/mesa2020-113030
8. Bettencourt, L.A., Gwinner, K.P., Meuter, M.L.: A comparison of attitude, personality, and knowledge predictors of service-oriented organizational citizenship behaviours. J. Appl. Psychol. **86**(1), 29 (2001). https://psycnet.apa.org/, https://doi.org/10.1037/0021-9010.86.1.29
9. Birnberg, J.G., Luft, J., Shields, M.D.: Psychology theory in management accounting research. In: Hopwood, A.G, Chapman, C.S. (eds.) Handbook of Management Accounting Research. Elsevier, Amsterdam (2007). https://doi.org/10.1016/S1751-3243(06)01004-2
10. Bonner, S.E., Sprinkle, G.B.: The effects of monetary incentives on effort and task performance: theories, evidence, and a framework for research. Account. Organ. Soc. **27**(4–5), 303–345 (2002). https://doi.org/10.1016/S0361-3682(01)00052-6
11. Campanale, C., Cinquini, L.: Emerging pathways of colonization in healthcare from participative approaches to management accounting. Crit. Perspect. Account. **39**, 59–74 (2016). https://doi.org/10.1016/j.cpa.2015.12.001
12. Campion, M.A., Medsker, G.J., Higgs, A.C.: Relations between work group characteristics and effectiveness: implications for designing effective work groups. Pers. Psychol. **46**(4), 823–847 (1993). https://doi.org/10.1111/j.17446570.1993.tb01571.x

13. Cattaneo, C., Bassani, G.V.: Il processo di budget e l'interiorizzazione dei valori: il caso di un ospedale italiano. In: Marchi, L., Lombardi, R., Anselmi L. (eds.) Il governo aziendale tra tradizione e innovazione, FrancoAngeli, Milano (2016)
14. Chenhall, R.H., Brownell, P.: The effect of participative budgeting on job satisfaction and performance: role ambiguity as an intervening variable. Account. Organ. Soc. **13**(3), 225–233 (1988). https://doi.org/10.1016/0361-3682(88)90001-3
15. Chong, V.K., Chong, K.M.: Budget goal commitment and informational effects of budget participation on performance: a structural equation modeling approach. Behav. Res. Account. **14**(1), 65–86 (2002). https://doi.org/10.2308/bria.2002.14.1.65
16. Chong, V.K., Johnson, D.M.: Testing a model of the antecedents and consequences of budgetary participation on job performance. Account. Bus. Res. **37**(1), 3–19 (2007). https://doi.org/10.1080/00014788.2007.9730055
17. Corsi, K., Ezza, A., Fadda, N., Giovanelli, L., Pinna, M., Rotondo, F.: Modelli di management nel settore sanitario. Criticità e prospettive. Giappichelli Editore (2016)
18. Covaleski, M.A., Evans, J.H., III., Luft, J.L., Shields, M.D.: Budgeting research: three theoretical perspectives and criteria for selective integration. J. Manag. Account. Res. **15**(1), 3–49 (2003). https://doi.org/10.2308/jmar.2003.15.1.3
19. da Silva Zonatto, V.C., Lunardi, M.A., Degenhart, L.: Antecedents that influence participatory budgetary configuration and its effects on vertical information sharing and managerial performance. Adv. Sci. & Appl. Account. **12**(1) (2019). https://doi.org/10.14392/ASAA.2019120108
20. De Nicola, M., Anees, U.: Why more CSR disclosure does not mean more favourable CSR perception? Insights from fast fashion industry of Italy. In: Za, S., Consorti, A. (eds.) Organizing in a Digitized World: Diversity, Equality and Inclusion, Lecture Notes in Information Systems and Organisation, in press (paper presented at XVII Conference of the Italian Chapter of AIS (Association for Information Systems – www.aisnet.org). https://doi.org/10.1007/978-3-030-86858-1_8
21. Demartini, C., Trucco, S.: Are performance measurement systems useful? Perceptions from health care. BMC Health Serv. Res. **17**(1), 96 (2017). https://doi.org/10.1186/s12913-017-2022-9
22. Derfuss, K.: Reconsidering the participative budgeting–performance relation: a meta-analysis regarding the impact of level of analysis, sample selection, measurement, and industry influences. Br. Account. Rev. **48**(1), 17–37 (2016). https://doi.org/10.1016/j.bar.2015.07.001
23. Doll, W.J., Torkzadeh, G.: Developing a multidimensional measure of system-use in an organizational context. Inf. & Manag. **33**(4), 171–185 (1998). https://doi.org/10.1016/S0378-7206(98)00028-7
24. Douthit, J., Majerczyk, M.: Subordinate perceptions of the superior and agency costs: Theory and evidence. Account. Organ. Soc. **78**, 101057 (2019). https://doi.org/10.1016/j.aos.2019.07.003
25. Eldenburg, L., Soderstrom, N., Willis, V., Wu, A.: Behavioral changes following the collaborative development of an accounting information system. Account. Organ. Soc. **35**(2), 222–237 (2010). https://doi.org/10.1016/j.aos.2009.07.005
26. Evans, J.H., III., Moser, D.V., Newman, A.H., Stikeleather, B.R.: Honor among thieves: Open internal reporting and managerial collusion. Contemp. Account. Res. **33**(4), 1375–1402 (2016). https://doi.org/10.1111/1911-3846.12181
27. Ferris, K.R.: A test of the expectancy theory of motivation in an accounting environment. Account. Rev. 605–615 (1977) http://www.jstor.org/stable/246080
28. Fleishman, E.A., Harris, E.F.: Patterns of leadership behavior related to employee grievances and turnover. Pers. Psychol. **15**(2), 43–56 (1962). https://doi.org/10.1111/j.1744-6570.1962.tb01845.x
29. Fowler, F.J., Jr.: Survey Research Methods. Sage publications (2013)
30. Francis-Gladney, L., Little, H.T., Magner, N.R., Welker, R.B.: Does organization-mandated budgetary involvement enhance managers' budgetary communication with their supervisor? In: Advances in Management Accounting. Emerald Group Publishing Limited (2004). https://doi.org/10.1016/S1474-7871(04)13007-4

31. Garelick, A., Fagin, L.: The doctor-manager relationship. Adv. Psychiatr. Treat. **11**(4), 241–250 (2005). https://doi.org/10.1192/apt.11.4.241
32. Gorden, W.I., Infante, D.A.: Test of a communication model of organizational commitment. Commun. Q. **39**(2), 144–155 (1991). https://doi.org/10.1080/01463379109369792
33. Hall, M.: Realising the richness of psychology theory in contingency-based management accounting research. Manag. Account. Res. **31**, 63–74 (2016). https://doi.org/10.1016/j.mar.2015.11.002
34. Hassel, L.G., Cunningham, G.M.: Budget effectiveness in multinational companies: an empirical examination of environmental interaction on cognitive and affective effect of two dimensions of budgetary participation. Scand. J. Manag. **9**(4), 299–318 (1993). https://psycnet.apa.org/, https://doi.org/10.1016/0956-5221(93)90026-O
35. Iedema, R., Degeling, P., Braithwaite, J., White, L.: 'It's an interesting conversation I'm Hearing': the doctor as manager. Organ. Stud. **25**(1), 15–33 (2004). https://doi.org/10.1177/0170840604038174
36. Ilies, R., Fulmer, I.S., Spitzmuller, M., Johnson, M.D.: Personality and citizenship behaviour: the mediating role of job satisfaction. J. Appl. Psychol. **94**(4), 945–959 (2009). https://psycnet.apa.org, https://doi.org/10.1037/a0013329
37. Ives, B., Olson, M.H., Baroudi, J.J.: The measurement of user information satisfaction. Commun. ACM **26**(10), 785–793 (1983). https://doi.org/10.1145/358413.358430
38. Jacobs, K., Marcon, G., Witt, D.: Cost and performance information for doctors: an international comparison. Manag. Account. Res. **15**(3), 337–354 (2004). https://doi.org/10.1016/j.mar.2004.03.005
39. Jones, C.A., Dewing, I.P.: The attitudes of NHS clinicians and medical managers towards changes in accounting controls. Financ. Account. & Manag. **13**(3), 261–280 (1997). https://doi.org/10.1111/1468-0408.00037
40. Kaiser, H.F.: The varimax criterion for analytic rotation in factor analysis. Psychometrika **23**(3), 187–200 (1958). https://doi.org/10.1007/BF02289233
41. Kaptein, M.: Developing and testing a measure for the ethical culture of organizations: The corporate ethical virtues model. J. Organ. Behav.: Int. J. Ind. Occup. Organ. Psychol. Behav. **29**(7), 923–947 (2008). https://doi.org/10.1002/job.520
42. Kenno, S.A., Lau, M.C., Sainty, B.J.: In search of a theory of budgeting: a literature review. Account. Pers. **17**(4), 507–553 (2018). https://doi.org/10.1111/1911-3838.12186
43. Kidwell, R.E., Scherer, P.M.: Layoffs and their ethical implications under scientific management, quality management and open-book management. J. Bus. Ethics **29**(1), 113–124 (2001). https://doi.org/10.1023/A:1006455228312
44. Kim, S.: Participative management and job satisfaction: lessons for management leadership. Public Adm. Rev. **62**(2), 231–241 (2002). https://doi.org/10.1111/0033-3352.00173
45. Kyj, L., Parker, R.J.: Antecedents of budget participation: leadership style, information asymmetry, and evaluative use of budget. Abacus **44**(4), 423–442 (2008). https://doi.org/10.1111/j.1467-6281.2008.00270.x
46. Kominis, G., Emmanuel, C.R.: The expectancy–valence theory revisited: developing an extended model of managerial motivation. Manag. Account. Res. **18**(1), 49–75 (2007). https://doi.org/10.1016/j.mar.2006.10.002
47. Kuang, X., Li, Z., Yang, D.: The effects of transparency and voice on managerial decisions and employee effort in hierarchical organizations. Eur. Account. Rev. 1–25 (2021). https://doi.org/10.1080/09638180.2021.1896370
48. Lau, C.M., Buckland, C.: Budgeting—The role of trust and participation: a research note. Abacus **37**(3), 369–388 (2001). https://doi.org/10.1111/1467-6281.00092
49. Lau, C.M., Scully, G., Lee, A.: The effects of organizational politics on employee motivations to participate in target setting and employee budgetary participation. J. Bus. Res. **90**, 247–259 (2018). https://doi.org/10.1016/j.jbusres.2018.05.002
50. Lega, F., Vendramini, E.: Budgeting and performance management in the Italian national health system (INHS): assessment and constructive criticism. J. Heal. Organ. Manag. **22**(1), 11–22 (2008). https://doi.org/10.1108/14777260810862371

51. Lehtonen, T.: DRG-based perspective pricing and case-mix accounting – exploring the mechanisms of successful implementation. Manag. Account. Res. **18**, 367–395 (2007). https://doi.org/10.1016/j.mar.2006.12.002
52. Libby, T., Lindsay, R.M.: Beyond budgeting or budgeting reconsidered? A survey of North American budgeting practice. Manag. Account. Res. **21**(1), 56–75 (2010). https://doi.org/10.1016/j.mar.2009.10.003
53. Llewellyn, S.: Two-way windows': clinicians as medical managers. Organ. Stud. **22**(4), 593–623 (2001). https://doi.org/10.1177/0170840601224003
54. Locke, E.A., Latham, G.P.: A Theory of Goal Setting & Task Performance. Prentice-Hall (1990)
55. Longo, F., Mele, S., Salvatore, D., Tasselli, S., Monchiero, G., Pinelli, N.: Il governo dei servizi territoriali: budget e valutazione dell'integrazione: Modelli teorici ed evidenze empiriche. Egea, Milano (2013)
56. Lukka, K.: Budgetary biasing in organizations: theoretical framework and empirical evidence. Account. Organ. Soc. **13**(3), 281–301 (1988). https://doi.org/10.1016/0361-3682(88)90005-0
57. Macinati, M.S.: NPM reforms and the perception of budget by hospital clinicians: lessons from two case-studies. Financ. Account. & Manag. **26**(4), 422–442 (2010). https://doi.org/10.1111/j.1468-0408.2010.00509.x
58. Macinati, M.S., Rizzo, M.G.: Partecipazione, commitment e informazioni di budget I risultati di una ricerca empirica. Mecosan **82**, 25–41 (2012). https://doi.org/10.3280/MESA2014-092004
59. Macinati, M.S., Rizzo, M.G.: Budget goal commitment, clinical managers' use of budget information and performance. Health Policy **117**(2), 228–238 (2014). https://doi.org/10.1016/j.healthpol.2014.05.003
60. Macinati, M.S., Anessi-Pessina, E.: Management accounting use and financial performance in public healthcare organisations: evidence from the Italian National Health Service. Health Policy **117**(1), 98–111 (2014). https://doi.org/10.1016/j.healthpol.2014.03.011
61. Macinati, M.S., Rizzo, M.G.: Exploring the link between clinical managers involvement in budgeting and performance: insights from the Italian public health care sector. Health Care Manag. Rev. **41**(3), 213–223 (2016). https://www.jstor.org/stable/48516220
62. Macinati, M.S., Bozzi, S., Rizzo, M.G.: Budgetary participation and performance: the mediating effects of medical managers' job engagement and self-efficacy. Health Policy **120**(9), 1017–1028 (2016). https://doi.org/10.1016/j.healthpol.2016.08.005
63. Macinati, M.S., Cantaluppi, G., Rizzo, M.G.: Medical managers' managerial self-efficacy and role clarity: How do they bridge the budgetary participation–performance link? Health Serv. Manag. Res. **30**(1), 47–60 (2017). https://doi.org/10.1177/0951484816682398
64. Magner, N., Welker, R.B., Campbell, T.L.: Testing a model of cognitive budgetary participation processes in a latent variable structural equations framework. Account. Bus. Res. **27**(1), 41–50 (1996). https://doi.org/10.1080/00014788.1996.9729530
65. Mahlendorf, M.D., Schäffer, U., Skiba, O.: Antecedents of participative budgeting – a review of empirical evidence. Adv. Manag. Account. **25**, 1–27 (2015). https://doi.org/10.1108/S1474-787120150000025001
66. Maiga, A.S.: Antecedents and consequences of budget participation. Adv. Manag. Account. **14**(1), 211–231 (2005). https://doi.org/10.1016/S1474-7871(05)14010-6
67. Maiga, A.S., Jacobs, F.: Budget participation's influence on budget slack: the role of fairness perceptions, trust and goal commitment. J. Appl. Manag. Account. Res. **5**(1), 39–58 (2007)
68. Maignan, I., Ferrell, O.C., Hult, G.T.M.: Corporate citizenship: Cultural antecedents and business benefits. J. Acad. Mark. Sci. **27**(4), 455–469 (1999). https://doi.org/10.1177/0092070399274005
69. Mancini, D., Iacoviello, G., De Nicola, M.: L'impatto della crisi pandemica sui sistemi di controllo di gestione: un'analisi empirica. Manag. Control **1**, 105–127 (2021). https://doi.org/10.3280/MACO2021-001006
70. Marchi, L.: Dalla crisi allo sviluppo sostenibile. Il ruolo dei sistemi di misurazione e controllo. Manag. Control **3** (2020). https://doi.org/10.3280/MACO2020-003001

71. Marchi, L., Mancini, D. (a cura di): Gestione informatica dei dati aziendali. III edizione, FrancoAngeli (2009)
72. Marcon, G., Panozzo, F.: Reforming the reform: changing roles for accounting and management in the Italian health care sector. Eur. Account. Rev. **7**(2), 185–208 (1998). https://doi.org/10.1080/096381898336448
73. McNulty, T., Ferlie, E.: Process transformation: Limitations to radical organizational change within public service organizations. Organ. Stud. **25**(8), 1389–1412 (2004). https://doi.org/10.1177/0170840604046349
74. Mia, L.: Managerial attitude, motivation and the effectiveness of budget participation. Account. Organ. Soc. **13**(5), 465–475 (1988). https://doi.org/10.1016/0361-3682(88)90017-7
75. Michel Sørup, C., Jacobsen, P.: Healthcare performance turned into decision support. J. Health Organ. Manag. **27**(1), 64–84 (2013). https://doi.org/10.1108/14777261311311807
76. Milani, K.: The relationship of participation in budget setting to industrial supervisor performance and attitudes: a field study. Account. Rev. **50**, 274–284 (1975)
77. Mount, M.K., Barrick, M.R., Scullen, S.M., Rounds, J.: Higher-order dimensions of the big five personality traits and the big six interest types. Pers. Psychol. **58**, 447–478 (2005). https://doi.org/10.1111/j.1744-6570.2005.00468.x
78. Nyland, K., Pettersen, I.J.: The control gap: the role of budgets, accounting information and (non-) decisions in hospital settings. Financ. Account. & Manag. **20**(1), 77–102 (2004). https://doi.org/10.1111/j.1468-0408.2004.00187.x
79. Nouri, H., Parker, R.J.: The relationship between budget participation and job performance: the roles of budget adequacy and organizational commitment. Account. Organ. Soc. **23**(5–6), 467–483 (1998). https://doi.org/10.1016/S0361-3682(97)00036-6
80. Numerato, D., Salvatore, D., Fattore, G.: The impact of management on medical professionalism: a review. Sociol. Health Illn. **34**(4), 626–644 (2012). https://doi.org/10.1111/j.1467-9566.2011.01393.x
81. Oppi, C., Campanale, C., Cinquini, L., Vagnoni, E.: Clinicians and accounting: a systematic review and research directions. Financ. Account. & Manag. **35**(3), 290–312 (2019). https://doi.org/10.1111/faam.12195
82. Organ, D.W.: Organizational citizenship behavior: the good soldier syndrome. Lexington Books/DC Heath and Com (1988)
83. Organ, D.W., Ryan, K.: A meta-analytic review of attitudinal and dispositional predictors of organizational citizenship behaviour. Pers. Psychol. **48**(4), 775–802 (1995). https://doi.org/10.1111/j.1744-6570.1995.tb01781.x
84. Osbourne, A.: How do they manage? A study of the realities of middle and front-line management work in healthcare. Cranfield University, School of Management, pp 1–4 (2011)
85. Pettersen, I.J.: Accountable management reforms: why the Norwegian hospital reform experiment got lost in implementation. Financ. Account. & Manag. **15**(3–4), 377–396 (1999). https://doi.org/10.1111/1468-0408.00090
86. Pettersen, I.J., Nyland, K.: Management and control of public hospitals—the use of performance measures in Norwegian hospitals. A case-study. Int. J. Health Plan. Manag. **21**(2), 133–149 (2006). https://doi.org/10.1002/hpm.835
87. Prenestini, A., Sartirana, M., Lega, F.: Involving clinicians in management: assessing views of doctors and nurses on hybrid professionalism in clinical directorates. BMC Health Serv. Res. **21**(1), 1–11 (2021). https://doi.org/10.1186/s12913-021-06352-0
88. Raucci, D., Paolini, M.: Soddisfazione lavorativa e work engagement nelle budgeting practices delle aziende sanitarie pubbliche. Una verifica empirica. Manag. Control **1**, 13–32 (2021). https://doi.org/10.3280/MACO2021-001002
89. Raucci, D., Dyczkowski, T., Agostinone, S.: Seeking performance-based accountability in Italian Public Healthcare Organizations. Transylv. Rev. Adm. Sci. **17**(63), 151–174 (2021). https://doi.org/10.24193/tras.63E.8
90. Raucci, D., Lepore, D.: The role of participation in the design of time equations in the time-driven activity based costing-a systematic review of the literature. J. Appl. Econ. Sci. **10**(3), 337–352 (2015)

91. Rawlins, B.: Give the emperor a mirror: toward developing a stakeholder measurement of organizational transparency. J. Public Relat. Res. **21**(1), 71–99 (2008). https://doi.org/10.1080/10627260802153421
92. Rea, M.A.: Le aziende sanitarie pubbliche. Giappichelli, Torino (1998)
93. Riketta, M.: Organizational identification: a meta-analysis. J. Vocat. Behav. **66**(2), 358–384 (2005). https://doi.org/10.1016/j.jvb.2004.05.005
94. Rivière, A., Commeiras, N., Loubès, A.: Nouveau Management Public, tensions de rôle et stress professionnel chez les cadres de santé. Revue de gestion des ressources humaines **2**, 3–20 (2019)
95. Rizzo, M.G.: La relazione tra il livello di coinvolgimento nel processo di budget, il commitment verso gli obiettivi, la soddisfazione lavorativa ei relativi risvolti sulla performance manageriale. I risultati di un caso studio. Manag. Control **1**, 9–34 (2014). https://doi.org/10.3280/MACO2014-001002
96. Ruiz-Pérez, F., Lleó, Á., Viles, E., Jurburg, D.: Enhancing participation through organizational drivers. TQM J. **33**(4), 823–840 (2021). https://doi.org/10.1108/TQM-01-2020-0012
97. Sargiacomo, M.: Comportamento manageriale e best-practices nell'azienda USL. Giappichelli, Torino (2003)
98. Schiavone, F., Mancini, D., Leone, D., Lavorato, D.: Digital business models and ridesharing for value co-creation in healthcare: a multi-stakeholder ecosystem analysis. Technol. Forecast. Soc. Chang. **166**, 120647 (2021). https://doi.org/10.1016/j.techfore.2021.120647
99. Shields, M.D., Young, S.M.: Antecedents and consequences of participative budgeting: evidence on the effects of asymmetrical information. J. Manag. Account. Res. **5**(1), 265–280 (1993)
100. Sholihin, M., Pike, R., Mangena, M., Li, J.: Goal-setting participation and goal commitment: examining the mediating roles of procedural fairness and interpersonal trust in a UK financial services organisation. Br. Account. Rev. **43**(2), 135–146 (2011). https://doi.org/10.1016/j.bar.2011.02.003
101. Smidts, A., Pruyn, A.T.H., Cess, B.M.V.R.: The impact of employee communication and perceived external prestige on organizational identification. Acad. Manag. J. **44**(5), 1051–1062 (2001). https://doi.org/10.5465/3069448
102. Solstad, E., Petterson, I.J.: Middle managers' roles after a hospital merger. J. Health Organ. Manag. (2019). https://doi.org/10.1108/JHOM-09-2018-0269
103. Solstad, E., Pettersen, I.J., Robbins, G.: Hospitals as professional organizations and the perception of distances. Financ. Account. & Manag. **37**(1), 20–36 (2021). https://doi.org/10.1111/faam.12234
104. Stock, J.H., Watson, M.W.: Introduzione all'econometria. Pearson, Italia (2005)
105. Szczesny, A., Ernst, C.: The role of performance reporting system characteristics for the coordination of high-cost areas in hospitals. Eur. Account. Rev. **25**(4), 635–660 (2016). https://doi.org/10.1080/09638180.2016.1210525
106. Tajfel, H., Turner, J.C.: The social identity theory of intergroup behavior. In: Worchel, S., Austin, W.G. (eds.) The Psychology of Intergroup Relations, pp. 7–24. Nelson-Hall, Chicago (1986)
107. Vagnoni, E., Maran, L.: Il controllo di gestione nelle aziende sanitarie pubbliche, vol. 103, Maggioli Editore (2013)
108. Van Knippenberg, D.: Work motivation and performance: a social identity perspective. Appl. Psychol. **49**(3), 357–371 (2000). https://doi.org/10.1111/1464-0597.00020
109. Vroom, V.H.: Work and Motivation (1964)
110. Wentzel, K.: The influence of fairness perceptions and goal commitment on managers' performance in a budget setting. Behav. Res. Account. **14**(1), 247–271 (2002). https://doi.org/10.2308/bria.2002.14.1.247
111. Wibbeke, L.M., Lachmann, M.: Psychology in management accounting and control research: an overview of the recent literature. J. Manag. Control 1–54 (2020). https://doi.org/10.1007/s00187-020-00302-3

112. Whitener, E.M., Brodt, S.E., Korsgaard, M.A., Werner, J.M.: Managers as initiators of trust: an exchange relationship framework for understanding managerial trustworthy behavior. Acad. Manag. Rev. **23**(3), 513–530 (1998). https://doi.org/10.5465/amr.1998.926624
113. Wong-On-Wing, B., Guo, L., Lui, G.: Intrinsic and extrinsic motivation and participation in budgeting: antecedents and consequences. Behav. Res. Account. **22**(2), 133–153 (2010). https://doi.org/10.2308/bria.2010.22.2.133
114. Yammarino, F.J., Skinner, S.J., Childers, T.L.: Understanding mail survey response behavior - a meta-analysis. Public Opin. Q. **55**(4), 613–639 (1991). https://doi.org/10.1086/269284
115. Zia-ur-Rehman, M., Latif, K., Mohsin, M., Hussain, Z., Baig, S.A., Imtiaz, I.: How perceived information transparency and psychological attitude impact on the financial well-being: mediating role of financial self-efficacy. Bus. Process. Manag. J. (2021). https://doi.org/10.1108/BPMJ-12-2020-0530

COVID-19 Pandemic and New Cardiology Telemonitoring Organization: How to Cast the Others

Alberto Zanutto, Diego Ponte, and Enrico Maria Piras

Abstract Over the last decade, ICT innovation in healthcare have been explored and extensively tested. While such implementation and use were not straightforward, the COVID-19 pandemic has accelerated a widespread use of new online services like telemonitoring. This paper takes a closer look at the cardiology telemonitoring to shed light on the technology adoption in the healthcare system. While, on the one hand, healthcare professionals have known how to quickly gear up to respond to the new constraints, on the other it seems that the stakeholders of the system show mixed feelings about them. Looking at two different cardiology departments, the paper highlights that this resilience can be allied with organizational innovations underway and in some cases assume an acceleration that is not easily predictable.

Keywords Telehealth · ICT · Organizational change · Telemonitoring

1 Introduction

The recurrent pandemic waves of COVID-19 provide an important opportunity to investigate the responses of public health systems to adapt to an increasingly unstable environment. The pandemic has required health organisations to perform part of their work through Information and Communication Technologies (ICTs) most of which pre-existed but were seldom used in clinical practice. Such technologies on the one hand have allowed work to be performed in accordance with social distancing protocols, and on the other to be transformed through the rearrangement of usual practices. One of the opportunities that have emerged in this period are televisit and

A. Zanutto (✉) · D. Ponte
Department Economy and Management, University of Trento, Trento, Italy
e-mail: alberto.zanutto@unitn.it

D. Ponte
e-mail: diego.ponte@unitn.it

E. M. Piras
Fondazione Bruno Kessler, Trento, Italy
e-mail: piras@fbk.eu

S. Za et al. (eds.), *Sustainable Digital Transformation*, Lecture Notes in Information Systems and Organisation 59, https://doi.org/10.1007/978-3-031-15770-7_8

telemonitoring interventions. This practice has made it possible to maintain important monitoring and control functions in various areas of health. Thus, during lockdowns established by governments, facilities have identified different strategies to respond to the needs of health departments.

In so far, the more the process of advancement of telemedicine consolidated, the better were the effects in the patient management during the pandemic (Menardi et al. 2020). While short term expectations are not revolutionary, the increasing availability of devices and wearables could allow for a widespread adoption of telemonitoring for several cardiological conditions in the long run (Miller et al. 2020; Piro et al. 2020). The pandemic has generated a plurality of approaches leading to a rearticulation of patients-providers encounters due to a number of contingent factors (Badawy and Radovic 2020) such as regulatory constraints regarding safety protocols on the one hand, and on the other, the changing professional practices of health service provision. Interestingly, research is beginning to identify both organisational and clinical effects due to COVID-19 restrictions (Bertagnin et al. 2021).

This scenario offers us the opportunity to understand how digitisation processes were affected by the pandemic in the specific area of implantable cardiological devices such as pace makers and cardioverter defibrillators.

Organisational theory applied to healthcare infrastructures has been exploring these dynamics for some time and today, thanks to the pandemic that has sustained widespread use of new online services, it is possible to take a closer look at an increasingly consistent phenomenon (Bokolo 2021). We have considered both changes on the organizational side and on the implementation of IS. As we shall see, the current experiments have generated various direct and indirect effects on health care work organization and the reliability of IT infrastructures.

The paper aims to understand whether the acceleration triggered by the pandemic on the implementation of digitalisation projects will generate stable changes and to understand how organisations are positioned between resilience and innovation pressures. Indeed, the non-linear situation in project development suggests that these changes have different effects depending on the maturity of the contexts. For this reason, it should be possible to observe a gap between system management directions and the actual adoption of new information systems by health departments.

The fieldwork consisted of an analysis of the management of a regional health authority for about a year. The work carried out on the management side was geared towards implementing a telemonitoring system in two cardiology departments. The system aimed at facilitating the process of monitoring data transmitted from implantable devices. The system was developed by a public regional research organisation that over the years has promoted various systems for digitising healthcare practices. In this case under analysis the system was first deployed in a cardiology department during the first wave of the pandemic and subsequently implemented in a second cardiology department. The research work tried to compare the two departments and two different work organisations.

The paper is organised as follows. First, it briefly reviews the related work on telehealth and cardiology monitoring. Section three describes the case study and the methodological framework adopted for the telemonitoring system. An analysis of the outcomes is provided to understand which are the limits and possible barriers for a final inclusion of the service in the healthcare system beyond the COVID-19 contingency period.

2 Related Work: Telehealth and Telemonitoring

2.1 Telehealth

The World Health Organization defined telehealth as "the delivery of health care services, where distance is a critical factor, by health care professionals using information and communication technologies (ICT) for the exchange of valid information for diagnosis, treatment and prevention of disease and injuries, research and evaluation, and for the continuing education of health care providers, all in the interests of advancing the health of individuals and their communities" (WHO 2009).

Over the last decade, scientific literature has supported the idea that the use of ICTs might improve the overall efficiency of the healthcare system. Many case studies and experimentations show advantages and disadvantages for both the patients and the healthcare providers (Kruse et al. 2020). The most important benefits might be summarized as: improved access to health care, improved quality of services, decreased management costs and reduced duration of the services.

In the field of cardiology, the use of ICT has received a lot of attention and at the same time many technologies have been produced that can read the clinical condition of patients at a distance. Telemonitoring has become another field of improvement of health services offered to patients. The multiple variabilities between different patients, different contexts of use and different healthcare systems have led to further development of ICT in healthcare and in particular to an increase in remote monitoring tools. Telemonitoring has become an integral part of therapeutic processes in many fields including heart failure implants (Planinc et al. 2020; De Backer et al. 2003).

A boost to these implementations has been given by the COVID-19 pandemic that forced organizations and people towards their utilization (Bokolo 2021; Doraiswamy et al. 2020). Despite these benefits, the path to a real wide implementation and use of such technologies is still a long path as their adoption and integration in healthcare practices is very complex (Tersalvi et al. 2020).

2.2 Telemonitoring in Cardiology

Telemonitoring in cardiology is therefore a particularly interesting field of observation. It is an area where ICT-mediated communication between patient and provider is already an established practice. Remote monitoring of the parameters produced by implantable devices (i.e., pace makers, implantable cardioverter defibrillators) is not a novelty. However, pandemic offered the opportunity to extend monitoring to other facets of cardiological monitoring. Problems arising from poor adherence to treatment and the non-linear trend in patients' attention to cardiological health (exercise, diet, therapy) is a source of hospitalisation and worsening quality of life. During the pandemic, patients with heart failure were one of the most affected subgroups as face-to-face visits were all cancelled. Therefore, their vulnerability required specific measures to ensure follow-up visits while preventing accessing the hospital (Graham et al. 2006).

Various forms of telemedicine and remote monitoring were developed rapidly and widely implemented for these patients (DeFilippis et al. 2020). While telephone calls often replaced face-to-face visits, this led to some complexities and limitations that cannot be managed on a large scale by the current hospital organisation. In addition, telephone monitoring requires specific skills as it generates a large amount of data that must be managed by staff trained for this purpose and it is a time-consuming process (Angermann et al. 2012).

While these studies have demonstrated the effectiveness and positivity of remote monitoring in cardiology patients, the interpretation of the organisational phenomena that have accompanied these sudden transformations seems much more complex. Organisational resilience in these situations is one of the most difficult challenges in order to make the changes stable over time (Testa et al. 2022).

Our paper analyses how pandemic allowed for new forms of telemonitoring of cardiologic patients. Drawing on a pilot implementation carried out in an Italian region, we discuss the challenges in developing and scaling up a multiprofessional remote monitoring practice aimed at becoming a part of the healthcare service.

3 Context and Methodology: Cardiology Departments in Two Different Hospitals of the Same Public Health Company

The purpose of the empirical research was to capture the implementation, evolution and institutionalization of a telecardiological remote monitoring practice set up at the onset of COVID-19 pandemic. We adopted a qualitative research design to flank the phases of the evolution of the project from its design to its piloting, from its refinement to the redesign and scale up. To this aim, we conducted a longitudinal analysis involving the institutional stakeholders, the innovation managers in charge of the design of the remote monitoring system, two departments of cardiology, and the patients involved in the first piloting. In total, our informants were seven professionals (in brackets the number of times we interviewed each informant).

- The General Director of the Regional Health Department (1)
- The Director of technological innovation for the health sector of Regional Health Department (1)

- The Director of the Research Centre for health technology innovation (2)
- The Project manager of the Provider of technological infrastructure (2)
- The Project manager of the telemonitoring system (2)
- The Head of the Cardiology Department 1 (1)
- The Head of the Cardiology Department 2 (2).

The research has been conducted in two distinct phases. In the summer of 2020, we focused on the pilot implementation in Cardiology 1 through seven interviews with the stakeholders involved. In early 2021 we conducted four new interviews with the Director of technological innovation for the health sector of Regional Health Department, the Director of the Research Centre, the project manager, and the cardiologists of Cardiology 2.

Besides interviews, information about how departments are organized was gathered from scientific articles authored by the cardiologists and documentation regarding the remote monitoring system design and implementation was also analysed (Maines et al. 2020, 2021). Contextual information regarding the development of the project was gathered by the first and third authors of this paper which, at the time of the first piloting, worked in the Research Centre that developed the technological system.

Cardiology 1 is a department with a long history of experience with telemedicine and the associated organisational redesign. Patients with implantable devices are monitored by two dedicated nurses that perform a systematic check of the signals coming from the devices. The manufacturers of the devices allow health personnel to pick up specific alerts to monitor the situation in detail. Cardiology 2 belongs to another territorial hospital of the same health authority and it has a less mature and less institutionalised monitoring system in place. Monitoring is still performed by medical staff who check alerts from devices in their free time and between scheduled visits to the outpatient unit. Contact with patients is still mainly by telephone.

During the first pandemic wave a collaboration with the Research Centre led the design and implementation of some telemedicine systems. Cardiology 1 benefited from the first implementation of a telemonitoring system to allow routine visits to be performed online to comply with the social distancing protocols adopted by the hospital. The system was further developed and it integrates data from both the implantable devices and other sensors such as portable devices (e.g. smartwatch, scales) and it is now implemented in both piloting sites.

Previously, the signals from the devices were organised according to proprietary applications provided by the device manufacturers. The hypothetical number of patients with cardiac monitoring/support devices is about 5000 people in the territories covered by these cardiology services.

The paper attempts to compare the organisational processes triggered by the adoption of the telecardiology system. From an organisational point of view, it is interesting to understand how the same health authority interacts with two different of the cardiology services. Both services work to meet the needs of patients with implantable devices. Since COVID-19 has accelerated the organisational process, it is interesting to investigate these contexts in order to understand how the organisational transformations determined by the pandemic are the outcome of dynamics that affect the different internal articulation work. The institutionalised processes and the perception of the constraints posed by the healthcare system demonstrate how the work of articulation also generates a redistribution effect of organisational power that is not linear. We will try to understand in this regard why the two organisational models of Cardiology 1 and Cardiology 2 differ and why (Fig. 1).

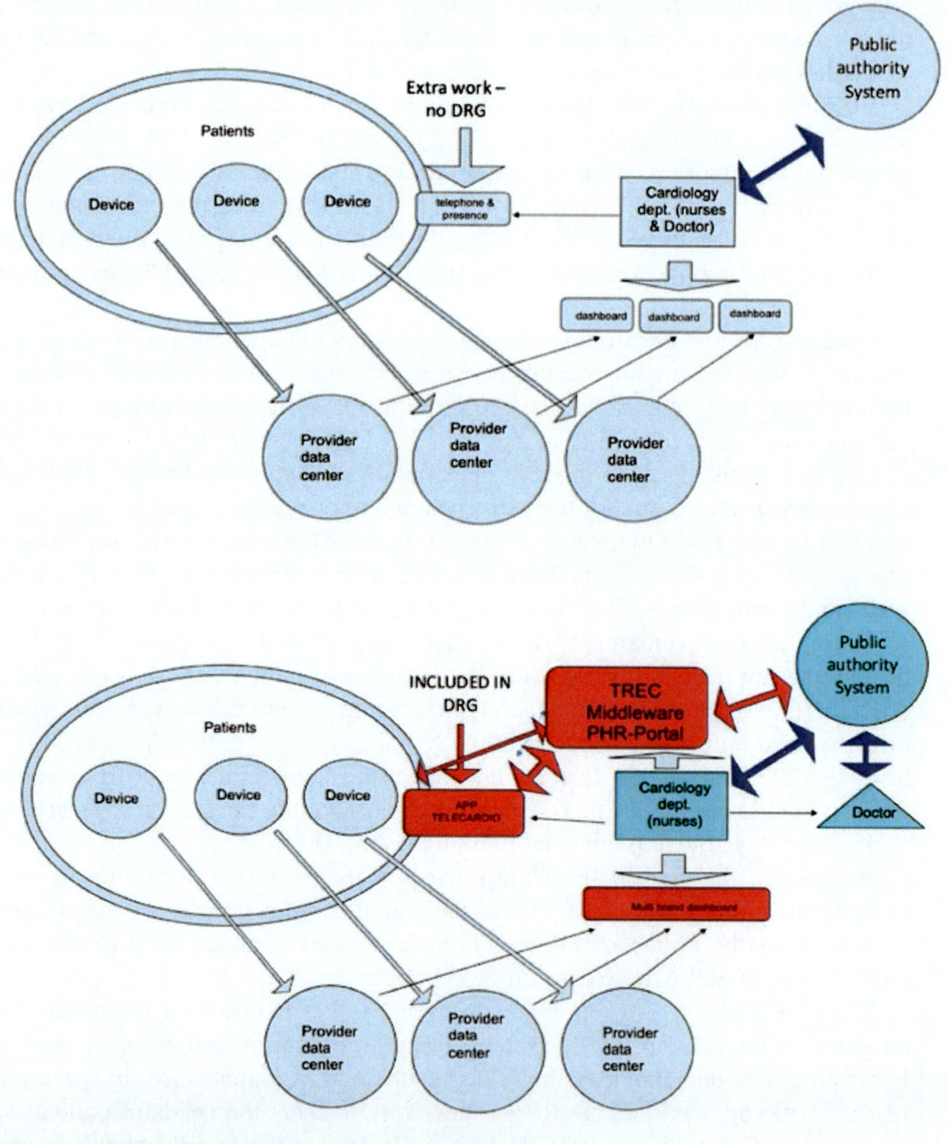

Fig. 1 Cardiology department 1 and 2

4 Findings

4.1 Organization Experience

The regional administration has a longstanding history of promotion of technological innovation in healthcare which has led over time to several telemonitoring projects. The partnership with the Research Centre, allowed the designing, piloting, and implementation of systems to connect patients and providers in several domains, from diabetology to cancer care, from asthma to peritoneal dialysis. Such endeavour has been largely made possible by adopting a common technological platform adapted and customized for each domain (Eccher et al. 2011).

Despite some success, the institutional stakeholders have mixed feeling with regards to the overall results of the innovation activities, blaming the healthcare trust for being not responsive enough in adapting to the possibilities offered by technology.

The director general of the Regional Health Department outlined several times in the interview that complexity "*is all in the field of the slowness of the health authority in adopting the proposed solutions*". At the same time, the director's interview revealed that the administrative structure does not understand much about the complexities of working in the health structure. These complexities appear much clearer to the Director of Innovation, who has always insisted on the point that transformations must be multi-stakeholder, although he admits: "*we are usually too slow in these processes, both in terms of development and in terms of adopting the various solutions*". The administration side, therefore, presents an approach that is a push for innovation but which alone is not enough.

In the two piloting settings the monitoring of patients has been traditionally carried by means of a telephone call that periodically allowed to check, through few questions, the patients' adherence to the therapies. Subsequently, implantable devices made monitoring possible via digital sharing of data accessed by clinicians through a proprietary dashboard created by manufacturers.

Thanks to the pandemic a new remote monitoring system provided patients with an app for monitoring and doctors with a dashboard to control the devices of all the implantable devices used. This application allows patients and nurses (or doctors) to perform televist as well. So, when requested by situation, patients and clinicians can interact with a dedicated infrastructure that can support traceability of the overall process.

At the time of writing this paper, in Cardiology 1, visits are scheduled when the need arises. This new way of monitoring patients has also allowed to reorganise the work of the staff. A first element that clarifies the effectiveness of the therapeutic model implemented can be derived directly from the account of the doctors of Cardiology 1 when they state that their experience has become the basis for the promotion of a Diagnostic-Therapeutic Care Pathways (DTCP) adopted by the regional health authority. Cardiology 1, in recent years, was able to receive additional resources and recruit two dedicated nurses trained in remote monitoring of devices.

"Our philosophy is the winning one (...) consider our model (DTCP) on heart failure: we started with heart failure patients which are the most delicate ones, which is just to manage a little bit like device carriers. We follow you, we monitor you all year round, there is a nurse who is available during working hours every day etc.

You can call them and manage situations. You have a problem, we schedule you a visit the week after... in short, if the doctors see the urgency immediately and sends you to the emergency room, if something that can be evaluated in the following days, we try to schedule the visit within 10 days, if there is no urge you can be seen even a month later. This is the paradigm shift in patient management, i.e., you no longer make the visit when you have scheduled it, but you make it when you need it". (Doctor1).

The reorganization is presented as a success story that allowed the redistribution of work within the department and the creation of a new approach to device data and patient management. This was made possible on the one hand with the support of the healthcare organisation, and on the other hand by the willingness to engage with private providers of heart failure devices.

In Cardiology 2, the situation is similar due to the availability of the technology provided by the public health company, but the organisation did not have a history of previous experimentation and therefore the doctors still must reorganise the department to make room for this new way of managing patient monitoring.

"As I understand it, the health administration aims to expand telemedicine. In practical terms, this means that the head nurse must remove two nurses from her shifts and devote them to the outpatient department, which I don't think she can do at the moment, otherwise she would have already done so. To relocate them, you have to define which are the essential services of the ward etc., *it is obvious that you cannot do that"*. (Doctor2).

In this situation, the introduction of technology has not brought any real benefit to the department in terms of redistribution of work, and therefore an intense articulation work is needed to define the "agreements" needed to provide the required service. The doctors' accounts highlight the fact that this work obliges them to use their free time at weekends and during breaks from work. In addition, the doctor coordinating the pilot project reports on his additional burden created by the new organisational model stressing that it is manageable as a pilot that involves 'just' 30–40 patients but that those numbers cannot be scaled up without additional dedicated workforce.

"At the moment, as far as telecardiology is concerned, at least as far as heart failure is concerned, it is almost zero... meaning that we have started with the app, we are making a few televisits, which basically means a phone call at the moment, but we do not have, for example, dedicated nurses, we do not have a preferential channel that allows us to enrol patients, to monitor them... that is, in my free time I read the reports of the app, but at the moment we have 30–40 patients, when there will be 200–300 I doubt that I will be able to keep up with this in my free time." (Doctor2).

In Cardiology 2, the ambiguity of the terms "adoption of new technologies" and "resilience" is brought out. Organisations never cease to be potentially conflictual and open fields in this regard. Telemedicine is represented by healthcare managers as a support to clinical practice and a viable way to increase organizational efficiency through a reorganization of internal resources. For clinicians, instead, telemedicine requires additional resources to make room for the additional time needed to perform additional monitoring. While Cardiology 1 has faced the problem in the past and it managed to secure additional staff, Cardiology 2 has yet to start to negotiate with the management and it struggles to manage the pilot performing unpaid overtime. The experimental nature of the project and the possibility that this innovation may change the approach to telemedicine, clashes with the "additive" nature of the change that cannot take place without a proportionate choice of resources and support from the organisation.

4.2 *The Double Face of Resilience in Organization*

While cardiology departments are urged to make room for experimentation, the framework of competencies takes on different dynamics between the pilot sites.

In the case of Cardiology 1, the greater experience and the reorganisation of the department allows doctors to envision new target groups eligible for telemedicine. The reorganisation has generated a new arrangement of people and technology. This shows a new "outlook" on the diagnostic pathways to be offered to patients who are currently treated by the department in traditional ways and not through the new monitoring system. As the doctor 1 reports, these organisational processes also require patients to change their perspective regarding being taken care of. For the new model to function, patients must systematically input personal data in a timely manner into the app to share them with the department. Committing to such a task implies recognising the dominance of the new technological system over the care process.

"In the philosophy of the app now, the philosophy has been to say let's start with the decompensated heart failure patients, because we have a project for that, but the philosophy afterwards is to extend [the model] to all the chronic. The strength of the app, in my opinion, lies in this, in educating the patient to manage these things, to give you the data and to be [active] part of his disease [management]... that is, it is not me who has to manage everything, it is you who are involved in the management because you have to weigh yourself, you have to do this, you have to give me the data, you have to call me if there is a problem. This is the winning thing here." (Doctor1).

In this perspective, the system must go through various moments of fragility and complexity for both the department and the patients, because the rules of engagement in the distribution of the various tasks of monitoring are changing. Moreover, the technology, as an experimental one, shows its vulnerabilities that can feed resilience in two directions. A first direction is that of the organisation not being able to rely 'entirely' on the new technology. In this case the resilience is of the health personnel who find suitable pathways to 'survival' and effective camouflage against technological innovation.

"But my philosophy will not be to use [so far] the televisit instead of the phone call because it's still a bit more cumbersome, it will only be when I can use the

app to make a phone call to the patient without having to give them advance notice, without having to go into the... [phone call] tell him that we're going to do it, because otherwise we'll lose more time." (Doctor1).

Moreover, until the new technological set-up has obtained sufficient guarantees of stabilisation, it is neither possible nor convenient to abandon the previous methods when adopting the new technological solutions. For example, since recruitment of patients is represented as a cumbersome and lengthy process doctors have decided to reduce the number of patients involved. Moreover, since the pilot did not foresee detailed inclusion/exclusion criteria, doctors enrolled patients deemed able to manage the app discarding other potential candidates. As the experimentation progressed, in fact, doctors realized that some skills and workarounds were needed to ensure the use of the app and some senior patients could not be relied upon if not properly assisted by a relative or a caregiver capable of using a smartphone.

"The televisit, for example, still has a problem in my opinion, because the way the app is structured requires me to phone patients, tell them to switch on [the phone], tell them to access the app, give consent, and do the tele visit. Yesterday the tele visit didn't work, because they changed something about the support, etc. *So, the technology needs to be a bit more stable. So, an 80-year-old with the mobile phone is not always mean eligible to have the app because if there's no family member with him [anti COVID-19 rules], if they can't remember the password, or maybe they can turn it on but to download the app the phone asks you for the password again... In short, technically it is not always feasible."* (Doctor2).

This last account helps us to understand how room is made available for resilience on the patients' side, especially if they are particularly old. There is, also, the resilience of some patients who do not accept this incorporation into monitoring systems and therefore try not to allow themselves to be included in a flow created by apps and devices.

"There is a 3% of patients with devices that do not have remote monitoring. There are some who don't want it because of strange beliefs or some who have old devices that cannot be monitored." (Doctor1).

4.3 The Technologies, the Choices, the People

While cardiologists provided a shop floor perspective of the implementation of the new monitoring system, the project manager was interviewed to position the initiative in the broader picture of a more comprehensive initiative to push telemedicine in the region. The primary challenge here is creating the conditions for direct adoption of the system. The attention is on the possibility of intercepting traditional monitoring practices and making them compatible with the automated ones of the system made available.

"So, we basically created a very simple platform, but during the year COVID was able to take on patients. We did an initial beta test with Cardiology 1, which lasted three to four months with about thirty patients. We then had an evaluation by the

internal sociologist staff, so I would say that the results were very comforting. In the beta test phase, we changed and optimised a few things with the development team, so that the app would be confident with both the patient part and the dashboard for the doctor." (PM1).

As this extract shows, there does not seem to be anything 'new' in the way technological solutions are proposed by the health authority, but the novelty this time is in the change of context generated by the pandemic. Telemedicine, having been regarded as a second-best option to provide care services, does not belong to a long distant future but it has become the only viable option to deal with the constraints of social distancing. The Research Centre that built the new telemedicine system became a relevant partner to provide services needed to grant the continuity of care during the emergency. The emergency allowed to push the boundaries and envision systems which do not simply allow to deal with the pandemic but aim at becoming a cornerstone of a new form of service provision by integrating external devices to have some monitoring work delegated to technological devices and wearables.

"We've done this with Apple Watch, we're coming out next week with the release of the Cardiology app with the ability to give direct download of data coming from Apple Watch... Apple Watch the latest version... There's also the ability to have a one-lead ECG that got FDA approval a couple of months ago regarding the diagnosis of atrial fibrillation." (PM3).

These experiments are combined with other experiments to gain a better understanding of how subgroups of patients act and to have retail technologies that are also considered acceptable by the authorities in the medical field, even for carrying out particularly sensitive biometric checks (e.g., FDA approval about Apple watch). This greatly reduces the resilience of medical staff, who usually do not trust patients' self-measurements. Patients have less and less work to feed the databases on which healthcare companies and private operators rely heavily. In seizing these opportunities, stakeholders recognise that "this time" the step seems firmer and more decisive to generate a paradigm shift with the patients involved. The system itself becomes a new opportunity for a new "digital therapy" prescription which they hope will soon be included in the procedures delivered by the health system.

"So, the app starts to become a digital therapy tool... this is the step we decided to take. The next step is to codify this service, because currently it is not codified... or rather, the telemonitoring is codified but the app is not codified as a service of the healthcare system. In the region, at the beginning of this year, we defined the DTCP for heart failure. The DTCP is basically a document for the diagnostic and therapeutic evaluation of certain chronic pathologies. We have reworked the DTCP for heart failure with the healthcare authority, and it is the first time in Italy that a DTCP has the possibility of integrating the care of a patient with technology. So, it is the first time in Italy that such wording appears." (PM1).

The new DTCP paved the way to semi-automated data monitoring by an algorithm and a limited intervention of healthcare professionals to check and validate a suggestion to be sent through the app to the patient. The PM, a cardiologist herself, represents this shift in terms of organizational challenges and opportunities. COVID-19 provided the opportunity for telemedicine services to find a legitimate space in the daily organisation of the workload. Some clinicians could work from home, the offices were empty and available for urgent, unpostponable visits, and the time for sanitization between visits was reduced. Beyond the pandemic, the cardiologists remarked the importance of organisational changes for a new technological approach to be successful. The introduction of the telemonitoring, in the medical areas involving cardiological consultation and monitoring, encouraged a shift from the traditional periodic visits to on-demand visits, where the patient is constantly remotely monitored and it is called for a face-to-face visit with the clinician only when a visit is needed, in a proactive way. In addition, the adoption of telemonitoring was perceived as a viable solution leading to a significant decrease of workload of health professionals on one side, and in terms of interfering with patients' agenda on the other.

"The big problem now is organisational change: if I have technology without organisational change, it is useless and creates even more confusion. In Cardiology 2, they managed to change the decompensation outpatient clinic by adding another nurse to the nurse who was following the telemonitoring patients on a part-time basis. Now it is [Cardiology 2] that has to make some choices, also from an organisational point of view, the number of nurses who follow and will follow these patients remotely." (PM1).

According to the project manager, the potential benefits are significant and range from the reduction of unnecessary visits, shortening of waiting lists, and the possibility to avoid face-to-face encounters when not strictly necessary. However, such results largely depend on how each department will confront the associated organizational challenges. Each department, in fact, is required to rearrange their working practices to accommodate the new technology (*"Now it is Cardiology 2 that has to make some of choices"*) to benefit from what the system can offer. Among the others, the system can provide some practical solutions to streamline work routines by providing a unique access point to several data sources. Before the introduction of the systems, in fact, the considerable complexity of cardiology monitoring of implanted devices in patients depended also on the different dashboards healthcare professionals had to switch between during the visits if they wanted to have an overall picture of their patients. In addition, the bureaucratic constraints associated with the administrative recognition of these services require that the work carried out by healthcare personnel be documented. This requires particularly intense "junction work" performed by staff (Piras and Zanutto 2016).

"They [healthcare professionals] had to enter all 4 dashboards, so it's a waste of time anyway. On the other hand, telecardiology service is now recognized as a legitimate service by the healthcare authority, but you have to prove that you have done that service. So, the nurse had to go to the portal of the healthcare authority, copy the PDF, the summary of the final PDF, and paste it in the healthcare IS which is the hospital system so that, at the annual reporting, they would say that the cardiology department has made a certain number telemonitoring visits to process to claim regional reimbursements from the Health Ministry..." (PM1).

Besides the mundane details of the technologies and the organizational constraints and challenges, the project manager presented the new initiative as a part of a broader strategy put forth by the regional healthcare authority to promote telemedicine leveraging on the opportunities offered by the pandemic. On the one hand, the emergency made it possible to strengthen the partnership between the regional government, the healthcare authority and the Research Centre. The funding for the project came from a COVID-19 dedicated funding scheme which allowed experimentation without investing a budget. On the other hand, the pandemic played a decisive role creating a fast lane for telemedicine projects aimed at reducing the risk of infection in hospitals during the critical phases of the infection.

"I admit that if it hadn't been for COVID, we probably wouldn't have reached this level. I mean that I often hold conferences, I often speak at courses, and I have seen a palpable difference between when I spoke before and when I speak now. Before the audience of doctors, when they heard about these things, was quite lukewarm if not reluctant, now I must say that the attitude has changed a lot. I don't expect 100% of decompensated and arrhythmic patients, hypertensive patients, post-infarction patients to be monitored with the app, not at all. I expect a proportion of these patients to be remotely monitored. Obviously, the amount will depend on the type of patient, on how many resources the hospital decides to include." (PM1).

The adoption of the system has allowed the healthcare authority to develop organisational potential both on the side of infrastructure and on the side of organisational behaviours and practices of healthcare personnel. This means that the solution adopted must be able to grow and be compatible with the different levels of maturity of the organisation so that it can be used with the appropriate patients for this new monitoring organisation. Clearly, this is largely dependent on making proprietary device data available in a way that is transparent to the patient, who no longer has to deal with it. At the same time, healthcare professionals can access this data without having to change interfaces and access protocols. This proved to be practically suitable for the target population, which often has low IT literacy, low commitment to specific data entry and limited resources from caregivers at home.

5 Discussion and Conclusion

According to a widely mistaken etymology, the Chinese word for "crisis" is (incorrectly) said to be composed of two characters signifying "danger" and "opportunity". Despite being a misinterpretation, the idea that an emergency creates room for a positive change has found significant echo in popular culture and it summarizes quite accurately the representations of the actors involved in the process of designing, deploying, testing, and scaling up a telemedicine solution described in the previous pages. All actors involved concur that while implementing telemedicine service requires lengthy and painstaking processes, the pandemic has offered an unparalleled opportunity not to be missed to take a giant step forward. The sense of urgency of clinicians and healthcare managers is largely due to the unparalleled alignment of loosening of institutional constraints, funding opportunities, and an overall favourable environment. The opportunity was seized firstly by re-adapting an existing system to the needs of cardiology, and subsequently by designing a specific layer to address the requests of the two departments. This strategy is consistent with the perceived need to 'strike the iron while it is hot' and introduce changes during the pandemic and work to make them permanent.

The first pilot conducted in 2020 highlighted several positive implications of adopting telemedicine such as the possibility of avoiding unnecessary travel and contacts during the COVID-19 epidemic; the possibility of reducing the organizational burden linked to visiting patients for simple routine follow-up visits at the clinic; the potential scalability of the tele visits and its adaptability in different departments.

Despite the overall positive results, however, there is one significant tension. Such tension stems directly from our analysis and it has been suggested by the comparison of the two trial sites and it relates to the different expectations regarding telemedicine by doctors and the healthcare organization. Datafication of healthcare is a phenomenon that predates the COVID-19 pandemic. Most likely, though, the prolonged emergency will boost the spreading of IT in different healthcare domains requiring new kinds of expertise, organizational change, data management practices just to name a few adjustments. As clinical practice becomes intermingled with "data work" ("*the activities related to creating, collecting, managing, curating, analyzing, interpreting, and communicating data*", Bossen et al. 2019) healthcare infrastructures and IT systems become a cornerstone of many services. IT systems, however, may be regarded quite differently by healthcare managers and clinicians. As illustrated by the excerpts presented above, they do not share the same perspective with regard to the effort needed to redesign the organizational processes implicated in the furnishing of telemedicine. Moreover, while managers envision a more efficient care delivery, clinicians represent telemedicine as a different way of working rather than a more productive one.

While managers claim that the increased volume of data received through devices will allow for personalized forms of care, clinicians are more likely to point to the additional resources needed to scrutinize those data. Doctors regard telemedicine as requiring the acquisition of additional skills. While data analysis can be assigned to nursing staff under medical supervision (Cartwright 2000), new staff needs to be hired to perform the additional data work. Such difference is well illustrated by the different way the pilots were handled in the two departments under scrutiny. While Cardiology 1 was able to secure new resources and assign them to telemedicine, Cardiology 2 did not yet manage to acquire new nursing staff leading doctors to practice telemedicine in his spare time.

Telemedicine schemes require patients to acquire new competences that go beyond the ability to deal with IT. Doctors involved in the pilots imply that a new therapeutic alliance needs to be established with patients. As one doctor put it "*it is you [the patient] who are involved in the management because you have to weigh yourself, you have to do this, you have to give me the data, you have to call me if there is a problem*" (see Sect. 4.2). The willingness to adopt a proactive approach, however, could not be taken for granted. However, remote monitoring assumes that professionals and patients play their part in dealing and sharing health information on a regular basis.

Involving patients in data collection, however, can be a daunting task and its success ultimately depends on making data collection a meaningful activity for patients and for the organization. The model envisioned by the departments, however, may not be suited to generate the desired patient engagement neither for the professionals. Patients with cardiac implantable devices have no access to the data automatically sent to the department and they would not be able to interpret them unless they were properly trained to do so.

At the same time, doctors and nurses must fit these new practices into a framework of meaning that is still unstable. Thus, the system is asked to consolidate a complex setting that still has to align all its allies.

In this sense the system can evoke the new but without being able to "generate" it. However, it has the capacity, by design, to redistribute work and to promote new ways of representing the working practices of the various human and non-human actors in health data management.

References

Angermann, C.E., Störk, S., Gelbrich, G., Faller, H., Jahns, R., Frantz, S., et al.: Mode of action and effects of standardized collaborative disease management on mortality and morbidity in patients with systolic heart failure: the interdisciplinary network for heart failure (INH) study. Circul. Heart Fail **5**, 25–35 (2012)

Badawy, S.M., Radovic, A.: Digital approaches to remote pediatric health care delivery during the COVID-19 pandemic: existing evidence and a call for further research. JMIR Pediatr. Parent. **3**(1) (2020). https://doi.org/10.2196/20049

Bertagnin, E., Greco, A., Bottaro, G., Zappulla, P., Romanazzi, I., Russo, M.D., Lo Presti, M., Valenti, N., Sollano, G., Calvi, V.: Remote monitoring for heart failure management during COVID-19 pandemic. Int. J. Cardiol. Heart & Vasc. **32**, 100724 (2021). https://doi.org/10.1016/j.ijcha.2021.100724

Bokolo, A.: Implications of telehealth and digital care solutions during COVID-19 pandemic: a qualitative literature review. Inform. Health Soc. Care **46**(1), 68–83 (2021). https://doi.org/10.1080/17538157.2020.1839467

Bossen, C., Pine, K. H., Cabitza, F., Ellingsen, G., Piras, E. M.: Data work in healthcare: an introduction. Health Inform. J. **25**(3), 465–474 (2019). https://doi.org/10.1177/1460458219864730

Cartwright, L.: Reach out and heal someone: telemedicine and the globalization of health care. Health **4**(3), 347–377 (2000). https://doi.org/10.1177/136345930000400306

De Backer, G., Ambrosioni, E., Borch-Johnsen, K., Brotons, C., Cifkova, R., Dallongeville, J., et al.: European guidelines on cardiovascular disease prevention in clinical practice. In: Third Joint Task Force of European and other Societies on Cardiovascular Disease Prevention in Clinical Practice; Eur. J. Cardiovasc. Prev. Rehabil. **10** (Suppl1), S1–S78 (2003)

DeFilippis, E.M., Reza, N., Donald, E., Givertz, M.M., Lindenfeld, J., Jessup, M.: Considerations for heart failure care during the coronavirus disease 2019 (COVID-19) pandemic. JACC Heart Fail **8**, 681–691 (2020). https://doi.org/10.1016/j.jchf.2020.05.006

Doraiswamy, S., Abraham, A., Mamtani, R., Cheema, S.: Use of telehealth during the COVID-19 pandemic: scoping review. J. Med. Internet Res. **22**(12) (2020). https://doi.org/10.2196/24087

Eccher, C., Piras, E.M., Stenico, M.: TreC–a REST-based Regional PHR. In: User Centred Networked Health Care, pp. 108–112. IOS Press (2011)

Graham, I.M., Stewart, M., Hertog, M.G.: On behalf of the cardiovascular round table task force: factors impeding the implementation of cardiovascular prevention guidelines: findings from a survey conducted by the European Society of Cardiology. Eur. J. Cardiovasc. Prev. Rehabil. **13**(5), 839–845 (2006). https://doi.org/10.1097/01.hjr.0000219112.02544.24

Kruse, C., Fohn, J., Wilson, N., Patlan, E.N., Zipp, S., Mileski, M.: Utilization barriers and medical outcomes commensurate with the use of telehealth among older adults: systematic review. JMIR Med. Inform. **8**(8), e20359 (2020)

Maines, M., Zorzi, A., Benetollo, P.P., Guarrera, G.M., Moz, M., Manica, A., Demattè, C., Del Greco, M.: Short-term outcome associated with remote evaluation (telecardiology) of patients with cardiovascular diseases during the COVID-19 pandemic. IJC Heart Vasc. **30**, 100625 (2020). https://doi.org/10.1016/j.ijcha.2020.100625

Maines, M., Tomasi, G., Moggio, P., Poian, L., Peruzza, F., Catanzariti, D., Angheben, C., Cont, N., Valsecchi, S., Del Greco, M.: Scheduled versus alert transmissions for remote follow-up of cardiac implantable electronic devices: clinical relevance and resource consumption. Int. J. Cardiol. **334**, 49–54 (2021). https://doi.org/10.1016/j.ijcard.2021.04.043

Menardi, E., Ballari, G.P., Racca, E., Gagliardi, M., Gonella, A., Sbarro, F., Musso, R., Cagliero, S., Baralis, G.: Telemedicine during COVID-19 pandemic. J. Arrhythmia **36**(4), 804–805 (2020). https://doi.org/10.1002/joa3.12381

Miller, J.C., Skoll, D., Saxon, L.A.: Home monitoring of cardiac devices in the era of COVID-19. Curr. Cardiol. Rep. **23**(1), 1 (2020). https://doi.org/10.1007/s11886-020-01431-w

Piras, E.M., Zanutto, A.: Tinkering around healthcare infrastructures: nursing practices and junction work. In: De Angeli, A., Bannon, L., Marti, P., Bordin, S. (eds.) COOP 2016: Proceedings of the 12th International Conference on the Design of Cooperative Systems, 23–27 May 2016, Trento, Italy, pp. 173–189. Springer International Publishing (2016). https://doi.org/10.1007/978-3-319-33464-6_11

Piro, A., Magnocavallo, M., Della Rocca, D.G., Neccia, M., Manzi, G., Mariani, M.V., Straito, M., Bernardini, A., Severino, P., Iannucci, G., Giunta, G., Chimenti, C., Natale, A., Fedele, F., Lavalle, C.: Management of cardiac implantable electronic device follow-up in COVID-19 pandemic: lessons learned during Italian lockdown. J. Cardiovasc. Electrophysiol. **31**(11), 2814–2823 (2020). https://doi.org/10.1111/jce.14755

Planinc, I., Milicic, D., Cikes, M.: Telemonitoring in heart failure management. Card. Fail. Rev. **6**, e06 (2020). https://doi.org/10.15420/cfr.2019.12

Tersalvi, G., Winterton, D., Cioffi, G.M., Ghidini, S., Roberto, M., Biasco, L., Pedrazzini, G., Dauw, J., Ameri, P., Vicenzi, M.: Telemedicine in heart failure during COVID-19: a step into the future. Front. Cardiovasc. Med. **7**, 612818 (2020). https://doi.org/10.3389/fcvm.2020.612818

Testa, S., Mayora-Ibarra, O., Piras, E.M., Balagna, O., Micocci, S., Zanutto, A., Forti, S., Conforti, D., Nicolini, A., Malfatti, G., Moz, M., Gios, L., Benetollo, P.P., Turra, E., Orrasch, M., Zambotti, F., Del Greco, M., Maines, M., Filippi, L., Ghezzi, M., Romanelli, F., Racano, E., Marin, M., Betta, M., Bertagnolli, E.: Implementation of tele visit healthcare services triggered by the COVID-19 emergency: the Trentino Province experience. J. Public Health **30**, 77–92 (2022). https://doi.org/10.1007/s10389-021-01609-8

WHO: Telemedicine: opportunities and developments in Member States. World Health Organization, Geneva (2009)

Smart and Inclusive Museums for Visitors with Autism: The App Case "A Dip in the Blue"

Luisa Varriale, Roberta Cuel, Aurelio Ravarini, Paola Briganti, and Giovanni Minucci

Abstract This paper aims to investigate how digital technologies can make museums 'smart' and 'inclusive' engaging visitors, especially people with special needs. Adopting a bottom-up approach and a participatory design, this exploratory and qualitative study describes the design and development of a specific App for children with Autism called 'A dip in the Blue' of archaeological museum located in Southern Italy (The Archaeological Museum of Paestum and Velia). Starting from a specific toolkit, a paper visual agenda, planned according to a specific format (forms, figures, colours, and emoticons), which made children and their parents to really enjoy the museum environment overcoming the barriers and limits that usually exist for them, the App provides a digital visual agenda and further services and facilities. Thus, after the first visits at the museum, the paper visual agenda became a virtual visual agenda that supports children with Autism and their family, as well as all the young visitors. The App has been designed and developed following all the specific standards and criteria of the Universal Design and considering the specific needs of the special visitors adopting a bottom-up approach, indeed, autistic children were actively involved in the design and development process with their families and all the operators. The paper provides some effective best practices for museums to become smarter and more inclusive through digital technologies and real users' needs.

L. Varriale (✉) · P. Briganti
Università Degli Studi Di Napoli "Parthenope", Naples, Italy
e-mail: luisa.varriale@uniparthenope.it

P. Briganti
e-mail: paola.briganti@uniparthenope.it

R. Cuel
Università Di Trento, Trento, Italy
e-mail: roberta.cuel@unitn.it

A. Ravarini
LIUC Università Carlo Cattaneo, Castellanza, Varese, Italy
e-mail: aravarini@liuc.it

G. Minucci
Il Tulipano Coop. Sociale, Naples, Italy
e-mail: info@iltulipanocoop.org

S. Za et al. (eds.), *Sustainable Digital Transformation*, Lecture Notes in Information Systems and Organisation 59, https://doi.org/10.1007/978-3-031-15770-7_9

Keywords Smart museums · Inclusive museums · Inclusion · Autism · Digital technologies · App · Social media

1 Introduction

Many museums develop or adopt solutions worldwide to be committed to accessibility and accommodations for the overall general public, such as ramps for wheelchair users or closed captions for the D/HH (deaf and hard-of-hearing) visitors. However, not all disabilities and disorders are visible.

Museum professionals face many challenges in developing solution to allow visitors with specific disabilities and disorders to really enjoy the museum experience [1]. Numerous museums already promoted and adopted special programs for people with specific disabilities or disorders. Studies about the benefits derived from museums for individuals with Autism are still scarce, as well as the additional features required, as services, provided by museums for meeting the specific needs of the individuals with Autism are still undeveloped.

Autism represents a disorder that specifically impacts on the individual's brain before the age of three years, creating much difficulties in communication and social skills, or also influencing the individual's behavior. Autism, which involves more boys than girls, constitutes one of the 5 brain disorders classified under the Autism Spectrum Disorders (ASD).[1] Individuals with Autism, generally with ASD, have difficulties in non-verbal and verbal communication language and difficulties to socialize. Therefore, museum environments could represent a very strong experience for these visitors becoming stressful and dangerous. Too much noise, flashing lights, etc., stimulate too much making the environment uncomfortable and agonizing for these individuals [1–6]. Museums increasingly adopt technological solutions to improve their offer to visitors, becoming smart museums, where technologies have been adopted making the visit experience unique and attracting tourists as well as people with special needs [6–8]. Museums have been eliminating the physical barriers, but thanks digital technologies they can be able to eliminate the sensory barriers, becoming really and much more inclusive.

This exploratory and qualitative study, adopting a research driven research model, through a bottom-up approach and a participatory design, aims to investigate museums in the perspective of being smart and inclusive through the adoption of digital technologies for children with Autism and their families. To achieve

[1] The Autism Spectrum Disorders (ASD) includes 5 different brain disorders: Autism, Asperger Syndrome, Childhood Disintegrative Disorder, Persuasive Developmental Delay-Not Otherwise Specified (PDD-NOS), and Rett Syndrome (WebMD). More specifically, due to the variety of symptoms and the complexity in providing a coherent and homogeneous clinical definition, it is more common to correctly use the expression Autism Spectrum Disorders (ASD, Autistic Spectrum Disorders) which includes a whole series of pathologies or syndromes having the aforementioned behavioral characteristics as a common denominator, albeit at varying degrees or levels of intensity. In this study we generally talk about "children/young teenagers with Autism" or "children/young teenagers with ASD", by distinguishing between low, medium or high level of functioning.

this goal, we follow a two-step research process. First, we conduct a review by analyzing and summarizing the most relevant contributions in the research on smart and accessible and inclusive museums, and specifically museums and visitors with Autism. We systematize and underlie the main research orientations of scholars providing a clear scenario about the gaps still existing in the research, especially with regard to the adoption of technological solutions addressed to people with Autism. Second, we design and develop a specific App as a virtual visual agenda investigating several visits at the Archaeological Museum of Paestum and Velia in Southern Italy, Campania Region. Also, the importance to adopt a collaborative orientation, with a participatory design, and to develop effective managerial and didactic/pedagogical practices for achieving the maximum social inclusion has been evidenced, as well as it has been outlined the need to effectively train and educate all the people involved in the museum visits and the design process for children with Autism, including parents, museum staff and operators.

In summary this study describes the design process drawn from a multidimensional approach (bottom-up approach and participatory design) to conceptualize and design an accessible and inclusive museum-based app.

The reminder of the paper is structured as follows. The Sect. 2 describes the methodology adopted, that is a two-step research process. In the Sect. 3, a brief review of the main contributions in the literature has been conducted for clearly explaining the concept of smart and inclusive museums through the digital technologies. Then, the subsequent Sect. 3.1. focuses on the specific link between museums and visitors with Autism with the contribution of technologies. Section 4 provides details about the design and development of the specific App for the museum experience visit. Finally, the Sect. 5 provides concluding comments, limitations and future perspectives of the study.

2 Method

This paper consists of two-step study process. Firstly, we conduct a deep review of the literature for analysing and summarising the most relevant contributions existing on museums considering two main related topics, that is smart museums and inclusive museums. Smart museums consist of a symbiosis between technology and exhibitions, where the adoption of digital technologies aims to improve the delivery to visitors of the large and complex cultural heritage, also creating the conditions for enhancing their interaction allowing creative processes. In this case, several advanced technological applications have been developed and implemented, like Internet of Things (IoT), Augmented Reality (AR), Augmented Virtuality (AV) and so forth. Inclusive museums concern the accessibility and usability of the museums, for all the visitors by overcoming all the physical, cognitive or sensory barriers making visitors with disability, and in general with special needs, able to completely and successfully experience museum visit. We consider only published studies clearly focused on smart museums, inclusive museums, social inclusion, disability and Autism over a 20-year period (1998–2020). The online search adopted and combined the key words "museum", "smart museum", "inclusive museum", "accessible museum", "autism friendly museum", "autism", "managerial solutions for accessible museums", "managerial solutions for inclusive museums", "pedagogical and didactic practices", "teaching solutions". This was performed in two main freely accessible web search engines specifying in academic contributions, that is the ISI Web of Science (WoS) and Google Scholar (GS). Specifically, the online search in both websites was conducted in two main phases: 1. The key words 'smart', 'inclusive' and 'accessible' were combined with the term museum ("smart" OR "inclusive" OR "accessible" AND "museum"). Here, we obtained 15.900 results in GS and 2755 results in WoS; 2. The previous key words were combined with the terms 'autism' and 'autism friendly museum' ("smart" OR "inclusive" OR "accessible" AND "museum" AND "autism" AND/OR "autism friendly museum"). Here, we obtained 3.500 results in GS and 25 results in WoS. 3. We matched the results from both websites and only we considered papers and chapters in English language with at least one key word in the title corresponding to "museum", "smart", "inclusive", "accessible", "autism". Finally, we had about 355 results. In more detail, the papers have been selected using the criteria described below. First, we consider only papers in academic journals and chapters published during the last two decades, 1998–2020. Second, the papers had to be published in English and contain at least one of the selected words and terms directly or indirectly in their titles. Third, the papers had to have dealt with research issues and the most relevant keywords, i.e., "smart museum", "accessible museums", "inclusive museum" and "autism friendly museum", need to be included. All the identified studies were analysed to identify relationships between the issues investigated. The abstract of each paper has been briefly read by the authors and then undertook a complete reading of each paper after outlining its relevance for our research.

Secondly, we investigate the experience of one specific App, the Project 'A dip in the blue', designed and developed within the program Autism friendly realized in one archaeological museum, located in Paestum (Salerno) in the Southern Italy, in Campania Region, the Archaeological Museum of Paestum and Velia. The Archaeological Museum of Paestum and Velia was chosen for two main reasons. First, this museum pays an increasing attention to accessibility issues and especially to the social inclusion, mostly in the last years where it is possible to observe numerous interventions in this direction, e.g. the introduction of ramps for wheelchair visitors, the proposal of specific programs for blind or deaf visitors. Second, this museum records a significant growth of its visitors. Indeed, in the last four years, in Italy, especially in the Southern regions, like Campania, museums record a significant growth of their visitors and profits. In particular, in 2017 the Archaeological Museum of Paestum is among the most visited by tourists in Italy with 441,037 visitors with an increase of about 15.10% compared to 2016 (about 382.172 visitors) [9].

The research study was conducted through a partnership between local public universities in Campania Region in the Southern Italy that is 'Parthenope' and 'Federico II' University, the Archaeological Museum of Paestum in Southern Italy, and a local social enterprise involved in social services for people with disability, especially individuals with Autism, the social enterprise 'Il Tulipano', and the all associations of families with children with Autism.

This App has been designed and developed thanks to the numerous experiences gained previously through the visits at the museum planned and carried out for families with children with Autism using specific programs (didactic and managerial solutions) supported by the toolkit "visual agenda" for the kids. The App represents the translation of the paper visual agenda used during the first visits at the museum, in digital visual agenda with several advanced functions for improving the involvement and interaction of the kids. The App has been designed and developed thanks to the data and information collected during the previous visits at the museum through interviews, questionnaires, personal schedules, focus groups directly with the families with children with Autism, museum staff and operators. The App considers and can be used by children/young teenager with Autism, with low, middle, and high-functioning abilities (low being low verbal skills and high being Asperger syndrome). The design and development of the App were based on the didactic program and all the previous visit experiences following always a bottom-up approach, in fact, all the actors (researchers, museum staff, operators and parents of children/young teenagers with Autism) participated, through planned meetings (specific focus group) for discussing and defining contents and putting together different ideas strictly taking into account the concrete needs of the participants, responded to interviews and questionnaires, and compiled fact sheets for the visitors. According to previous studies on the topic [1, 2, 4, 5, 10, 11, 13–15] and past practical directed and undirected experiences already documented [10–12], the App is, therefore, the result of a deep analysis and further development of the original entire program (the visual agenda used during the visit, the steps of the museum visit path, and the instruments used for evaluating the overall initiative) using digital technologies. Hence, the current App project was realized thanks to previous studies and experiences on the topic and also of an opened discussion directly involving all the partners and players. An integrative schema for analysing the museum visit "Autism friendly" was developed, firstly defining the program (visual agenda) used during the visit of one specific area of the archaeological museum for the children with Autism. The original paper visual agenda consists of a little book created for kids with images representing parts to visit in the museum, emoticons for making the kids able to express their feeling and emotion about the visit, colours and forms for supporting kids in their visit in making the museum environment more comfortable and friendlier for them. The App can represent digitally the paper visual agenda.

3 Smart and Inclusive Museums

In the last decades, museums have been changing their way to serve visitors catching the attention of the tourists and to respond to their interests, museums provide innovative solutions, like interactive and personalized museum tours, using also advanced digital technologies, like IoT (which can involve the extension of the Internet to small and low-cost "things" thought to create smart environments to provide new services to the users), AR or AV applications (which could support to appreciate art more deeply and make it more accessible to everyone), and so forth. In this perspective, museums become "smart", where heterogeneous technologies make the museum environment much more interactive, innovative and accessible. Museums develop and implement apps able to facilitate the visitors in their fruition process, making information available, more or less automatically additional, in the form of text, audio or video files, images, that the museum intends to make available for specific part of its environment [6, 8, 12–14, 16–18]. Smart museums provide additional services and support to their visitors becoming much more attractive and giving real interactive experiences, using digital technologies with multiple applications able to give different and useful services.

In this direction, there are many interesting examples that we can considered as expressions of smart museums experiences. For instance, Alletto and colleagues [8] in their study designed and validated an indoor location-aware architecture for enhancing the museum user's experience. This wearable device uses "combines image recognition and localization capabilities to automatically provide the users with cultural contents related to the observed artworks" [8: 244]. The device uses a system which is based on a mix of elements, such as a Bluetooth low energy (BLE) infrastructure for the localization information, the Cloud to store multimedia contents produced by the users and to share environment-generated events on their social networks. All the services provided interact with physical devices through a multiprotocol middleware. The effectiveness of the system, designed also for being used with other IoT technologies, was evaluated in the MUST Museum in Southern Italy.

Otherwise, a novel smart museum concept was proposed by López et al. [6] considering intelligent services able to enrich the museum's collection, including knowledge acquired from museum's experts and visitors. This novel concept for smart museums adopts the smart spaces approach for an IoT museum environment proposing a semantic infrastructure. Other scholars try to understand user's onsite physical behaviors outlining that IoT allows to understand visitors' information needs [19]. Also, a specific further architecture was proposed by Mighali et al. [20] able to improve the users' cultural experience including connectivity, wearable devices, mobile devices, multimedia data in the cloud and a processing centre. Going beyond these important contributions for implementing the smart museum where the focus is on technological developments, others focus much more on visitors' interaction. For example, López et al. [6] have explored "alternative forms of interaction which take advantage of the virtual continuum, able to include real objects in museum's exhibitions making it behave like a smart object" [6: 3]. Overcoming the real environment, the virtual continuum goes from real environments to virtual environments at the other, where thanks to the virtuality users can fully immerse within a digital synthetic world. Also, mixed Reality (MR) in the middle of the virtual continuum can allow real-world and virtual objects to interact and being displayed in a combined way [21]. In this scenario, AR increases information from the reality with digital content, while AV incorporates visualizations of real objects within a virtual environment [21].

Beyond being smart museums, as well as all informal learning institutions (e.g. zoos, art museums, science centres), have been increasingly paying their attention for improving access and inclusion for people with disabilities, overcoming any kind of barriers [3, 22, 23], also using much more digital technologies.

Although museums promoted and implemented numerous actions for making their environment more accessible and inclusive, people with disabilities still report feeling excluded from museums [3, 5, 24, 25]. Full inclusion concerns cognitive and social dimensions, as well as physical, following the overall thoughts in the informal science education field [23]. Focusing the attention on criteria for inclusion, learners are able to "physically interact with and perceive the space, cognitively engage with the materials, and socially interact with one another" [23: 15]. Otherwise, inclusion efforts mostly focus on physical and cognitive inclusion and less on social inclusion [23, 24].

The international community, including institutions, academics, and firms, argues that museums should be "open to the public" [5, 26, 27]. Specifically, museums should be also accessible to all people with disabilities, overcoming any kind of barriers, that is physical, cognitive or sensory obstacles [28–30]. For trying to be accessible and inclusive museums also tend to adopt much more digital technologies, otherwise, Asensio and Asenjo [31] argued that technology represents a useful tool able to mediate between people and their own heritage messages [33].

Ramírez and Domínguez [34] investigate the case of Appside in Spain, an App developed thanks to the collaboration with GVAM and Orange Foundation. This specific App was designed for hearing and visually impaired visitors, and is consisting in the development of autonomous and details routes for visiting the museum through various languages, maps and sound and visual recordings. These technologies were co-designed and tested by over 200 disabled people in Spain, Austria and the UK [35].

Other examples of technological solutions developed and implemented for making museums much more accessible and inclusive are tools like are tactile digital replicas and interactive gesture-based audio guides, capable to enrich the tactile experience through digital interaction especially for visually and blind impaired people with audio feedback activated touching objects [36]. Other museum tools concern the use of 3D-printed models, laser cutting and the use of reliefs for sculptures and paintings, like for instance the laser cutting and 3D printing tools were developed in the Australian art galleries by Holloway and colleagues (2019), providing to all visitors, especially disabled people, a better texture of the sculptures. Furthermore, Cavazos et al. [37] designed a prototype combining 3D tools, plus other sensory experiences called 2.5D, with printed elements in thermoform, elements such as audio, wind or heat, and verbal elements for supporting above all the blind public. In most of these technological solutions the goal is always to improve and support the blind visitors' autonomy and dependence in living the cultural experience also involving the artists during the p process of the tools [38]. In this direction, we mention also the 'Façade project' consisting of tactile representations by means of

3D printing for blind people [39], or the 'SeeingVR project' representing a virtual reality which combines visual and audio zoom for low vision public [40].

Other interesting experiences come from the USA, like USA, the 'Incluseum project', based in Seattle, Washington, which propones new ways of being a museum through critical discourse, community building and collaborative practice related to inclusion in museums (Incluseum 2015 cit. in [41]) creating a community, like a digital environment, between museums and public and technology experts, where the solutions and progress in the field of cultural inclusion are shared, stimulating informal partnerships for promoting inclusive practices. Ad well as in Spain, regarding the virtual museum collections, the DOMUS platform is capable to consolidate a Digital Network of Museum Collections in the entire country, which is currently CER.ES [42]. An interesting study by Vaz et al. [43] provides an evaluation about the use of technologies comparing experiences in museums and exhibitions worldwide, investigating the way for designing and implementing facilities and digital media in order to improve the experience, especially for disabled people. Thus, wearable technologies, like smart watches, are considered as nonintrusive and lightweight solutions that are able to improve the visitor experience generating new and different emotions paying attention to different features during the visit [11].

3.1 Technological Solutions for Inclusive Museums: Focus on Visitors with Autism

Social inclusion, which is essential for all museum's inclusion efforts, is very important especially regarding a subset of the disability community, that is individuals with ASD and their families [3]. ASD presents different expressions from person to person, but this kind of disability usually concerns challenges with social communication and interaction, along with the presence of narrow and repetitive behaviours, interests, or activities [44]. Thus, individuals with Autism spectrum can present different characteristics ranging from having no or minimal verbal language to having well-developed language skills, or from having cognitive disability to above average IQ, and from needing only some support to function in daily life to needing substantial support. Museums need to deeply consider the inclusion issue for visitors with ASD. People with ASD, more than other people with disabilities, experience several barriers in museums settings [1, 4, 32]. Indeed, museum environments generally can be distressful for people with Autism, because of many factors beyond the noise, for instance, flashing lights from a screen, children with loud voices, machines dinosaurs with too big roars, and heavy crowds [1]. These factors can make the museum visit for individuals with ASD a source of anxiety and sometimes panic, they can experience negative feelings related to the museum visit because the environment is not comfortable, without adequate accommodations and appropriate sound and light solutions, as well as quiet and inclusive setting. In this case, something that seems fun becomes for individuals with ASD very dangerous and sad. In the last decades, museums are paying a significant attention to the needs of people with Autism, trying to become more comfortable for them also thanks to the participation and partnerships with external institutions and specialized organizations [1] and also through the design and development of useful and effective technological solutions [10, 11]. Otherwise, numerous studies show that the integration into the community, as well as through the museum visit experience, is very beneficial for children with disabilities, especially for children with ASD, as shown significant results from analysis of parent's perceptions of their children's participation in museum visits [45–47], but these studies are still scarce.

Although there are numerous studies in the literature about the accessibility and inclusion of museums environments, most research focuses on visitor motivations and identity related to visitors at large, compared to studies about people with disabilities (including families with children with ASD), which are still less numerous and so researchers are beginning to explore this area more [3], as well as the research on the adoption of technologies for making the museums much more accessible and inclusive for people with ASD is still scarce.

Otherwise, many museums worldwide, especially in the United States, have been implementing special programs and other educational experiences for better meeting the needs and preferences of individuals with ASD, and specifically with Autism [31]. In many cases, the museum efforts promote "sensory-friendly" solutions for providing a welcoming environment which is better in line with individuals with ASD because it is not over-stimulating, indeed, the sound or light features are limited in exhibits, programs, or performances. Other museums plan special events for individuals with ASD, such as the Opening Our Doors offered thanks a partnership between the Museum of Fine Arts, Museum of Science, and Boston Children's Museum in Boston [48], or another special event consists of webinars and workshops hosted by some museums, for instance the American Alliance of Museums [1]. These special efforts play a crucial role because can contribute to the social participation of people with ASD, who usually are less frequently involved in social activities and experience limited activities in the community [49, 50].

In this scenario briefly described, most programs developed and implemented by the museums worldwide described and investigated by scholars adopt some specific technologies.

Indeed, several scholars have evaluated the technology-based programs in the area of Autism [51, 52], but the usability of such digital platform is still underrepresented [10, 53–55]. It is no easy to design and develop interfaces for autistic groups because of their impact on children's behaviors and attitudes with high risk that the technology program is not able to fit autistic users' needs [56, 57]. In order to overcome these limits, it is necessary: to adopt much more inclusive design approaches and best practices in designing these technologies [53–56]; and also, to really understand autistic people's needs involving them in the design process [38, 58].

In this direction, the active involvement in technology development have advantages for both autistic users and designers and represents the most effective solution [10, 52]. Participatory design (PD) implies the active involvement of end-users in the design process requiring continuously their ideas and opinions also reflecting and using the prototypes [8, 52, 59]. This process generates ideas interactively refining the design through the user's feedback, needs and desires [60]. This approach allows to identify possible limitations, enhance functionality and test the validity of the interface, giving a very useful support for the successful design of new technologies.

Over the past ten years, the technologies for autistic children have been significantly increasing adopting mostly a child-centered approach to design products and novel work platforms involving autistic children in the design process [61]. Thus, PD has been considered as "a well evidence-based practice to involve the end-users and other stakeholders within the context of the design process and to identify how novel platforms can work in real situations" [60]. In this case, autistic children operate assuming several roles, that is co-designer, tester, user and informant [62]. In the autism field, this specific approach has been mostly adopted developing useful interactive technology platforms with the children's input also for the museums.

Indeed, other studies provide an assessment of 'MicroCulture', a digital and tangible installation created directly involving children with ASD and bridging history learning across museums and schools in the perspective of game based learning [63, 64]. Also, Giaconi and colleagues [65], adopting the principles of universal design, explored the potential of digital technologies, specifically virtual and augmented reality, for supporting inclusive practices in museums and co-planned and implemented actions with people with ASD to increase their participation during the visit experience. In particular, unpredictable and chaotic contexts in the museum were redesigned, developing a technological prototype for creating an accessible virtual museum tour with important benefits, that is the improvement of empowerment of people with disabilities and the cultural rights of the whole community [65].

Furthermore, other scholars help people with ASD to enjoy their museum experience thanks to digital technologies, especially specific digital solutions developed directly involved the special visitors, like Wearable Immersive Virtual Reality (WIVR) and Wearable Immersive Social Stories (WISS) adopting a digital storytelling approach [66], or a museum-based application tailored to autistic children's needs [67].

"Most of the projects were designed by incorporating user-centered techniques and collaborating with indirect stakeholders, such as parents, autistic children, teachers, and assistive technology practitioners throughout the process" [10: 5]. For instance, the co-designed tablet applications developed by [68], helped autistic children to improve their social skills, as well as in the ECHOES project [69], the focus was on the process of the co-design sessions instead of the outcomes.

Also, a narrative story and sensory exploration through different techniques contributed to effective participation [69]. In the IDEAS framework, based on TEACCH (a structured teaching intervention approach), the designers supported significantly an effective and creative involvement of participants with ASD [70, 71]. Furthermore, Malinverni et al. [72] investigated the way PD activities can help the validation of initial designs, collecting new ideas by autistic children and assessing aspects able to motivate children.

4 The App Case

The study described in this paper was built adopting a bottom-up approach and a participatory design as already outlined considering previous studies on the phenomenon and experiences carried out with focus on the relevance to create the conditions in the museum environment to be comfortable and welcoming to parents and their children with Autism, responding to their special needs.

Firstly, several visits at the museum were carried out with parents and their children/young teenagers with Autism supported and guided by trained operators and social therapists with an identified support tool, that is a "paper visual book". This tool was developed by the researchers, operators and all staff involved in the study, taking into account the special needs of visitors with Autism, that is their specific ways to communicate and socially interact with others, so images, forms, colours and emoticons were introduced into the "paper visual agenda" which each child had during the visit and helped him/her to follow the narration of operas of the archaeological museum.

The visits regarded the "Tomba del Tuffatore" ("The diver's tomb") located at the Archaeological Museum of Paestum and Velia. As already said, for supporting parents and their children with Autism to experience museum visit a didactic program was built and realized thanks a continuous and active discussion between all the partners involved (researchers, museum staff, operators, therapists, families).

The proposal provides for the presentation of a story calibrated on the real one of the "Tomba del Tuffatore" which will be narrated by an operator (the content of the story was previously shared with all the partners). The children/young teenagers with Autism were able to follow the narration, also using an activity notebook (a paper visual agenda) that was provided to them at the beginning of the guided tour and which could take home as a tangible element of the museum visit. The narration in the notebook was supported by images, colours, forms and emoticons that the participants could freely choose based on their interests and accompanied by the sounds. There was a key concept to guide and support the participants in their museum visit, that is the water, with connected other relevant objects used during the narration, for example, the jar, the wine, and so forth, these elements for supporting the narration during the visit were reported in the visual notebook with the images of the operas (see Fig. 1).

On each page of the paper visual notebook the five plates in the room of the "Tomba del Tuffatore" were shown: for each plate there will be an explanation of the meaning for the image and some individual elements will be highlighted and examined in the image. The narration will be set up based on those specific elements. The language used is simple, immediate, non-allegorical and direct in order not to carry too many verbal stimuli that could lead the participants to excessive load.

After the several visits experienced (6 visits were carried out) at the museum through the specific program with the toolkit of the paper visual agenda, the team thought to adopt technological solutions in order to much more involve the autistic

Fig. 1 Page examples of the paper visual book

children and make their visit experience really useful in terms of social participation and funny time.

The digital path ‘A dip in the Blue’ (“Un Tuffo nel Blu”—“Tulipano Art” project) (conceived by the cooperative company ‘Il Tulipano’ in collaboration with two universities, Parthenope and Federico II in Naples, realized with the co-financing of the Campania Region POR Campania Fesr 2014–2020) has as its specific and primary objective the proposal of a method of digital use, scientifically validated, for people with autism at the Archaeological Museum of Paestum and Velia and at the network of Campania Museums called ‘Tulipano Art Friendly’ promoted and coordinated by ‘the Tulipano’ organization.

The path ‘Un tuffo nel Blu’, downloadable at the ‘Tulipano Art Platform’ through the specific App ‘A Dip in the Blue’, is the transposition of the methodology and instrumentation conceived and created in the homonymous project, active at the Archaeological Museum of Paestum and Velia since 2018 and aimed at people with Autism to enjoy a visit at the museum. The project aimed at creating new models in visiting museum through the support of digital technologies.

Regarding the details of the structure of the specific App, starting from the previous experiences in visiting the museum using the paper visual agenda, the tour is developed with the aid of a digital application, downloadable easily on the smartphone or tablet by autistic children (supported by the Android and macOS system), which acts as a digital visual agenda and where the previously identified elements are recalled for each individual work selected and validated by the scientific research group, useful for being understood by the users of the tour, who were previously involved in designing and developing the same App.

Specifically, regarding the opera to visit 'La Tomba del Tuffatore', this proposal provides for the presentation of a social story inspired by the story of the discovery of this famous artistic opera by an 'archaeologist' represented by an educator, through the technique of storytelling.

Visitors, especially autistic children and their families, can follow the narration in person in the 'museum environment' with a digital application via tablet and/or remotely with connection to a special digital platform called 'Tulipano Art' conceived and created by the partner 'Il Tulipano' for inclusive itineraries in hybrid mode.

The narration is supported by images and sounds and is inspired by specific elements of each plate (highlighted with drawings/photos that represent them in order to capture the attention and motivation of visitors with autism).

The digital visual notebook created with the App reproduces and depicts the five slabs presented in the room dedicated to the opera, for each of them there is an explanation of the meaning of that image and some single elements that are found on the image are highlighted.

The App allows visitors to identify the individual elements to highlight and simplifies and guides young visitors, especially autistic children, through images, colors and sounds appropriately selected and combined.

The educational visit available through the App represents an inclusive proposal that can be used by all: it allows the participation in the museum hall of people with autism together with their family members and/or classmates with whom they can interact and live a positive learning experience and socialization.

At the end of the narration through the storytelling of each work shown on the digital visual agenda (App), visitors are presented with the five basic emotions (represented by emoticons), and they are asked to identify one that represents their state of mind in relation to all the route taken (see Fig. 2).

The emotions and elements selected by visitors during the visit and reported on the visual agenda (App) are the memory of the visit also for a possible subsequent work at home and/or at school, allowing visitors to continue to review the images and experience the emotions and sensations perceived during the tour.

Visitors as users of this App are invited to write down a questionnaire (information sheet) for analyzing the specific needs before starting the visit supported by the App and at the end of the visit. The questionnaires aim to collect data and information about autistic children knowing their specific needs, as well as the motivation to participate of the families, satisfaction, previous experience at the museum, and so forth.

Fig. 2 Examples of the digital visual book

4.1 The App: Specific Aim and Characteristics

This App project can contribute to develop much more the research about the technological solutions adopted by museums for making themselves much more inclusive, comparing the results between the use of paper visual diary and digital visual diary. Otherwise, this App can enhance the educational offer of inclusive museum services to implement the territorial offer of proposals and activities for visitors with special needs with positive effects on the school and cultural tourism chain system.

Specifically, this App project aims to create:

- a tool for living the Museums and specifically the Archaeological Museum of Paestum and Velia for people with autism and their families (both have been involved with museum staff, operators, therapists in the planning phase of the activities and in the fruition phase through the compilation of the questionnaire booking and especially all of them, especially autistic children and their families were involved in the design process of the App) and the museum operators who will be trained in sharing the project and acquiring communication and management methods shared with the designers;
- a data monitoring and measurement tool aimed at the different groups involved, that is autistic children whose response data and perceptions are monitored and evaluated to analyse their visit by measuring the duration, frequency, latency times during the activities in order to improve the proposal based on their specific needs emerged; parents and families of autistic children, the perception of the model developed and applied, also in terms of impact on participation or social inclusion;

the museum staff and all the actors involved for assessing the level of satisfaction and participation in the proposal.

In addition, regarding the live management and operation for the App, some useful details are provided below:

- Dashboard management or control panel, through which to program, manage and control all aspects and functions of the virtual live;
- Live virtual tour scheduling date and time of live sessions, managing access and invitation methods for participants;
- Invitation and reminder via email to participants in live session events, that the platform will send automatically;
- One-click Live to start the virtual tour with a simple click;
- Conduction management of a media library dedicated to the museum in which to store and manage documents, textual and multimedia contents (audio and video) that can be shared with the participants in the live during the virtual tour;
- Moderation management service that can be used to moderate comments, questions and polls during the virtual tour;
- Virtual waiting room;
- Live recordings in MP4 of all live virtual tours;
- Report & Analytics of live shows with reference to actual participation of autistic children, students and families, duration of each live and access statistics.

Furthermore, this App project aims to contribute to make museums a very inclusive environment also for people with Autism, making possible to enjoy it using technological solutions.

Regarding the technical and functional features and graphic customization related to the App especially with concern of visiting museums remotely, here below there are some details:

- Social integration: to broadcast the live streams of the virtual tour also directly on YouTube and Facebook;
- One-click Social Sharing: users can share the virtual tour directly and easily on their social profiles;
- Live Media Sharing: museum operators interact with participants during the virtual tour by sharing documents, multimedia materials (audio and video), presentations, pdfs on the screen, thus making the remote live tour increasingly interactive;
- Screen Sharing: visitors can share with their desktop, an open document or a web page to all connected participants, stimulating engagement and improving learning during the virtual tour;
- Interactive whiteboard: visitors can take notes or comment live presentations and documents, using an interactive whiteboard-style drawing tool, to create graphics, drawings or insert notes;
- Question Time: organizers can make question and answer sessions, with moderation functionality of the conductor and textual or live answers;

- Live Surveys: visitors can take part in real-time surveys during virtual tours, stimulating active participation and involvement;
- Text and voice chat: participants can communicate through a public chat and in real time, with both text and voice messages;
- Request to speak: participants can speak during the tour session using a virtual "show of hands" tool, to speak live or share their screen (from desktop) or text or multimedia content.

This App briefly described has been already tested by few autistic children during a remote visit of the museum and by students from schools.

5 Concluding Remarks

This research provides a deep analysis of one interesting application of technologies in creating a virtual visual agenda for museums by children/young teenagers with Autism and their parents. The overall program used for the museum visit was built adopting a bottom-up approach and a participatory design directly involving all the partners and players of the research team, that is parents, operators and museum staff, especially autistic children for really know and meet their special needs.

Thanks to the self-reported questionnaires, focus group, interviews and direct observations in this first step of the App project, we can outline that there is totally satisfaction and good participation of parents, operators, staff, and especially the children/young teenagers with Autism. Although there are still some criticisms to manage for improving the App, also because limited to one specific area of the museum, the participants express positive opinion and consider their experience in being involved and actively participating to this project really comfortable, welcome and inclusive, having the opportunity to use an effective technological support for visiting the museum considering their specific needs.

In the future, we would like to incorporate the voices of the young individuals with Autism by collecting data from children, as well as their parents and teachers, as already some previous studies did [1, 4]. In this exploratory study we already collect some direct opinions by children thanks to the support of their parents and caregivers because it is very important and represents a unique and significant contribution to the field by investigating the families' motivations and needs when visiting museums [1, 4], especially for designing and developing technological solutions as useful support tools for making museums much more inclusive. Otherwise, as already outlined, some interesting studies outline the effectiveness and the positive impact in terms of social inclusion about the use of web-based resources and technologies in supporting individuals with ASD and specifically Autism in their museum visits [73–75].

In addition, in the next step of the entire project, the App will be completely and broadly used for visiting the Archeological Museum of Paestum and Velia, as well as in the future development of the research we should consider the idea to further develop the App with specific sections addressed to much more stimulate and involve the special visitors.

References

1. Varner, R.: Museums and visitors with autism: an overview of programs (2015)
2. Kulik, T.K., Fletcher, T.S.: Considering the museum experience of children with autism. Curator: Mus. J. **59**(1), 27–38 (2016)
3. Lussenhop, A., Mesiti, L.A., Cohn, E.S., Orsmond, G.I., Goss, J., Reich, C., Osipow, A., Pirri, K., Lindgren-Streicher, A.: Social participation of families with children with autism spectrum disorder in a science museum. Mus. Soc. Issues **11**(2), 122–137 (2016)
4. Langa, L.A., Monaco, P., Subramaniam, M., Jaeger, P.T., Shanahan, K., Ziebarth, B.: Improving the museum experiences of children with autism spectrum disorders and their families: an exploratory examination of their motivations and needs and using Web-based resources to meet them. Curator: Mus. J. **56**(3), 323–335 (2013)
5. Poria, Y., Reichel, A., Brandt, Y.: People with disabilities visit art museums: an exploratory study of obstacles and difficulties. J. Herit. Tour. **4**(2), 117–129 (2009)
6. López, B.B., Sánchez, I.M., Sánchez, G.M., Prakash, E.C., Buitrago, D.F.L., Navarro-Newbal, A.A.: Towards the smart museum: challenges from lab experimentation to deployment. Research Gate (in press)
7. Korzun, D., Varfolo-meyev, A., Yalovitsyna, S., Volokhova, V.: Semantic infrastructure of a smart museum: toward making cultural heritage knowledge usable and creatable by visitors and professionals. Pers. Ubiquitous Comput. **21**(2), 345–354 (2017)
8. Alletto, S., Cucchiara, R., Del Fiore, G., Mainetti, L., Mighali, V., Patrono, L., Serra, G.: An indoor location-aware system for an IoT-based smart museum. IEEE Internet Things J. **3**(2), 244–253 (2016)
9. Mibact – Ufficio statistica: Report visite e incassi musei statali italiani (2018)
10. Magkafa, D., Newbutt, N., Palmer, M.: Implementing co-design practices for the development of a museum interface for autistic children. In: Recent Advances in Technologies for Inclusive Well-Being: Virtual Patients, Gamification and Simulation, pp 421–443 (2021)
11. De Prado, J.E.L., Gago, A.R.A.: Education and ICT in inclusive museums environments. Int. J. Disabil. Dev. Educ. 1–15 (2020)
12. Varriale L., Briganti P., Ferrara M., Minucci G.: Archaeological museums for sustainable actions: one inclusive experience for children with austism. In: 19th Annual Conference European Academy of Management (EURAM), Lisboa University, 26–28 June 2019, Lisboa, Portugal (2019)
13. López-Martínez, A., Carrera, Á., Iglesias, C.A.: Empowering museum experiences applying gamification techniques based on linked data and smart objects. Appl. Sci. **10**(16), 5419 (2020)
14. Porfireanu, A., Ungurean, A., Dascălu, A., Iftene, A., Gîfu, D.: Smart museums with augmented reality. In: 5th Proceedings of the Conference on Mathematical Foundations of Informatics, pp. 258–294 (2019)
15. Rappolt-Schlichtmann, G., Daley, S.G.: Providing access to engagement in learning: The potential of Universal Design for Learning in museum design. Curator: Mus. J. **56**(3), 307–321 (2013)
16. Siountri, K., Skondras, E., Vergados, D.D.: Towards a smart museum using BIM, IoT, blockchain and advanced digital technologies. In: 2nd International Symposium on Computers and Communications (ISoCC 2019) (2019)
17. Ardito, C., Buono, P., Costabile, M.F., Desolda, G., Matera, M., Piccinno, A.: Towards enabling cultural-heritage experts to create customizable visit experiences. In: AVI* CH (2018)
18. Chianese, A., Piccialli, F.: Designing a smart museum: When cultural heritage joins IoT. In 2014 eighth international conference on next generation mobile apps, services and technologies (pp. 300–306). IEEE. (2014).
19. Hashemi, S.H., Kamps, J., Hupperetz, W.: Busy versus empty museums: effects of visitors' crowd on users' behaviors in smart museums. In: Tkalcic, M., Thakker, D., Germanakos, P., Yacef, K., Paris, C., Santos, O. (eds.) Adjunct Publication of the 25th Conference on User Modeling, Adaptation and Personalization (UMAP '17), pp. 333–334. ACM, New York, NY, USA (2017)

20. Mighali, V., Del Fiore, G., Patrono, L., Mainetti, L., Alletto, S., Serra, G., Cucchiara, R.: Innovative IoT-aware services for a smart museum. In: Proceedings of the 24th International Conference on World Wide Web (WWW '15 Companion), pp. 547–550. ACM, New York, NY, USA (2015)
21. Azuma, R.: Overview of augmented reality. In: ACM SIG-GRAPH 2004 Course Notes, SIGGRAPH 04, New York, NY, USA (2004)
22. National Federation of the Blind. National Federation of the Blind Resolutions for 2016|National Federation of the Blind (2016). https://nfb.org/2016-resolutions
23. Reich, C., Price, J., Rubin, E., Steiner, M.: Inclusion, disabilities, and informal science learning: a CAISE inquiry group report. Center for Advancement of Informal Science Education (2010)
24. Reich, C., Lindgren-Streicher, A., Beyer, M., Levent, N., Pursley, J., Mesiti, L.A.: Speaking out on art and museums: a study on the needs and preferences of adults who are blind or have low vision. Research Report #2011-3. Museum of Science, Boston, MA (2011). http://www.informalscience.org/sites/default/files/2013-07-03_Speaking_Out_110718.pdf
25. Linton, S.: My Body Politic: A Memoir. University of Michigan Press, Ann Arbor, MI (2006)
26. Canadian Museums Association. Museum definition. Canadian Museum Association (2007). Accessed 25 Nov 2018. http://www.museums.ca/en/info_resources/reports_guidlines/museum_defintion/
27. Platt, T.: What are museums for? Museums, object and representations. Anthropol. Today **3**(4), 13–16 (1987)
28. Soren, B.J.: Meeting the needs of museum visitors. In: Lord, G.D., Lord, B. (eds.) The Manual of Museum Planning, pp. 55–65. HMSO, London (1999)
29. Thompson, P.: Visitor with special needs. In: Lord, G.D., Lord, B. (eds.) The Manual of Museum Planning, pp. 69–74. HMSO, London (1999)
30. Stanfield, G.: Education and interpretation in natural history museums. In: Stanfield, G., Mathias, J., Reid, G. (eds.) Manual of Natural History Curatorship. HMSO, London (1994)
31. Asensio, M., Asenjo, E. (ed.) Blue light ties: Museums and technologies 1, 2 y 3.0 (7). UOC, Barcelona (2011)
32. Lidwell, W., Holden, K., Butler, J.: Universal Principles of Design, Revised and Updated: 125 Ways to Enhance Usability, Influence Perception, Increase Appeal, Make Better Design Decisions, and Teach Through Design. Rockport Publishers, Beverly, Massachusetts (2010)
33. Rodríguez, J.P.: Reflections on sustainable museography. Museos.es: Magazine of the Subdirección General De Museos Estatales **1**(7–8), 182–189 (2011)
34. Ramírez, J.S., Domínguez, M.G.M.: Reinventing the concept of the guided tour accessible through apps. Her&Mus. Heritage & Museography **16**, 141–150 (2015)
35. Garcia, H., Diaz, J., Krall, R., Sisinni, F.: Cultural differences in ARCHES: a European participatory research project—working with mixed access preferences in different cultural heritage sites. Int. J. Incl. Mus. **12**(3), 33–50 (2019)
36. Andrade, E.C., Delgado, R., Hauptner, B., Kerschbaum, F., List, R., Pobežalová, P., Wögerbauer, S.: Inclusive technologies in museums: For a better access to culture for blind and visually impaired people. Project AMBAVis, Vienna, Austria (2015). http://www.ambavis.eu/wp-content/uploads/2016/11/AMBAVis-Broschuere_BF_V01_EN_bf.pdf
37. Cavazos, L., Iranzo, J., Lee, S., Han, E., Kim, S., Cho, J.: An interactive multimodal guide to improve art accessibility for blind people. In: Proceedings of the 20th International ACM SIGACCESS Conference on Computers and Accessibility, pp. 346–348. ACM (2018). https://dl.acm.org/doi/10.1145/3234695
38. Friedman, B., Hendry, D.G., Borning, A.: A survey of value sensitive design methods. Found. Trends® Hum.–Comput. Interact. **11**(2), 63–125 (2017)
39. Guo, A., Kim, J., Chen, X.A., Yeh, T., Hudson, S.E., Mankoff, J., Bigham, J.P.: Facade: autogenerating tactile interfaces to appliances. In: Proceedings of the CHI Conference on Human Factors in Computing Systems, pp. 5826–5838. ACM, Denver, CO (2017). https://doi.org/10.1145/3025453.3025845
40. Zhao, Y., Cutrell, E., Holz, C., Morris, M.R., Ofek, E., Wilson, A.D.: Seeing VR: a set of tools to make virtual reality more accessible to people with low vision. In: Proceedings of the

CHI Conference on Human Factors in Computing Systems, vol. 111, pp. 1–14. AMC. Glasgow, Scotland UK (2019). https://www.microsoft.com/en-us/research/uploads/prod/2019/01/SeeingVRchi2019.pdf
41. Coleman, C.: In touch with culture: Inclusive engagement in museums for children with visual impairment in mainstream schools. In: Eleventh International Conference on the Inclusive Museum Inclusion as Shared Vision: Museums and Sharing Heritage. Granada, Spain (2018). https://onmuseums.com/assets/downloads/museum/Z18-Final-Program.pdf
42. Veloso, A.: Design and application of technological solutions in the information management of the museum project of the computer museum. Doctoral dissertation, Universitat Politècnica de València (2019). https://n9.cl/c7j1
43. Vaz, R.I.F., Fernandes, P.O., Veiga, A.C.R.: Interactive technologies in museums: How digital installations and media are enhancing the visitors' experience. In: Handbook of Research on Technological Developments for Cultural Heritage and eTourism Applications, pp. 30–53. IGI Global (2018)
44. APA (American Psychiatric Association): The Diagnostic and Statistical Manual of Mental Disorders: DSM 5. BookpointUS, Washington, DC (2014)
45. Antonetti, A., Fletcher, T.: Parent perceptions of museum participation: a comparison between parents of children with and without autism spectrum disorders. Inclusion **4**(2), 109–119 (2016)
46. Stahmner, A.C., Akshoomoff, N., Cunningham, A.B.: Inclusion for toddlers with autism spectrum disorders: the first ten years of a community program. Autism **15**(5), 625–641 (2011)
47. Lam, S., Wong, B.P.H., Leung, D., Ho, D., Au-Yeung, P.: How parents perceive and feel about participation in community activities: the comparison between parents of preschoolers with and without autism spectrum disorders. Autism **14**(4), 359–377 (2010)
48. Alexander, J.M., Kollmann E., Iacovelli S.: Opening our doors to visitors with autism through museum educator professional development. Museum of Science, Boston, MA (2012)
49. Little, L.M., Rojas, J.P., Bard, A., Luo, Y., Irvin, D., Rous, B.: Automated measures to understand communication opportunities for young children with autism in the community: a pilot study. OTJR: Occup. Particip. Health **39**(2), 124–130 (2019)
50. Orsmond, G.I., Krauss, M.W., Seltzer, M.M.: Peer relationships and social and recreational activities among adolescents and adults with autism. J. Autism Dev. Disord. **34**(3), 245–256 (2004)
51. Kagohara, D., Van der Meer, L., Ramdoss, S.S., O'Reilly, M., Lancioni, G., Davis, T., Rispoli, M., Lang, R., Marschik, P., Sutherland, D., Green, V., Sigafoos, J.: Using iPods and iPads in teaching programs for individuals with developmental disabilities: a systematic review. Res. Dev. Disabil. **34**(1), 147–156 (2013)
52. Parsons, S., Cobb, S.: Reflections on the role of the 'users': challenges in a multi-disciplinary context of learner-centred design for children on the autism spectrum. Int. J. Res. Method Edu. **37**(4), 421–441 (2014)
53. Davis, M., Dautenhahn, K., Powell, S., Nehaniv, C.: Guidelines for researchers and practitioners designing software and software trials for children with autism. J. Assist. Technol **4**(1), 38–44 (2010)
54. Putnam, C., Chong, L.: Software and technologies designed for people with autism: what do users want? In: International Conference of the 10th International ACM SIGACCESS Conference on Computers and Accessibility, pp. 3–10 (15) (2008)
55. Millen, L., Edlin-White, R., Cobb, S.: The development of educational collaborative virtual environments for children with autism. In: Proceedings of 5th Cambridge Workshop on Universal Access and Assistive Technology (CWUAAT 2010), pp. 1–7 (2010)
56. Ploog, B., Scharf, A., Nelson, D., Brooks, P.: Use of computer- assisted technologies (CAT) to enhance social, communicative and language development in children with autism spectrum disorders. Autism Dev. Disord. **43**, 301–322 (2013)
57. Rogers, Y., Sharp, H., Preece, J.: Interaction Design: Beyond Human-Computer Interaction, 3rd edn. Wiley, Chichester (2011)
58. Brown, D.J., McHugh, D., Standen, P., Evett, L., Shopland, N., Battersby, S.: Designing location-based learning experiences for people with intellectual disabilities and additional sensory impairments. Comput. Educ. **56**(1), 11–20 (2011)

59. Spinuzzi, C.: The methodology of participatory design. Tech. Commun. **52**(2), 163–174 (2005)
60. Muller, M.J., Druin, A.: Participatory design: the third space in HCI. In: Jacko, J. (ed.) The Human-Computer Interaction Handbook, 3rd edn., pp. 273–291. Taylor & Francis, New York (2011)
61. Fails, J.A., Guha, M.L., Druin, A.: Methods and techniques for involving children in the design of new technology for children. Found. Trends Hum. Comput. Interact. **6**(2), 85–166 (2012)
62. Druin, A.: The role of children in the design of new technology. Behav. Inf. Technol. **21**(1), 1–25 (2002)
63. Marchetti, E., Valente, A: A tangible digital installation in the classroom: role play and autistic children. In: European Conference on Games Based Learning, p. 346. Academic Conferences International Limited (2015)
64. Marchetti, E., Valente, A.: What a tangible digital installation for museums can offer to autistic children and their teachers. Int. J. Game-Based Learn. (IJGBL) **6**(2), 29–45 (2016)
65. Giaconi, C., Ascenzi, A., Del Bianco, N., D'Angelo, I., Capellini, S.A.: Virtual and augmented reality for the cultural accessibility of people with autism spectrum disorders: a pilot study. Int. J. Incl. Mus. **14**(1) (2021)
66. Garzotto, F., Matarazzo, V., Messina, N., Gelsomini, M., Riva, C.: Improving museum accessibility through storytelling in wearable immersive virtual reality. In 2018 3rd Digital Heritage International Congress (DigitalHERITAGE) held jointly with 2018 24th International Conference on Virtual Systems & Multimedia (VSMM 2018), pp. 1–8. IEEE (2018)
67. Magkafa, D., Newbutt, N.: The process of involving children with autism in the design of a museum-based application. MW18: MW 2018 (2018)
68. Hourcade, J.P., Bullock-Rest, N.E., Hansen, T.E.: Multi- touch tablet applications and activities to enhance the social skills of children with autism spectrum disorders. Pers. Ubiquit. Comput. **16**(157–168), 36 (2012)
69. Frauenberger, C., Good, J., Alcorn, A., Pain, H.: Supporting the design contributions of children with autism spectrum conditions. In: Proceedings of the 11th International Conference on Interaction Design and Children, pp. 134–143. ACM (2012)
70. Benton, L., Johnson, H., Ashwin, E., Brosnan, M., Grawemeyer, B.: Developing IDEAS: supporting children with autism within a participatory design team. In: Proceedings of the SIGCHI Conference on Human Factors in Computing Systems, pp. 2599–2608 (2012)
71. Benton, L., Vasalou, A., Khaled, R., Johnson, H., Gooch, D.: Diversity for design: a framework for involving neurodiverse children in the technology design process. In: Proceedings of the SIGCHI Conference on Human Factors in Computing Systems, pp. 3747–3756. ACM (2014)
72. Malinverni, L., Mora-Guiard, J., Padillo, V., Mairena, M., Hervás, A., Pares, N.: Participatory design strategies to enhance the creative contribution of children with special needs. In: Proceedings of the 2014 Conference on Interaction Design and Children, pp. 85–94. ACM (2014)
73. Graham, H.: All Access Digital Arts camp report. Unpublished manuscript. Smithsonian Institution, Washington, DC. Retrieved from http://museumstudies.si.edu/Helen percent20Graham percent20All. (2011).
74. Graham, H.: Museums and how to know about access. New Form. **79**(79), 64–82 (2013)
75. New Learning Institute All Access: The Smithsonian Institution Multimedia Camp for High School Students with Cognitive or Intellectual Disabilities. Unpublished manuscript, Smithsonian Institution, Washington, DC (2011). http://newlearninginstitute.org/all-access-smithsonian-institutionmultimedia-camp-high-school-studentscognitive-or-intellectual

Smart City's Internationalization and International Management Strategies in the Digital Era: A Systematic Literature Review

Filippo Marchesani, Lea Iaia, Francesca Masciarelli, and Michael Christofi

Abstract The impact of the smart city concept in the urban landscape has been the subject of considerable attention over the last few years. Cities are changing their development strategies by trying to attract not only capital but also knowledge and talent. This change has led cities to turn increasingly to the outside world by developing international strategies and raising their internationalization process towards the global context. The purpose of the paper is to develop a systematic overview of the literature examining the relationship between smart cities and the internationalization process. Emphasis will be placed on global management strategies for the international development of smart cities. The study aims to examine existing research through the adaptation of the Systems Literature Review (SLR). As a result, new knowledge on the state of the art in policy, practice, and academia can be generated to identify significant theoretical insights and knowledge gaps for future research. We provide a descriptive analysis, a state of the art of research topic, and an integrative vision of the development of smart cities concerning international management and the internationalization process.

Keywords Smart cities · Internationalization · Systematic literature review · International strategies

F. Marchesani (✉) · L. Iaia · F. Masciarelli
Department of Management and Business Administration, University of Gabriele 'd Annunzio Chieti-Pescara, Chieti, Italy
e-mail: filippo.merchesani@unich.it

L. Iaia
e-mail: lea.iaia@unich.it

F. Masciarelli
e-mail: francesca.masciarelli@unich.it

M. Christofi
School of Management and Economics, Cyprus University of Technology, Limassol, Cyprus
e-mail: michael.christofi@cut.ac.cy

S. Za et al. (eds.), *Sustainable Digital Transformation*, Lecture Notes in Information Systems and Organisation 59, https://doi.org/10.1007/978-3-031-15770-7_10

1 Theoretical Background

The expression 'smart city' has recently become important in discussions about the city and urban development [1]. The term 'smart' has commonly been used to explain a new vision of city development. Harrison et al. [2] defines a smart city as a city that connects physical infrastructure, IT infrastructure, social infrastructure, and business infrastructure to leverage the collective intelligence of the city. As this paper explains, the Internet of Things (IoT), Information and communication technology (ICT) and the internationalization process are changing the way cities organize policy-making and urban growth [3].

Smart Cities base their international developing strategies on the adoption of IoT and ICT in several fields such as economy, environment, mobility, sustainability, citizens engagement, and governance to transform the infrastructure and services of the city [1].

In today's contemporary urban context, policymakers, and governance in cities around the world are increasingly seeking strategies through concepts and channels in the attempt to engage and connect with their stakeholders [4]. In particular, much hope is placed on the use of IoT, ICT, web 2.0 interactivity and, social media which for the first time provide channels for connecting the city governance to the various stakeholders such as company, citizens, entrepreneurs, and policymakers [5]. Consequently, smart cities strongly rely on international strategies and solutions enabled by ICTs directly involving local governments, citizens, and communities [6] and moving toward more comprehensive and global governance [7].

In recent years there has been an exponential growth of projects for the international development of the city [8]. For example, Barcelona has an established reputation as a pioneering European smart city and has integrated a series of municipal government initiatives to promote the intersection of "international promotion," "international collaboration," and "local projects" [9]. Furthermore, in a recent study related to the competitive urbanism, Buck and While [10] combine information about firms and governments to find effective and transferable demonstrations of advanced urban technology. By examine initiatives by the UK national government focusing on London, Glasgow, Bristol and Peterborough, this study evaluates the urban technological innovation through a range of national and international strategies, particularly the TSB Future Cities Demonstrator Competition, to explore opportunities and tensions in the practical realization of the smart city concept.

For cities, the development through the evolution of IoT and ICT represents a fundamental driver for their economic growth [11]. This expansion highlights that cities are becoming more and more digitally dependent [12] and competitive in terms of social policies [13]. besides, the role of international management strategies and the internationalization process in the smart city context is still considered an unexplored theme as well as the impact of new technologies on smart city development in the digital era [14]. As for global businesses, cities' internationalization process requires strategies and planning to be globally competitive and attract knowledge, capital, and human capital [15].

To fill this gap in the literature, this article reviews the impact of international management strategies on the smart city over 11 years (2009–2020) by aiming to provide a more comprehensive understanding of the role played by city management strategies in the smart city context. The objectives of this paper are to develop a systematic review on the theme in order to review the existent research, provide new knowledge on the state of art for policies, practitioner, and academics, and finding the relevant theoretical insights for future research. As a main part of our work, to gasps the relationship among international management strategies and the development of smart cities, we consider the widely accepted classification of international management research highlighted by Pisani [15, 16] as a central element of our work.

Based on this view, we aim to systematically review the existing literature and discuss the different potential implications for researchers, managers and policymakers with concrete suggestions for this field. In doing this, our manuscript is structured as follows. We begin with a analysis and discussion of the key methodological options used in our review. We explain the research criteria such as database sources, keywords, inclusion and exclusion criteria, and the main steps used to identify the final sample of studies. Following that procedure, we also provide qualitative information on journal details, year of publication, and field of research.

We rely on the widely accepted classification of international management research highlighted by Pisani [15, 16] to group articles and have a clear picture of the current publications. This led to a better understanding of the main city's international management strategies and their relationship to the development of smart cities. The last section provides the theoretical and practical implications that arise from studies that consider and advise other topics for future research.

The systematic literature review is motivated by a defined research question, from which the search strategy for identifying the related articles is determined based on a dialogue between the authors as regards to: the identification of the research gaps; the evaluation of the role of a new field such as international management strategies in smart city development, and the importance to underline a comprehensive overview of the topic. To achieve this research aim, we undertake a systematic literature review of international strategies into the smart cities development and pose the following research question: "*How do internationalization and international management influence the smart city development into the global panorama?*".

Through a systematic process of research, this review contributes to provide policy advice, practice and theoretical recommendations and future avenues that governments of smart cities, practitioners and scholars could use for the smart cities development into internationalization process.

2 Methodology

In this manuscript, we used the systematic literature review methodology in reviewing existing research, as it considered a robust method to review key findings of large and multifaceted research area [17]. Adding to this, it provides the method to identify, select, analyze and synthesize existing literature in a rigorous and replicable manner, and permit us to provide robust conclusions about the outcomes as well as a depth analysis of the reviewed area itself [18, 19].

To conduct the analysis, we relied on EBSCOhost's Business Source Premier database as the main source of research as it offers solid coverage of key reference journals [20]. Following the literature review practice, we performed a keyword search on the study titles, abstracts, and subject terms [21]. Our keyword selection is based on an analysis of previous literature reviews published in major reference journals concerning international strategies also used in other literature review [21, 22] and the notion of Smart Cities [23]. We have chosen to use the city's international marketing strategies (which include keywords on internationalization) to gain a wider understanding of the city's international strategies. Follow the previous protocol, 1608 potentially relevant studies emerged from this research.

To better understand the international dimension of smart cities, we decided to exclude national studies. Thus, our research was redesigned to include studies focusing on the international vision of smart cities and the process of internationalization of the city itself due to improve our understanding of smart city development strategies on the international scene. Finally, we determined the exclusion and inclusion criteria by referring to the key practices used in the systematic reviews [24].

We excluded non-academic and non-peer-reviewed articles, articles written in a language other than English as well as articles not related to the economic and managerial context. Concerning the time frame, our research considered the timeline from 2009 to 2020. We established a cutoff point from 2009, following the evolution of the smart city concept at global level and due to the international development of the smart city policy and strategies [25]. Starting from this point, an increasing number of studies followed, which used the smart city concept into the city context as we intend it now [1, 25].

The application of these exclusionary criteria limited the results of our sample to 630 selected studies. Based on these 630 studies, we used a quality criterion to better identify our sample. Manuscripts were identified by leading international journals to capture the main components of our research question [21]. In particular, we considered only the studies published in a top journal to ensure a high level of quality. Thus, we only considered studies published in rating 3, 4, and 4* journals of all categories in the 2018 academic guide of the Association of Business Schools (www.charteredabs.org).

Using this criterion, 53 articles with classification 3, 4 and, 4* were identified. Further analysis was done by reading the abstracts, introductions, and conclusions of the identified studies to asset the topic of the international management field and to ensure the rigorous procedure. This process yielded a total of 42 studies. Of these, 10 were subsequently excluded on the basis of the reading of the integral text, leaving 32 relevant articles. In addition, we also adopt the cross-references analysis [26] to make sure we did not ignore any articles checking each reference in the selected studies. This additional process added 9 items to our sample. The identified articles were reviewed and eligibility for inclusion was determined through the same process as previously. Following this step, 9 articles were found to be in line with our research process, highlighting a final sample of 41 articles.

3 Results

Using the SLR methods in this paper we provide a descriptive analysis, a state of the art about the research topic, and an integrative vision of the development of smart cities concerning international management and the internationalization process. Moreover, this paper captures the evolution of scientific production at the intersection of smart cities and internationalization strategies by systematically tracking the evolution of these topics in the selected documents.

3.1 Descriptive Analysis

Since 2009, the number of articles published over the years, except the first period due to the not clear understanding of the smart city concept, had an increasing trend. Table 2 shows a growing trend, with a peak of the number of articles published during the last years in 2018 (N = 7), 2019 (N = 4) and in the first part of 2020 (N = 7 until 31 August).

Even though this research domain was initiated in the past decades, the findings show that as a research area especially in terms of IoT and Information Communication Technology ICT is at a youth stage and grows to a fast degree. More specifically, the findings in Table 1 show that scholarly research has intensified in the second half of the past decade (2015), which is the reference period for the existence of this stream of research. Interestingly, 71% of papers were published in journals in the past five years and 41% of papers were published in the last three years.

Furthermore, as we can see in Fig. 1, extant research had been published in a wide array of publication outlets (15 journals ranked 3,4 and 4* ABS) from various disciplines, including different research are such as Regional Studies, Planning and Environment (N = 14), Information Management (N = 13), Operations and Technology Management (N = 3), General Management, Ethics, Gender and Social Responsibility, Innovation and Public Sector and Health Care (N = 4) and Economics, Econometrics and Statistics (N = 1). This reflects a growing interest in regional and city development as well as its managerial interpretation and the spread of publications on the field of information management in recent years. This conception takes on increasing importance in the development and strategies of cities, which broaden their national and international development field through internationalization strategies.

Table 1 Research area and years of publication

	Regional. Studies, Plan, and Env	Info man	Ethics-CSR-Man	Innovation	OPS & Tech	Pub sec	Econ	Tot
2009	1							1
2010								
2011		1						1
2012		1						1
2013	2							2
2014	3	1		1	1			6
2015	4					1		5
2016		1	3			1		5
2017	2	2						4
2018		2		1	1	2		6
2019	1	3						4
2020	1	2		1	1		1	6
Tot	14	13	3	3	3	4	1	41

3.2 *International Management Perspective in Cities*

To understand the relation between smart cities strategies and international management strategies, we considered a widely accepted classification of international management research, as reported, and briefly summarized in Table 2, and coded articles accordingly. In the following classification, we used 12 categories to organize and group works related to International Management (IM) research [16, 26, 27]. The list is quite comprehensive because it includes all the principal aspects of international management. While it should not be considered a conclusive classification of IM research, it can be regarded as a well-organized framework to categorize articles in this field and it is still used in numerous researches in the most important journals [16, 27]. Table 3 briefly synthesize the outcomes of the classification of our sample according to the 12 categories of international management research.

As we can see in Table 3, the principal international management categories observed are global business environment (51% N = 21) [3], e.g. [29, 30] by evaluating the "global economy, global markets, political and regulatory environments, and international risk" represent one of the most important areas to connect international management and smart city governance.

It is also interesting looking at the categories "transfer of knowledge" and "Internationalization" which represent respectively 22% (N = 9) and 19% (N = 8) of our sample. Several papers looking at the relation between smart city context and stakeholder [31], e.g. [32] by focusing on the development and implementation of the knowledge process in the city itself. Besides, the internationalization process

Table 2 Categories of international management research

Global business environment	Global economy, global markets, political and regulatory environments, and international risk
Internationalization	Description and measurement of internationalization, antecedents, and consequences of internationalization
Entry mode decisions	Predictors of entry mode choices, predictors of international equity ownership levels, and consequences of entry mode decision
International joint ventures	International joint venture partner selection, partner relations, and consequences of international joint ventures
Foreign direct investment	The timing, motivations, location of foreign direct investment, and firm and host country consequences
International exchange	International exchange, determinants of exporting, export intermediaries, and consequences of exporting
Transfer of knowledge	Antecedents of knowledge transfer, processes of knowledge transfer, and consequences of knowledge transfer
Strategic alliances and networks	Strategic alliance relationships, networks of strategic alliances, and outcomes of strategic alliances
Multinational enterprises	Multinational enterprise strategies and policies, and models and descriptions of the multinational enterprise
Subsidiary-headquarters relations	Subsidiary role (including subsidiary strategies and typologies), subsidiary control, and subsidiary performance
Subsidiary and multinational team management	Subsidiary human resource management practices, subsidiary behaviours, multinational negotiations, and multinational team management
Expatriate management	Expatriate human resource management, issues for expatriates, and expatriate and repatriate reactions

Sources Pisani [16], Werner [28]

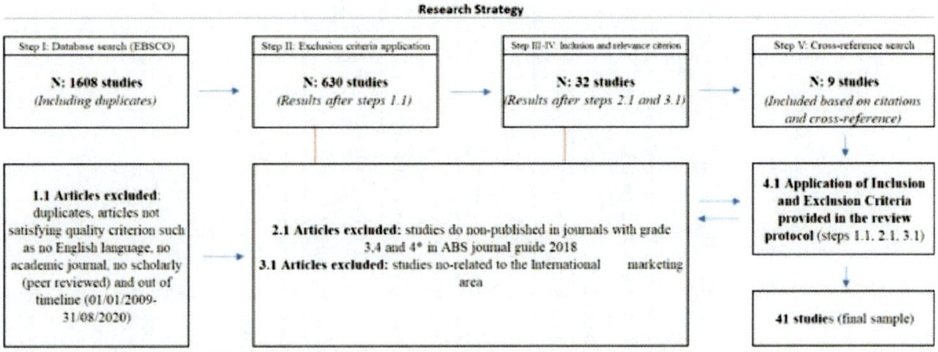

Fig. 1 Search strategy

Table 3 International management categories per years

Categories	2009	2010	2011	2012	2013	2014	2015	2016	2017	2018	2019	2020	Tot
Global business environment					2	3	2	2	3	3	3	3	21
Internationalization				1		1	1			3	1	1	8
Transfer of knowledge	1		1				2	1	1	1		2	9
Entry mode decisions								1				1	2
Strategic alliances and networks								1					1
Multinational enterprises													0
Subsidiary-headquarters relations													0
Subsidiary and multinational team management													0
Expatriate management													0
International joint ventures													0
Foreign direct investment													0
International exchange													0
	1	0	1	1	2	6	5	5	4	6	4	6	41

represents a key element of growth and development of the smart city concept by following the impact of IoT and Communication technologies into the smart city policy [32–34], e.g. [35].

The rest of the studies rely on "entry mode decision" (5%) and "strategic alliance and networks" (3%). No articles were grouped in the other categories although these perspectives may also be relevant for smart city research. For instance, the international exchange could be an interesting field of research in terms of city network and international management strategies between smart city dynamics.

Consequently, the government and policymakers must consider not only the internal management of the city but also the global competition and well-defined international management strategies [36] based on the currently existing tools such as IoT and ICT. These findings indicate the importance of the role played by policymakers and government in the life of smart cities and the close relationship between smart city governance and city stakeholders.

3.3 Methodology Applied in the International Management Area

The present section proceeds to evaluate the principal methodologies implemented in our sample by the categories of international management.

The theoretical articles capture about 30%. As consequence, the majority of paper are empirical (63%) especially focusing on the qualitative method (48%), followed by mixed methods (13%) and quantitative methods (7%). The rest of the paper are a literature review (7%). Moreover, the distribution of these methodologies over the years is particularly appealing.

The research evolution beginning with qualitative methods and theoretical publications as we can see in Table 4. In this sense, the peak of publications within the years, 2015–2016 were theoretical and qualitative research, (25%). Thus, because of the great development of the concept of smart city is in the following years as quantitative studies have been implemented in this research area. likewise, there is a strong increase in terms of quantitative (20%) studies in recent years.

This short description has made the case that smart city research is at a relatively early stage regarding its theoretical development and empirical understanding. While the term has increased popular traction amongst academics, businesses, government and media, the concept itself tends to be more theoretical than practice and need futures empirical evidence in the next years. Given how quickly the smart city concept has gained traction and been translated into different forms of networked urbanism, reshaping city administration and urban economic development it is important to push the research stream into the practice of smart city.

As noted previously, the "Global business environment" encompasses most of the research that emerged in our sample. Research in this category is mainly theoretical and qualitative, with a large number of interviews and case studies. In the "Transfer of

Table 4 International management categories per methodology

Categories	Theoretical	Review	Empirical			Total
			Quantitative	Qualitative	Mixed-Methods	No. %
Global business environment	7	2	1	10	1xzz	21
Transfer of knowledge	3			3	3	9
Internationalization	2		1	5		8
Entry mode decisions			1	1		2
Strategic alliances and networks	1					1
International joint ventures						0
Foreign direct investment						0
International exchange						0
Multinational enterprises						0
Subsidiary-headquarters relations						0
Subsidiary and multinational team management						0
Expatriate management						0

knowledge" category, theoretical, qualitative, and mixed methods are implemented by the research equally. In the "Internationalization" and "Entry mode decisions" categories, the first qualitative studies were carried out mainly in recent years.

These data show that the relationship between international marketing and smart cities is still in a preliminary stage, where theoretical and qualitative studies attempt to study this phenomenon. Interestingly, recent empirical demonstrations combined with the theoretical framework produced by academics and practitioners provide evidence of the central role of internationalization strategies in the development of smart cities.

4 Conclusion and Discussion

Our analysis shows a growing development of the relation between international management and the development of smart cities underlying the strong openness of cities to the international context. The international context leads cities to compete in different areas such as human capital, knowledge, financial capital, tourism, and innovation. This work provides an initial overview of the role of international management in the development of smart cities.

The existing literature shows that international city management strategies are currently in a preliminary phase. Even though cities are evolving towards a digital and increasingly competitive environment, the development of international strategies is still embryonic. This awareness is confirmed by the analysis of the literature that demonstrates mainly theoretical and qualitative papers combined, only in recent years, by growing empirical research on the subject. From this perspective, the principal drivers emerging from this analysis mainly concern three categories: Global business environment, Internationalization, and Transfer of knowledge, which summarize the current need for cities to move from a local to an international and competitive context in order to attract knowledge, human and financial capital.

Cities should build their smart city models from an entrepreneurial point of view with well-defined strategies to be competitive and develop on a national and international level [22, 37].

This study is a valuable insight into the development and implementation of international strategies to promote smart cities. Strategies can drive this new wave of change in redefining the relationship between the city and its stakeholders nationally and internationally [38]. To increase synergy and push towards a development increasingly aimed at international openness, professionals in the sector must improve coordination between policymakers and the various actors involved using technological and innovative tools increasingly present in Smart Cities [39, 40].

The emerging picture shows a growing corporate vision of the city and its need to be developed, supported, and promoted both locally and internationally [41]. Moreover, this study provides valuable information to policymakers and government by illustrating the effective impact of international management strategies on the opening of smart cities in the global panorama. Therefore, government and policymakers must invest in ICT and IoT to sustain national and international strategies and improve relationships with our stakeholders.

This research, like any other systematic review, is subject to structural limitations. Firstly, we privileged reading in an international key, to the exclusion of some valid articles that did not fall within the concept of international development. Secondly, the use of keywords in the search formula and the use of specific databases may have resulted in a lack of potentially relevant literature. However, we believe firmly that the identified publications are representative of the current literature on the subject.

Moreover, the perspective of international management is still in a rather preliminary phase. Although the concept of internationalization and international strategies of the city has attracted scholars and practitioners in recent years, there is still no univocal vision regarding the management and development of smart cities' strategies from a managerial point of view. For this reason, we have decided to implement a widely accepted classification at the academic level to consider cities as companies that compete in the global landscape.

Future research could study this emerging relationship not only by assessing the relationship between governance and the city's international development but also in terms of emerging global competitiveness. In addition, as emerges from our sample, future research should focus on quantitative research that is useful for confirming, modifying, or consolidating the essentially theoretical developments observed so far.

References

1. Albino, V., Berardi, U., Dangelico, R.M.: Smart cities: definitions, dimensions, performance, and initiatives. J. Urban Technol. (2015)
2. Harrison, C., et al.: Foundations for smarter cities. IBM J. Res. Dev. **54**(4) (2010)
3. Gil-Garcia, J.R., Zhang, J., Puron-Cid, G.: Conceptualizing smartness in government: an integrative and multi-dimensional view. Gov. Inf. Q. **33**(3), 524–534 (2016)
4. Nam, T., Pardo, T.A.: The changing face of a city government: a case study of Philly311. Gov. Inf. Q. **31**(SUPPL.1), S1–S9 (2014)
5. Kumar, S., Mookerjee, V., Shubham, A.: Research in operations management and information systems interface. Prod. Oper. Manag. **27**(11), 1893–1905 (2018)
6. Silva, B.N., Khan, M., Han, K.: Towards sustainable smart cities: a review of trends, architectures, components, and open challenges in smart cities. Sustain. Cities Soc. **38** (2018)
7. Vinod Kumar, T.M.: Smart environment for smart cities. In: Advances in 21st Century Human Settlements (2020)
8. Romão, J., Kourtit, K., Neuts, B., Nijkamp, P.: The smart city as a common place for tourists and residents: a structural analysis of the determinants of urban attractiveness. Cities **78**, 67–75 (2018)
9. de Falco, S., Angelidou, M., Addie, J.P.D.: From the 'smart city' to the 'smart metropolis'? Building resilience in the urban periphery. Eur. Urban Reg. Stud. **26**(2), 205–223 (2019)
10. Buck, N.T., While, A.: Competitive urbanism and the limits to smart city innovation: the UK future cities initiative. Urban Stud. **54**(2), 501–519 (2017)
11. Lamberton, C., Stephen, A.T.: A thematic exploration of digital, social media, and mobile marketing: Research evolution from 2000 to 2015 and an agenda for future inquiry. J. Mark. **80**(6), 146–172 (2016)
12. Camboim, G.F., Zawislak, P.A., Pufal, N.A.: Driving elements to make cities smarter: evidences from European projects. Technol. Forecast. Soc. Change **142**, 154–167 (2019)
13. Herrschel, T.: Competitiveness and sustainability: can 'smart city regionalism' square the circle? Urban Stud. **50**(11), 2332–2348 (2013)
14. Krishnan, B., Arumugam, S., Maddulety, K.: Critical success factors for the digitalization of smart cities. Int. J. Technol. Manag. Sustain. Dev. **19**(1), 69–86 (2020)
15. Ismagilova, E., Hughes, L., Dwivedi, Y.K., Raman, K.R.: Smart cities: advances in research—an information systems perspective. Int. J. Inf. Manag. (2019)
16. Pisani, N.: International management research: investigating its recent diffusion in top management journals. J. Manag. **35**(2), 199–218 (2009)
17. Denyer, D., Tranfield, D.: Producing a systematic review. In: The SAGE Handbook of Organizational Research Methods (2009)
18. Gaur, A., Kumar, M.: A systematic approach to conducting review studies: An assessment of content analysis in 25 years of IB research. J. World Bus. (2018)
19. Atewologun, D., Kutzer, R., Doldor, E., Anderson, D., Sealy, R.: Individual-level foci of identification at work: a systematic review of the literature. Int. J. Manag. Rev. (2017)
20. Bhimani, H., Mention, A.L., Barlatier, P.J.: Social media and innovation: A systematic literature review and future research directions. Technol. Forecast. Soc. Change (2019)
21. Leonidou, E., Christofi, M., Vrontis, D., Thrassou, A.: An integrative framework of stakeholder engagement for innovation management and entrepreneurship development. J. Bus. Res. (2018)
22. İpek, İ.: The relevance of international marketing strategy to emerging-market exporting firms: from a systematic review towards a conceptual framework. Int. Mark. Rev. (2020)
23. Yigitcanlar, T., Kankanamge, N., Vella, K.: How are smart city concepts and technologies perceived and utilized? A systematic geo-twitter analysis of smart cities in Australia. J. Urban Technol. (2020)
24. Danese, P., Manfè, V., Romano, P.: A systematic literature review on recent lean research: state-of-the-art and future directions. Int. J. Manag. Rev. (2018)
25. Paskaleva, K.A.: Enabling the smart city: the progress of city e-governance in Europe. Int. J. Innov. Reg. Dev. (2009)

26. Nofal, A.M., Nicolaou, N., Symeonidou, N., Shane, S.: Biology and management: a review, critique, and research agenda. J. Manag. (2018)
27. Pisani, N., Ricart, J.E.: Offshoring of services: a review of the literature and organizing framework. Manag. Int. Rev. **56**(3), 385–424 (2016)
28. Werner, S.: Recent developments in international management research: a review of 20 top management journals. J. Manag. (2002)
29. Gibbs, D., Krueger, R., MacLeod, G.: Grappling with smart city politics in an era of market triumphalism. Urban Stud. **50**(11), 2151–2157 (2013)
30. Chatfield, A.T., Reddick, C.G.: A framework for Internet of Things-enabled smart government: a case of IoT cybersecurity policies and use cases in U.S. federal government. Gov. Inf. Q. **36**(2), 346–357 (2019)
31. Berrone, P., Ricart, J.E., Carrasco, C.: The open kimono: toward a general framework for open data initiatives in cities. Calif. Manag. Rev. **59**(1), 39–70 (2016)
32. Stock, W.G.: Informational cities: analysis and construction of cities in the knowledge society. J. Am. Soc. Inf. Sci. Technol. (2011)
33. Paskaleva, K., Cooper, I.: Open innovation and the evaluation of internet-enabled public services in smart cities. Technovation **78**, 4–14 (2018)
34. Kumar, M., Graham, G., Hennelly, P., Srai, J.: How will smart city production systems transform supply chain design: a product-level investigation. Int. J. Prod. Res. **54**(23), 7181–7192 (2016)
35. El-Haddadeh, R., Weerakkody, V., Osmani, M., Thakker, D., Kapoor, K.K.: Examining citizens' perceived value of internet of things technologies in facilitating public sector services engagement. Gov. Inf. Q. **36**(2), 310–320 (2019)
36. Sofronijevic, A., Milicevic, V., Ilic, B.: Smart city as framework for creating competitive advantages in international business management. Manag. - J. Theory Pract. Manag. **19**(71), 5–16 (2014)
37. Cohen, B., Amorós, J.E.: Municipal demand-side policy tools and the strategic management of technology life cycles. Technovation **34**(12), 797–806 (2014)
38. Kitchin, R.: Making sense of smart cities: addressing present shortcomings. Camb. J. Reg. Econ. Soc. **8**(1), 131–136 (2015)
39. Gagliardi, D., Schina, L., Sarcinella, M.L., Mangialardi, G., Niglia, F., Corallo, A.: Information and communication technologies and public participation: interactive maps and value added for citizens. Gov. Inf. Q. **34**(1), 153–166 (2017)
40. Fortino, G., Russo, W., Savaglio, C., Shen, W., Zhou, M.: Agent-oriented cooperative smart objects: From IoT system design to implementation. IEEE Trans. Syst. Man Cybern. Syst. **48**(11), 1949–1956 (2018)
41. Reinartz, W., Wiegand, N., Imschloss, M.: The impact of digital transformation on the retailing value chain. Int. J. Res. Mark. (2019)
42. Christofi, M., Iaia, L., Marchesani, F., Masciarelli, F.: Marketing innovation and internationalization in smart city development: a systematic review, framework and research agenda. Int. Mark. Rev. **38**(5), 948–984 (2021). https://doi.org/10.1108/IMR-01-2021-0027

Sustainability in Digital Transformation

Assessing Capabilities to Embrace Digital Transformation: The Case of Southern Italy

Nabila Abid, Filippo Marchesani, Federica Ceci, and Francesca Masciarelli

Abstract Southern Italy has been confronting dire economic and resource scarcity challenges to keep up with the national growth. Digitalization is a changing phenomenon that transforms the firm's structure and enhances production, operational, and service efficiency helping to reduce economic and geographical disparity. Firms play a crucial role in the development of an economy. In the recent decade, digital transformation has emerged as a driver for economic growth and urban development by transitioning the firms' processes. However, firms need sufficient institutional support during the digital transition process. The Italian government has taken substantial initiatives to stabilize and boost the economic structure of southern Italy. This study aims to determine the existing relationship between southern Italian cities' digitalization and firms' financial capabilities and institutional support. We have applied correlation and regression models to examine the relationship between cities' digitalization, local firms' financial capabilities, and institutional support. Our results highlight the significant relationship between cities' digitalization, firms' financial capabilities, and institutional support in southern Italian cities. This paper produces policy suggestions for the government to extend the institutional financial support toward the southern firms. As the transformation of cities will increase the operational and production efficiency of the firms, which will add to the regional and national economic development.

Keywords Digital transformation · Financial capability · Institutional support · Cities' digitalization

N. Abid (✉) · F. Marchesani · F. Ceci · F. Masciarelli
Department of Business Administration, University of Gabriele d'Annunzio Chieti-Pescara, Chieti, Italy
e-mail: nabila.abid@unich.it

F. Marchesani
e-mail: filippo.marchesani@unich.it

F. Ceci
e-mail: Federica.ceci@unich.it

F. Masciarelli
e-mail: Francesca.masciarelli@unich.it

S. Za et al. (eds.), *Sustainable Digital Transformation*, Lecture Notes in Information Systems and Organisation 59, https://doi.org/10.1007/978-3-031-15770-7_11

1 Introduction

The last two decades have witnessed rapid economic and societal developments. The changes in economic and societal domains worldwide are catalyzed by the increased deployments of information and communication technologies [1, 2]. A country's national or regional transition to technological advancements accompanied by the dissemination of digital technologies is a prerequisite for the economic and societal transformation to the new stages of development [3].

The evolution of economic processes is changing the competitive business environment. In such a hostile environment, digital technologies and innovation are considered to enhance processes, operational efficiency, and communication in the business sector [4]. Cities' need to embrace digitalization because technologies like big data, ICTs, blockchain, and the internet of thing (IoT) is going to have far-reaching consequences. For the business and economic world [5, 6]. However, an effort is also required by the firms located in the cities area to do so.

Local firms need to have the financial capabilities to develop strategies and plans to finance digital transformation to improve organizational processes that positively impact local economic conditions [7, 8]. Firms' readiness to adapt to the surrounding challenges is of utmost importance [9]. Firms' capabilities are embedded in their financial resources [10]. In a volatile business environment, assessing firms' financial readiness to adopt advanced technologies is crucial. It is termed a financial commitment by the firm's management to change for which they implement strategies and plans to channel to create a more responsive and receptive innovation context [11]. According to Heeks et al. [12], besides firms' financial readiness, institutional support plays a significant role in driving digital technologies in a city because firms need sufficient institutional help during the cities' digital transition process. [13, 14] defined institutions as formal and informal regulatory bodies crucial to achieving economic and societal well-being in a country, region, or city. According to Büchi et al. [15], digitalization should happen at an equal level across cities in a country; otherwise, it can lead to digital inequalities if the relevant bodies inside a city fail to embrace the phenomenon compared to others.

This study explores the firms' financial capability in 12 southern cities to examine if it channels the city digitalization and how institutional support affects city digitalization. Urbanization enhances firms' productivity and outcomes, thereby, promotes economic growth in this geographical location [16]. Firms' financial capability is crucial as it ensures their readiness to transit traditional organizational structure and adopt more digital technology [17]. Institutions play an important role in driving business activities, whether related to the formulation of laws, environmental performance, or financial activities [18]. Thereby, it is crucial to understand the relationship between the aforementioned variables.

The empirical context is particularly relevant for this study because those cities are economically less developed and lag behind digitalization adoption in the operational and services process. Studying the geographical location or region is crucial to analyze the economic and development differences. Compared to northern Italy, which has undergone massive industrialization, southern Italy is underdeveloped with natural and financial resources constraints [19]. The Italian government has taken the initiative to fund the industrial and economic development process [20, 21]. A researcher, Arokszallasi et al. [22], have explored the organizational financial readiness for digitalization on country-level statistics. Still, Li et al. [23] argue that the firm's response to digitalization adoption is mixed across firms and places. Therefore, we aim to fill the gap in the research to explore the possibilities for southern Italy to harness the digitalization opportunities to enhance firms and societal well-being.

This study offers the following critical contributions to the existing body of literature. First, by focusing only on the southern Italian firms, this study produces insights into whether the south Italian firms can transform their traditional organizational process into digitalized ones. Second, most previous research has employed institutional supporters' moderator or mediator variables in either new businesses [24] or multinational joint ventures [25], which has produced a controversial result that cannot be generalized. Our study, however, considers the individual impact of institutional support on a cities' readiness to embrace digitalization. Third, along with possible policy implications, we have provided comprehensive directions for future research.

2 Literature Review

2.1 Theoretical Framework

The southern Italian region has been facing diverse economic and development crises for decades now. The Italian government has taken a severe initiative to promote regional development across Italy with different funding programs for industrial and economic growth [20]. Still, the economic output ratio difference between the southern and other Italian regions is visible [19]. Digitalization is an emerging phenomenon that has captured the attention of global leaders striving to excel in their countries' economic growth and development [26].

The empirical context is particularly relevant for this study because the economically less developed cities lag behind digitalization adoption in the business sectors. Studying the geographical location or region is crucial to analyze the economic and development differences. Compared to northern Italy, which has undergone massive industrialization, the southern part is industrially underdeveloped with less natural and financial resources [21].

Institutions are an integral part of a society that stimulates people's behaviors and actions and regulates business with specific ethical codes and policies [27]. Chang et al. [28] stated that inside one country, the same institutions could promote economic growth at one level in the region, state, or city, which may differ from the other area, state, or city. Institutional support is defined as the extent to which government bodies provide sufficient support to firms to decrease the negative impacts of the firms on the environment and people and increase the industrial efficiency to contribute to national reserves. The institutional support includes financial or technical support, policy, and programs [29]. Considering the importance of business industries in adding to the national GDP, many governments worldwide initiated different funding programs and policies to support the firms to evolve digitally. Henceforth, government institutions play a crucial role in devising plans, programs, and procedures to help the city and the city firms with inadequate resources adopt competitive practices with the help of advanced digital technologies [30–32].

Governmental Institutions play a significant role as institutions can affect a firms' financial capabilities to embrace a specific type of transition. Institutions can help firms with different phenomena, e.g., lower machinery or deployment taxes, financial assistance, and financing the deployment of advanced technology [33]. Firms can excel with improved productivity, environmental concerns, and state and national economic growth by adopting digital practices. However, firms in less developed areas face financial constraints to go digital, as digital transformation requires enormous installation and service costs. Thereby, institutional support (financial aid) holds crucial importance in increasing organizational capability and channel a firm's readiness to adopt digital operation, communication, and production processes.

2.2 *Financial Capability and Digitalization*

For decades, a firm's financial capability to transition from one operational and functional state to another has been of utmost importance [34, 35]. The firms' sensitivity towards resources to transit the traditional organizational practices depicts the significance of financial capabilities. Firms' financial capability is a critical dimension of firms' readiness [36], help firms strengthen their operation and production processes. Thereby, the financial capability or financial readiness is defined as the "firm's available monetary resources to buy and pay for installation cost of any object relating to the operational enhancement or production improvements and the subsequent charges during the practice" [36]. The evolution of economic growth processes is changing the competitive business environment. In such a hostile business environment, when digital technologies are considered to enhance processes, operational efficiency, and communication, it is becoming crucial for firms to embrace the phenomenon to excel in their activities [4].

Economic developments and digitalization are interlinked, which is observed to impact the social aspect, which can be seen in society's health and education sector. Evangelista et al. [37] argued that digital transformation and technologies in a city channel the structural change process in the economy. Garzoni et al. [38] stated that digitalization refers to the inclusion of digital technologies in the business. Del Río Castro et al. [39] indicated that digitalization is embracing all spheres of society, making it essential for the firms to update their traditional operations to digitalized ones. A company can adopt digital practices if it's already happening in the community. Digital business is ranked among the top three business priorities

[40], subsequently is it crucial for firms to adopt digitalization. Digitalization in a country is positively associated with industrial and societal realms [41] and affects all spheres of human society at the micro and macro level [42]. The international organization highlights the importance of digitalization in accelerating economic and social growth in a country [43].

The world bank emphasized the inclusion of digitalization in the national plan. It benefits the business firms and people [44] by tailoring more jobs, time-saving, effective operational efficiency, and less environmental impact. In international cross-sectoral research. The digital activities of businesses have far-reaching implications for an economy. Therefore, it is crucial to map the digitalization in a country, state, or region [45, 46]. The city's digitalization is proven to boost economic growth; however, the impact of digitalization developments and its impact on the economy differ from place to place. The leading five cause of such difference is embedded in the economic and societal structure of the developed and developing regions [47]. It's not easy for a society to transit from a static context to a more complex and digital process as it requires massive investment and time. Still, it is beneficial to deal with persistent economic, business, and societal challenges in the developing areas [48]. Ritter and Pedersen [49] argued that a firm's capability to adopt digitalization could vary across industries and the urban regions in a country. Hence, it is essential to study how firms' financial capability or readiness affects cities' digitalization and act as a prerequisite for societal, environmental, and organizational efficiency to stay competitive in the hostile economic and business environment [50, 51].

In the light of the above literature, we, therefore, propose the following hypothesis:

H1: Firms financial capabilities in cities is positively related to the cities' digitalization.

2.3 Institutional Support and digitalization

Institutions are responsible for economic, social, and environmental well-being [13, 52]. It shapes the behavior of relevant factors and makes them behave in devised constraints. North [14] defined institutions as formal and informal regulatory bodies which play a crucial role in achieving economic growth and societal well-being in a country, region, or city. Institutions are an integral part of a society that stimulates people's behaviors and actions and regulates business with specific ethical codes and policies [27]. Chang et al. [28] stated that inside one country, the same institutions could promote the economic growth at one level at a point in the region, state, or city, which may differ from the economic growth level of the other region state, or city.

When a society undergoes tremendous development or infrastructure changes, institutions offer support to relevant stakeholders and businesses to help them transit for the national long-run benefits [53]. In an underdeveloped society, firms don't have sufficient resources to normalize the advanced business practices by deploying digital technologies and, therefore, face huge constraints and challenges [54]. The academic and practitioner world has realized the importance of digitalization, but some firms can still not digitally transform their organizations. Digitalization can change the organizational structure, but it requires enormous investment to deploy advanced communication and production technologies [55]. Firms' financial readiness helps to efficiently deploy digitalization to compete in domestic and international markets [56]. Thereby, the lack of sufficient financial support hinders the deployment rate of digital infrastructure in economically deprived areas and its firms [57].

In the past few studies [58, 59] have reported institutional support passively associated with cities' digitalization, while others [60, 61] have found a negative impact [62]. In most studies, institutional supports are used as mediation or moderation variables that can channel the relationship between two variables, and the findings of such moderation and mediation are mixed and cannot be generalized [29, 63]. The varying results can explain the different sizes of study samples or the difference in the theoretical approach and the various geographical contexts and diverse policies [29, 64]. The significant impacts of institutional support on a particular firms' perspective are not well explored [65].

In the light of the above gap and mixed results, this research focuses on exploring the effect of institutional support on cities' digitalization. According to Ingram and Silverman [66], institutions under specified constraints channel the transitioning processes in a city from traditional infrastructure to digitalized ones. Based on the above literature, we, therefore, proposed the following hypothesis (Fig. 1).

H2: The institutional support positively related to the cities' digitalization.

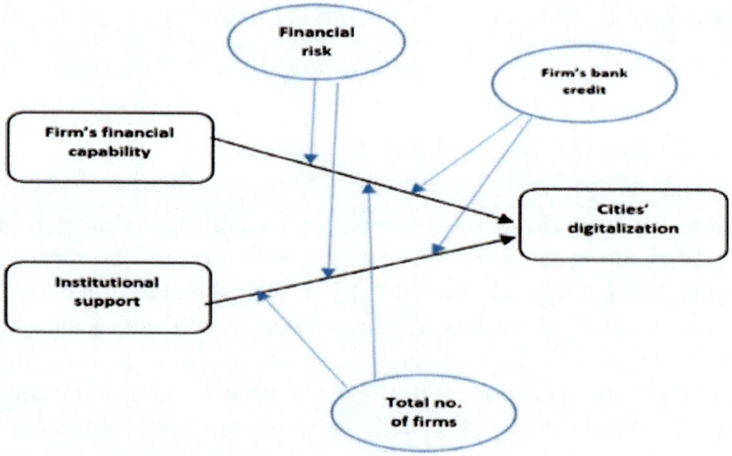

Fig. 1 Conceptual framework

3 Methodology

3.1 Sample and Data Collection

In this study, we focused on 12 cities in the center-south of Italy, traditionally considered less developed both technologically [38] and economically [67] compare to the northern cities, for a period ranging from 2012 to 2019. To select the center-south Italian cities, we considered the statistical territorial units of Italy NUTS used for statistical purposes at the European Union level (Eurostat). According to this ranking, the least the cities are Rome concerning Italy's center; Naples, Salerno, Bari, Lecce, Cosenza, Reggio Emilia, Foggia, and Caserta concerning the south of Italy and Messina and Catania concerning the Island.

The city-level data used to analyze the financial capability, firms' statistics, and R&D investment were collected by the Italian National Institute of Statistics (ISTAT) through the firms' regional analysis. Data is mainly related to the digitalization process. Cities are based on an index considering nine indicators based on data sources such as ISTAT, FPA, and AGCOM to represent technological advances in cities and the technological services offered to their stakeholders.

This analysis is conducted using the ordinary least squares method (OLS) to verify the research framework and hypotheses. We analyzed 12 Italian cities during an 8 year period (2012–019). The Hypothesis testing is conducted using a panel data regression analysis model that intends to predict the extent of the strength of the impacts of both independent variables on the dependent variable.

3.2 Operationalization of the Variable

The digitalization index is our dependent variable. This index aims to measures the technological development of the cities based on a set of indicators that covered a large panel of technological services. These indicators include online services, broadband access, municipal app, home banking, diffusion, digital transparency, digital openness, social public administration, public wi-fi, and IoT development in cities to produce an index that measured the proportion of digitalization in a city. This variable is usually used to assess the technological advance in cities to understand the impact of technologies in the urban area [68].

Our model includes two independent variables: financial capability and institutional support. The first independent variable is the financial capability; in this variable, we consider the firms' financial capability in each city based on access to appropriate financial services evaluates using the differential of active lending rates on cash loans of firms in cities. The firms' abilities to raise capital from existing shareholders, the public, and easy access to bank financing, also considering the geographical position, are usually related to advantage on firm's competitiveness within an industry [69].

Table 1 Descriptive statistics

Variable	Obs	Mean	Std. Dev	Min	Max
Digitalization index	96	0,339	0,128	0,152	0,768
Financial capability	96	0,402	0,274	−0,062	1,001
Institutional support	96	107,896	258,820	4764	1059
Firms bank credit	96	1,322	1,931	0,005	5,247
Total firms	96	0,084	0,011	0,068	0,116

Table 2 Correlation model

	Variable	[1]	[2]	[3]	[4]	[5]	[6]
[1]	Digitalization index	1					
[2]	Financial capability	−0,291	1				
[3]	Institutional support	0,514	−0,391	1			
[4]	Financial risk	−0,133	0,353	0,136	1		
[5]	Firms bank credit	0,463	−0,361	0,964	0,148	1	
[6]	Total firms	0,464	−0,314	0,698	−0,063	0,678	1

Our second independent variable, institutional support, considers each city's public expenditure in R&D over the city's population. The institutional support perspective is usually consistent with the notion that access to tangible and intangible resources from both government and private individuals is a crucial enabler of entrepreneurial activity [70].

In the regression model, we controlled several factors at both the city and firms' levels. All variables are continuous variables, and the model specification includes the following indicator as a control variable. To assess the financial development of firms in cities, we looked at the financial risk of a firm's city, using the percentage of the decay rate of the financial loan. We also control bank credit by considering the Total value of banker's credit lines used by firms in cities over the population. Moreover, we also use the total firms in the city by considering the total number of firms registered in the Chamber of Commerce over the population of each city.

Table 1 presents the summary statistics of the variables used in the regressions, and Table 2 the correlation matrix related to this model.

3.3 Results

This article is focused on exploring the relationship between cities' digitalization, local firms' financial capability, and institutional support in southern Italian cities in the presence of two control variables, financial risk, and bank credit, respectively. Table 1 describes the data statistics, and Table 2 presents the correlation matrix. The weak correlation between local firms' financial capability and cities' digitalization is explained by the scenario of the southern Italian firms. According to Lukonga [71], firms require enormous financial resources to shift traditional operations to digitalized ones. Firms need institutional support to fund the shift. Chen et al. [54] describe institutional support as financial aid provided by the government to the local businesses to adopt advanced technological operations to protect the environmental, economic, and societal concerns.

The results of the regression matrix are presented in Table 3. Collinearity in regression leads to an increase in the variance of coefficients and thereby produces unbiased results. To avoid multicollinearity, we deployed the VIFs (variance inflation factors). For all four-study models, the maximum and mean VIF values are less than the threshold of 3.5. Therefore, no collinearity in the study model is confirmed, and the study results are compelling and unbiased.

Although all models depict the significant relationship between study variables, the negative value of local firms' financial capability reveals the inability of the southern firms to embrace digitalization as the firms lack sufficient funds. The positive association of institutional support and cities' digitalization does not imply the strong position of the firms in the region. According to Acemoglu and Robinson [53], institutions in a country affect the different economic areas differently; subsequently, institutional support in southern Italy is not as significant as other Italian regions [19]. Suppose the Italian government extends institutional financial support in southern Italian cities and provides them with sufficient support and resources. In that case, these cities and the firms inside them can embrace digitalization, positively affecting firms' output and economic and societal progress.

Table 3 Regression matrix

	Model I	Model II	Model III	Model IV
Financial capability		−123,17*		−106,94*
		[54,11]		[53,53]
Institutional support			2177,84**	1952,91**
			[811,75]	[816,332]
Financial risk	−24,56**	−14,44	−29,11**	−20.130*
	[9,24]	[10,05]	[9,03]	[9.954]
Firms bank credit	−7,23	−1.26	−5.24**	−5,299**
	[1,18]	[1,18]	[1,98]	[1,945]
Total firms	7388.23***	6992.35***	4843.98*	4813,93*
	[2040,67]	[2032,86]	[189,11]	[2311,75]
No. of observation	96	96	96	96
R-squared	0,189	0,147	0,221	0,162

Note Digitalization Index, dependent variable. $P < 0.10$; * $P < 0.05$; ** $P < 0.01$; *** $P < 0.001$

4 Conclusion and Implications

The present study attempted to explore the relationship between cities' digitalization, firms' financial capabilities, and institutional support in southern Italian cities. We find a positive yet weak correlation between local firms' financial capability and cities' digitalization, which directs our attention towards economic development and institutional resource availability in southern cities of Italy.

Our results show that southern Italian cities are less reactive to digitalization. The analysis results reveal that institutional shares a significant positive relationship with a firm's capability and city digitalization which is in line with the study findings of Shu et al. [63]. However, the negative yet significant relationship between local firms' financial capability and cities' digitalization implies that the institutional support is not substantial to drive digitalization in southern Italy like other Italian regions. Therefore, we proposed the following policy suggestions. First, the Italian government must devise plans to promote regional economic development in southern Italy. Second, the Italian government must allocate sufficient budget and resources to local institutions to channel the digitalization in southern Italian firms.

Our research offers several implications for the firms. Notably, the study has investigated the local firms' financial capability to embrace the digital footprint. It has proved that digital transformation and firms' financial capabilities are strongly linked. A firms' financial capability can be a central source to drive digitalization. However, it requires substantial institutional support if firms are not financially capable of the transition. Together the business can develop a platform to raise their concern for business, society, and environmental efficiency and ask for the proper institutional support from the central government. Collective efforts can be helpful to draw sufficient budgets to fund the digital transformation in the firms.

4.1 Limitation and Future Research

This study has several limitations and suggests some directions for future research. First, the study indicators are limited and do not incorporate every aspect of the firms' capabilities. While financial capability can be the central driver for digitalization, another technical and human resource capability can also be effective. The firms' capabilities can be studied in future research to develop a comprehensive taxonomy. Second, the sample is limited to the southern Italian firms and thus, produces results that can be generalized to a similar economic and organizational setup. However, a large and variant sample can generate meaningful and new insights on this topic for future research. Future research can also study the strategic and management perspective of the firms toward digitalization. Third, although institutional support is a much-required phenomenon an organization needs for their technological or digital transformation, future research can look up to other external societal or state factors like capturing the impact on the firms' digitalization. Cross-sectional data and other external factors can help to dig deeper to examine the longitudinal path towards digitalization.

References

1. De Groen, W.P., Lenaerts, K., Bosc, R., Paquier, F.: Impact of digitalization and the on-demand economy on labor markets and the consequences for employment and industrial relations. CEPS Spec. Rep. 1–76 (2017). https://www.ceps.eu/system/files/EESC_Digitalisation.pdf
2. Vrchota, J., Maříková, M., Řehoř, P., Rolínek, L., Toušek, R.: Human resources readiness for industry 4.0. J. Open Innov. Technol. Mark. Complex. **6**(1), 1–20 (2020)
3. Zaborovskaia, O., Nadezhina, O., Avduevskaya, E.: The impact of digitalization on the formation of human capital at the regional level. J. Open Innov. Technol. Mark. Complex. **6**(4), 1–24 (2020)
4. Yudina, T.N.: Digital segment of the real economy: digital economy in the context of analog economy. **12**(2), 7–18 (2019)
5. Wedel, M., Kannan, P.K.: Marketing analytics for data-rich environments. J. Mark. **80**(6), 97–121 (2016)
6. Ng, I.C.L., Wakenshaw, S.Y.L.: The internet-of-things: review and research directions. Int. J. Res. Mark. **34**(1), 3–21 (2017)
7. Kane, G.C., Palmer, D., Phillips, A.N., Kiron, D., Buckley, N.: Aligning the organization for its digital future. MIT Sloan Manag. Rev. **58180**, 1–29 (2016)
8. Svahn, F., Mathiassen, L., Lindgren, R.: Embracing digital innovation in incumbent firms: how Volvo Cars managed competing concerns. MIS Q.: Manag. Inf. Syst. **41**(1), 239–253 (2017)
9. Armenakis, A.A., Harris, S.G., Mossholder, K.W.: Creating readiness for organizational change. Hum. Relat. **46**(6), 681–703 (1993)
10. Barney, J.: Firm resources and sustained competitive advantage. J. Manag. **17**(1), 99–120 (1991)
11. Holt, D.T., Armenakis, A.A., Harris, S.G.: Research in organizational change and development. Res. Organ. Chang. Dev. **16**, 289–336 (2016)
12. Heeks, R., Molla, R., Boateng, A., Hinson, R.: Advancing e-commerce beyond readiness in a developing country: experiences of Ghanaian firms. J. Electron. Commer. Organ. **9**(1), 1–16 (2011)
13. Acemoglu, D., Johnson, S., Robinson, J.: Institutions as the fundamental cause of long-run growth. Working Paper 10481, Cambridge (2004). https://www.nber.org/papers/w10481
14. North, D.C.: Institutions, Institutional Change and Economic Performance. Cambridge University Press, Cambridge (1990)
15. Büchi, M., Festic, N., Latzer, M.: How social well-being is affected by digital inequalities. Int. J. Commun. **12**, 3686–3706 (2018)
16. Oestreicher-Singer, G., Zalmanson, L.: Paying for content or paying for community? The effect of social computing platforms on willingness to pay in content websites. SSRN Electron. J. (2011)
17. De Carolis, A., Macchi, M., Negri, E., Terzi, S.: A maturity model for assessing the digital readiness of manufacturing companies. IFIP Adv. Inf. Commun. Technol. **513**, 13–20 (2017)
18. Abid, N., Ikram, M., Wu, J., Ferasso, M.: Towards environmental sustainability: exploring the nexus among ISO 14001, governance indicators and green economy in Pakistan. Sustain. Prod. Consum. **27**, 653–666 (2021)
19. Felice, E.: The socio-institutional divide: explaining Italy's long-term regional differences. J. Interdiscip. Hist. (1), 1–28 (2018)

20. Essays, U.: Disparities between north and south italy history essay (2018). https://www.ukessays.com/essays/history/disparities-between-north-and-south-italy-history-essay.php?vref=1. Accessed 20 April 2021
21. Musolino, D.: The North-south divide in Italy: reality or perception? Eur. Spat. Res. Policy **25**(1), 29–53 (2018)
22. Arokszallasi, Z., Kotian, J., Rzentarzewska, K.: Digitalization and higher R&D readiness—way to foster income convergence in CESEE. Focus Eur. Econ. Integr. **Q3–18**, 34–42 (2018)
23. Li, L., Su, F., Zhang, W., Mao, J.Y.: Digital transformation by SME entrepreneurs: a capability perspective. Inf. Syst. J. **28**(6), 1129–1157 (2018)
24. Li, H., Zhang, V.: The role of managers' political networking and functional experience in new venture performance: evidence from China's transition economy. Strat. Manag. J. **28**(8), 791–804 (2007)
25. Ménascé, D., Vincent, C.E., Moreau, M.M.: Smart cities and new forms of employment. Field Actions Sci. Rep. **2017**(Special Issue 16), 16–21 (2017)
26. Krause, O., Opitz, M., Schreiber, B., Pfirsching, V., González, A., Gnirs, T., Mohr, G., Peintner, S.: Digital transformation—how to become digital leader. Digit. Transform. (2016). Accessed 15 May 2021
27. Dobreva, J.G.: The role of institutions of institutions, business, and society in shaping the modern economy. J. Int. Sci. Publ. **12**, 119–125 (2018)
28. Chang, H.J.: Institutions and economic development: theory, policy, and history. J. Inst. Econ. **7**(4), 473–498 (2011)
29. Li, H., Atuahene-Gima, K.: Product innovation strategy and the performance of new technology ventures in China. Acad. Manag. J. **44**(6), 1123–1134 (2001)
30. Kraja, Y.B., Osmani, E., Molla, F.: The role of the government policy for support the SME-s. Acad. J. Interdiscip. Stud. **3**(2), 391–396 (2014)
31. Park, S., Lee, I.H., Kim, J.E.: Government support and small- and medium-sized enterprise (SME) performance: the moderating effects of diagnostic and support services. Asian Bus. Manag. **19**(2), 213–238 (2020)
32. Pelletier, C., Cloutier, L.M.: Conceptualising digital transformation in SMEs: an ecosystemic perspective. J. Small Bus. Enterp. Dev. **26**(6–7), 855–876 (2019)
33. Lewin, W., Cartwright, K.: Field theory in social science: selected theoretical paper. Psychology 520–521 (1951)
34. Lewin, K.: Frontiers in group dynamics: II. Channels of group life; social planning and action research. Hum. Relat. **1**(2), 143–153 (1947)
35. Iacovou, C.L., Benbasat, I., Dexter, A.S.: Electronic data interchange and small organizations: adoption and impact of technology. MIS Q. **19**(4), 465–485 (1995)
36. Evangelista, R., Guerrieri, P., Meliciani, V.: The economic impact of digital technologies in Europe. Econ. Innov. New Technol. **23**(8), 802–824 (2014)
37. Garzoni, A., De Turi, I., Secundo, G., Del Vecchio, P.: Fostering digital transformation of SMEs: a four-level approach. Manag. Decis. **58**(8), (2020)
38. Del Río Castro, G., González Fernández, M.C., Uruburu Colsa, Á.: Unleashing the convergence amid digitalization and sustainability towards pursuing the Sustainable Development Goals (SDGs): a holistic review. J. Clean. Prod. **280**, (2021)
39. Gartner: New Business Executive; Insights From the 2018 CIO Agenda Report (2017)
40. Gray, J., Rumpe, B.: Models for the digital transformation. Softw. Syst. Model. **16**(2), 307–308 (2017)
41. Kaplan, J., Truex, B., Wastell, D.P., Wood-Harper, D., DeGross, A.T.: Information Systems Research: Relevant Theory and Informed Practice. Boston (2004)
42. Dobrolyubova, E., Alexandrov, O., Yefremov, A.: Is Russia ready for digital transformation? Commun. Comput. Inf. Sci. **745**, 431–444 (2017)
43. Soppe, A.: Sustainable corporate finance. J. Bus. Ethics **53**(1), 213–224 (2004). https://doi.org/10.1023/B
44. The World Bank: Digital dividends (2016). https://doi.org/10.1596/978-1-4648-0728-2

45. Mentsiev, A.U., Engel, M.V., Tsamaev, A.M., Abubakarov, M.V., Yushaeva, R. S.-E.: The concept of digitalization and its impact on the modern economy. Proc. Int. Sci. Conf. "Far East Con" (ISCFEC 2020). **128**(Iscfec), 2960–2964 (2020)
46. Mueller, S.C., Bakhirev, A., Böhm, M., Schröer, M., Krcmar, H., Welpe, I.M.: Measuring and mapping the emergence of the digital economy: a comparison of the market capitalization in selected countries. Digit. Policy, Regul. Gov. **19**(5), 367–382 (2017)
47. Friedrich, R., El-Darwiche, B., Singh, M., Koster, A.: Digitization for economic growth and job creation: regional and industry perspectives (2017)
48. Khan, S., Aftab, M.: Digitization and its impact on economy. Int. J. Digit. Libr. Serv. **1142**, 138–149 (2015)
49. Ritter, T., Pedersen, C.L.: Digitization capability and the digitalization of business models in business-to-business firms: past, present, and future. Ind. Mark. Manag. **86**, 180–190 (2020). https://doi.org/10.1016/j.indmarman.2019.11.019
50. Hanafizadeh, P., Hanafizadeh, M.R., Khodabakhshi, M.: Taxonomy of e-readiness assessment measures. Int. J. Inf. Manag. **29**(3), 189–195 (2009)
51. Mutula, S.M., van Brakel, P.: An evaluation of e-readiness assessment tools with respect to information access: towards an integrated information-rich tool. Int. J. Inf. Manag. **26**(3), 212–223 (2006)
52. Douglass, C.N.: Institutions, Institutional Change and Economic Performance (Political Economy of Institutions and Decisions). Cambridge University Press, Cambridge (1990)
53. Acemoglu, D., Robinson, J.: The role of institutions in growth and development. Rev. Econ. Inst. **1**(2), 1–33 (2010)
54. Chen, C.L., Lin, Y.C., Chen, W.H., Chao, C.F., Pandia, H.: Role of government to enhance digital transformation in the small service business. Sustainability **13**(3), 1–26 (2021)
55. Sundaram, R., Sharma, R., Shakya, A.: Digital transformation of business models: a systematic review of the impact on revenue and supply chain. Int. J. Manag. **11**(5), 9–21 (2020). https://doi.org/10.34218/IJM.11.5.2020.002
56. Matricano, D.: Digital business transformations. 173–195 (2021)
57. Chang, A., et al.: Taiwan's digital imperative: how a digital transformation can re-ignite economic growth, pp. 6–9 (2017). http://mckinseychina.com/wp-content/uploads/2017/10/McKinsey_Taiwans-Digital-Imperative-EN.pdf
58. Durmuşoğlu, S.S., Apfelthaler, G., Nayir, D.Z., Alvarez, R., Mughan, T.: The effect of government-designed export promotion service use on small and medium-sized enterprise goal achievement: a multidimensional view of export performance. Ind. Mark. Manag. **41**(4), 680–691 (2012)
59. Shamsuddoha, A.K., Yunus Ali, M.: Mediated effects of export promotion programs on firm export performance. Asia Pac. J. Mark. Logist. **18**(2), 93–110 (2006)
60. Faroque, A.R., Takahashi, Y.: Export marketing assistance and early internationalizing firm performance. Asia Pac. J. Mark. Logist. **27**(3), 421–443 (2015)
61. Njinyah, S.Z.: The effectiveness of government policies for export promotion on the export performance of SMEs cocoa exporters in Cameroon. Int. Mark. Rev. **35**(1), 164–185 (2016)
62. Falahat, M., Lee, Y.Y., Ramayah, T., Soto-Acosta, P.: Modelling the effects of institutional support and international knowledge on competitive capabilities and international performance: evidence from an emerging economy. J. Int. Manag. **26**(4), 100779 (2020)
63. Shu, C., Wang, Q., Gao, S., Liu, C.: Firm patenting, innovations, and government institutional support as a double-edged sword. J. Prod. Innov. Manag. **32**(2), 290–305 (2015)
64. Sheng, S., Zhou, K.Z., Lessassy, L.: NPD speed vs. innovativeness: the contingent impact of institutional and market environments. J. Bus. Res. **66**(11), 2355–2362 (2013)
65. Zhang, S., Wang, Z., Zhao, X., Zhang, M.: Effects of institutional support on innovation and performance: roles of dysfunctional competition. Ind. Manag. Data Syst. **117**(1), 50–67 (2017)
66. Ingram, P., Silverman, B.S.: Introduction: the new institutionalism in strategic management. In: Ingram, P., Silverman, B.S. (eds.) The New Institutionalism in Strategic Management, pp. 1–30. Emerald Publishing Limited (2000)

67. Ciani, E., Torrini, R.: The geography of Italian income inequality: recent trends and the role of employment. Politica Economica **35**(2), (2019)
68. Pittaway, J.J., Montazemi, A.R.: Know-how to lead the digital transformation: the case of local governments. Gov. Inf. Q. (2020)
69. Fonseka, M.M., Tian, G.L., Li, L.C.: Impact of financial capability on firms' competitiveness and sustainability: evidence from the highly-regulated Chinese market. Chinese Manag. Stud. **8**(4), 201
70. Stephan, U., Uhlaner, L.M., Stride, C.: Institutions and social entrepreneurship: the role of institutional voids, institutional support, and institutional configurations. J. Int. Bus. Stud. **46**(3), 308–331 (2015)
71. Lukonga, I.: Harnessing digital technologies to promote SMEs and inclusive growth in MENAP region. IMF working paper. Middle East and Central Asia department

Getting Digital Technologies Right—A Forward-Looking Maturity Model for Enterprise Performance Management

Jörg H. Mayer, Markus Esswein, Moritz Göbel, and Reiner Quick

Abstract Enterprise performance management (EPM) helps in executing a company's strategy. As transformations towards digital EPM are challenging, the objective of this paper is to develop a forward-looking maturity model to help companies digitalize their EPM. We apply a "zero-quartile" approach. In contrast to the best practices of top performing companies ("first quartile"), a zero-quartile defines the expected (collectively deemed best possible) state of a future EPM leveraging digital technologies. We employ the Rasch algorithm on data of a survey of 203 participants and based on a maturity model, we come up with four design guidelines to help companies digitalize their EPM. (1) A digital enterprise platform is the future single source of truth for planning, budgeting, and forecasting. Backing managers' experience with data, it combines harmonized ERP outcomes with insights from market analyses, social media, and other sources. (2) Predictive analytics is the first opinion for planning, budgeting, and forecasting. Yet, managers have to learn to accept such outcomes so that they can focus more on irregularities. (3) Standard reports and analyses as well as standard comments will be automated. User-centricity is the "new" normal for a more natural working modus. (4) Managers should overcome their reluctance to work with data and start analyzing in a self-service fashion. Technology will support them from a global view to a line-item level.

Keywords Enterprise performance management (EPM) · Maturity model (MM) · Benchmarking · Digital technologies · Survey · Rasch algorithm · Design science research in information systems

J. H. Mayer · M. Esswein (✉) · M. Göbel · R. Quick
Darmstadt University of Technology, Karolinenplatz 5, 64289 Darmstadt, Germany
e-mail: markus.esswein@unidue.de

J. H. Mayer
e-mail: jhmayer@tonline.de

S. Za et al. (eds.), *Sustainable Digital Transformation*, Lecture Notes in Information Systems and Organisation 59, https://doi.org/10.1007/978-3-031-15770-7_12

1 Introduction

"From bookkeeper to business partner" is a statement often used when talking about the finance function. *Enterprise performance management (EPM)* is particularly affected by this development because it integrates financial and non-financial information for planning and decision support [1].

Companies often compare their own performance against competitors. In doing so, *benchmarking* is a continuous process of identifying the highest standards of excellence for products, services, and processes [2]. Most often a "first quartile" approach is applied [3]. It depicts the best practices of top performing companies.

Given that time series from the past define the first quartile, benchmarking is backward-looking. Accordingly, it cannot consider the potential of latest *digital technologies* such as automation, analytics, and digital enterprise platforms. In other words, digital is disruptive and thus distorts the philosophy of today's benchmarking in its very essence [4]. We propose a more forward-looking approach, the *"zero" quartile* benchmarking [5]. In contrast to the best practices of top performing companies, a zero quartile defines the *expected* (collectively deemed best possible) *state of a benchmarking object*.

To make this approach more operational, especially to describe a company's path toward such a future state, we rely on the concept of *maturity models (MMs)*. As maturity can be defined as "the state or quality of being perfect, complete, or ready" [6], MMs are conceptual models that consist of a sequence of discrete maturity levels and represent an anticipated, desired, or typical path of evolution [7].

Examining the body of knowledge, Röglinger et al. [8] and Ahmad et al. [9] mentioned the *lack of forward-looking MMs* providing "…improvement measures in the sense of good or best practices for each stage." In turn, practitioner journals described the impact of digital technologies on finance per se [10–12] or they evaluated single digital technologies such as automation [13]. However, these studies often lack a rigorous foundation [14]. Consequently, the objective of this paper is to develop a *forward-looking MM*[1] *to help companies digitalize their EPM*. The proposed model will not only serve as a self-assessment for companies to evaluate their as-is situation, but also to derive design guidelines based on substantial differences between different EPM MM levels. We raise two research questions:

- Which digital technologies are most relevant for EPM at what maturity level?
- How can one achieve the next level of Digital EPM?

To create things that serve human purposes [16], we follow Design Science Research (DSR) in Information Systems [17, 18], for which the publication scheme from Gregor and Hevner [19] gave us direction. We motivate this article with

[1] Considering the four types of Design Science Research (DSR) in IS artifacts identified by March and Smith [15]—constructs, models, methods, and instantiations—we propose a *model*. It should serve as an assessment for companies wishing to evaluate their IS investments, ultimately to prepare their implementations through mere experience and gut feeling.

current challenges associated with EPM leveraging digital technologies (*introduction*). Building on the state of the art, we highlight research gaps (*literature review*). Addressing these gaps, we apply the Rasch algorithm with data from a survey (*method*) and consolidate our findings in a MM—ultimately to lay out four design guidelines that should help companies digitalize their EPM (*artifact description*). Emphasizing a staged research process with "build" and "evaluate" activities, we review our MM in a next publication with the help of a case study [20]. Comparing our results with prior work and examining how they relate back to the article's objective and research questions, we close with a summary, limitations of our work, and avenues for future research (*discussion and conclusion*).

2 Literature Review

Following Webster and Watson [21], we started our literature review with a (1) *journal search* focusing on leading IS research and accounting journals, complemented by proceedings from major IS conferences.[2,3,4] Since our subject of research is also of practical interest, we additionally considered practitioner journals such as MIS Quarterly Executive and the Harvard Business Review. For our (2) *database search*, we used ScienceDirect, EBSCO host, Springer Link, AIS eLibrary, and Google Scholar.

Assessing the publications through their titles, abstracts, and keywords, we performed an iterative (3) *keyword search* with the following search string: Enterprise performance management (EPM) OR business process management (BPM) OR corporate performance management (CPM) AND digital technology OR digital transformation AND maturity model OR stage model OR capability model. We also tested variations of this string with singulars, plurals, and abbreviations.

Our first search results were articles such as Ongena and Ravesteyn [25] on the relationship of BPM maturity to company process performance, size and sector, Williams et al. [26] on developing a digital MM for SMEs, Comuzzi and Patel [27] and Imgrund et al. [28] on a big data and digital transformation MM, respectively. Furthermore, we found 24 practitioner articles such as Accenture [12] and The Hackett Group [3]. Finally, we conducted (4) a *backward and forward search*.

---

[2] Based on the AIS senior scholars' basket of leading IS Journals [22]: European Journal of Information Systems; Information Systems Research; Information Systems Journal; Journal of the Association for Information Systems; Journal of Information Technology; Journal of Management Information Systems; Journal of Strategic Information Systems; MIS Quarterly.

[3] In order to focus on leading accounting journals, we used the Scimago Journal Ranking [23]. We selected the subject area "Business, Management, and Accounting" and, herein, the subject category "accounting." The resulting top 50 journal ranking includes outlets such as Accounting Review, Journal of Accounting Research, and the Journal of Finance.

[4] We followed the AIS' list of leading IS conferences [24]: Americas Conference on Information Systems; European Conference on Information Systems; International Conference on Information Systems; Pacific and Asia Conference on Information Systems.

Following the "citation pearl growing" approach, we complemented our search whenever we examined relevant new aspects in the retrieved publications [29]. With references from all relevant publications, we identified another 20 publications such as Hess et al. [30] talking about achieving a digital transformation strategy by following their guidelines and ended up with *69 publications* in total.

For our **gap analysis**, we structured these publications with respect to two topics: The *benchmarking object* encompasses three EPM process activities: that is planning, budgeting, and forecasting, followed by business performance reporting, and finally, analysis and decision support [31]. "Others" subsume articles that do not focus on a specific EPM process activity. (2) The cluster "*peer-group partner*" refers to what the benchmarking object is compared to [32].

(1) Benchmarking object: EPM, also known as corporate performance management (CPM), business performance management (BPM), and business process management (BPM), aims to improve the performance of the entire company [33]. Examining different domains, *EPM* addresses internal decision makers [34] and is often at the center of attention [35].

EPM is based on the hypothesis that the better the information available to decision makers, the better their decision should be. This stems from the theory of the *homo economicus* which has been expanded to the field of neuroeconomics [36]. The performance measurement ensures the alignment of performance with the strategy of the company [37] and has to balance human intuition with the relevant data [38, 39]. This can be achieved by setting more data-driven goals to translate the complex structure of a business into something understandable and actionable [40, 41].

Furthermore authors such as Eckerson [33] or Yaghi et al. [42] began highlighting the integration of IS support in the form of *dashboards* as a cornerstone of a successful EPM. Not only the underlying data landscape, structure, and contents of data are changing [43], also the visualization of data plays an important role [44]. This technology-based future of performance management is an essential component of leading successful digital transformation, making it more data-driven, more flexible, more continuous, and more development-oriented [43]. Accordingly, today, digital technologies such as finance bots are examined to *automate* processes like budgeting, forecasting, and analyses [45] or *predictive analytics* to handle forecasts more fact-driven [46].

In line with Williams et al. [26] we examined that the majority of MMs focuses on digitalizing the production and logistics domain, rather than EPM and clustered articles such as Akdil et al. [47] and Colli et al. [48] as "Industry 4.0" papers. Eckerson [33] described the impact of IS for EPM whereas Cokins [31] examined effects of the "digital revolution" on EPM. Pinto [49] as well as Ongena and Ravesteyn [25] researched the correlation between business process maturity and a company's business performance. Another fourteen articles such as Plaschke et al. [13] focused on single EPM activities such as planning, budgeting, and forecasting and eleven articles elaborated on standard reporting and analysis.

Detailing digital technologies with automation, analytics, and digital enterprise platform, we followed Mergel et al. [50] and Mayer et al. [51]. We found twenty-one articles covering the impact of *automation* on EPM. With a focus on standard reporting, companies have already started to automate routine tasks [12]. In doing so, Robotic Process Automation (RPA) is suitable for high-volume, standardized processes [52]. Practitioners such as Eckerson [33] and Cokins [31] predicted a substantial usage of *analytics* when companies have the capability to easily access all their financial data as well as data from social media listening and the internet of things. Pearson [53] suggested that analytics will increase company productivity, since planning, budgeting, and forecasting processes will no longer require months of negotiating targets, calculating figures in spreadsheets, and performing endless iterations to close gaps between top-down targets and bottom-up budgets. Accordingly, Comuzzi and Patel [27] proposed a MM for measuring organizations leveraging big data analytics in their business processes. Shifting EPM towards a more proactive, forward-looking steering, *digital enterprise platforms* help as a single source of truth of a company's data [11, 31]. "Data lakes" contribute to a broader data base [54]. The necessary master data management was examined by Spruit and Pietzka [55].

Accordingly, we derive our first takeaway and, based on that, we propose to expand the body of MMs with a more *forward-looking EPM model—based on the zero-quartile definition.* In doing so, we will examine the impacts of automation, analytics, and digital enterprise platforms on EPM process activities (for details, see Sect. 3).

(2) Peer-group partner: The term "peer-group partner" refers to whom the organization is compared to in a cluster of similar organizations or other structured entities based on preselected attributes [32, 56, 57]. *Internal benchmarking* compares different organizational units of a company such as sites [58]. Atkinson [59] is the only article we found on this kind of benchmarking. He carried out a case study at a health care provider where he constructed a framework to plan, act, review, and revise strategies and objectives. This enabled the organization to compare their goals against the fulfillment and adjust objectives, which is similar to how planning is usually conducted in businesses but offered little comparative value for benchmarking.

In turn, we found 68 articles referring to *external benchmarking*. Of these, industry benchmarking looks at trends within a group of companies of the same industry or market [60]. Ifenthaler and Egloffstein [61] is a good example since they examined digital transformation in the European education sector, a crucial topic due to homeschooling in the past two years, with an n = 222. They opted for a six-dimensional model based on a Likert scale, rating the adopted technology, the strategy, and, industry-specific, the digital learning and teaching capabilities, among other factors, to sort the participants into five maturity categories derived from literature.

Finally, *generic benchmarking* focuses on processes across industries [2]. 54 out of 68 articles employed such a benchmarking with notable examples such as Imgrund et al. [28] who constructed a digital transformation maturity model for BPM in SMEs and used the existing process and enterprise maturity model (PEMM) which accounts for the heterogeneity of SMEs in different industries. They adapted the model by adding a digital perspective to it. Som and Gamroth [62] constructed a model to measure the digital transformation level in the HR departments of multiple industries across continents with a special focus on data integrity and using a MM with seven dimensions.

In order to ensure sufficient data for our novel form of benchmarking, we propose a *generic benchmarking across industries* (Sect. 3).

3 Method

Since we aimed to create a MM to benchmark a company's EPM across industries, which requires a large amount of company-specific data, we opted for a survey-based approach. This is in line with what we also identified as method from several of the MMs reviewed and our synthesis of Sect. 2. With a pre-study we tested the usability of the underlying questionnaire with two EPM process experts from multinational companies and a subject-matter expert from the department of accounting and auditing at Darmstadt University of Technology [63]. For the main study, we opted for an *online survey*.

We asked members of a manager working group hosted by the Schmalenbach working group "Digital Finance" [64] who regularly meet to discuss trends in digital finance and extended the survey to a broader group of practitioners based on the mailing list of a special interest group. 25% of people who accessed the survey decided not to participate while only 2% abandoned after starting the survey. On average, people spent 15 min answering all questions. The survey was closed after 5 weeks. The characteristics of the data sample are given in Table 1. We differentiated between Industry (manufacturing), Services, Banking and Insurance, IT as well as Public sector and other. Finally, we complement our analysis with *design guidelines* based on substantial differences between MM levels within the individual EPM process activities.

3.1 Questionnaire

Combining Frolick's [34] framework and IMA [65] we detailed EPM in terms of **three process activities: (1) Planning** determines key business drivers and measures business success such as market shares and product margins, in order to create the 3–5 year (strategic) plan [34]. Translating the strategic plan into action, budgeting is the annual planning process for preparing the budgets in terms of sales, earnings, manpower, expenditures for the next year. Forecasting develops, reviews, and consolidates the year-end and rolling outlook reports. Furthermore, forecasting examines gaps between the current performance and the forecast targets, in order to finally set up actions for closing these gaps. **(2) Standard reporting and monitoring** measures the day-to-day business performance with standard and simple ad-hoc reporting, including management support systems, balanced scorecards, etc. [34]. **(3) Analysis**

Table 1 Sample characteristics

Sector	No	%	Position	No	%	Market cap. [bn $]	No	%
Industry (manufacturing)	68	33	CxO, executive managers	75	37	<100 m	73	36
Services	55	27	Finance department	28	14	<5 bn	94	46
Banking and insurance	14	7	Analytics competence center	52	25	<20 bn	18	9
IT	26	13	(Internal) consultants	18	9	>20 bn	18	9
Public sector and other	40	20	IT	30	15			
Total	203	100	Total	203	100	Total	203	100

and decision support focus on non-regular analyses such as root-cause analyses, what-if, and how-to-achieve requests. Typically performed only a few times a year, this also covers complex special issue analyses regarding pricing or costs [59].

Then, the participants were asked to provide their primary **value-creation target** for each of the three processes activities. We distinguish between three factors:

(1) **Efficiency** covers the monetary effects of digital technologies, assuming equal quality. It reflects cost savings such as processing the same number of reports with fewer people or reduced effort. We operationalize cost savings threefold by reducing *full-time equivalents* (FTE), lowering *cost* by operating expenditures reductions in terms of ordinary and necessary expenses (OPEX) and capital expenditure (CAPEX) reductions as well as increased *speed* by time savings [20].

(2) **Effectiveness** reflects the ability to offer new products and services or reach new customers through a better understanding of their behavior. This consists of five items: (a) *Better insights* covers the degree to which new information (reports, analyses, KPIs) meet the requirements of the addressees and improve business decisions. (b) *Flexibility* describes the ability to react to new, but mainly anticipated requirements [66]. We include agility, which additionally covers responses to unexpected requirements [67]. (c) *Accuracy* covers the provision of correct data [68]. (d) *Consistency* refers to the integrity of data stored in different sources. (e) *Security* comprises secure data even in heterogeneous ERP/BI system architectures or the cloud [69].

(3) **Experience** covers learning effects within the organization or setting up future economies of scale when implementing digital technologies. In order to support efficiency and effectiveness, we differentiate twofold: (a) The use of digital technologies paves the way for future cost and/or FTE reduction (*enabling*

Standard reporting and monitoring: measure the day-to-day business performance with standard and simple ad-hoc reporting, including management support systems, balanced scorecards, etc.

Applying digital technologies, state your primary target of value creation: efficiency, effectiveness (better insights, flexibility, accuracy, consistency, or security), experience	

	Today					2025				
	1	2	3	4	5	1	2	3	4	5
Automation										
Analytics										
Digital enterprise platform										

Fig. 1 Excerpt of the online questionnaire

efficiency). (b) *Enabling effectiveness* addresses how digital technologies shape future organizations.

Ultimately, we focus on **three digital technologies**, that is **automation, analytics, and digital enterprise platform** (Sect. 2).

Following the structure of the three process activities of EPM, we created questions with a subdivision into three parts each, accommodating the three technologies. For each question, the participants had to rate the use of a technology now and their expected state in 2025 based on a five-point Likert-scale. Figure 1 shows an excerpt of the questionnaire structure for the third process activity.

3.2 Rasch Algorithm

The Rasch [70] algorithm was initially proposed for measuring discrete dichotomous data, generally about individual performance success or failure when completing certain tasks. The model assumes that answers depend on individual ability, along with the item difficulty. Accordingly, we suggest that highly skilled companies much better implement more difficult items than unskilled ones [71]. Using the Rasch algorithm on our proposed zero quartile benchmarking, the original model was modified in three ways [72]: (1) In order to express opinions rather than simple right or wrong answers, we applied a five-point Likert scale. This conversion uses the approach of a partial credit model [73], which transforms binary values into a floating scale with subordination-probabilities for each category instead of a "yes or no" probability. (2) Secondly, as the impact of a digital technology might not increase monotonically but be limited by an upper bound, we asked the respondents not only to rate their current *as-is level,* but also to express their expected *to-be level* for implementing a digital technology. In order to derive an MM that is valid for the complete population, the median was used as the commonly desired to-be level across all companies. The delta between the common expected value (median $\widehat{D}_i$) and the company's individual actual value (B_{ci}) represents the anticipated improvement (for positive values). The larger the positive gap, $X_{ci} = \widehat{D}_i - B_{ci}$, the more difficult an item. To obtain valid item estimates, we re-coded the differences, collapsing them into five categories (Z_{ci}) labelled ascendingly from difficult to easy items. (3) Thirdly, as the Rasch algorithm does not yield maturity levels, but only a single ordinal scale representing the maximum log-likelihood estimates (logit values) of each item and company, we defined **five maturity levels** based on the logit values, representing the difficulty of implementing them for companies.

Applying the aforementioned modifications, we used the eRM package in R [74] in order to create our partial credit model. Evaluating the validity of our results, we used the infit and outfit statistics, which are included in the eRM package to assess our model. Variations around a company's own maturity level are represented by the *infit* statistic, whereas *outfit* is more sensitive to items that are located far from a company's maturity level (outliers). Both values should be around one, and a value greater than two or smaller than 0.5 is regarded as critical and should be removed [75]. In our case, the statistics were all within a range of 0.75 (outfit for standard reporting and digital enterprise platform, infit for ad-hoc analyses and analytics) and 1.47 (outfit for strategic planning and automation). Hence, we were able to retain all items. In addition to the logit values of the Rasch model, we calculated means for all Likert-scale items to observe the maturity level at which the majority of surveyed participants are positioned.

4 Artifact Description

Enriched by results from our descriptive statistics (Table 2), our MM and its levels following the logit values are presented in Table 3. The descriptive statistics cover distinct parameters measuring the skill of a particular person and are in line with the difficulty β of an item. When the capability is higher than β, a person is more likely able to complete the task. Furthermore, Table 3 highlights advancements that companies should strive for to achieve the next maturity level (▲ symbol). Logit values (model betas) indicate these critical steps as "β (technology, Likert-scale item)".

Table 2 Results from our descriptive statistics

		Never		Rarely		Sometimes		Often		Always	
		Now	2025	Now	2025	Now	2025	Now	2025	Now	2025
Planning, budgeting, and forecasting	AUT	61%	13%	24%	24%	12%	27%	3%	33%	0%	3%
	ANA	32%	1%	36%	10%	21%	25%	8%	47%	3%	16%
	DEP	18%	1%	28%	4%	29%	15%	18%	43%	7%	37%
Standard reporting and monitoring	AUT	51%	13%	24%	17%	19%	24%	4%	33%	1%	12%
	ANA	36%	4%	32%	20%	21%	24%	9%	38%	2%	15%
	DEP	17%	1%	27%	5%	26%	14%	23%	39%	7%	40%
Analysis and decision support	AUT	67%	18%	20%	30%	10%	26%	2%	23%	1%	3%
	ANA	40%	4%	33%	16%	16%	26%	10%	41%	2%	13%
	DEP	23%	2%	29%	9%	24%	17%	18%	40%	6%	32%

Table 3 MM for enterprise performance management

	I - Digital Beginner	II - Digital Student	III - Digital Practitioner	IV - Digital Driver	V - Digital Master
Planning, budgeting, and forecasting			Level of **automation** is increased, especially for data preparation. *β (AUT, rarely) = -0.29* ▲	Use of **automation** is further increased. *Data is intelligently processed to enable recommended actions for some areas.*	**Automation** is used often to prepare and consolidate the results. β (AUT, often) = 2.57 ▲
		Analytics is sometimes used, mostly in a prototype status. *Market insight data is systematically acquired for certain uses. β (ANA, sometimes) = -0.92* ▲	**Analytics** use is operationalized for planning and covers more domains. *More sophisticated data base with first uses of predictive analytics.*	**Analytics** is always used for value driver, market, and other analyses. *Data incorporates past, present and predictive data. β (ANA, always) = 2.28* ▲	
	DEPs are used often to provide the base data. Essential planning data is stored at a central hub, but there is still much use of Emails or other shared folders. β (DEP, often) = -2.31 ▲	**DEPs** are always used, intuitive front-ends make navigation easy. *All available data is easily accessible and updated at one place.*			
Standard reporting and monitoring			**Automation** is slowly introduced to address specific use cases. *Some rough budget constraints can be suggested.*	Use of **automation** is largely increased. *Budgets are mostly progenerated and accepted by humans. β (AUT, often) = 1.74* ▲	**Automation** is always used to prepare and consolidate the results. *β (AUT, always) = 5.17* ▲
		Analytics is sometimes used, mostly in a prototype status. *Market intelligence data as well as order data are aggregated. β (ANA, sometimes) = -0.79* ▲	**Analytics** use is operationalized for budgeting and covers more data. *β (ANA, sometimes) = -0.12* ▲	Analytics is always used for value driver, market, and other analyses.	
	DEPs are used often to provide the base data for budgeting. *This is often in the form of an early collaboration platform with important cornerstones of data stored. β (DEP, often) = -1.6* ▲	**DEPs** are always used, intuitive front-ends make navigation easy.			
Analysis and decision support			Level of **automation** is increased, especially for data preparation. *β (AUT, sometimes) = -0.34* ▲	Use of **automation** is further increased. *This ties in with the use of analytics so that forecasts are automated and only adjusted for exceptions.*	**Automation** is always used to prepare and consolidate the results. *β (AUT, always) = 4.10* ▲
		Analytics identifies relevant factors and improves forecast accuracy but is rarely used. *β (ANA, rarely) = -1.01* ▲	**Analytics** is often used, gradually replacing gut feeling with data-driven decisions.	**Analytics** is always used as a baseline and managers mainly adjust for exceptions. *β (ANA, always) = 1.79* ▲	
		DEPs are used often to provide the base data for forecasting. β (DEP, often) = -1.11 ▲	**DEPs** are always used. *All forecasting data is available at a glance.*		

Following Esswein et al. [5], for maturity level I "*digital beginners*", the item logit values are between −1.73 (Table 3, first column third row for the digital enterprise platform) and −1.6 (Table 3, first column sixth row for the digital enterprise platform), depending on the EPM process activity and the preselected three digital technologies. Such companies are newcomers in leveraging digital technologies and represent 5.8% of our survey participants. Maturity level II incorporates items with logit values between −1.56 and −0.61. In such *student companies* (21.8% of the survey participants), some early analytics use-cases are explored—but so far, without substantial competitive advantages. Assessment items with a logit between −0.49 and 0.41 define maturity level III and represents the majority of our survey participants (54.9%). These *digital practitioners* are confident with our preselected three digital technologies, as they have already entered the stage of rollout and mass adoption for analytics and are exploring some initial automation use-cases on a digital enterprise platform. Maturity level IV covers the broader adoption of analytics and a high degree of automation in *digital driver* companies. Logit values range from 0.58 to 2.36, and 17.5% of our participants can be found here. Maturity level V covers *digital masters*. Such companies are strongly committed to making the most of digital technologies, whilst addressing even highly difficult use cases (reflected by logit values as high as 4.11 in Table 3, fifth column fourth row for automation). The Rasch algorithm did not put any of our surveyed companies into this category.

In order to make the results of our artefact design more concrete, we finally summarize the key findings in *four design guidelines* that provide guidance on how to achieve the next levels of maturity. We argue in three steps: (1) We first elaborate on the primary target (efficiency, effectiveness with its subcategories) for each activity. (2) We then combine the descriptive statistics of the present levels of implementation and Rasch-model betas for each of the technologies. (3) Finally, we complement the results with accompanying feedback from the participants and our own interpretation.

4.1 Planning, Budgeting, and Forecasting: Intuition Enriched by Data Insights—A Prime Example of Human–Computer Interaction

Starting with process activity #1 "planning, budgeting, and forecasting," the majority (62%) of the survey participants stated that *effectiveness* is the primary target for using digital technologies. Among these answers, 57% targeted future value creation on *better insights* (31%) and *speed* (26%). As many companies still rely on traditional spreadsheets, their plans are often too slow or too unrealistic.

85% of the participants answered that they never (61%) or rarely (24%) use **automation** today Table 2, first row (AUT), ("now"). We allocated them to the first three levels of our MM, since the difficulty of using automation in a prototype stage is ranked quite high at $\beta = 0.9$. Even in 2025, about 64% of these companies believe they will never (13%), rarely (24%), or only sometimes (27%) use automation. This indicates that maturity levels IV and V are reserved for companies willing to invest considerably more time and effort than the rest of the surveyed population. This is also apparent in one of the highest logit scores for "always" ($\beta = 2.57$, Table 3, fifth column, first row).

While our results show that today, more than two thirds of the surveyed participants use **analytics** rarely (36%) or never (32%), in 2025, the participants respond that analytics will be their focus technology for these activities. 63% replied that they will use analytics often (47%) or even always (16%). This is reflected in our MM through the fact that analytics is key to achieving maturity level II for use "sometimes", leading to a more widespread use at level III. To consolidate analyses such as value-driver simulations or market analyses, at maturity level IV, analytics is always used. There is no distinction between maturity levels IV and V for analytics since it is already used to its full potential by level four companies. This levelling off is evident in all of the technologies which are mastered below the current level. The unexceptional use of analytics can entail social media listening and market analyses being fed into the strategy formation process, which is then executed manually or automatically.

Moving towards digital EPM, the **digital enterprise platform** is a cornerstone for companies as their new single source of truth and central IT backbone. Today, about 50% of the surveyed companies already use such a platform, sometimes (29%), often (18%) or always (7%). In 2025, more than 80% will probably have a digital enterprise platform in use often or always. As a result, a digital enterprise platform can be considered a precondition for achieving higher maturity levels in strategic (business) planning, as it offers quick and better access to company data from a single source.

Accordingly, our first result is that planning, budgeting, and forecasting will no longer solely rely on the intuition of the management. Companies will progressively leverage their unparalleled access to data stored in the *ERP* and connect other sources such as customer relationship management to one single source of truth. Even *third-party data sources* such as market analyses or social media will be included in the new digital enterprise platform. We thus present our first design guideline.

First design guideline*: A digital enterprise platform is the future single source of truth for planning, budgeting, and forecasting. Backing a managers' experience with data, it combines harmonized ERP outcomes with insights from market analyses, social media, and other sources.*

Based on our information regarding company size, when it comes to forecasting supported by analytics, larger companies with a market capitalization of more than 20 bn EUR are more advanced than mid-sized (<20 bn EUR) and smaller companies (<5 bn EUR). Some critics might argue that predictive analytics neither foresaw the economic crisis of 2008/2009 nor the outbreak of Coronavirus in 2020. Mitigating this issue, for digital-driver companies, analytics provides an efficient baseline forecast, and managers can adjust for known exceptions of which the machine cannot be aware. This process should be flexible and modified rapidly, even over just a month.

Second design guideline*: Predictive analytics is the first opinion for planning, budgeting, and forecasting. Yet, managers have to learn to accept such outcomes so that they can focus more on irregularities.*

4.2 Standard Reporting and Monitoring—In Real-Time Where Needed

Regarding process activity #2 "standard reporting and monitoring," the surveyed participants stated that *efficiency* (46%) and *effectiveness* (50%) are de facto equal. Of the participants who answered "effectiveness", 62% stated that *better insights* (39%) and *speed* (22%) are the main drivers of digitization. Currently, 75% never (51%) or rarely (24%) use **automation**. This is reflected in a β of 0.07 for maturity level III which is higher than about half of the participants' ability logit values. However, for 2025, 45% predicted using it often (33%) or always (12%). This coincides with the progression through our maturity levels, for which, starting from level III, automation is gaining importance at every level (Table 3). Real-time information will be the new normal where it is needed. Standard reports such as sales reports delivered once a day are fully automated. Finally, at maturity level V, automation is always used for generating most standard reports and analyses, and just the push of a button away.

Analytics was attributed a similar level of importance. Today, companies use analytics never (36%), rarely (32%), or sometimes (21%). For 2025, 53% answered that they will use analytics often (38%) or always (15%), with a β of 0.04 and 1.8 respectively. For 79% of the surveyed participants, the **digital enterprise platform** will be a conditio sine qua non for "modern" standard reporting and monitoring, as it will be used often (39%) or always (40%) in 2025 (Table 2, 6th row). Analytics development starts with helping to comment on standard reports (maturity level II). It is improved at levels III and IV regarding the quantity of use in daily business.

Based on a digital enterprise platform, we believe that pull reports will replace the push reports. Management will gain access to required data with the help of smart frontends ("visual analytics") and a self-service reporting architecture, even mobile solutions are available for kind of approvals.

Third design guideline: *Standard reports and analyses as well as standard comments will be automat-ed. User-centricity is the "new" normal for a more natural working modus.*

4.3 Analyses and Decision Support—Event-Driven Self Service from Global to Line-Item Level

The majority (65%) of the survey participants stated that *effectiveness* is the primary target for using digital technologies. Herein, they specified that *better insights* (41%), *speed* (25%) and *flexibility* (19%) are the main drivers.

Presently, **automation** is never (67%) or rarely (20%) used. In 2025, automation will be more widely adopted among early adopters, companies plan to do so often (23%, $\beta = 0.9$, digital driver) or sometimes (26%, $\beta = -0.3$, digital practitioner). Hence, companies will employ semi-automated ad-hoc analyses, for example, by a causal combination of data sources in order to analyze a problem from different perspectives without manual data collection. Today, companies never (40%) or rarely (33%) use **analytics**. As they answered often (41%) and always (13%), for 2025, they will evidently increase their usage (even in comparison to automation). This indicates that more data will be analyzed at a line-item level, processed and used to model scenarios with as much information as possible. This is considered in our MM (Table 3), marking the key steps for maturity levels II (β (sometimes) $= -1.0$) and III (β (often) $= 0.35$). Visual analytics and predictive analytics will go hand in hand at these levels. At present, a digital enterprise platform is used sometimes (24%) or often (18%). In 2025, a digital enterprise platform will be used by 89% sometimes (17%), often (40%), or always (32%).

Ad-hoc analysis is a non-standard activity, which is often triggered by an event. A digital enterprise platform is needed to be able to perform individual requests

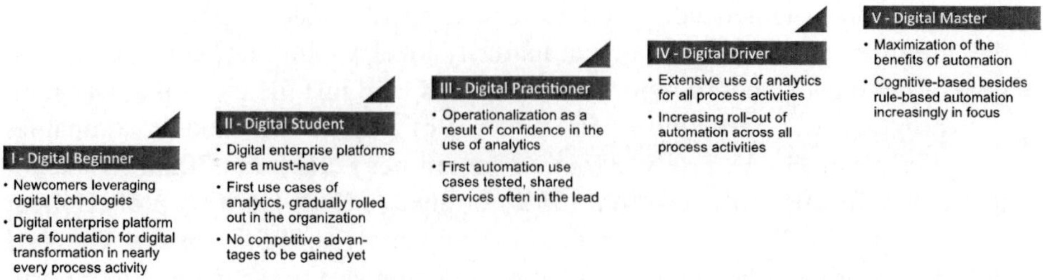

Fig. 2 Key elements to drive in our MM

by drill downs aimed at gaining a deeper understanding of the underlying reasons, and ultimately deriving meaningful business advice. Experienced companies will incorporate ad-hoc analyses even into managers' workflows, so as to become more flexible rather than adhering to a regular reporting cycle. Today, managers are not often skilled in such analyses, but that will change along the path towards digital EPM. In a digital economy, much will relate to the data needed to offer transparent, and flexible algorithms to answer business questions.

Fourth design guideline*: Managers should overcome their reluctance to work with data and start analyzing in a self-service fashion. Technology will support them from a global view to a line-item level.*

Summarizing our findings, Fig. 2 depicts the key elements that drive our MM. In stage I, the surveyed companies started to implement a digital enterprise platform supporting a joint IT architecture for all process activities. In stage II they made progress, having their ERP harmonized and external data sources connected. Furthermore, these companies have some initial analytics use-cases with a prototype status.

In stage III, companies are more confident with analytics. Some predictive analytics use-cases, such as net sales forecasts, are implemented and they started testing automation. In stage IV, companies use analytics quite extensively for all researched EPM process activities and they push forward to roll-out automation. In stage V, companies focus on maximizing the benefits of each digital technology. In parallel to this, they aim to realize synergies combining all three digital technologies. In this stage the advanced use of automation is pushed by adding cognitive automation.

5 Discussion and Conclusion

Applying a "zero-quartile" benchmarking approach and taking EPM as our case example, the objective of this paper was to develop a *forward-looking MM*. We detailed EPM with three process activities and evaluated the use of automation, analytics, and the digital enterprise platform along different levels of maturity (RQ1).

Data for the Rasch algorithm was obtained from a survey. In answering RQ2, we derived four design guidelines.

For practice, these design guidelines should help companies evolve towards digital EPM. In comparison to approaches such as Eckerson [33] and Joo et al. [76], our MM goes beyond the traditional (backward-looking) benchmarking. Reflecting the fact that automation is not the starter technology in the EPM domain, this is contrary to other finance processes such as order-to-cash, purchase-to-pay or record to report [77]. For *research purposes*, our method mix including the Rasch algorithm constitutes a rigorous starting point for examining digital technologies even beyond EPM. Our approach is more comprehensive than Blumenberg [78], who covers only single EPM process activities. In comparison with practitioners like Plaschke et al. [13], who focus on efficiency, we complement it with effectiveness and experience evaluation criteria.

Our research inevitably reveals certain *limitations*. Accordingly, there are several avenues for future research. With a sample size of 203, our data base is quite sound. However, a first future avenue would be to test for *moderating effects* of different demographic attributes. Analyses of different working styles, age, gender, education, IS experience, culture, and motivation should complete the results on hand. A second avenue would be to examine the *impact* of our MM. It should provide companies with a clear direction of their digitalization. Thus, our research should become more multifaceted by initiating *use cases* applying our MM. Such a subsequent evaluation should indicate whether our findings could be converted into action.

A further limitation of our work lies in the definition of maturity levels across the three technologies and three process activities. The uneven spread of companies across all five levels introduces a bias towards maturity levels II–IV. By choosing *equal logit values* as thresholds for all three technologies, this bias would have been even stronger. While infit and outfit statistics showed that the Rasch results are valid, different thresholds could have skewed the results towards higher or lower maturity levels respectively.

Last, but not least, we advise to *continuously update our results* as the pace of digitization is high and there could be more unpredictable developments beyond the current COVID-19 pandemic. For companies, we suggest a continuous benchmarking of their "as is" status in order to track digital progress over time.

References

1. Cokins, G.: Performance Management: Finding the Missing Pieces (to Close the Intelligence Gap). Wiley and SAS Business Series, vol. 2. John Wiley & Sons Inc, Hoboken, NJ, USA (2004)
2. Bhutta, K.S., Huq, F.: Benchmarking—best practices: an integrated approach. Benchmarking: Int. J. **6**(3), 254–268 (1999)
3. The Hackett Group: Finding the Right Best Practices Benchmarking Provider. https://www.thehackettgroup.com/best-practices-benchmarking/ (2018). Accessed 9 June 2021

4. Chanias, S., Hess, T.: How digital are we? Maturity models for the assessment of a company's status in the digital transformation. Manag. Rep./Institut für Wirtschaftsinformatik und Neue Medien **2016**(2), 1–14 (2016)
5. Esswein, M., Mayer, J.H., Razaqi, T., Quick, R.: Zero-Quartile Benchmarking—a novel method accommodating the impact of digital technologies. In: Baskerville, R., Nickerson, R. (eds.) Bridging the Internet of People, Data, and Things. Proceedings of the Thirty-Eight International Conference on Information Systems (ICIS, 2018), San Francisco, CA, USA, pp. 1–17
6. Neufeldt, V., Guralnik, D.B.: Collier's Dictionary. K to Z, 2nd ed. P. F. Collier & Son, New York City (1986)
7. de Bruin, T., Freeze, R., Kulkarni, U., Rosemann, M.: Understanding the main phases of developing a maturity assessment model. In: Proceedings of the 16th Australasian Conference on Information Systems (ACIS, 2005), Sydney, Australia, pp. 8–19
8. Röglinger, M., Pöppelbuß, J., Becker, J.: Maturity models in business process management. Bus. Process Manag. J. (Emerald Group Publishing Limited) **18**(2), 328–346 (2012)
9. Ahmad, M., Botzkowski, T., Klötzer, C., Papert, M.: Behind the blackbox of digital business models. In: Proceedings of the 53rd Hawaii International Conference on System Sciences (HICSS, 2020), Wailea, Hawaii, USA, pp. 4547–4557
10. Axson, D.A.: Finance 2020: death by digital: the best thing that ever happened to your finance organization. https://www.accenture.com/t00010101T000000Z__w__/_acnmedia/PDF-21/Accenture-Finance-2020-PoV-v2.pdf (2015). Accessed 9 June 2021
11. Lucas, S.: The Benefits of the SAP digital enterprise platform. https://blogs.saphana.com/2016/02/03/the-benefits-of-the-sap-digital-enterprise-platform/ (2016). Accessed 9 June 2021
12. Accenture: From bottom line to front line. https://www.accenture.com/_acnmedia/pdf-85/accenture-cfo-research-global.pdf (2020). Accessed 9 June 2021
13. Plaschke, F., Seth, I., Whiteman, R.: Bots, algorithms, and the future of the finance function. Risk Manag. (McKinsey on Finance) **65**, 18–23 (2018)
14. Lasrado, L.A., Vatrapu, R., Andersen, K.N.: Maturity models development in IS Research: a literature review. In: Selected Papers of the Information Systems Research Seminar in Scandinavia (IRIS, 2015), Oulu, Finland, pp. 1–12
15. March, S.T., Smith, G.F.: Design and natural science research on information technology. Decis. Support Syst. **15**(4), 251–266 (1995)
16. Simon, H.A.: The Science of the Artificial, 3rd edn. MIT Press, Cambridge, Mass (1996)
17. Hevner, A.R., March, S.T., Park, J., Ram, S.: Design science in information systems research. MIS Q. **28**(1), 75–105 (2004)
18. vom Brocke, J., Winter, R., Hevner, A., Maedche, A.: Accumulation and evolution of design knowledge in design science research—a journey through time and space. J. Assoc. Inf. Syst. **21**(3), 520–544 (2019)
19. Gregor, S., Hevner, A.R.: Positioning and presenting design science research for maximum impact. MIS Q. (Management Information Systems Research Center, University of Minnesota) **37**(2), 337–355 (2013)
20. Mayer, J.H., Hebeler, C., Esswein, M., Göbel, M., Quick, R.: Evaluating a forward-looking maturity model for enterprise performance management. In: Aier, S., Rohner, P. (eds.) Festschrift für Robert Winter. LNISO, vol. 38, pp. 137–153. Heidelberg, New York, Dordrecht (2022)
21. Webster, J., Watson, R.T.: Analyzing the past to prepare for the future: writing a literature review. MIS Q. (Management Information Systems Research Center, University of Minnesota) **26**(2), xiii–xxiii (2002)
22. AIS: Senior Scholar's Basket of Journals. https://aisnet.org/page/SeniorScholarBasket (2020). Accessed 14 July 2020
23. SJR: Scimago Journal & Country Rank. https://www.scimagojr.com/journalrank.php?area=1400&category=1402 (2020). Accessed 6 June 2021
24. AIS: Conferences. https://aisnet.org/page/Conferences (2020). Accessed 14 July 2020
25. Ongena, G., Ravesteyn, P.: Business process management maturity and performance. Bus. Process Manag. J. (Emerald Publishing Limited) **26**(1), 132–149 (2020)

26. Williams, C., Boardman, L., Lang, K., Schallmo, D.: Digital maturity models for small and medium-sized enterprises: a systematic literature review. In: Proceedings of the 30th International Society for Professional Innovation Management (ISPIM, 2019), Florence, Italy, pp. 1–15
27. Comuzzi, M., Patel, A.: How organisations leverage Big Data: a maturity model. Ind. Manag. Data Syst. (Emerald Group Publishing Limited) **116**(8), 1468–1492 (2016)
28. Imgrund, F., Fischer, M., Janiesch, C., Winkelmann, A.: Approaching digitalization with business process management. In: Proceedings of the 26th Multikonferenz Wirtschaftsinformatik (MKWI, 2018), Ilmenau, Germany, pp. 1–12
29. Rowley, J., Slack, F.: Conducting a literature review. Manag. Res. News **27**(6), 31–39 (2004)
30. Hess, T., Benlian, A., Matt, C., Wiesböck, F.: Options for formulating a digital transformation strategy. MISQE **15**(2), 123–139 (2016)
31. Cokins, G.: Enterprise performance management (EPM) and the digital revolution. Perform. Improv. Conf. - Expert Perspect. **56**(4), 14–19 (2017)
32. Schmaus, P.A.: Peer group benchmarking for the relative performance evaluation of companies. University of St Gallen, Business Dissertations. Epubli GmbH, Berlin, pp. 128 (2018)
33. Eckerson, W.: Best Practices in Business Performance Management: Business and Technical Strategies. TDWI report series, pp. 1–32 (2004)
34. Frolick, M.N., Ariyachandra, T.R.: Business performance management: one truth. Inf. Syst. Manag. **23**(1), 41–48 (2006)
35. Suša Vugec, D., Ivancic, L., Milanovic Glavan, L.: Business process management and corporate performance management: does their alignment impact organizational performance. Interdiscip. Descr. Complex Syst.: INDECS (Croatian Interdisciplinary Society) **17**(2), 368–384 (2019)
36. Santos, L.R., Chen, M.K.: The evolution of rational and irrational economic behavior. In: Glimcher, P.W. (ed.) Neuroeconomics: Decision Making and the Brain, 1st edn., pp. 81–93. Academic Press, London, San Diego, CA (2009)
37. Auguinis, H.: Performance management, 2nd edn. Dorling Kindersley Publishing Pvt. Ltd., Noida (2009)
38. Kahneman, D.: Maps of bounded rationality: psychology for behavioral economics. Am. Econ. Rev. (American Economic Association) **93**(5), 1449–1475 (2003)
39. Vezard, A.: Understanding the interplay between cognitive and affective decision making processes: Implications for management accounting based on neuroeconomic evidence. Master's Thesis, Julius-Maximilians-Universität (JMU, 2015)
40. Vroom, V.H.: Work and Motivation. Wiley, New York, NY, USA (1964)
41. Locke, E.A., Cartledge, N., Koeppel, J.: Motivational effects of knowledge of results: a goal-setting phenomenon? Psychol. Bull. **70**(6, Pt. 1), 474–485 (1968)
42. Yaghi, B., Youell, N., Neely, A.D.: Enterprise performance management: the global state of the art. SSRN J. Oracle Report/Cranfield University (2008)
43. Schrage, M., Kiron, D., Hancock, B., Breschi, R.: Performance management's digital shift. MIT Sloan Manag. Rev. 1–23 (2019)
44. Farahdel, S.: A visual performance management framework to improve decision making using Lean Six Sigma. Master's Thesis, Concordia University (CU, 2020)
45. Moskalenko, V., Fonta, N.: The cascading subsystem of key performance indicators in the enterprise performance management system. In: Nechyporuk, M., Pavlikov, V., Kritskiy, D. (eds.) Integrated Computer Technologies in Mechanical Engineering—2020: Synergetic Engineering. Lecture Notes in Networks and Systems, vol. 188, 1st edn., pp. 704–715. Springer International Publishing; Imprint, Springer, Cham (2021)
46. Zou, T., Bai, S.: Enterprise performance optimization management decision-making and coordination mechanism based on multiobjective optimization. Math. Probl. Eng. **2021**(1), 1–12 (2021)
47. Akdil, K.Y., Ustundag, A., Cevikcan, E.: Maturity and readiness model for industry 4.0 strategy. In: Ustundag, A., Cevikcan, E. (eds.) Industry 4.0: Managing The Digital Transformation. Springer Series in Advanced Manufacturing, pp. 61–94. Springer International Publishing, Cham (2018)

48. Colli, M., Berger, U., Bockholt, M., Madsen, O., Møller, C., Wæhrens, B.V.: A maturity assessment approach for conceiving context-specific roadmaps in the Industry 4.0 era. Annu. Rev. Control **48**(1), 165–177 (2019)
49. Pinto, J.L.: Assessing the relationship between bpm maturity and the success of organizations. NOVA Information Management School (2020)
50. Mergel, I., Edelmann, N., Haug, N.: Defining digital transformation: results from expert interviews. Gov. Inf. Q. **36**(4), (2019)
51. Mayer, J.H., Quick, R., Towara, T.: Digital Technologies for Managers: A Maturity Model from their Business Perspective. In: Krause, S. and Pellens, B. (ed) Betriebswirtschaftliche Implikationen des wirtschaftlichen Wandels. 75 Jahre Arbeitskreise der Schmalenbach-Gesellschaft für Betriebswirtschaft e.V., Sonderheft 17 der Zeitschrift für betriebswirtschaftliche Forschung und Praxis (ZfbF), pp. 241–263 (2017)
52. The Hackett Group: CFO Agenda: Finances Four Imperatives to Accelerate Business Value. https://www.thehackettgroup.com/key-issues-fin-1801-thankyou/ (2018b). Accessed 8 October 2020
53. Pearson, M.: Strategies for aligning manufacturing with business and supply chain goals. Logist. Manag. 20–21 (2012)
54. Karunagaran, S., Mathew, S.K., Lehner, F.: Differential cloud adoption: a comparative case study of large enterprises and SMEs in Germany. Inf. Syst. Front. **21**(4), 861–875 (2019)
55. Spruit, M., Pietzka, K.: MD3M: the master data management maturity model. Comput. Hum. Behav. **51**(2), 1068–1076 (2015)
56. Bizjak, J.M., Lemmon, M.L., Naveen, L.: Does the use of peer groups contribute to higher pay and less efficient compensation? J. Financ. Econ. **90**(2), 152–168 (2008)
57. Albuquerque, A.: Peer firms in relative performance evaluation. J. Account. Econ. **48**(1), 69–89 (2009)
58. Spendolini, M.J.: The benchmarking process. Compens. Benefits Rev. **24**(5), 21–29 (1992)
59. Atkinson, M.: Developing and using a performance management framework: a case study. Meas. Bus. Excell. **16**(3), 47–56 (2012)
60. McNair, C.J., Leibfried, K.H.J.: Benchmarking: a tool for continuous improvement. John Wiley & Sons (1992)
61. Ifenthaler, D., Egloffstein, M.: Development and implementation of a maturity model of digital transformation. TechTrends **64**(2), 302–309 (2020)
62. Som, O., Gamroth, P.N.: Assessing the digital maturity of human resource management. In: Proceedings of the 30th International Society for Professional Innovation Management (ISPIM) Conference, pp. 1–29 (2019)
63. Department of accounting and auditing at Darmstadt University of Technology. https://www.rcw.wi.tu-darmstadt.de/; https://www.tu-darmstadt.de/index.en.jsp. Accessed 25 July 2021
64. Schmalenbach working group "Digital Finance". https://www.linkedin.com/showcase/ak-digital-finance/?originalSubdomain=de; https://www.schmalenbach.org/index.php/arbeitskreise/finanz-und-rechnungswesen-steuern/digital-finance. Accessed 25 July 2021
65. IMA: Enterprise Performance Management: Management Accountants Perceptions. https://www.imanet.org/insights-and-trends/performance-measurement-incentives-and-alignment/enterprise-performance-management?ssopc=1 (2014). Accessed 9 June 2021
66. Winter, R., Schelp, J.: Towards a methodology for service construction. In: 40th Annual Hawaii International Conference on System Sciences (HICSS, 2007), Waikoloa Village, HI, USA, pp. 1–7
67. Yusuf, Y., Sarhadi, M., Gunasekaran, A.: Agile manufacturing: the drivers, concepts and attributes. Int. J. Prod. Econ. **62**(1), 33–43 (1999)
68. Belhiah, M., Bounabat, B., Achchab, S.: The impact of data accuracy on user-perceived business service's quality. In: 10th Iberian Conference on Information Systems and Technologies (CISTI), pp. 1–4 (2015)
69. Takabi, H., Joshi, J.B., Ahn, G.-J.: Security and privacy challenges in cloud computing environments. IEEE Secur. Privacy Mag. **8**(6), 24–31 (2010)

70. Rasch, G.: Studies in Mathematical Psychology: I Probabilistic Models for Some Intelligence and Attainment Tests. Danmarks Paedagogiske Institut, Copenhagen (1960)
71. Bond, T.G., Fox, C.M.: Applying the Rasch Model: Fundamental Measurement in the Human Sciences. Routledge Taylor & Francis Group, New York (2015)
72. Lahrmann, G., Marx, F., Mettler, T., Winter, R., Wortmann, F.: Inductive Design of Maturity Models: Applying the Rasch Algorithm for Design Science Research, vol. 6629, pp. 176–191 (2011)
73. Masters, G.N.: A Rasch model for partial credit scoring. Psychometrika **47**(2), 149–174 (1982)
74. Mair, P., Hatzinger, R.: Extended Rasch Modeling: The eRm Package for the Application of IRT Models in R. Research Report Series/Department of Statistics and Mathematics, vol. 47, no. 1. Department of Statistics and Mathematics, WU Vienna University of Economics and Business (2007)
75. Linacre, B., Beck, M.: What do infit and outfit, mean-square and standardized mean? https://www.rasch.org/rmt/rmt162f.htm (2002). Accessed 9 June 2021
76. Joo, S.-J., Nixon, D., Stoeberl, P.A.: Benchmarking with data envelopment analysis: a return on asset perspective. Benchmarking **18**(4), 529–542 (2011)
77. Berger, S., Bitzer, M., Häckel, B., Voit, C.: Approaching digital Transformation—development of a multi-dimensional Maturity Model. In: Proceedings of the 28th European Conference on Information Systems (ECIS, 2020), Marrakech, Morocco, pp. 1–18
78. Blumenberg, S.: Benchmarking financial chain efficiency—the role of economies of scale for financial processes. In: Proceedings of the 8th Pacific Asia Conference on Information Systems (PACIS, 2004), Shanghai, China, pp. 972–985

Data Ecosystem and Data Value Chain: An Exploration of Drones Technology Applications

Cristina De Simone, Federica Ceci, and Cristina Alaimo

Abstract The drones' market is anticipated to grow significantly because of its increasing use for commercial and professional purposes. They are currently used in many industries and the next frontier is represented by the automotive industry. The volume of disposable data is growing exponentially, reaching more than 44 zettabytes of valuable data in 2020. In order to be able to fully reap the value of data available, firms must delve in big data and Data Value Chain (DVC) discipline. This paper explores the ecosystem formation as well as the challenges and criticalities encountered by Dronus and Here in their interaction and exchange of data. Ecosystems are network of distributed companies that shows multiple links toward their environment that interact via standard and business rules which permit them to be independent but also connected. Data have been collected through multiple sources, i.e. semi-structured interviews with firm's representatives and direct observation. This study will give a contribution for future literature as it focuses on the analysis and research of an important gap that sees knowledge of bottlenecks as a way of conscious and efficient growth. In this way, firms and ecosystems that have successfully understood the importance of these variables found will be able to better answer to changes becoming more agile. Successful big data integration, accessibility and standard business rules, as we identify as the main roadblocks, will allow firms in data-driven sectors, and in particular in computer vision-based data set, to be efficient in the interconnection and to become more agile.

Keywords Data ecosystem · Data value chain · Digital transformation

C. De Simone
Dipartimento di Impresa e Management, Luiss University Rome, Rome, Italy

F. Ceci (✉)
Department of Business Administration, University G. d'Annunzio Chieti-Pescara, Chieti, Italy
e-mail: federica.ceci@unich.it; f.ceci@unich.it

C. Alaimo
Department of Political Sciences, Luiss University Rome, Rome, Italy
e-mail: calaimo@luiss.it

S. Za et al. (eds.), *Sustainable Digital Transformation*, Lecture Notes in Information Systems and Organisation 59, https://doi.org/10.1007/978-3-031-15770-7_13

1 Introduction

Drones are growing in their importance in nowadays lives and applications [1]. They are currently used in agriculture, industries, oil and gas, real estates, public safety, energy, delivery, and the next frontier is to use them in the automotive industry [2–4]. Firms are increasingly utilizing drone-acquired data in their business operations to accelerate their service delivery and to expand the universe of possible applications [5]. The volume of data available is growing exponentially, arriving to more than 44 zettabytes (44 trillion GB) of useful data in 2020 [6]. To obtain full advantage of the huge quantity of data produced, firms are delving into the technological field of big data. However, big data need to be processed to gain strategic validation; to do so, they are often included in a Data Value Chain (DVC) [7]. A value chain is composed by a series of subsystems each with inputs, processes of transformation and outputs [8, 9]. With DVC we refer to the information flow within a big data system, composed by a series of steps needed to generate value and useful insights from data. The DVC enables the appropriation of value from the data [10].

Such technological advancements require to established firms and startups a reorganization of their relations and collaborations, in order to match the new technological and organizational requirements. In fact, in an increasingly interconnected world, economic value is less and less created by one firm alone but rather through a combination and enrichment of data by various actors in their so-called data ecosystems [11]. Ecosystems are network of organizations involved in the delivery of a product or a service thought both competition and cooperation creating a constantly evolving relationships in which each firm must be flexible and adaptable to survive and predominate, as in biological ecosystems. A successful data ecosystem shows seamlessly interactions of all the stakeholders within a digital single market, leading to business opportunities, easier access to knowledge and capital. A well-functioning data ecosystem must bring together the key stakeholders with a clear benefit for all [10]. Previous literature, especially the one focusing on ecosystems and their structure [12, 13], explored the new forms of organizations in a digital environment. However, the debate on how to bridge business transformation with big data analytics for value creation and to accelerate on the sustainable development of the society is still open [14].

This paper explores the structure of relationships a nascent DVC, i.e., the navigation systems. More specifically, we provide a fine-grained analysis focusing on the process of relation building in one specific link of the DVC, composed by a drone producer and a firm operating the navigation sector. The study is positioned in the literature, in between data-driven technology and formation of ecosystems, with specific attention to the optimization of acquired knowledge to make exchange of data between ecosystem participants more efficient. The diffusion of connectivity software made it clear that ecosystem actors can't be seen in isolation, but all of them need to interact and collaborate to create sharable knowledge. That's why we focus our research on the ecosystem, starting from its creation and center to the final structure. We analyze the initial activities implemented by the two players in the process of ecosystem formation, to identify challenges and criticalities emerged during the first phases of its creation. We have found that in the initial steps of Dronus/Here relationship, the two companies have sternly focused their attention on succeeding in the exchange of data to arrive to a shared interaction procedure, in order to minimize bottlenecks during the chain. Then we have explored the core ecosystem interaction in order to find the exact challenges which the two firms have faced to find standard procedures and to exchange consistent data.

2 Theoretical Framework: Data Value Chain and Ecosystem Formation

2.1 Data Value Chain

The Data Value Chain (DVC) describes the evolution of data from collection to analysis, dissemination, and the final impact of data on decision making [15]. Through its analysis, a decision support tool will be created to model the chain of activities that an organization performs in order to deliver a valuable product or service to the market [8]. The value chain categorizes the generic value-adding activities of an organisation allowing them to be understood and optimized. A value chain is made up of a series of subsystems each with inputs, transformation processes, and outputs. Rayport and Sviokla [16] were one of the first to apply the value chain metaphor to information systems within their work on Virtual Value Chains. The inclusion of DVC in a smart environment increases the performances of firms that have successfully understood the great importance of data. The process of DVC [10, 17] is reported in Fig. 1. It is possible to identify 5 phases, briefly described as follows:

- *Data Acquisition*: process by which the data are gathered, filtered and cleaned to generate an element that can be insert in the Data Warehouse to carry out the necessary analysis;
- *Data Analysis*: process that involves the exploration, transformation and modelling of data with the aim of making data useful for strategic purpose;
- *Data Curation*: process by which involved data management is obtained by ensuring that the required quality of data has been met over the entire life cycle [19];

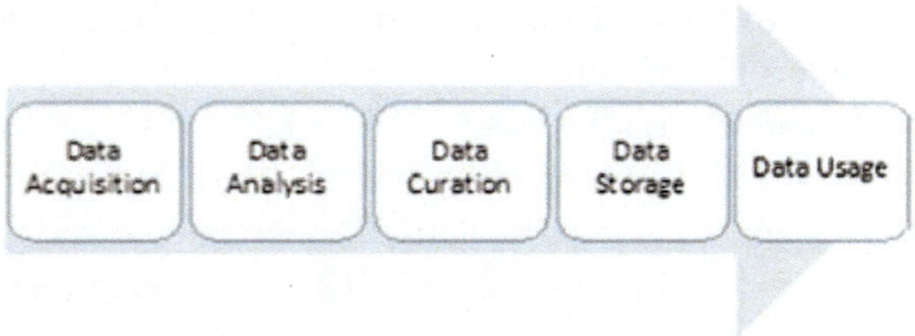

Fig. 1 Authors representation from Curry [18]

- *Data Storage*: process by which the data are correctly clustered and stored in a scalable way in order to be quickly and efficiently accessed by firms and actors that need them;
- *Data Usage*: activity of proactive integration of the data analysis in the business processes though tools that are aimed at supporting the analysis and the access to storage data.

The DVC has been proposed to model high level activities within information systems, assuming more interconnections than in traditional Value Chain, and is placed in the core of the Data Ecosystem at a micro level, while multiple stakeholders exist at the meso and macro level [20]. When referring to big data and business analytics, the term ecosystem describes the environment created and supported by the numerous actors, that generate perpetual data along with their interactions and interrelations. Such ecosystems already exist in the industry within or between different sectors (e.g., Apple, Google, Intel, Microsoft). However, giving the fast progress of data, there is a need to evolve existing ecosystems, or develop new ones, to be more dynamic and actively include more stakeholders, taking into account both their capabilities and needs. Because of modern digital technologies, also conventional business environments are turning into digital ecosystems, where dependencies and interconnections are increasingly constituted by digital connectivity. New capabilities need to be developed in order to correctly face digital customer orientation, which is the customization and enrichment of experience provided to customer of the service offered by the company [18].

In this way, firms will establish a more intimate and personalized relation with the customers being able to better know their needs thanks to data-driven methodologies. The contributions given by Knabke and Olbrich [21] and Mikalef and Gupta [22] in fact, highlight the potential of capabilities in increasing business intelligence and value, thus improving academic understanding on how firms may evolve their role and position in current big data and business analytics ecosystems. A strong analytics capability is crucial to foster digital transformation, as organizations that want to compete in the digital economy will have to invest in various resources including people, processes, technologies and organizational design [17, 23].

2.2 Ecosystem Formation

The diffusion of connectivity services and software allow firms to redesign their environment towards a structure that shows less strict discrepancy between what is internal and what is external, making the boundaries of firms more blurred. This phenomenon has been often analyzed troughs the lens of the ecosystems literature [24–27]. In managerial literature, an ecosystem is a complex network of affiliated organizations whose activities and outputs are linked in multilateral ways that cannot be reduced to the sum of bilateral connections between ecosystem participants, but show dependencies running across many participants and along several dimensions

[12]. Studies tend to concur that ecosystems are not hierarchically managed, but few have specifically looked at the rules governing membership and relationships [28]. Participants are linked together by several resource or product/service dependencies that confer to them distinct advantages that would have otherwise not emerged [12]. Ecosystem actors can't be seen in isolation, instead all of them need to actively interact and collaborate with each other to create knowledge and innovate [14, 29].

The continuous interaction between players and the exchange of strategic data which can achieve uniqueness when merged and analyzed in combination, can lead the ecosystem to an absolute advantage that have the possibility to shape the future designs of the ecosystem in these sectors, thus capable to drive the market from then on [30]. In complex networks, actors interact and collaborate with each other to find, archive, publish, consume, or reuse data as well as to foster innovation, create value, and support new businesses with the aim to create added value for all the actors involved in the flow [31]. Thus, to guarantee the interconnection of different actors given by data exchange, the ecosystem needs to develop various roles with different functions [32]. Researchers define a role as a function performed by an actor within the ecosystem [31]. In some ecosystem we can identify the existence of a central role ("keystone" actor) which can be responsible for the real success of the ecosystem, which is embodied by the firm that has been able to reap the wave of innovations and that will shape the design of the market from then on [33]. The emergence of a dominant design, in fact, is a very important moment, significantly affecting firms' strategies and performances. That's why it is so important that an organization is able to shape the technological trajectory succeeding over the other players [34, 35]. It seems appropriate to highlight a common characteristic between ecosystems, known as "co-evolution", which is crucial in the phase of ecosystem formation because the players that have decided to combine data to create valuable knowledge, start a process of growth that is reciprocally shaped [12, 36]. When a standard of exchange has been created thanks to joint decisions, players set up a process of continuous, interdependent development that led to cooperative and competitive relationships simultaneously in the ecosystem—also known as coopetition [37].

With consciousness about the different types of configurations between companies, Subramaniam et al. [38] have suggested a strategic option in order to leverage new opportunities from digital ecosystem, which are "Digital Hybrids". They are in the middle between consumption and production ecosystem, thus reaping the advantage of customization of service offering and the positive network effects though interactions among complementary entities. In the automotive sector firms are beginning to unlock new value from cars' product-in-use information as predictive maintenance services, voice-activated technology or the equipment of parking lots with sensor [38].

Ecosystems have different layers depending on the interconnections and the strategic role that each participant possess; thus, actors develop a multitude of links which go far beyond the bi-lateral one of traditional firms. As reported in Fig. 2, the ecosystems modelled by Cavanillas et al. [10], is represented by:

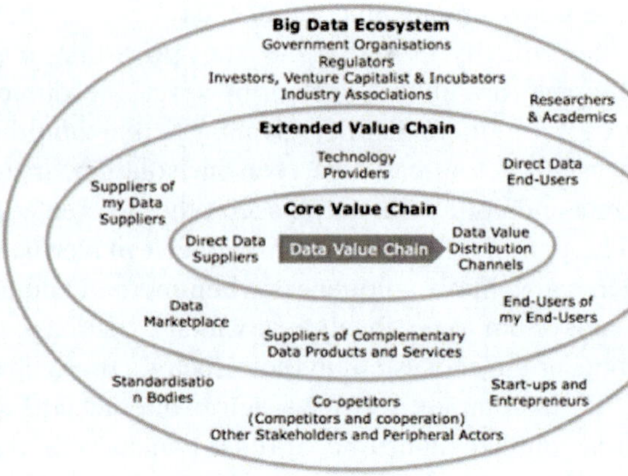

Fig. 2 The micro, meso, and macro levels of a big data ecosystem [20]

- *Big Data Ecosystem*: the macro level, able to exogenously shape the context. It is composed by: regulators for data privacy and legal issues; standardization bodies which define technological standards (both official and de facto); investors, venture capitalists, and incubators; researchers who investigate new algorithms, technologies, methodologies, and business models.
- *Extended Value Chain* is the middle level of the network, with the potential of change market dynamics thanks to the availability of data. Actors included in this level are: (i) data providers: people or organizations that create, collect, aggregate, and transform data from both public and private sources; (ii) technology providers: typically organizations that provide tools, platforms, services, and know-how for data management; (iii) data end users: people or organizations from different industries that leverage on big data technologies; (iv) data marketplace: people or organizations that host data from publishers and sell them to end users; (v) start-ups and entrepreneurs that develop innovative data-driven technologies, products, and services.
- *Core Value Chain*: the fulcrum of the ecosystem is the interconnections between the direct data supplier and the data value distribution channels which give value to the data, deciding on business implications.

The focus of this paper relies in the micro level, i.e. the two players that generate the first and more important interaction: the supplier of data and the data distributor. Their expectations are to succeed in the collection, development and supply of data, to be able to sell them globally, making the technology be known worldwide. This level represents the "heart" of the entire process, requiring the two players the development of appropriate technical skills. Players usually show deep understanding of large-scale analytical data and good knowledge in statistics and machine learning, which is crucial to make data valuable.

3 Method

3.1 *Empirical Context: Dronus and Its Surrounding Ecosystem*

Big data ecosystem is composed by multiple levels, that can be differently important depending on the focus we are looking for. In the present work, we focus our attention on one specific link of the value chain, composed by the relationship of Dronus and Here. Dronus is an Italian start-up specialized in the production of highly precise drones used in professional applications which is developing innovative solutions for the charging of drones and their possibility of flying for wide distances with a network of distributed nests. Moreover, Dronus is fostering the precision in the photogrammetry and in the construction of highly precise Digital Surface Model (DSM) and Digital Terrain Model (DTM) for multiple commercial purposes (i.e. security, agriculture, automotive). Here is a multinational firm, leader in the navigation sector. Here innovating efforts aims at building a highly precise map that can be used for the implementation of the autonomous vehicle software insert in car's system.

In our case, there is a strategic reciprocal importance of Dronus, firm specialized in the production of highly precise drones used in professional applications, and Here, specialized in the production of navigation systems. Dronus, is responsible of the generation of data, acquired throughout the use of drones and transferred to Here to be sized and cleaned to generate a cloud of points that will constitute a highly precise picture (photogrammetry) of the territory for automotive application. As these two players interact together (Micro Level), other actors, in bigger layers (Marco Level) enter in the fields and shows interest in this connection.

The results of this collaboration will change the landscape of the automotive sector that we currently know, allowing Here to collect enough data needed to build an integrated map at high definition (42 Megapixel) of almost all the cities in the world, for the new frontier of the automotive world: the autonomous driving. In fact, in the past, data were collected with GPS and airplanes, signifying that the precision was sacrificed and that the update of the maps was missing.

The big challenge that Here needs to address will be, thanks to the partnership with Dronus, to arrange flights that are on-demand and real time. These surveys will be executed by Dronus, that will become a strategic partner in the collection of data for the implementation of this innovative, potentially worldwide, project. Dronus and Here aim is to reduce the costs associated with airplane flights thanks to the possibility of a lower-altitude flight, on demand, which can fly over urban areas and therefore certified, which has higher definition cameras than GPS with fixed points geo-localized. To reduce costs and have highly precise images thanks to Here recognition systems and Artificial Intelligence, it will make two advances: (i) modify and improve its content; (ii) recognize some details that neither from the satellite nor with specialized machines Here have been able to obtain (e.g., improve the presence of pedestrian crossings or identify holes on the roads) since with the drone it is possible to obtain a weekly or monthly update, on demand and in real time.

Dronus and Here have the potentiality to shape the technological trajectory of the future in multiple sectors being the first movers on this type of experimentation, having even reached strategic agreements with the National and International legislation entities. The interactions between the two players will be explained analyzing the process that allowed them to perform an experimental flight over Biella (Italy), the target city, to collect data that will be used by Here to build a highly precise map. Such map will be the starting point for implementing a radically improved version of the autonomous driving software insert in car's system.

3.2 Data Collection

We collected data though multiple sources, that can be divided in semi-structured interviews with firm's representatives and direct observation. We started from the collection of secondary data to structure an interview protocol that has been used for conducting personal interviews. The advantage of personal interviews is that they deal with personal and direct contact between the interviewer and the interviewee, thus eliminating the no-answer probability. Moreover, the structure of a protocol allows us to develop a good flow and pattern of data and information eliminating misalignments and deviation from the pre-specified research aims and targets. All the interviews focused on the DVC in the market of drones and automotive, on the Big Data Ecosystem, on the expectation of the players involved, problems and issues that firms have encountered in the various stage of the process. The aim of the interviews has been to clearly identify opinions, real life applications and enlighten explanations on Dronus/Here ecosystem formation in order to identify major roadblocks to be further analyzed and expanded deep inside. All the collected data has been analyzed individually and then discussed together to be structured in an organic way. All the interviews have been recorded. The analysis aimed at identifying the main bottlenecks encountered in the process. A list of interviews is reported in Table 1.

We have collected data using a semi-structured questionnaire, which has been used as a guideline for the researcher and interviewer. An interview protocol (reported in Appendix) has been prepared in order to smooth and facilitate the trend of the speeches and leaving space to further develop subject born in the conversation which weren't in the programmed list and lineup.

Meetings with the company's representatives were held during the 1st semester of 2021. In this way, the interviewer has had the possibility to fully shape its ideas in order to ask the right questions to the right person. In fact, being a very specific and untouched sector, it has been crucial to identify precise vertical competences within employees so to reap their entire cultural baggage.

Thanks to a multitude of time, with data extrapolation and concepts enrichment has been possible the realization of a really deep understanding of the subjects declared by our interviewees.

Table 1 List of interviews

#	Interviewee	Role	Firm	Day	Lenght
1	Giulio Segurini	Co-Founder Business Development AeroSpace Engineering	Dronus	16/02/2021 10/03/2021 15/04/2021	3 h 2 h 1 h
2	Alessandro Zullo	Practice Director/Senior Account Executive	Here	15/03/2021	3 h
3	Marco Ballerini	Dronus CEO—Head of R&D Founder	Dronus	10/03/2021	30 min
4	Stefano Pettini	Location Platform/Big Data Architect	Here	20/03/2021	30 min
5	Michele Feroli	CEO SiraLab Co-Founder	Dronus	01/04/2021	30 min
6	Laura Minore	Senior Local Data Intelligence Analyst	Here	10/04/2021	45 min
7	Riccardo Benedetti	Dronus Director Head of Program Co-Founder	Dronus	12/03/2021	30 min
8	Simone Menicucci	Certification Manager	Dronus	05/03/2021	1 h

3.3 Data Analysis

Content analysis was used to analyze and examine data that has been gathered from personal interviews. Data have been categorized in themes and sub-themes in order to make them comparable. The main advantage of this methodology of analysis is that data collected are simplified and cleaned in order to be effectively managed by actors and employees that need them and in order to give to qualitative data structure in a way that satisfy the objectives of the research.

However, the possibility of human error is highly probable given the fact that researchers can interpret data in different ways based on past experience, culture and internal/contextual biases.

Moreover, employees and representatives have been fully informed regarding the objectives of the research and they were granted the confidentiality and academic-only purpose of the information, thus creating a climate of comfort and mutual esteem.

4 Results and Discussion

This paper investigates the initial activities of a newborn ecosystem, i.e. the navigation system, and its relations within the DVC. The aim of this paper is to explore, focusing on the relationship between two actors, the ecosystem in its initial phase and to identify challenges and criticalities emerged during the first phases of its creation.

In all ecosystem formation, numerous challenges need to be faced by the key players, which have to decide and define common standards on which to align on in order to act independently in the daily business. In the formation of Dronus/Here relationship, the two firms worked hard to find the best way to exchange data and to reach shared interaction procedure, aimed at minimizing problems and bottlenecks during the process. Yet, they experienced numerous challenges. We grouped them in the following three categories: (i) data integration; (ii) accessibility; (iii) data architectures; (iv) standard business rules.

The biggest problem encountered by Dronus and Here is the definition of an aligned format for data sharing, i.e. data integration. To be more precise, the complexity of data integration and their interoperability, provide a scenario where multiple levels of data storage and integration are needed to be able to structure a single data entity. Dronus and Here understand the importance of managing their data effectively but struggled with the step involved in structuring, transforming and maintaining access to valid and reliable information. Thus, data integration activities required additional effort and time to work. Another challenge is represented by the need of integrating disparate data sources into a centralized database that can be accessed by all the employees of Here and Dronus. To solve this issue, the firms created a platform containing all the shared data. The platform database is composed by data of high-level precision that constitute the photogrammetrical tables georeferenced. The tables will permit to implement Digital Surface Model (DSM), Digital Terrain Model (DTM) and Building Information (BI) models needed by the autonomous vehicle to perform defined framework. Integrating data from a source system to another database requires Application Programming Interfaces (APIs) in a format that the system can read. So, if Dronus and Here don't have expertise in specific solution to be used, they may have to develop workarounds to get data passing correctly on the flow. To be more precise, APIs are security system which are connected to internal and external environment. This permits to Dronus and Here to determine and agree on the destination points of the data. APIs serve as data connector and guarantee that data move in secure way and give to their owner control on who is allowed to access them. For instance, if Here need to update its application with fresh data, automatically the software will "ask" information to Dronus database and data will be transferred to the end-user thanks to APIs authority. The final goal of data integration is to understand the outcome, i.e. what firms want to achieve. An intelligence solution needs a platform that can support real-time/right-time data streaming where algorithms will be applied guaranteeing uploading and storage of data in an effective way.

The second element is represented by "accessibility". Collect source data on a regular basis and in an effectively manner is a challenging task. Being sure that the complexities required for data integration won't invalidate the idea of open source is the center of the accessibility defiance. To make the source code accessible for everyone into a secure network, firms need to identify clearly what are the data that can be easily shared and the one that need to be retained in the firm. Firms must prefer to keep internally data that can be a source of distinctive advantage and know-how. Moreover, it will be difficult to fly over cities with high frequency to allow the software to be updated in "real time". Indeed, the increase of storage capacity makes hard to measure realistically the dependency of efficient integrations with the big calculation effort. More data are processed and storage, more organizations require a "piecemeal" approach, wherein they examine the data points individually and evaluate their value in the integration strategy.

The third problem faced by the firms related to "data architectures", that is a direct consequence of the size and maturity of the players. Players with big size and old establishments tend to be more hierarchical, schematics and with standard business rules, meanwhile players which are slender tend to be more fluid and blur. Data architectures refers to the overarching system used to ingest and process enormous amount of data that can be analyzed for business purpose. Data architectures are developed to deal with batch processing of data sources, real-time processing of data, predictive analysis and machine learning. Big challenges deriving from the orchestration of big data are related to: (i) data quality, that means that Dronus and Here need to ensure that data formats match and that they don't have duplicate problems, (ii) scaling, because the larger the volume, the more difficulty in handling them increases, so if they haven't designed in advance a solid standard business architecture, they can quickly run into problems, (iii) security, considering that there is a huge volume of sensitive information that are shared in their big data, cybercriminal could mine the flow of data.

The last challenge is constituted by "standard business rules". Identification of business rules across business units and make sure that accurate versions of the correct standard apply to each, so that everyone is aligned on corporate culture. A deep understanding of responsibilities and tasks can help the process of exchange, making the flow smoother and more fluid. In fact, although the employees in the firms understand the value their data can bring, once they are analyzed, many still struggle with effective solution and general efficiencies based on a conduit between Dronus source data and Here target database.

Table 2 reports some excerpts from the interviews, Fig. 3 reports a graphical representation of the challenges.

5 Conclusion

Firms are increasingly utilizing drone-acquired data in their business operations to accelerate their service delivery and to expand the universe of possible applications [5].

To obtain full advantage of the huge quantity of data produced, firms are delving into the technological field of big data. However, big data need to be processed to gain strategic validation; to do so, they are often included in a Data Value Chain (DVC) [7]. A value chain is composed by a series of subsystems each with inputs, processes of transformation and outputs [8, 9].

Table 2 Excerpt from the interviews

Issues	Quotes
Data integration	*A problem that we face constantly when we exchange data regards the integration of different streams and flow into a common and shared Data warehouse. It affects all the dimensions of data, starting from the format to the volume, to the meaning we attribute to it*
Accessibility	*We are open firms that believe in progress and future. We want to make everyone participate to the internal dynamic but is delicate to define what are the data boundaries needed for each role. The aim of our ecosystem is to be able to create an integrated micro-world in which data are shared real-time and on-demand with a continuous flow*
Data architecture	*Data Architecture is a big challenge for technological companies. In our past, we had been thorough many difficulties due to incompatibility of data quality, scale and different layers of security. All the players toward we are opening our boundaries need to share our "philosophy" of business, or at least they must be firmly clear in showing us their business rules and habits. We are a transparent and blur company, and we want to establish a network that reflects our inner characteristics, but it will pose us a multitude of obstacles during the path*
Standard business rules	*We want to create a lean data value chain and we are stressing on training and coaching in order to clearly make our employees understand what their roles and responsibilities are. In unstructured process, effectiveness is reached when every gusset of the chain has understood what the rules are. Only in this way the flow can become smooth and efficient*

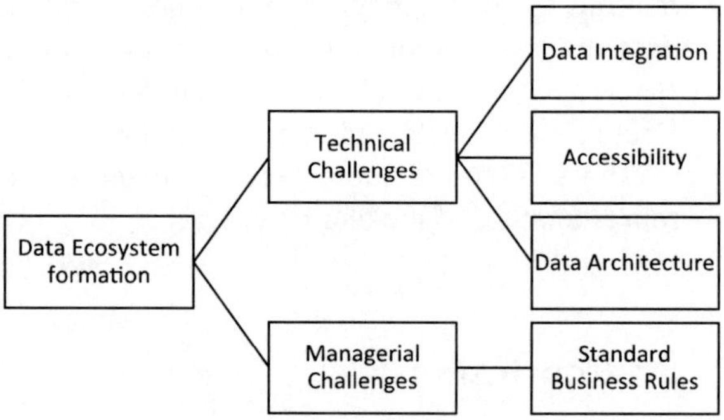

Fig. 3 A graphical representation of data ecosystems formation challenges

The approach of Data Value Chain allows to describe the path of data from their collection to analysis, and to deeply understand the final impact on strategic decisions. The diffusion of software and connectivity allowed firms to better design their environment shifting from an isolated world to a structure in which interconnection play the most important role thanks to mutual dependence. This phenomenon has been studied and described troughs the lens of the ecosystem's literature, which show it as a network of organizations linked in multilateral ways and along several dimensions.

We analyzed the activities implemented by the two players in the process of ecosystem formation in order to identify criticalities born in the first stages of its creation. We discovered that in the initial phase of Dronus/Here relationship, they have focused deeply on succeeding in the exchange of data to constitute a shared and interconnected process with the aim of minimizing bottlenecks in each step of the chain. Then we have explored the core ecosystem in order to find the proper challenges that the two firms have faced to find standard procedures interfaced to exchange consistent and modular data.

The research presented in this work has presented the problems encountered by Dronus and Here in building their own DVC. Data have been collected through the analysis of the interviews with the firm's representatives. The main challenges which have been extrapolated and that need to be handled, are: (i) Data Integration, (ii) Accessibility (iii) Data Architecture and (iv) Standard Business Rules. We consider that is crucial to fully know the difficulties encountered in the ecosystem formation in order to be prepared and to design a data architecture which transposes it and that is firm enough to overtake them.

Successful big data integration, accessibility and standard business rules will allow firms in data-intense sectors, to be completely efficient in the exchange of information and to become more and more flexible and agile.

DVC and Ecosystem provide exciting possibility for the future in the drone industry as well as for a multitude of other sectors. The field is still very row and untouched, thus giving the possibility to researchers to develop multiple theories and discoveries. In fact, the literature has just stretched the potential of this innovative process and drone's organization external design. We give though this research a very new and illuminating perspective on how to deal with the exchange of data and on what kind of problem can be encountered in the formation of a new business relationship data-based in order to make companies ready to be responsive to bottlenecks to speed up procedures. Companies, thanks to our contribution, can anticipate criticalities, knowing how they are formed, and can reap the full advantage of a fluid process of data, being ahead of competition.

With the increasing need for integrated and shared data sets and infrastructures to support DVC, we expect their impact on organizations performances to increase. As data quality and interconnection become a significant issue in data management, we hope this work offers a guideline for practitioners when investigating developments of data-driven ecosystem.

The constrained existing knowledge available make the subject both innovative in terms of possible applications and limited by the absence of conspicuous literature making more challenging the modality of retrieval of information and the channeling towards a correct and well-founded interpretation.

Yet firms are increasingly interconnecting and utilizing drone acquire-data in their business operations whit the aim of speed up processes making the future of ecosystem of drone organizations decidedly bright.

Appendix

Interview Protocol

1. What do you think are the main advantage and disadvantage of Ecosystem formation?
2. What encouraged you to enter in contact with Dronus/Here?
3. What do you think will be the output of your interconnection?
4. What will be the evolution of automotive sector and drones? What are your expectations for the future?
5. What do you think will be the main roadblocks encountered during the exchange of data?
6. Is there any kind of platform or digital standardization adopted in order to facilitate and smooth the process of exchange?
7. In your view, what are the improvement that your company can put in place in order to increase efficiency?
8. Ecosystem standards can give you help in shaping the methodology of interfacing, do you think there are other measure you can adopt internally in order to open the company toward a more blur structure?
9. What is your relationship with Dronus/Here in terms of formalization, bureaucracy and in depth comprehension?
10. What is, in your opinion, the most innovative way in the field of drones to construct photogrammetrical model?

References

1. Floreano, D., Wood, R.J.: Science, technology and the future of small autonomous drones. Nature **521**(7553), 460–466 (2015)
2. Dutta, G., Goswami, P.: Application of drone in agriculture: a review. Int. J. Chem. Stud. **8**(5), 181–187 (2020). https://doi.org/10.22271/chemi.2020.v8.i5d.10529
3. Hassanalian, M., Abdelkefi, A.: Classifications, applications, and design challenges of drones: a review. Prog. Aerosp. Sci. **91**, 99–131 (2017)
4. Ma, K.Y., Chirarattananon, P., Fuller, S.B., Wood, R.J.: Controlled flight of a biologically inspired, insect-scale robot. Science **340**(6132), 603–607 (2013)
5. Giordan, D., et al.: The use of unmanned aerial vehicles (UAVs) for engineering geology applications. 3437–3481 (2020)
6. Sivarajah, U., Kamal, M.M., Irani, Z., Weerakkody, V.: Critical analysis of big data challenges and analytical methods. J. Bus. Res. **70**, 263–286 (2017). https://doi.org/10.1016/j.jbusres.2016.08.001
7. Chiang, R.H.L., Grover, V., Liang, T., Guest, D.Z.: Special issue: strategic value of big data and business analytics. J. Manag. Inf. Syst. **35**(2), 383–387 (2018). https://doi.org/10.1080/07421222.2018.1451950
8. Porter, M.E.: The value chain and competitive advantage. Underst. Bus. Process. **2**, 50–66 (2001)
9. Hansen, M.T., Birkinshaw, J.: The innovation value chain. Harv. Bus. Rev. **85**(6), 121 (2007)

10. Cavanillas, J.M., Curry, E., Wahlster, W.: New Horizons for a Data-Driven Economy: A Roadmap for Usage and Exploitation of Big Data in Europe (2016). https://doi.org/10.1007/978-3-319-21569-3
11. Gelhaar, J., Groß, T., Otto, B.: A Taxonomy for Data Ecosystems, pp. 6113–6122 (2021)
12. Jacobides, M.G.: Towards a Theory of Ecosystems, pp. 2255–2276 (2018)
13. Adner, R., Kapoor, R.: Value creation in innovation ecosystems: how the structure of technological interdependence affects firm performance in new technology generations. Strateg. Manag. J. **31**(3), 306–333 (2010)
14. Pappas, I.O., Mikalef, P., Giannakos, M.N., Krogstie, J., Lekakos, G.: Big data and business analytics ecosystems: paving the way towards digital transformation and sustainable societies. Inf. Syst. E-Bus. Manag. **16**(3), 479–491 (2018). https://doi.org/10.1007/s10257-018-0377-z
15. Watch, O.D.: The data value chain: moving from production to impact. no. 1985, pp. 1–8 (2017)
16. Rayport, J.F., Sviokla, J.J.: Exploiting the virtual value chain. McKinsey Q. **1**, 20–36 (1996)
17. Alaimo, C., Kallinikos, J., Aaltonen, A.: Data and value. In: Handbook of Digital Innovation. Edward Elgar Publishing (2020)
18. Kopalle, P.K., Kumar, V., Subramaniam, M.: How legacy firms can embrace the digital ecosystem via digital customer orientation. J. Acad. Mark. Sci. **48**(1), 114–131 (2020). https://doi.org/10.1007/s11747-019-00694-2
19. Pennock, M., Pennock, M., Pennock, M.: Digital curation: a life-cycle approach to managing and preserving usable digital information. 1–3 (2007)
20. Curry, E.: The big data value chain: definitions, concepts, and theoretical approaches. In: New Horizons for a Data-Driven Economy, pp. 29–37. Springer, Cham (2016)
21. Knabke, T., Olbrich, S.: Exploring the future shape of business intelligence: mapping dynamic capabilities of information systems to business intelligence agility. In: 2015 Americas Conference on Information Systems, AMCIS 2015 (2015)
22. Mikalef, P., Gupta, M.: Artificial intelligence capability: conceptualization, measurement calibration, and empirical study on its impact on organizational creativity and firm performance. Inf. Manag. **58**(3), 103434 (2021). https://doi.org/10.1016/j.im.2021.103434
23. Chivaka, R.: Organisational design and development (2018)
24. Baldwin, C.Y.: Organization design for business ecosystems. J. Organ. Des. **1**(1), (2012)
25. Kapoor, R., Agarwal, S.: Sustaining superior performance in business ecosystems: evidence from application software developers in the iOS and Android smartphone ecosystems. Organ. Sci. **28**(3), 531–551 (2017)
26. Um, S., Yoo, Y., Wattal, S.: The evolution of digital ecosystems: a case of WordPress from 2004 to 2014 (2015)
27. Alaimo, C., Kallinikos, J.: Computing the everyday: social media as data platforms. Inf. Soc. **33**(4), 175–191 (2017). https://doi.org/10.1080/01972243.2017.1318327
28. Puranam, P., Puranam, P.: Meta-organizational design: rethinking design in inter-organizational and community contexts (2012). https://doi.org/10.1002/smj.1975/abstract
29. Spagnoletti, P., Ceci, F., Bygstad, B.: An investigation on the generative mechanisms of Dark Net markets (2018)
30. Blijleven, V., Van Angeren, J., Jansen, S., Brinkkemper, S.: An evolutionary economics approach to ecosystem dynamics (2013). https://doi.org/10.1109/DEST.2013.6611323
31. Oliveira, M.I.S., Lima, G.d.F.B., Lóscio, B.F.: Investigations into data ecosystems: a systematic mapping study. Knowl. Inf. Syst. 1–42 (2019)
32. Hanssen, G.K.: A longitudinal case study of an emerging software ecosystem: implications for practice and theory. J. Syst. Softw. **85**(7), 1455–1466 (2012). https://doi.org/10.1016/j.jss.2011.04.020
33. Kapoor, R., Iansiti, M., Levien, R.: Ecosystems: broadening the locus of value creation. Harv. Bus. Rev. **82**(1), 12 (2004)
34. Abernathy, W.J., Utterback, J.M.: Patterns of industrial innovation. Technol. Rev. **80**(7), 40–47 (1978)
35. Tushman, M.L., Anderson, P.: Technological discontinuities and organizational environments. Adm. Sci. Q. **31**(3), 439–465 (1986)

36. Rong, K., Lin, Y., Li, B., Burström, T., Butel, L., Yu, J.: Business ecosystem research agenda: more dynamic, more embedded, and more internationalized. Asian Bus. Manag. **17**(3), 167–182 (2018). https://doi.org/10.1057/s41291-018-0038-6
37. Moore, J.F.: Business ecosystems and the view from the firm. Antitrust Bull. **51**(1), 31–75 (2006)
38. Subramaniam, M., Iyer, B., Venkatraman, V.: Competing in digital ecosystems. Bus. Horiz. **62**(1), 83–94 (2019)

Towards an Understanding of the Platform Phenomenon: An Agent-Based Simulation Approach

Marius Schmid

Abstract Despite the omnipresence of platforms and the breadth of related research, predicting the outcomes of platforms remains challenging. To reach a critical mass of complementary partners innovating on their platform, platform owners must foster both generativity and profitability on their platform. The conditions under which these objectives may be achieved have yet to be delineated, however. The study at hand theorizes that the impact of platforms' promised capabilities is delineated by the conditions in the competitive environment. Through simulation, explicitly designed to understand system-level behavior, this theorization can be tested. The developed agent-based simulation model captures a platform within its surrounding business ecosystem. It accounts for platforms' value proposition to lower search costs and resource costs associated with innovation, as well as related governance decisions faced by platform owners. Importantly, conditions in the competitive environment, namely environmental complexity, may also be adjusted for experimental testing. The simulation model thereby enables a flexible investigation of platform governance decisions and broader environmental conditions. Experimentation results reveal platforms as ineffective at fostering generativity and profitability in low complexity environments, implying platforms to not be uniformly promising or disruptive in all kinds of competitive environments. Thus, this study's main contribution is an agent-based simulation model to help understand and predict outcomes of platforms as complex phenomena.

Keywords Platforms · Agent-based simulation · Complex adaptive systems

1 Introduction

Platforms are becoming increasingly relevant across industries, irrespective of size and domain [1]. Whereas newly established firms like AirBnB or Kickstarter are platform-native, several more traditional companies launch platforms and convert

M. Schmid (✉)
Institute of Information Management, University of St. Gallen, St. Gallen, Switzerland
e-mail: marius.schmid@unisg.ch

S. Za et al. (eds.), *Sustainable Digital Transformation*, Lecture Notes in Information Systems and Organisation 59, https://doi.org/10.1007/978-3-031-15770-7_14

their current businesses into platform ecosystems [2]. Examples of this include General Electric [2], SAP [3, 4], and Salesforce [5]. Naturally, such transitions in organizing logic bring along several challenges.

Managing a platform ecosystem requires the orchestration of a network of complementary third-party innovation to integrate functionalities on the platform and to co-create value with customers who source their services on the platform [6]. The crucial factor for the sustained success of orchestrating a platform ecosystem is the network effect in reaching a critical mass of complementary platform partners to foster innovation [6, 7]. Platform ecosystems can be attractive not only for platform partners owing to access to new markets and higher profits, but also for customers due to the access to a wide range of innovative solutions. Platform ecosystems must thus address the need for both creation and capture of additional value [8]. In turn, platform owners must orchestrate value creation and value capture in a way that is attractive to both customers and partners.

This orchestration entails several decisive governance decisions. Platform owners must define aspects like revenue sharing arrangements [8], and the level of investments in platform-related capabilities like recommender systems [9], or modularity [10], for example. Search costs [11] and resource costs [12] associated with the process of innovation may be decreased depending on the level of such investments. Platform owners may also decide to enter the market of their own platform and thus directly compete with platform partners [13]. Here, research disagrees on whether complementary innovation is positively or negatively impacted [13]. Similarly, there are conflicting findings on whether a higher number of partners is beneficial or detrimental to platforms [10, 14, 15]. Thus, despite the critical role of network effects for the platform logic [16–18], it is not entirely clear how to optimize them. Ultimately predicting the success or failure of a platform is thereby still challenging [1]. Fundamentally, we lack insights into the conditions under which platforms are particularly advantageous [19] and when additional investments in platforms stop paying off [3]. This study theorizes that the impact of platforms' promised ability to decrease firms' search costs and resources costs varies in different competitive environments and for different designs of governance mechanisms.

To enable this theorization, simulation is leveraged as a research method that allows to generate large amounts of data and conduct what-if analyses for various scenarios [20]. Thus, this study presents an extendible agent-based simulation model of a platform and its surrounding business ecosystem. By characterizing platforms and the broader business ecosystems as complex adaptive systems [21], the simulation model aims to help illustrate and explain the underlying system-level behavior. It enables the testing of governance decisions faced by platform owners, as well as the environmental conditions that apply in the surrounding business ecosystem. The impact of these varying conditions on relevant performance metrics can thus be tested extensively. Thereby, the simulation model allows platform researchers and managers to better understand platforms as complex phenomena and assists the latter in predicting outcomes of platform design decisions.

2 Conceptual Foundation

2.1 *Digital Platforms as Enablers of Value Creation and Value Capture*

Being situated at the center and as the enabler of a platform ecosystem, a digital platform is crucial to the success of the corresponding platform ecosystem. From a sociotechnical perspective, platforms comprise both technical and organizational elements [1, 22]. It is the technological core, typically provided by the platform owner, that can be extended by autonomous and self-organized third parties (platform partners) to jointly create value in the form of innovations for customers [6, 7, 10, 23]. Apple and Google provide the mobile operation systems of their respective iOS and Android platforms that may be extended to develop apps for customers, for example. Similarly, SAP provides fundamental technologies, data, and processes to enable complementary innovation on its Business Technology Platform. The digital platform thus serves as the basis of a platform ecosystem that comprises complementary platform partners whose resources are bundled to create value in the form of innovative solutions to solve customers' problems. The main platform actors are the platform owner, complementary partners, and customers [24].

Within platform literature, there is a common understanding that sufficient value creation is a prerequisite for the success of the entire ecosystem [6, 23]. Enabling the joint value creation among platform partners represents a platform's generativity [25], which is the "overall capacity to produce unprompted change driven by large, varied, and uncoordinated audiences" [26, p. 1980]. Put simply, the demand for a given platform increases with the availability and quality of available complements [17]. Thus, a platform's generativity for value creation and innovation, to offer a wide range of solutions to platform customers, is vital for platform success.

Next to, and as important as, value creation is the appropriation (capture) of the created value [8, 27] that sustains an economic benefit from innovation [28]. Platform partners, as third-party innovators, must perceive the participation in the platform ecosystem as beneficial to join and integrate their resources, and remain on the platform over time. If partners cannot appropriate sufficient value from the platform, they will feel free to conduct business off-platform or offer their resources on rival platforms. Similarly, the platform owner must derive an economic benefit from orchestrating the platform ecosystem. Platform owners must invest significantly and these investments should pay off in terms of value capture [3]. Platform owners ideally want to maximize value appropriation without limiting generativity as the underlying mechanism of value creation [23]. Thus, both value creation and value capture play central roles for the success of platforms.

2.2 Platform Governance

Governing a platform and its surrounding ecosystem is therefore a challenging task [29, 30]. As an orchestrator of the platform ecosystem, the platform owner typically has a variety of governance mechanisms it can apply to govern the platform and its participants [23, 30, 31]. Platform owners may decide to employ a greater degree of openness of their platform to external innovation, for example [32]. This may increase the diversity of contributed innovations [33] but also may yield a loss of control over the content provided that may result in a lower quality of offerings [16]. Platform owners typically employ boundary resources, i.e., software tools and regulations, to steer generated innovations [7] and may adjust their policies over time. Although realizing network effects is a fundamental aspect of platforms [16, 17], it is not clear to which extent an increased number of partners is beneficial. Research suggests both positive attention spillover effects [34], as well as negative crowding effects [14] as a result of an increased number of partners operating on a platform. Platform governance is thus also impeded by the fact that desired outcomes are not entirely clear.

Another central task for platform owners is deciding how to distribute the generated revenue and thereby setting a framework for value capture on the platform [8]. Platform owners will typically define a revenue sharing arrangement for transactions on their platform [8, 35], as Apple does on the App Store (30%) or Salesforce does on its AppExchange (15%), for example. The empirical example of SAP suggests that defining the revenue sharing arrangement may be adapted over time. On its recently launched Business Technology Platform (BTP), SAP merges existing platform offerings and offers only a single revenue sharing arrangement [36]. Platform governance thus entails decisions that may have to be revoked or adapted over time.

2.3 The Role of Search Costs and Resource Costs

Platform literature thus presents contradictory findings on the implications of platform governance decisions. Similarly, empirical examples suggest platform owners continuously adjust their governance mechanisms. Understanding why platforms succeed may thus require expanding the scope to the greater context in which platforms are situated. In broader innovation ecosystems [37], firms have alternatives to organizing around a platform and may decide to interact without the aid of a platform. Following the resource-based view of the firm, resources are assumed to be valuable, rare, and not perfectly imitable or substitutable [38]. Furthermore, it is generally understood that not all firms are endowed with all resources [39]. In business ecosystems, innovation is typically distributed within a network of upstream and downstream firms [37], searching for and integrating each other's resources.

Search, as a process in itself, is hence an integral part of value creation and innovation that comes at a certain cost [11]. This is where digital platforms and platform ecosystems can contribute in effectively facilitating and optimizing solution and resource matching through their search matching function. Search matching capabilities, in the form of two-sided recommender systems, have been found to improve the performance of platform agents [9]. More specifically, they aid in taming the complex search matching in platform ecosystem settings [9]. Thus, investing in search matching capabilities can reduce the search costs of both platform partners and customers. Such a capability incentivizes both platform partners and customers to conduct their business on the platform, as opposed to alternative organizing logics, and thereby affects the sustained success of a platform ecosystem.

Similar to the search process, creating and maintaining resources is also associated with a relevant cost [12]. Here, the level of modularity has direct implications [10]. If a platform offers a high degree of modularity, resources can be decomposed and recombined to a greater degree, yielding a higher reusability of resources [10]. In effect, this decoupling of resources through investments in a modular architecture enables a higher flexibility in generating outputs on a platform, stimulating generativity and leveraging economies of scale [10]. It is precisely the decrease in resource costs through such reusability that is an inherent part of the value proposition of platforms in general. Even though platforms can evidently lower both search costs and resource costs, joining a platform is a decision associated with risk for potential partners. Partners that consider joining the platform effectively weigh the benefits of reduced search costs and resource costs against the risks such as not getting paid sufficiently, for example.

The sustained success of a platform ecosystem is thus contingent on how much the platform owner invests in search matching and modularity to reduce search costs and resource costs for platform partners and customers. Further, the platform owner can employ revenue sharing as a governance lever to increase the attractiveness of conducting business on the platform for partners, but also adjust the own profitability. Accounting for such factors is vital to understand the fundamental logic of platforms and ultimately why they may fail or succeed. Nevertheless, there are also aspects outside of the control of the platform owner. This study therefore opts for considering the conditions in the surrounding competitive environment, i.e., the broader innovation ecosystem, as well. The aim is to investigate the effect of platform governance decisions in different competitive environments and thereby delineate the conditions under which platforms are particularly promising.

To understand both internal platform factors and external factors in the surrounding environment, the complex adaptive systems (CAS) view is applied as a starting point. Recent studies in platform literature have drawn on CAS theory to characterize and analyze platforms as CAS [9], or investigate how a product platform transitioned into a platform ecosystem [40]. Thus, CAS theory is evidently suitable to investigating platforms and existing approaches may be complemented by adopting a system-level view that incorporates the surrounding business ecosystem, as elaborated in the subsequent section.

3 Research Method

3.1 Simulation-Based Research

A research method that lends itself well to understanding system behavior, particularly in the context of complex adaptive systems, is simulation [41, 42]. Simulation-based research is established across various fields and has made significant contributions particularly to disciplines like the natural sciences [41, 43]. It is commonly defined as "a method for using computer software to model the operation of real-world processes, systems, or events" [44, p. 481]. In effect, a simulation is a simplified, computational representation of a world and its central underlying constructs [44]. Thus, through simulation, researchers create an abstraction of a given phenomenon of interest and translate it into software for experimentation. Importantly, this allows for investigating individual aspects or constructs of a phenomenon in isolation and generating large amounts of artificial data for analysis, which may be difficult or infeasible in empirical contexts [43]. Although the application of simulation techniques in the field of information systems (IS) is not as widespread as in other fields, recent studies highlight its potential for IS research [41, 43]. Agent-based simulation, as one of the most common simulation techniques, is deemed particularly suitable for analyzing complex systems with emergent properties and nonlinear behavior [44, 45]. Thus, this study sets out to develop an agent-based simulation model of the complex system under investigation. The model development process leans on common simulation guidelines [46] and existing models [45, 47]. More precisely, the development process consists of the conceptual development, operational simulation development and validation, and conducting experiments and analysis [45].

3.2 Conceptual Model Design

The conceptual model creates the basis for any computational operationalization [45, 46]. The basic setting at hand is a business ecosystem of partners and customers, within which a digital platform is situated. As discussed, the platform owner typically provides this extendible technological core [6, 48]. Partners and customers may decide to conduct business and source their required services on- or off-platform, depending on which option they perceive to be more beneficial (see solid arrow lines and dotted arrow lines in Fig. 1, respectively). For the innovating partners, this means resources for integration to develop new services may be sourced on-platform or off-platform in the broader ecosystem (see solid arrow lines and dotted arrow lines in Fig. 1, respectively). To account for the investments into search matching and modularity as an effort by the platform owner to increase the platform's attractiveness, levels of search costs and resource costs on the platform may vary. Similarly, the

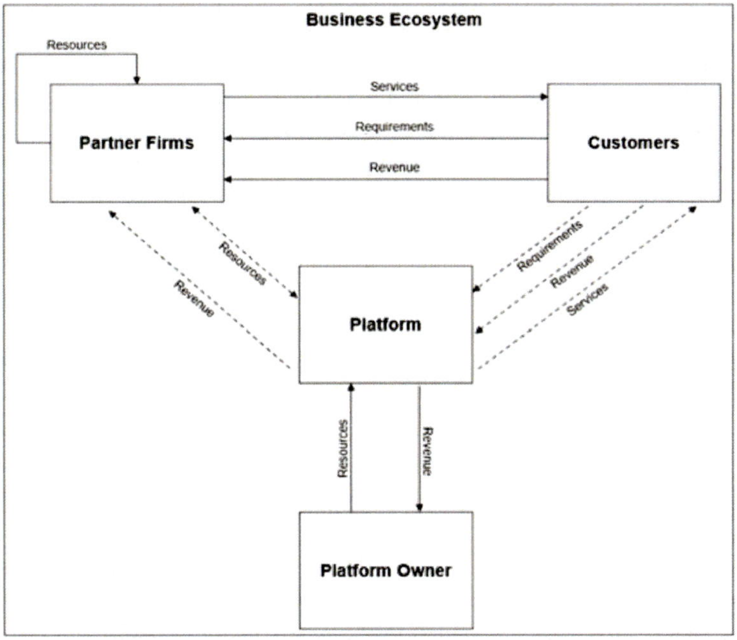

Fig. 1 Abstract model design

revenue share obtained by the owner depends on the defined revenue sharing arrangement. This basic conceptualization also leans on an existing agent-based simulation of a digital platform [9] that conceptualizes a multi-sided platform as a complex adaptive business system. The resulting setting is depicted in Fig. 1.

Operationalizing this basic concept into a simulation model requires a more precise definition of the model components. From a CAS perspective, *agents*, *interactions*, and the *environment* are the critical elements in this regard [42].

Agents. Formally, agents may represent different entities, like individuals, groups of individuals, or entire organizations [42]. They are equipped with unique attributes and behavioral rules that define their operationalization [42, 45]. Based on the abstract model design, the simulation model contains the platform owner, partners, and customers as central agents, as well as combinable resources and resulting services. As a main attribute, customers are equipped with service requirements for which they search for matching services. This accounts for the fundamental premise that innovations are designed to meet customer demands [49], be it mobile applications or analytics services. Naturally, aside from meeting the requirements, services must also be affordable for customers. The services are in turn created by partners that combine and integrate resources [37, 39].

Similarly, the platform owner supplies an extendable core for complementary innovation [50], i.e., offers core resources as a basis for generating services on-platform. Next to extendable resources, platform owners also make dedicated investments into search matching [9] and modularity [10] to lower search costs and resource costs on the platform, respectively. Owner, partners, and customers may all be characterized as learning- and utility-based agents that choose to maximize their utility function [45, 51]. Customers search for services that they can afford, partners intend to make profits with their generated innovations, and the platform owner aims to orchestrate a platform that fosters both value creation and value capture. Resources and services on the other hand are reflex agents [45, 51] that are designed and used by other actors.

Interactions. Importantly, these described agents also interact in different ways. Aside from the agents themselves, interactions in CAS generally comprise the connections or links between given agents and the flows of resources among them [42, 45]. In other words, the premise for interaction among agents is being connected and exchanging something along this connection. In the described conceptual model, interactions are driven by innovation as a search process in the broader business ecosystem [52]. Whereas customers search for services that match their requirements, partners search for resources to integrate in order to meet customers' requirements. Following established conceptions of search in other simulation contexts [37, 53, 54], the basic search process is divided into local search and distant search. Thus, agents search both their immediate neighborhood (local search) and conduct *long-jumps* beyond their immediate neighborhood (distant search) [37, 53, 54] that are associated with higher risk and may therefore be more costly [53].

Adopting this logic to the presented setting, both customers' and partners' search may thus be divided into local search and distant search. The immediate neighborhood as a setting for local search is then the existing network of partners and customers, whilst conducting distant search means moving beyond this local network, i.e., searching the entire business ecosystem of actors. Searching the broader business ecosystem also includes the possibility to search on-platform. Partners that innovate may thus also search for and integrate the resources offered on-platform, and customers may source services on-platform. These interactions may be facilitated through the mentioned investments by the platform owner. Thus, conceptually, partners and customers may also be connected to the platform owner through the platform.

Environment. The medium in which these agents interact is considered the environment [42, 45]. Based on Fig. 1, the surrounding business ecosystem conceptually presents the environment. However, the conditions in the competitive environment may vary and such variations must be accounted for. Thus, this study leans on existing simulation models [45, 47] to account for environmental complexity as a decisive factor for the conditions in the competitive environment. In effect, the competitive environment is shaped by the complexity of customer requirements. Innovation, that is ultimately designed to meet customer requirements [49], becomes increasingly challenging as the complexity of these requirements increases, especially when not all firms are endowed with all resources [39]. Therefore, the complexity of customer requirements requires an adaptation by the other agents in the business ecosystem, delineating the conditions in the surrounding competitive environment. With the conceptual model and its constituent components outlined, the focus turns towards the operationalization of the simulation model and experimentation.

4 Operationalization and Experimentation

4.1 Operational Model Logic

In the conceptual model, partners combine and integrate their resources to form services as the basic process of innovation and can choose to do so on-platform or off-platform. Operationally, the approach from existing studies that use binary vectors of 0 s and 1 s [37, 47], as well as "?"s [45] is adopted. Ganco et al. [37] specifically model upstream and downstream firms mixing-and-matching their components, i.e., 5-bit vectors of 0 s and 1 s to form a product. To account for resource features left open for improvisation [45], some features are represented by "?"s and may be improvised to become either a 1 or 0. For example, the resource [0110?] may be interpreted as [0110**1**] or [0110**0**]. In our digital platform context, the recombination of components is applied so that four resources as 5-bit vectors are combined and integrated to form services as 20-bit vectors. Thus, the resources [1101?], [1100?], [0010?], and [1010?] may be combined to form the service [1101**0**1100**1**0010**0**1010**1**].

As the developed innovations must ultimately meet customers' requirements [49], services must be tested for their fit to given requirements. Again, the operationalization leans on existing models that capture opportunities as binary vectors of 0 s and 1 s that, if met, yield a random payoff [45, 47]. In our setting, opportunities for partners are equated to customers' requirements. If partners meet a given requirement, they receive a payoff for the successful transaction. To enable a comparison of requirements and services, the former are also operationalized as 20-bit binary vectors of 0 s and 1 s. Importantly, the complexity of customer requirements determines how many matches there must be between a service and a requirement for the service to match the requirement [45, 47]. Thus, resources are combined to form services and the resulting services are tested for their match with requirements, leaning on existing approaches [37, 45, 47].

4.2 Definition of Variables and Parameters

The computational model is subsequently developed using the agent-based simulation software NetLogo, a software designed particularly to model complex phenomena [55]. After the translation of the described conceptual model, several parameters can be defined and adjusted to test their impact on output variables of interest. Based on the conceptual foundation of platforms, value creation and value capture are vitally important. The modeling context allows making these factors concrete and measurable. The platforms' value creation capacity, or generativity, may thus be measured in terms of the number of services generated on-platform. Similarly, value capture may be captured in the form of platform agents' profitability by considering the revenues generated and costs incurred. Partners' profitability on the platform may be of particular interest in delineating their decision to innovate on-platform versus off-platform in the broader business ecosystem. Thus, profitability and generativity serve as suitable outcome variables.

These outcome variables may be impacted by several factors. The discussed investments into search matching and investments into modularity can be concretized by lowering search costs and resource costs on-platform. This is operationalized as a cost reduction by a factor of 0.00–1.00, respectively. Similarly, the revenue sharing agreement between platform owner and partners may vary. In the simulation model, the platform owner's revenue share can thus be adjusted freely between 0 and 100% per transaction. Lastly, the environmental complexity in the broader business ecosystem, induced by the complexity of customer requirements, may be varied between 0 and 20. In effect, simulation enables an investigation of all of these factors individually and jointly, allowing for a more nuanced analysis of the impact on the outcome variables of interest. How is generativity impacted when the platform owner opts for a revenue share of 50%, compared to 25%? How effective are investments into search matching and modularity when the competitive environment is highly complex? Table 1 summarizes the discussed variables and variations as a basis for a first round of simulation experiments. Table 2 summarizes the remaining initialization parameter settings required for operationalization.

4.3 Experimentation

The definition of the main variables lays the foundation for experimentation. In a first round of experiments, all discussed variables are varied simultaneously to test their impact on profitability and generativity. In total, the defined parameter ranges in Table 1 yield $2 \times 3 \times 3 \times 21 = 378$ unique parameter combinations that were tested 25 each for a total of $25 \times 378 = 9{,}450$ simulation runs. Each simulation run in turn comprises 1,000 time steps. Figure 2 captures an excerpt of these results, displaying how varying levels of the platform owner's revenue share impact profitability and generativity in low and high complexity environments. To this end, the platform owner's revenue share (for every transaction within one simulation run) is varied across the entire range from 0–100% in increments of 5%. Complexity, varying from 0–20, is fixed at a level of 5 (low) and 15 (high). To account for the impact of investments into search matching and investments into modularity, both factors are fixed at medium levels (0.5) in the displayed results. This basic setup helps to understand whether the discussed investments are worthwhile in different kinds of environments.

Evidently, environmental complexity fundamentally impacts profitability and generativity outcomes on-platform. Generativity, i.e., the number of services created, is at or below 3 in low complexity environments, and profitability, i.e., value capture,

Table 1 Experiment parameter settings

Variable name	Range	Tested values	Description
Environmental complexity	0–20	5; 15	More complex customer requirements are more challenging to meet, i.e., require more feature matches with a given service. Customer requirements thus delineate the complexity of partners' competitive environment
Investments into search matching	0.00–1.00	0.00; 0.50; 1.00	Through dedicated investments into search matching, the platform owner may decrease search costs on the platform by a factor of 0.00–1.00
Investments into modularity	0.00–1.00	0.00; 0.50; 1.00	Through dedicated investments into modularity, the platform owner may decrease search costs on the platform by a factor of 0.00–1.00
Owner's revenue share	0–100%	0–100% in increments of 5%	The platform owner's revenue share for transactions on-platform may vary
Generativity	*N.A*		As a proxy for value creation, the simulation model tracks the number of unique services developed on-platform
Profitability	*N.A*		As a proxy for value capture, the simulation model tracks partner firms' generated revenues and incurred costs, as well as the resulting profitability

is accordingly low (aside from a few outliers).[1] In high complexity environments, however, generativity is notably higher, reaching levels of 800 and beyond. Profitability, though not sharing the same curve progression, is also significantly higher.

[1] Individual services may be highly profitable. This may explain the few outliers displayed for profitability in a low complexity environment, despite low generativity levels.

Table 2 Initialization parameter settings

Parameter	Description	Default value
Time steps	Each simulation run comprises a defined number of time steps	1,000
Number of customers	The number of customers and partners in the entire business ecosystem must be defined initially	1,000
Number of partners		100
Initial platform market share	The model assumes the platform owner providing the technological core to be a significant player in the business ecosystem	25%
Resources per partner	Each partner is equipped with a number of resources	4
Owner's resources	The platform owner provides a number of extendable core resources	30
Resource costs	Resources are costly to produce and maintain and thus associated with a cost	5–15
Level of improvisation of resources	Resources are assumed to leave some room for improvisation when combining them (i.e., a number of the 5 features is not fixed)	1
Requirement payoff	Each met customer requirement is associated with a payoff	$\mu = 110$, $\sigma^2 = 10$
Requirement duration	Customers' requirements disappear after a number of time steps in the model	$\mu = 20$, $\sigma^2 = 5$
Service duration	Services disappear after a number of time steps in the model without being requested by customers	$\mu = 30$, $\sigma^2 = 10$
Customer-partner links	Customers and partners are assumed to have an existing local network. These links may also disappear after a number of time steps without interacting, i.e., local networks are not infinitely stable	2
Partner-partner links		1
Life of links		100–150
Search costs	Search costs for resources and services may vary, particularly between local and distant search	20–80
Renewal of resources	To account for continuous innovation, as well as the possibility to retire existing resources, after a number of ticks, partners renew and replace one of their resources	100

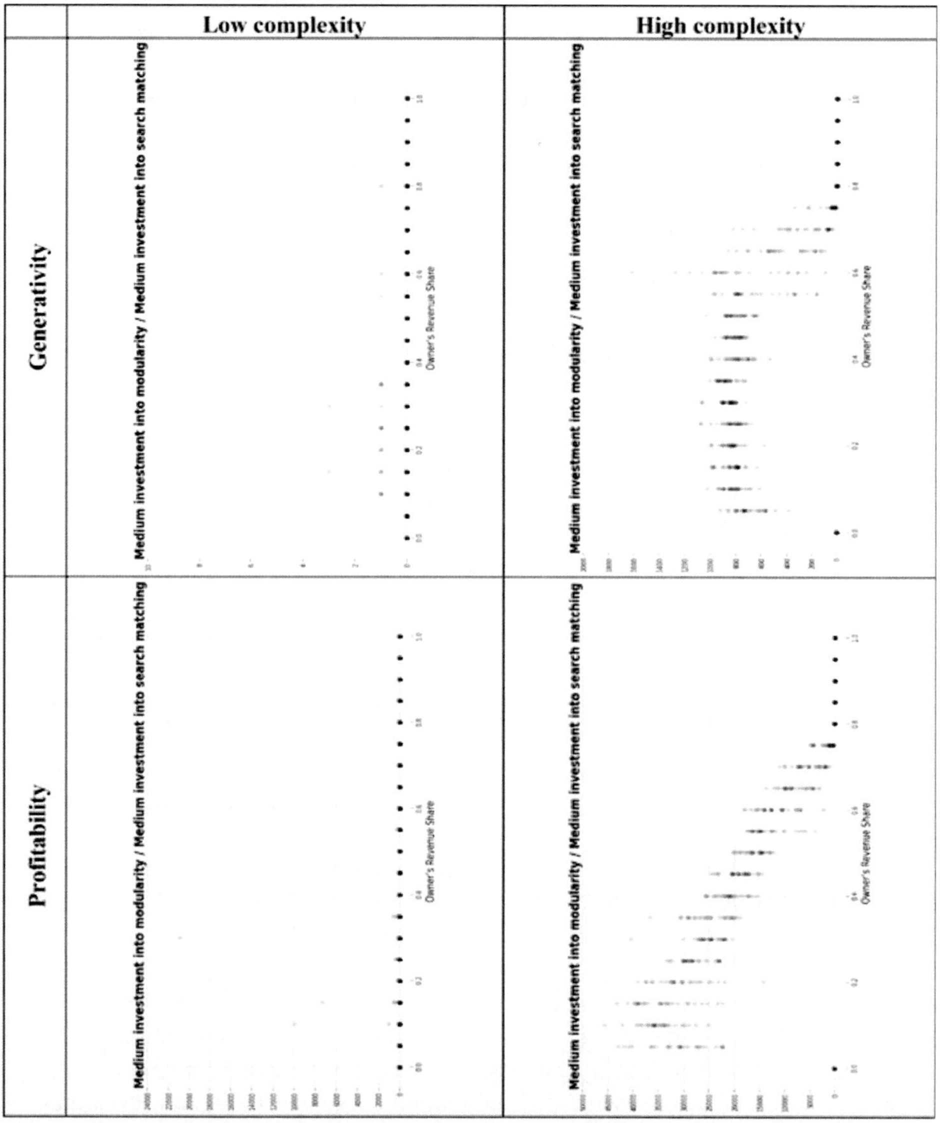

Fig. 2 Profitability and generativity in low and high complexity environments

Interestingly, generativity levels are still stable when the platform owner's revenue share is increased to around 50%, where partners' profitability is already significantly decreasing. This may imply that although the value capture capacity for partners decreases on-platform, this does not automatically decrease their value creation capacity. More broadly, these findings suggest investments into search matching and investments into modularity may not be feasible in low complexity environments. In high complexity environments, however, such investments may be promising, even when the platform owner's revenue share increases beyond the discussed empirical examples of Apple (30%) and Salesforce (15%).

Validation of these results and the model in general stems partially from building on existing models [45, 47]. In addition, results like partners' profitability decreasing with an increasing platform owner's revenue share or generativity levels maximizing around 15–35% whilst tapering off at the extremes are intuitive or in line with empirical examples.

5 Discussion and Conclusion

The aim of this study was to address some of the timely research gaps in platform literature, particularly contributing to the discussion on why platforms may fail or succeed and delineating the underlying conditions. Current research informs us that attracting a critical mass of complementary partners is critical to foster innovation [6, 7] and so platform owners must orchestrate their platform ecosystem accordingly. Related studies point out that an increased number of partners on a platform may also have negative impacts like competitive crowding, however [14]. Such contradictory findings suggest that there is a lack of understanding for the underlying mechanisms that impact the ultimate success of platforms. This study posits that the external environment plays a non-trivial role. Thus, an extendible agent-based simulation model is developed that enables the flexible testing of governance decisions and environmental conditions in the platform context to better understand why platforms may fail or succeed.

The model itself builds on some of the fundamental premises of platforms, e.g., their ability to decrease participants' search costs and resource costs associated with innovation. The study theorizes that the impact of decreased resource costs and search costs is delineated by platform owners' governance decisions and the competitive environment. Experimentation results indeed suggest that the complexity of the competitive environment significantly impacts relevant performance indicators of platforms. Investments into search matching, which have been found to improve performance in form of two-sided recommender systems [9], and investments into modularity, which are designed to increase flexibility [10], do not appear to fulfill the desired effect in low complexity environments. Similarly, as the platform owner requires a greater or lower revenue share for the transactions on the platform, partners' performance is clearly impacted. Thus, the developed simulation model helps to delineate under which conditions platforms are particularly advantageous and thereby also assist practitioners in predicting the feasibility of costly platform-related investments.

In its current form, the model may be used to further investigate how value creation (in terms of the number of created services) and value capture (in terms of the profitability levels of platform partners) are affected by governance decisions regarding the investments into search matching and modularity, and at different levels of environmental complexity. In a first step, the parameter combinations may be extended to include values across the entire range of all main variables. This would serve as a basis for conducting regression analyses on the individual and joint impacts of these variables and thus enable an extension of the developed findings. It would also require further validation efforts, i.e., extending the testing of the initialization parameters outlined in Table 2. Additionally, to compare performance in the broader business ecosystem, generativity and profitability can be tracked off-platform to better understand the ecosystem-level dynamics.

The model may also be extended in several ways. For one, to investigate competition between platforms, additional platforms may be modeled within the broader business ecosystem. This would allow for a deeper investigation of multihoming by platform partners under different environmental conditions, or the implications of different governance decisions for the performance of competing platforms, for example. In addition, the model could be extended by accounting for the explicit entry of a platform owner [13], through the acquisition of complementors or the integration of certain service offerings, for example. Again, the impact of such strategic decisions on crucial outcome variables like the overall generativity on the platform can thus be tested for different competitive environments. As platform evolution is a central topic in platform literature that needs further research [1], one may also investigate the impact of adapting these governance mechanisms over time by using the model to collect data throughout simulation runs, rather than at one point in time. In general, the model thus lends itself to several avenues of future research in the platform context.

Acknowledgements This work has been supported by the Swiss National Science Foundation (SNSF).

References

1. de Reuver, M., Sørensen, C., Basole, R.C.: The digital platform: a research agenda. J. Inf. Technol. **33**(2), 124–135 (2018)
2. Constantinides, P., Henfridsson, O., Parker, G.G.: Platforms and infrastructures in the digital age. Inf. Syst. Res. **29**(2), 381–400 (2018)
3. Hein, A., Schreieck, M., Riasanow, T., Soto Setzke, D., Wiesche, M., Böhm, M., Krcmar, H. Digital platform ecosystems. Electronic Markets (30), 87–98 (2020)
4. Schmid, M., Haki, K., Tanriverdi, H., Aier, S., Winter, R. Platform over market—when is joining a platform beneficial? In: 29th European Conference on Information Systems (ECIS 2021): A Virtual AIS Conference (2021)
5. Staub, N., Haki, K., Aier, S., Winter, R., Magan, A. Evolution of B2B platform ecosystems: what can be learned from salesforce? In: 29th European Conference on Information Systems (ECIS 2021): A Virtual AIS Conference (2021)
6. Ceccagnoli, M., Forman, C., Huang, P., Wu, D.J.: Cocreation of value in a platform ecosystem: the case of enterprise software. MIS Q. **36**(1), 263–290 (2012)
7. Eaton, B., Elaluf-Calderwood, S., Sorensen, C.: Distributed tuning of boundary resources: the case of Apple's iOS service system. MIS Q. **39**(1), 217–243 (2015)
8. Karhu, K., Gustafsson, R., Lyytinen, K.: Exploiting and defending open digital platforms with boundary resources: android's five platform forks. Inf. Syst. Res. **29**(2), 479–497 (2018)

9. Malgonde, O., Zhang, H., Padmanabhan, B., Limayem, M.: Taming complexity in search matching: two-sided recommender systems on digital platforms. MIS Q. **44**(1), 49–84 (2020)
10. Yoo, Y., Henfridsson, O., Lyytinen, K.: The New organizing logic of digital innovation: an agenda for information systems research. Inf. Syst. Res. **21**(4), 724–735 (2010)
11. Benslimane, Y., Plaisent, M., Bernard, P.: Investigating search costs and coordination costs in electronic markets: a transaction costs economics perspective. Electron. Mark. **15**(3), 213–224 (2005)
12. Alexy, O., West, J., Klapper, H., Reitzig, M.: Surrendering control to gain advantage: reconciling openness and the resource-based view of the firm. Strateg. Manag. J. **39**(6), 1704–1727 (2018)
13. Foerderer, J., Kude, T., Mithas, S., Heinzl, A.: Does platform owner's entry crowd out innovation? Evidence from Google photos. Inf. Syst. Res. **29**(2), 444–460 (2018)
14. Li, J., Netessine, S.: Higher market thickness reduces matching rate in online platforms: evidence from a quasiexperiment. Manage. Sci. **66**(1), 271–289 (2020)
15. Boudreau, K.J.: Let a thousand flowers bloom? An early look at large numbers of software app developers and patterns of innovation. Organ. Sci. **23**(5), 1409–1427 (2012)
16. Casadesus-Masanell, R., Hałaburda, H.: When does a platform create value by limiting choice? J. Econ. & Manag. Strat. **23**(2), 259–293 (2014)
17. Markovich, S., Moenius, J.: Winning while losing: competition dynamics in the presence of indirect network effects. Int. J. Ind. Organ. **27**(3), 346–357 (2009)
18. Cennamo, C., Santaló, J.: Generativity tension and value creation in platform ecosystems. Organ. Sci. **30**(3), 617–641 (2019)
19. Kretschmer, T., Leiponen, A., Schilling, M., Vasudeva, G. Platform ecosystems as meta-organizations: implications for platform strategies. Strat. Manag. J. (forthcoming)
20. Nan, N., Tanriverdi, H.: Unifying the role of IT in hyperturbulence and competitive advantage via a multilevel perspective of IS strategy. MIS Q. **41**(3), 937–958 (2017)
21. Anderson, P.: Complexity theory and organization science. Organ. Sci. **10**(3), 216–232 (1999)
22. Ghazawneh, A., Henfridsson, O.: A paradigmatic analysis of digital application marketplaces. J. Inf. Technol. (Palgrave Macmillan) **30**(3), 198–208 (2015)
23. Wareham, J., Fox, P.B., Giner, J.L.C.: Technology ecosystem governance. Organ. Sci. **25**(4), 1195–1215 (2014)
24. Blaschke, M., Haki, K., Aier, S., Winter, R. Capabilities for digital platform survival: insights from a business-to-business digital platform. In: 39th International Conference on Information Systems (ICIS2018), pp. 1–17. San Francisco, CA: Association for Information Systems (2018)
25. Tilson, D., Lyytinen, K., Sørensen, C.: Research commentary—digital infrastructures: the missing IS research agenda. Inf. Syst. Res. **21**(4), 748–759 (2010)
26. Zittrain, L.J.: The Generative Internet. Harv. Law Rev. **119**(7), 1974–2040 (2006)
27. Jacobides, M.G., Knudsen, T., Augier, M.: Benefiting from innovation: value creation, value appropriation and the role of industry architectures. Res. Policy **35**(8), 1200–1221 (2006)
28. Garcia-Castro, R., Aguilera, R.V.: Incremental value creation and appropriation in a world with multiple stakeholders. Strateg. Manag. J. **36**(1), 137–147 (2015)
29. Gawer, A., Cusumano, M.A. Platform leadership: how Intel, Microsoft, and Cisco Drive industry innovation, 1st edn, p. 336. Boston, Mass: Harvard Business Review Press (2002)
30. Halckenhaeusser, A., Foerderer, J., Heinzl, A. Platform governance mechanisms: an integrated literature review and research directions. In: 28th European Conference on Information Systems (ECIS 2020): A Virtual AIS Conference (2020)
31. Tiwana, A., Konsynski, B., Bush, A.A.: Platform evolution: coevolution of platform architecture, governance, and environmental dynamics. Inf. Syst. Res. **21**(4), 675–687 (2010)
32. Benlian, A., Hilkert, D., Hess, T.: How open is this platform? The meaning and measurement of platform openness from the complementors' perspective. J. Inf. Technol. **30**(3), 209–228 (2015)
33. Tiwana, A.: Platform ecosystems: aligning architecture, governance, and strategy. Morgan Kaufmann, Amsterdam (2014)

34. Li, Z., Agarwal, A.: Platform integration and demand spillovers in complementary markets: evidence from Facebook's integration of Instagram. Manage. Sci. **63**(10), 3438–3458 (2017)
35. Ghazawneh, A., Henfridsson, O.: Balancing platform control and external contribution in third-party development: the boundary resources model. Inf. Syst. J. **23**(2), 173–192 (2013)
36. Sahasrabudhe, J. How partners enable customer success through a unified technology platform: part two (2021). Available from: https://news.sap.com/2021/03/part-two-unified-technology-platform-partners-enable-customer-success/, 09.08.2021
37. Ganco, M., Kapoor, R., Lee, G.K.: From rugged landscapes to rugged ecosystems: structure of interdependencies and firms' innovative search. Acad. Manag. Rev. **45**(3), 646–674 (2020)
38. Bowman, C., Ambrosini, V.: Value creation versus value capture: towards a coherent definition of value in strategy. Br. J. Manag. **11**(1), 1–15 (2000)
39. Gavetti, G., Helfat, C.E., Marengo, L.: Searching, shaping, and the quest for superior performance. Strategy Science **2**(3), 194–209 (2017)
40. Sandberg, J., Holmström, J., Lyytinen, K.: Digitization and phase transitions in platform organizing logics: evidence from the process automation industry. MIS Q. **44**(1), 129–153 (2020)
41. Spagnoletti, P., Za, S., Winter, R., Mettler, T.: Exploring foundations for using simulations in IS research. Commun. Assoc. Inf. Syst. **42**(1), 268–300 (2018)
42. Nan, N.: Capturing bottom-up information technology use processes: a complex adaptive systems model. MIS Q. **35**(2), 505–532 (2011)
43. Beese, J., Haki, M.K., Aier, S., Winter, R.: Simulation-based research in information systems: epistemic implications and a review of the status Quo. Bus. Inf. Syst. Eng. **61**(4), 503–521 (2019)
44. Davis, J.P., Eisenhardt, K.M., Bingham, C.B.: Developing theory through simulation methods. Acad. Manag. Rev. **32**(2), 480–499 (2007)
45. Haki, K., Beese, J., Aier, S., Winter, R.: The evolution of information systems architecture: an agent-based simulation model. MIS Q. **44**(1), 155–184 (2020)
46. Sargent, R.G. Verification and validation of simulation models. In: Winter Simulation Conference. Orlando, Florida, pp. 130–143 (2005).
47. Davis, J.P., Eisenhardt, K.M., Bingham, C.B.: Optimal structure, market dynamism, and the strategy of simple rules. Adm. Sci. Q. **54**(3), 413–452 (2009)
48. Blaschke, M., Brosius, M. Digital platforms: balancing control and generativity. In: 39th International Conference on Information Systems (ICIS 2018). San Francisco, United States (2018)
49. Ahuja, G., Lampert, C.M., Tandon, V.: Moving beyond Schumpeter: management research on the determinants of technological innovation. Acad. Manag. Ann. **2**(1), 1–98 (2008)
50. Gawer, A.: Platforms, markets and innovation. Edward Elgar Publishing, Cheltenham (2011)
51. Russel, S., Norvig, P. Artificial intelligence: a modern approach, 3rd edn. Essex, UK: Pearson (2009)
52. Ganco, M., Kapoor, R., Lee, G. From rugged landscapes to rugged ecosystems: structure of interdependencies and firms' innovative search. Academy of Management Review Published Online, 4 Nov 2019 (2019)
53. Levinthal, D.A.: Adaptation on rugged landscapes. Manage. Sci. **43**(7), 934–950 (1997)
54. Kauffman, S.A.: The origins of order: self-organization and selection in evolution. Oxford University Press, New York, NY (1993)
55. Tisue, S., Wilensky, U. Netlogo: a simple environment for modeling complexity. In: International Conference on Complex Systems, pp. 16–21. Boston, MA (2004)

Implementation of Platform Governance Mechanisms: Insights From a B2B Platform Ecosystem

Nicola Staub

Abstract Platform ecosystems are complex ecologies of firms with individual, sometimes conflicting, interests and goals. A platform owner as orchestrator of the ecosystem needs to constantly align the ecosystem actors' individual interests towards common objectives. To achieve such alignment of interests, platform owners rely on a purposefully defined governance structure, which is implemented through a set of governance mechanisms. Despite a variety of mechanisms being discussed in the existing research, little is known about platform owners' main activities to implement such mechanisms in their specific platform contexts, particularly in a B2B platform ecosystem context. To bridge this gap, we conduct an in-depth study of Salesforce, a thriving B2B platform ecosystem in the enterprise software industry. We find that the platform owner made significant resource investments to implement governance mechanisms based on innovative activities and we provide detailed empirical accounts on each of the main activities. Our findings indicate that governance mechanisms are implemented differently in B2B platform ecosystems compared to consumer-focused platform ecosystems, which should be examined in more detail by future research.

Keywords Digital platform · Platform ecosystem · Platform governance

1 Introduction

Platform ecosystems are becoming the new organizing logic of many industries as illustrated by telecommunications (e.g., iOS, Android), video games (e.g., PlayStation, Xbox), and enterprise software (e.g., Salesforce, SAP) [1, 2]. In a platform ecosystem, a *platform owner* offers a digital platform as a software-based technological foundation upon which third-party *complementors* can produce complementary applications [3, 4]. Ultimately, *customers* derive certain values from the offerings jointly provided by the platform owner and the complementors. As each of

N. Staub (✉)
University of St. Gallen, St. Gallen, Switzerland
e-mail: nicola.staub@unisg.ch

S. Za et al. (eds.), *Sustainable Digital Transformation*, Lecture Notes in Information Systems and Organisation 59, https://doi.org/10.1007/978-3-031-15770-7_15

these actors pursue their own, sometimes conflicting interests and goals, a platform owner, as the ecosystem's orchestrator, needs to align the actors' diverse interests toward achieving collective objectives [5]. Hence, managing a digital platform and the various actors in its ecosystem is a dynamic process that requires substantial resources [6, 7].

To allocate these resources in a structured way, platform owners rely on a purposefully designed governance structure, enabling them to attract, coordinate, and control different groups of actors [7]. As complementors are generally not dependent on a single platform, platform owners need to incentivize complementors to provide their applications on the platform rather than directing them with command-and-control structures known from traditional organizations [7]. Such a governance structure is usually implemented through a portfolio of mechanisms [8–10].

A fragmented set of studies in existing platform research has discussed various governance mechanisms as enablers of effective design and management of digital platforms [e.g., 11–13], resulting in a growing body of implicit knowledge accumulated from different platform types. However, scholars have recently asked for a more detailed view on the implementation of platform governance mechanisms to gain a deeper understanding of the specific activities available to platform owners to implement each mechanism [10, 14, 15]. Therefore, the existing body of knowledge needs a consolidated view to illustrate how the major mechanisms can be implemented in specific platform contexts.

One important platform type that received considerably less attention in existing research is the B2B platform ecosystem. The implementation of governance mechanisms in the B2B context may differ from other contexts (e.g., consumer-focused platform ecosystems like Apple's iOS or Google's Android) due to several of the distinct characteristics of B2B platform ecosystems, which make the platform owner more dependent on complementors and customers [e.g., 16–18]. For example, the provision of highly complex products and services, which require diligent integration of resources from the ecosystem's various actors. Therefore, as B2B incumbent firms from several industries (e.g., manufacturing, real estate, chemical) aim to transition into the platform economy [19], it is of value for both research and practice to obtain a coherent understanding of how governance mechanisms can be implemented in a B2B platform ecosystem context.

To bridge this gap, this study aims to provide insights into B2B platform owners' main activities to implement the major governance mechanisms which are discussed in the existing platform research. Therefore, we specify the following research question: *How are platform governance mechanisms implemented by platform owners in a B2B platform ecosystem context*? To answer the research question, we conduct an in-depth study of Salesforce, a B2B platform ecosystem that has thrived considerably over the last years. We find that Salesforce relies on several major proprietary developments and acquisitions to implement the major platform governance mechanisms and provide detailed empirical accounts of Salesforce's activities to achieve this implementation. We further provide initial insights about how the implementation of these governance mechanisms might differ in B2B platform ecosystems as compared to consumer-focused platforms, which should be examined in more detail by future research.

2 Research Background

In this section, we present our conceptualization of platform ecosystems, the main discourses on platform governance, and the particularities of B2B platform ecosystems.

2.1 Platform Ecosystems

Platform ecosystems are complex ecologies of firms with individual and collective, intertwined interests [5]. Each platform ecosystem is marked by a central digital platform that provides a software-based technological foundation upon which third-party actors can produce their complementary extensions [1, 3, 4]. Actors of a platform ecosystem include the platform owner (i.e., operator), complementors (e.g., developers), and customers. Even though the engaged actors pursue their own, sometimes conflicting, interests and goals, they have a common interest in the survival and prosperity of the platform for materializing and selling their own products and/or services [20].

2.2 Governance

Governance in organizational contexts has been defined from different perspectives. From a corporate governance point of view, governance is defined as "providing the structure for determining organizational objectives and monitoring performance to ensure that objectives are attained" [9]. From an IT governance standpoint, governance refers to "specifying the decision rights and accountability framework to encourage desirable behavior in using IT" [9] in order to ensure that individual IT decisions are consistent with a firm's strategic objectives [21]. Both these two perspectives illustrate the use of a set of mechanisms to encourage desirable behavior [9, 22]. Consequently, a *mechanism* can be conceptualized as a means to implement a governance structure [e.g., 10].

However, governance in the context of platform ecosystems differs from traditional organizational contexts [3, 7]. The survival of a platform ecosystem is considerably contingent on the contributions provided by loosely coupled and independent third-party complementors that each pursue their own interests and goals [7, 20]. Therefore, the platform owner needs to *incentivize* complementors to create their complementary applications rather than direct them with command-and-control structures. One major challenge of platform owners is to simultaneously facilitate complementors' value co-creation (i.e., generativity) while retaining sufficient stability over how their interactions take place (i.e., control) [3, 12, 23]. Ultimately, platform governance encompasses the need for innovative governance mechanisms to align the platform owner's own interests with those of the complementors [8, 10].

Tiwana (2014) applied the concept of governance to platform ecosystems and derived three dimensions of platform governance, namely the allocation of decision rights to decide how responsibility is divvied up among the ecosystem's actors, the configuration of a control portfolio to ensure sufficient complement quality, and pricing to ensure each of the actors receive their fair share of the revenue generated on the platform [7]. Another major contribution was Ghazawneh and Henfridsson's (2013) boundary resources model which refers to the resources that should be provided by platform owners to complementors to encourage them to make their contributions [12]. Table 1 provides an overview of the major mechanisms discussed in the literature. These mechanisms are accumulated from studies focusing on different platform contexts. As their implementation may differ across different platform contexts, we aim to complement the existing research by providing insights on the implementation of these mechanisms in the understudied context of B2B platform ecosystems.

2.3 B2B Platform Ecosystems

To study the implementation of governance mechanisms in a specific context, our focus is on B2B platform ecosystems. The latter are particularly suitable to answer our research question because of their distinct characteristics, which make the platform owner more dependent on the other ecosystem actors (i.e., complementors and customers), therefore requiring a specific approach to governance and potentially resulting in novel insights on the implementation of appropriate mechanisms. Some of these particularities are as follows: the provision of highly complex and industry specific products and services to customers that requires diligent integration of complementary resources contributed by various ecosystem actors; the broad spectrum of complementary resources provided by the external actors (e.g., development, implementation, or consultancy); the negligible power distance between the ecosystem actors as the platform owner (e.g., Salesforce), complementors (e.g., Accenture), and customers (e.g., ABB) are often all big players in their respective industry [16–18, 28–33].

3 Methodology

The investigation of how platform governance mechanisms manifest in the B2B context requires the in-depth study of a B2B platform ecosystem from the perspective

Table 1 Governance mechanisms in digital platform ecosystems[1]

Governance mechanism	Definition	References
Boundary resources	*Refer to resources that are provided by the platform owner to complementors to support their development work*	[12, 17]
Programming resources	*Refer to resources that help complementors build their applications (e.g., software tools, software development kits)*	
Interfaces	*Refer to resources that help complementors connect with the platform core (e.g., application programming interfaces)*	
Knowledge resources	*Refer to resources that help complementors understand the platform ecosystem (e.g., documentation, workshops)*	
Pricing & revenue sharing	*Refers to the degree to which the platform extracts revenue that is co-created with the complementors as well as to the creation of financial incentives for complementors to provide their complements*	[7, 24]
Gatekeeping (i.e., input control)	*Refers to the degree to which platform owners apply predefined criteria to decide which complementors are allowed into the platform ecosystem*	[7, 25, 26]
Relational control	*Refers to the degree to which the platform owner relies on the establishment of norms and values shared with complementors to influence their development work*	[7, 27]

of all engaged ecosystem actors [1, 34]. This would allow to gain detailed insights about a platform owner's specific activities to implement governance mechanisms. Therefore, we opt for a single case study approach [35] to gain insights on how the major governance mechanisms from the existing platform research manifest in a specific B2B platform ecosystem.

3.1 Case Selection and Description

We opt for Salesforce, a prime example of a thriving B2B platform ecosystem in the enterprise software industry. Salesforce has a more than 15 year long history as a platform ecosystem. In addition, due to the company's continuous development of the platform's technology and functionalities that considerably influenced the ecosystem

[1] These governance mechanisms are derived from a comprehensive literature review on platform governance mechanisms [10].

actors' contributions, the study of Salesforce specifically enables us to investigate how the ecosystem is governed through mechanisms.[2]

Salesforce is a leader in the global customer relationship management (CRM) market. While in Salesforce's early stages, its main value proposition was a sales-related software module (today known as *Sales Cloud*), Salesforce has since evolved into an integrated CRM offering (called *Customer 360*) with a broad range of modules related to sales, customer service, marketing, analytics, collaboration, and e-commerce. Besides this, complementors offer complementary applications in Salesforce's commercial marketplace for enterprise software applications called *AppExchange*. The latter has become the world's largest enterprise software marketplace, with more than 3,500 registered complementors as of today. These offerings jointly provided by the platform owner and complementors have attracted more than 150,000 customers, including both small businesses and multinational large enterprises. Customers can buy licenses for individual modules on a pay-per-use basis and can extend these modules with complementary applications. In the interplay of these different actors, Salesforce as platform owner orchestrates the ecosystem's actors with various targeted activities.

3.2 Data Collection

We collected data from July until October 2020 by means of semi-structured interviews in order to obtain first-hand insights from experts in the Salesforce ecosystem. We conducted 15 interviews with an average duration of 63 min per interview.

We derived interview questions based on the roles, interests, and concerns of the ecosystem's actors to explore each actor's perspective on Salesforce's platform governance decisions. More specifically, we collected data on the following points: How does each of the actors (i.e., platform owner, complementors, and customers) understand the ecosystem (e.g., the core and side offerings); What is each actor's role in the ecosystem and in relation to the other actors; What were the major developments in the ecosystem that considerably impacted the roles of actors and the values that they derive from the ecosystem; What are the platform owner's main activities to manage the ecosystem and align the various ecosystem actors' interests.

In the following, we describe the steps that we conducted as part of our interview series to ensure consistent data collection according to our research objective. To obtain a comprehensive understanding of all perspectives in the ecosystem, we collected data from all three engaged actor groups (i.e., platform owner, complementors, and customers). Owing to Salesforce's role as the ecosystem's orchestrator, we decided to conduct a large portion of the interviews with Salesforce employees in various roles. For identifying potential interviewees, requirements were business and/or technology roles in relation to Salesforce as well as in-depth familiarity with

---

[2] For a more detailed overview of Salesforce's history, please see the following article: https://www.salesforce.com/news/stories/the-history-of-salesforce/.

the Salesforce ecosystem. Table 3 in the appendix provides an overview of our interviewees and their organizations. We also developed a comprehensive interview guideline that contains the interview questions and an introduction to the research objectives. In accordance to our ecosystem view in data collection, we adapted the interview guideline and its constituent questions with the role of each interviewee's organization in the Salesforce ecosystem (owner, complementor, or customer). In the case of interviews with Salesforce employees, we also adapted the interview guideline depending on their functional area inside Salesforce. We shared this interview guideline several days in advance with interviewees along with an interviewee factsheet (to collect interviewee's demographic data such as position, department, location, and years of experience). Further, we recorded all interviews with the approval of the interviewees and later transcribed them verbatim, except for one interview for which we created notes during the session.

3.3 Data Analysis

To analyze the data, we relied on a-priori and open coding [35]. We used an a-priori coding scheme based on the governance mechanisms that we derived from the existing platform research (Table 1). This approach enabled us to capture all data directly related to each of the governance mechanisms. We also followed the approach of open coding to capture other aspects related to the general orchestrating initiatives of the platform owner. During this procedure, we maintained a broad perspective in the sense that we did not merely code aspects explicitly related to the governance mechanisms identified in the existing research. For instance, we also coded *transparency*, which was mentioned by several interviewees as a specific means that helped the platform owner incentivize complementors for their development work. In this regard, our multi-actor perspective was beneficial as it allowed us to capture relevant aspects from the perspective of all actors (i.e., platform owner, complementors, and customers). Subsequently, we categorized these open codes into the major governance mechanisms (Table 1) in a step-by-step coding of the data [35]. For instance, in the above-mentioned example of *transparency*, while the term was mentioned several times, we observed that transparency primarily relates to Salesforce's upfront communication before major releases, enabling complementors to prepare for important changes in advance. Therefore, we categorized *transparency* into the *boundary resources* mechanism, more specifically into the *knowledge resources* mechanism. This approach enabled us to capture all activities related to the platform owner's efforts to align the ecosystem's various actors.

4 Platform Governance Mechanisms at Salesforce

In this section, we present our results on how the governance mechanisms, which are discussed in the existing platform research, are implemented in the context of the Salesforce platform ecosystem. Specifically, we describe Salesforce's main activities to implement each of the major governance mechanisms (see Table 2 for an overview).

Table 2 Platform governance mechanisms in the Salesforce ecosystem

Governance mechanism		Platform owner's main implementation activities
Boundary resources	Programming resources	– A development environment upon which complementors build their applications (*Force.com*)
		– A more flexible development environment enabling complementors to access open source development languages (*Heroku*)
	Interfaces	– An API platform to enable complementors to connect their applications to the Salesforce core platform (*MuleSoft*)
	Knowledge resources	– Various complementor enablement programs with extensive support related to both technical and business aspects
		– An online learning system to enable complementors to gain a deeper understanding of Salesforce's various features (*Trailhead*)
Pricing & revenue sharing		– Salesforce's two major development environments can be used by complementors for a relatively small fee
		– A commission-based licensing revenue model that charges complementors only on actual applications sold
Gatekeeping		– A structured onboarding process with various obstacles that must be overcome in order to become a Salesforce complementor
Relational control		– Various social events during a major conference (*Dreamforce*) or as part of experience programs to facilitate the complementor community
		– An online voting system to enable complementors to provide feedback on ideas of other complementors (*Trailblazer*)

4.1 Boundary Resources

Salesforce provides several boundary resources to support complementors in their development work as well as to provide some standardization on how their interactions take place in the ecosystem.

Programming Resources. Salesforce provides several types of programming resources to complementors to facilitate their development work. To provide complementors with a technological foundation upon which they can create their own applications, Salesforce offers two main options. The first one is a proprietary development environment called *Force.com*. The *Force.com* usually has three releases each year and the applications can be created using an object-oriented programming language called *Apex*. To give more flexibility and additional options to complementors in their application development, Salesforce later acquired an additional development environment called *Heroku*, which enables complementors to use a variety of open source programming languages to build their applications. A Director of Applications at a large Salesforce customer described the benefits of *Heroku* for complementors as follows:

"You can also write applications outside the Force.com platform. You can use Heroku and you can run whatever, Heroku is just an environment to run Python or [...] other development platforms. And they will run on Salesforce modules. [...] You can write applications that are connected to Salesforce. Everything is possible." (Director Applications, Customer, CU-2)

Interfaces. To provide complementors with a standardized form of platform access as well as to facilitate data exchange and seamless integration, Salesforce acquired *MuleSoft*, a leading integration platform with several interface builders as well as its own marketplace for application programming interfaces (APIs) called *Anypoint Exchange*. MuleSoft enables complementors to connect any two IT systems both inside and outside of the Salesforce ecosystem and particularly supports complementors in connecting their applications to the Salesforce core platform.

Knowledge Resources. Salesforce also provides several knowledge resources to complementors. Specifically, Salesforce launched an online learning system called *Trailhead*, which contains various online courses and certificates that enable complementors to gain a deeper understanding of Salesforce's major functionalities and identify possible ways to extend these offerings:

"We recognized that we weren't reaching enough people to allow them to learn about Salesforce and our products. Trailhead came as a result of our desire to grow our footprint and knowledge in the wider business and technology communities. So, now you will see a lot of people that made their first experience at Salesforce [...] via Trailhead". (Senior Director, Solution Engineering, Platform owner, PO-4)

Besides this self-information tool, Salesforce actively provides information to complementors as part of their various complementor enablement programs focusing on both technical and business aspects. In this regard, Salesforce developed a four-tier model to distinguish between four levels of complementors; the higher the level, the more enablement services will be provided by Salesforce.

4.2 Pricing and Revenue Sharing

Salesforce's pricing and revenue sharing policies create incentives for complementors to produce their own applications in two main ways. First, the development environments *Force.com* and *Heroku* can be used for a relatively small fee. Second, complementors only need to pay a commission for applications that were actually sold. In general, complementors are able to sell their own licenses on top of Salesforce's basic *platform license.* In this regard, Salesforce makes an important distinction between two groups of complementors, namely independent software providers (ISVs) and original equipment manufacturer (OEMs). The former, ISVs, are registered in Salesforce's *AppExchange,* extend Salesforce's core products, and need to share 15% of their revenue generated through selling applications in the Salesforce ecosystem. The latter, OEMs, which merely access Salesforce's customer base to leverage their previously existing offerings (outside of the Salesforce ecosystem), need to share a higher amount of 25%.

4.3 Gatekeeping

To control for complement quality, Salesforce established a structured onboarding process which complementors must go through in order to be able to sell their applications in the *AppExchange.* This process includes both technical and business aspects. The technical part includes a compliance check, signing a distribution agreement, and a security review. Complementors must also meet certain business-related requirements, such as undergoing a business plan assessment or an alignment with upcoming changes to Salesforce's product roadmap.

4.4 Relational Control

Salesforce facilitates relational control in various ways by organizing social events and reinforcing a common identity among complementors. During its annual *Dreamforce* conference, several sessions are organized to foster exchange among Salesforce complementors. In addition, Salesforce launched various developer enablement programs, such as a program called *Developer Experience (DX)*, which plays an important role in connecting complementors among each other and further supports complementors with enablement services. A Vice President of Product Management at Salesforce explained the benefits of this program as follows:

"That was a big turn for our community [...]. For a very long time, we had focused on the end user configuring, but we had not done a lot of investment in developer tooling, sort of professional developer tooling to help them build around Salesforce implementations. [...] What we did, we went through a big program, worked a lot

with our partners around the types of developer tooling that they would need to really kind of take a professional developer lens on how to improve support for our platform. […] For years and years, we've been getting asked to build more declarative tools and services." (Vice President, Product Management, Platform owner, PO-3)

In addition, Salesforce offers several online forums to facilitate discussions and the exchange of ideas among complementors. For example, to enable complementors to contribute new feature ideas for future releases, Salesforce launched *Trailblazer*, an online voting system. *Trailblazer* allows complementors to post and upvote feature ideas, thereby contributing to Salesforce's product roadmap planning process.

5 Discussion and Conclusion

We started with the premise that the major governance mechanisms from the existing platform research need to be considered in specific platform contexts to gain a more detailed understanding of the required activities to implement these mechanisms. Despite the fact that B2B incumbents from various industries increasingly aim to transition into the platform economy [19], B2B platform ecosystems received relatively little attention in the existing research. By conducting an in-depth analysis of Salesforce, a thriving B2B platform ecosystem in the enterprise software industry, we shed light on B2B platform owners' activities to implement the major governance mechanisms. In the following, we discuss the results of our study, elaborate on their boundary conditions, and provide avenues for future research.

5.1 Contributions to Research

Our study provides two main contributions to the existing platform research. First, we provide an overview of the major governance mechanisms in the existing research and provide detailed empirical accounts on the implementation of each of the mechanisms in the B2B platform ecosystem context as one exemplary platform context (Table 2). Our findings illustrate that Salesforce as the platform owner put great emphasis on the implementation of these governance mechanisms as several of them required major proprietary developments or acquisitions. For example, to provide *knowledge resources* to complementors, Salesforce created an online learning platform (i.e., *Trailhead*) that helps complementors gain deep expertise about Salesforce's various features and identify possible ways to extend these features with complementary applications. Another example is the provision of *interfaces*, where Salesforce conducted a major acquisition of a leading integration technology (i.e., *MuleSoft*) with a marketplace for application programming interfaces (APIs) and several interface builders. These are just two examples to illustrate that Salesforce made significant resource investments to implement each of the governance mechanisms and planned required activities well in advance.

Second, we provide evidence that the implementation of several of the governance mechanisms may manifest differently in the B2B context compared to consumer-focused platform ecosystems (e.g., Apple's iOS, Google's Android). On the one hand, B2B platform ecosystems, similar to their consumer-focused counterparts, facilitate complementor and customer transactions through innovative activities (e.g., app stores, rating systems). On the other hand, there are important commonalities in the governance mechanisms between Salesforce and other B2B platform ecosystems such as SAP [e.g., 16] and Siemens *MindSphere* [e.g., 36], which do not apply to consumer-focused platforms: (a) In B2B platform ecosystems there are often multiple types of complementors. For example, in the Salesforce context, complementors include independent software vendors (ISVs), original equipment manufacturers (OEMs), and implementation consultancy services providers. In the Siemens *MindSphere* context, complementors further include data and hardware providers [36, 37]. Due to this, platform owners' governance mechanisms need to take the specific complementor groups into account. For example, Salesforce applies different licensing models to different types of complementors (i.e., ISVs are required to share 15% and OEMs 25% of their revenue generated in the Salesforce ecosystem). Salesforce further developed a four-tier model to incentivize complementors in different ways. The higher the level, the more enablement services will be provided by the platform owner. (b) Another aspect in which B2B platform ecosystems differ from consumer-focused platform ecosystems is the relatively higher need for integration of platform offerings with customers' diverse applications. To enable seamless integration, Salesforce conducted a major acquisition of a leading integration platform (i.e., *MuleSoft*). SAP also made considerable resource investments into its *SAP Integration Suite*, which ensures integration with other cloud or on-premise systems. (c) The onboarding process is slower in the B2B context due to relatively higher quality requirements. In contrast to, for example, Google's Android, which is considered as relatively open in various studies [e.g., 38], B2B platform ecosystems generally apply several predefined criteria to judge which complementors can access the ecosystem. Salesforce, for instance, relies on a structured onboarding process during which multiple technical (e.g., compliance check, signing a distribution agreement, and a security review) and business (e.g., business plan check) requirements must be met in order to be granted access to the platform ecosystem. Ultimately, all of these differences highlight the need for additional research on platform governance in the context of B2B platform ecosystems.

5.2 Contributions to Practice

Our study also provides recommendations for practitioners. We enable practitioners to learn from a platform leader like Salesforce as our detailed insights into Salesforce's activities to implement major governance mechanisms can support their own platform design and governance. Specifically, the main results of our study may guide B2B platform owners in defining an appropriate governance structure as a set of mechanisms and in implementing it with targeted activities. This is beneficial for both platform designers that aim to derive an initial governance structure and estimate potential activities to implement such a structure through appropriate mechanisms as well as for platform managers that aim to derive possible adjustment variants to alter their current portfolio of governance mechanisms.

5.3 Limitations

This paper also faces some limitations. While we are confident that our study captures Salesforce's current activities to implement the governance mechanisms, these activities may change over time. Such changes can either be due to the general evolution of the platform ecosystem (e.g., evolving needs and governance preferences) or by specific events during the evolution (e.g., regulatory changes such as the recent removal of *Parler* from Apple's App Store after its users increasingly published posts that spread misinformation and incited violence[3]). Further, we acknowledge that the data used in this study was only collected from a retrospective. While this may be of limited relevance with respect to the platform owner, the study may lack data on former complementors, which may have potentially resulted in additional insights on how Salesforce implemented the platform governance mechanisms.

5.4 Future Research

To overcome these limitations, we encourage future research to conduct longitudinal in-depth case studies to also capture the platform owner's changes in governance mechanisms to illustrate evolving governance needs and preferences. Another fruitful avenue for prospective research is to study other B2B platform ecosystems to provide additional insights on B2B platform ecosystems as well as on how they can be differentiated from other platform types based on their distinct governance practices. Lastly, future research may link platform owners' activities for implementing governance mechanisms to performance outcomes in certain contexts in order to obtain insights on systematic performance differences based on selected governance choices.

Acknowledgements This work has been supported by the Swiss National Science Foundation (SNSF).

[3] For more information about the *Parler* case, please visit the following article: https://www.nytimes.com/2021/01/09/technology/apple-google-parler.html.

Appendix

See Table 3

Table 3 Organizations and profiles of the interviewees

Ecosystem actors	Organization (or pseudonym); interviewee (position/unit/experience[4])
Platform owner (Salesforce)	*Platform owner* (Salesforce) – Program Architect Director/Customer Success/20, 5 (*PO-1*) – Senior Director, Product Management/Community Cloud/16, 5 (*PO-2*) – Vice President, Product Management/Developer Platform/19, 10 (*PO-3*) – Senior Director, Solution Engineering/Solution Consulting/30, 12 (*PO-4*) – Business Architect Director/Customer Service/32, 5 (*PO-5*) – Senior Executive, Global Services/Customer Success/29, 12 (*PO-6*) – Program Architect Director/Customer Service/20, 6 (*PO-7*) – Senior Executive, ISV Enablement/AppExchange/19, 16 (*PO-8*)
Complementors	*Complementor* #1 (Developer): A USA-based provider of an end to end DevOps solution with over 100 employees and offices in the US and Europe – Chief Technology Officer/Product Development/19, 7 (*CO-1*)
	Complementor #2 (Developer): A USA-based provider of industry-specific cloud and mobile software with more than 500 employees and offices in North America, Europe, Asia, and Latin America – Chief Digital Transformation Officer/Customer Success/25, 2 (*CO-2*)
	Complementor #3 (Developer): A USA-based provider of integration software for applications, data, and devices with more than 2,000 employees and offices in North America, Europe, and Latin America – Senior Customer Success Architect/Customer Success/23, 10 (*CO-3*)
	Complementor #4 (Implementation consultant): A Spain-based provider of Salesforce consulting with over 120 employees and offices in two countries – Chief Executive Officer/21, 12 (*CO-4*)
Customers	*Customer #1:* A Germany-based producer of building materials and construction systems with more than 35,000 employees and offices in over 85 countries – Senior Manager, Sales Excellence/Group Marketing/6, 6 (*CU-1*)
	Customer #2: An Ireland-based industrial gases and engineering firm with almost 80,000 employees in more than 100 countries – Director, Applications/IT/20, 15 (*CU-2*)
	Customer #3: A Kenya-based non-for-profit organization that has developed several funding programs to support education and to fight famine – Founder & Sponsor Development/30, 8 (*CU-3*)

[4] Years of professional experience, years of experience in current firm.

References

1. de Reuver, M., Sørensen, C., Basole, R.C.: The digital platform: a research agenda. J. Inf. Technol. **33**(2), 124–135 (2018)
2. Yoo, Y., Henfridsson, O., Lyytinen, K.: The new organizing logic of digital innovation: an agenda for information systems research. Inf. Syst. Res. **21**(4), 724–735 (2010)
3. Tiwana, A., Konsynski, B., Bush, A.A.: Platform evolution: coevolution of platform architecture, governance, and environmental dynamics. Inf. Syst. Res. **21**(4), 675–687 (2010)
4. Gawer, A.: Platforms, markets, and innovation. Edward Elgar, Cheltenham, Gloucestershire, UK (2009)
5. Cennamo, C., Santaló, J.: Generativity tension and value creation in platform ecosystems. Organ. Sci. **30**(3), 617–641 (2019)
6. Gawer, A.: Bridging differing perspectives on technological platforms: toward an integrative framework. Res. Policy **43**(7), 1239–1249 (2014)
7. Tiwana, A.: Platform ecosystems: aligning architecture, governance, and strategy. Morgan Kaufmann, Amsterdam (2014)
8. Schilling, M.A.: Strategic management of technological innovation. McGraw-Hill, Boston, MA (2005)
9. Weill, P., Ross, J.W.: IT governance: how top performers manage IT decision rights for superior results. Harvard Business Press, Boston, USA (2004)
10. Staub, N., Haki, K., Aier, S., Winter, R. Governance mechanisms in digital platform ecosystems. Paper under review
11. Benlian, A., Hilkert, D., Hess, T.: How open is this platform? The meaning and measurement of platform openness from the complementors' perspective. J. Inf. Technol. **30**(3), 209–228 (2015)
12. Ghazawneh, A., Henfridsson, O.: Balancing platform control and external contribution in third-party development: the boundary resources model. Inf. Syst. J. **23**(2), 173–192 (2013)
13. Schmeiss, J., Hoelzle, K., Tech, R.P.: Designing governance mechanisms in platform ecosystems: addressing the paradox of openness through blockchain technology. Calif. Manage. Rev. **62**(1), 121–143 (2019)
14. McIntyre, D.P., Srinivasan, A.: Networks, platforms, and strategy: emerging views and next steps. Strateg. Manag. J. **38**(1), 141–160 (2017)
15. Jacobides, M.G., Cennamo, C., Gawer, A.: Towards a theory of ecosystems. Strateg. Manag. J. **39**(8), 2255–2276 (2018)
16. Ceccagnoli, M., Forman, C., Huang, P., Wu, D.J.: Cocreation of value in a platform ecosystem: the case of enterprise software. MIS Q. **36**(1), 263–290 (2012)
17. Foerderer, J., Kude, T., Schuetz, S.W., Heinzl, A.: Knowledge boundaries in enterprise software platform development: antecedents and consequences for platform governance. Inf. Syst. J. **29**(1), 119–144 (2019)
18. Staub, N., Haki, K., Aier, S., Winter, R., Magan, A. Evolution of B2B platform ecosystems: what can be learned from salesforce? In: 29th European Conference on Information Systems (ECIS 2021): A Virtual AIS Conference (2021)
19. Hermes, S., Guhl, R., Schreieck, M., Weking, J., Krcmar, H. Moving beyond the build-or-join decision: a multiple case study on multi-platform strategies of incumbent firms. In: 54th Hawaii International Conference on System Sciences (HICSS 2021), pp. 6143–6152. Kauai, USA (2021)
20. Selander, L., Henfridsson, O., Svahn, F.: Capability search and redeem across digital ecosystems. J. Inf. Technol. **28**, 183–197 (2013)
21. Weill, P., Ross, J.: A matrixed approach to designing IT governance. MIT Sloan Manag. Rev. **46**(2), 25–34 (2005)
22. De Haes, S., Van Grembergen, W.: An exploratory study into IT governance implementations and its impact on business/IT alignment. Inf. Syst. Manag. **26**(2), 123–137 (2009)
23. Eaton, B., Elaluf-Calderwood, S., Sorensen, C.: Distributed tuning of boundary resources: the case of Apple's iOS service system. MIS Q. **39**(1), 217–243 (2015)

24. Oh, J., Koh, B., Raghunathan, S.: Value appropriation between the platform provider and app developers in mobile platform mediated networks. J. Inf. Technol. **30**(3), 245–259 (2015)
25. Boudreau, K.J.: Open platform strategies and innovation: granting access versus devolving control. Manag. Sci. **56**(10), 1849–1872 (2010)
26. Evans, D.S., Hagiu, A., Schmalensee, R.: Invisible engines: how software platforms drive innovation and transform industries. MIT Press, Cambridge, MA (2006)
27. Dhanaraj, C., Parkhe, A.: Orchestrating innovation networks. Acad. Manag. Rev. **31**(3), 659–669 (2006)
28. Hein, A., Weking, J., Schreieck, M., Wiesche, M., Böhm, M., Krcmar, H.: Value co-creation practices in business-to-business platform ecosystems. Electron. Mark. **29**, 503–518 (2019)
29. Riemensperger, F., Falk, S.: How to capture the B2B platform opportunity. Electron. Mark. **30**(1), 61–63 (2020)
30. Blaschke, M., Haki, K., Aier, S., Winter, R. Capabilities for digital platform survival: insights from a business-to-business digital platform. In: 39th International Conference on Information Systems (ICIS2018), pp. 1–17. San Francisco, CA: Association for Information Systems (2018)
31. Schreieck, M., Wiesche, M., Krcmar, H. The platform owner's challenge to capture value—insights from a business-to-business IT platform. In: 38th International Conference on Information Systems (ICIS 2017). Seoul, South Korea (2017)
32. Schmid, M., Haki, K., Tanriverdi, H., Aier, S., Winter, R. Platform over market—when is joining a platform beneficial? In: 29th European Conference on Information Systems (ECIS 2021): A Virtual AIS Conference (2021)
33. Staub, N., Haki, K., Aier, S., Winter, R. Taxonomy of digital platforms: a business model perspective. In: 54th Hawaii International Conference on System Sciences (HICSS 2021), pp. 6163–6172. Kauai, USA (2021)
34. Tilson, D., Lyytinen, K., Sørensen, C.: Research commentary—digital infrastructures: the missing IS research agenda. Inf. Syst. Res. **21**(4), 748–759 (2010)
35. Eisenhardt, K.M.: Building theories from case-study research. Acad. Manag. Rev. **14**(4), 532–550 (1989)
36. Petrik, D., Herzwurm, G. Boundary resources for IIoT platforms—a complementor satisfaction study. In: 42th International Conference on Information Systems (ICIS 2021). Hyderabad, India (2020)
37. Pauli, T., Fielt, E., Matzner, M.: Digital industrial platforms. Bus. Inf. Syst. Eng. **63**(2), 181–190 (2021)
38. Karhu, K., Gustafsson, R., Lyytinen, K.: Exploiting and defending open digital platforms with boundary resources: Android's five platform forks. Inf. Syst. Res. **29**(2), 479–497 (2018)

Digital Bridge or Tradeoff: Telehealth Adoption and Healthcare Service Quality. A Scoping Review

Layal N. Mohtar and Nabil Georges Badr

Abstract As the pressing need to expand the delivery of healthcare has surpassed the traditional limits of implementation, the substantial burden of the COVID-19 pandemic has placed the provision of healthcare services under duress. We explore the outcomes associated with the implementation of telehealth technology in healthcare ecosystems, we are mindful of the challenge in bridging the gap between the potential for extending healthcare technology to overcome the disruption in the provision of health services and the possible effect on the quality of healthcare services. This paper aims to learn from the literature on the impact of Telehealth diffusion on the delivery of quality care. We develop a scoping review and evaluate the outcome through the lens of the six aims of improvement of healthcare quality. We synthesize the literature around managing the disruption, identifying the risks of unintended consequences and factors affecting adoption. We also offer learnings and call to action.

Keywords Telehealth · COVID · Healthcare quality · Telemedicine

1 Introduction

After decades of measured implementation of telemedicine and telehealth [1], the COVID-19 pandemic has dramatically changed not only the frequency of patient-clinician visits conducted via technology across a distance, but also the urgency to practice at a distance, in order to prevent the spread of the pandemic [2]. Telehealth became a component of the personal protective equipment gear, designated as Electronic PPE (ePPE), in the medical practice [3], giving this new interaction experience a mainstream [4, 5]. Thus, bridging the digital divide for a tranche of the population and creating new challenges for others vulnerable sectors of society [6]. Hence, telehealth is a technology that built a new bridge between the patient and the

L. N. Mohtar · N. G. Badr (✉)
Higher Institute of Public Health, USJ, Beirut, Lebanon
e-mail: nabil@itvaluepartner.com

L. N. Mohtar
e-mail: layal.mohtar@net.usj.edu.lb

S. Za et al. (eds.), *Sustainable Digital Transformation*, Lecture Notes in Information Systems and Organisation 59, https://doi.org/10.1007/978-3-031-15770-7_16

service enabling a level of sustainability of the medical practice and the continuum of care. Now, clinicians could practice from the hospital and from home. While practitioners used teleconferencing equipment and connected remote devices to collect their patient's vitals and provide a remote assessment [7], patients were able to access their information through their mobile app, interfaced with the health record [8]. Technology implementers have joined the front line of the medical provider workforce to deploy and maintain the platforms that make these "at a distance" services possible.

The aims for healthcare quality imply that a Telehealth provisioned service shall be the equivalent to a traditional in person service in a healthcare setting when delivered virtually. It shall be safe, effective, patient-centered, timely, efficient, and responsive, offering an equitable and standardized service to all patient categories [9]. As we introduce technology to a new level of interaction between the care team and the care seekers, a new set of complexity arises. A tradeoff must be managed between the potential value added and the benefits in care quality as opposed to risks incurred through unintended consequences of the benefits. Therefore, we propose to answer the following questions: *How could we use telehealth to improve Care Quality? What does the literature inform on managing the potential disruption caused by the diffusion of telehealth? What learning can we conclude from the existing research?*

This paper summarizes the evidence from very recent and not-so-recent studies on telehealth quality and presents a wide literature review on works dealing with the adoption of telehealth, which in a nutshell, can be described as all the solutions built around digitals tools for providing healthcare services remotely. In our study, we identify some quality-of-care benefits and improvements of care outcome through telehealth using the lens of dimensions of quality of care. We also build the argument around the tradeoff that unintended consequences pose to this technological diffusion phenomenon. The underlying theory, building on sociotechnical systems theory [10], is that the implementation and use of the technological systems for a specific task will influence the device operators performing the tasks and their organizational setting.

2 Approach

We start this scoping review to explore the state of the literature in the context of telehealth deployment and consequential impact on quality of care. We follow the recommendations of [11] and similar studies in telehealth [12] to explore the potential of telehealth diffusion in addressing Care Quality. We also focus on understanding the disruption from telehealth diffusion while we aim at learning from the literature on how to address such challenges.

2.1 Scoping Review Criteria

As we prepare for our review, we identify relevant studies and develop a decision plan for where to search, which terms and what sources to use. The search encompasses online databases including but not limited to *PubMed, Journal of Telemedicine and Telecare, Journal of American College of Surgeons, International Journal of Medical Informatics, New England Journal of Medicine, JAMA Dermatology, NEJM Catalyst Innovations in Care Delivery, JMIR Public Health Surveillance, International Journal of Environmental Research and Public Health, and JAMA Intern Med.*

We base our inclusion criteria on the specifics of the research question and on new familiarity with the subject matter through reading the studies. In scanning the literature, we found that the terms telehealth and telemedicine are often used interchangeably. We then perform the searches twice, once using the filter of "*Telehealth*" AND "*Impact on Quality of Care*" in which 221 articles are retrieved and the second time using the filter of "*Telemedicine*" and "*Impact on Quality of Care*" in which 313 papers are returned. We then isolate and remove the duplicate papers and narrow down the search to 209 distinct articles. We screen the papers and identify relevant articles written in the English language. We read the articles in full and exclude duplicate findings in publications, citations, and student dissertations, then narrow our listing to 57 uniquely relevant articles. After independent review by each author individually, we document the body of literature on this topic. As a final step of this data collection effort, we catalog the findings based on outcome, context and findings related to impact on quality of care. We pay attention to the clarity and the nuances in the consulted studies then classify them based on a coding technique [11]. For better sense making and to effectively answer the research question we follow a coding technique that uses the framework of the six aims of improvement of healthcare quality that was introduced by Institute of Medicine (2001), in their seminal work, "*Crossing the Quality Chasm*" [9]. These aims stipulate that health care should be safe, effective, patient-centered, timely, efficient, and equitable, in order to be of quality (Table 1).

We make use of the six aims framework to help focus the study on the quality-of-care information as seen in practice and as a useful framework to advance quality of care [13]. We then follow up with discussion points that support our findings state of the literature. We enrich our findings through an investigation to identify means for potential managing the disruption, a review of factors affecting adoption, organizational considerations and close with learnings and recommendations from our review.

Table 1 The six aims of improvement of healthcare quality (Adapted from [9])

Aim for quality care	Concept—outcome
Safe	Avoiding injuries to patients from the care intended to help them—Potentially related to error reduction and prescription adherence
Effective	Providing services based on scientific knowledge to all who could benefit and refraining from providing services to those not likely to benefit (avoiding underuse and overuse)
Patient-centered	Providing care that is respectful of and responsive to individual patient preferences, needs, and values and ensuring that patient values guide all clinical decisions
Timely	Reducing waits and sometimes-harmful delays for both those who receive and those who give care
Efficient	Avoiding waste, in particular waste of equipment, supplies, ideas, and energy
Equitable	Providing care that does not vary in quality because of personal characteristics such as gender, ethnicity, geographic location, and socioeconomic status

3 Findings

To note, upon review of the papers, we find a rush in publications during the COVID-19 pandemic—slightly more than half of the works identified (112) published after 2020. Further, while most published literature discuss quality of life [14] in connection to telehealth; our study deepens the investigation into exploring the impact of Telehealth on Quality of Care, which is a concept that is larger in scope.

We find that most telehealth literature refer to telehealth as the broader practice of delivering healthcare services at a distance and to telemedicine as the term that describes the actual practice of medicine at a distance. For our purposes, Telehealth is the delivery of healthcare services by healthcare professionals using information and communication technologies, for the exchange of valid information for diagnosis, treatment, and injuries and prevention of disease, evaluation and research, and the healthcare providers' continuing education [15]. The modes of delivery of telehealth incorporates several means of delivery such as videoconferencing, mobile applications, and secure messaging. Telehealth services include provider-to-provider services with patient presence, provider to provider without patient presence, tele monitoring, and health education etc. [16].

3.1 Telehealth Use for Improvement of Care Quality—State of the Literature

The literature is scarce but vocal about how Telehealth improves the provisioning of quality care (Table 2).

Telehealth has made care safer, as evidenced by the reduction in mortality related to severe sepsis [17], and increase in prescription accuracy [18, 19]. Telehealth use helped prevent the potential of spread of disease [20], especially relevant in the era of the present-day COVID pandemic, and the need for the continuum of care [21, 22]. Telehealth was touted to improve compliance with clinical practice guidelines [23] care outcome [19, 24]; and quality of life in patients chronic conditions [25]. Thus, contributing to an effective means of providing quality care. Our review has also identified uses that help improve care service quality through patient engagement [17]. This patient centered approach increases ease and comfort for patients [26] and their satisfaction [28] while providing better access to personalized care [27]. Some authors recognized the benefits of timeliness, reducing wait time for care [29] and efficiency, reducing waste and costs [18, 31] and decreasing resource utilization

Table 2 Examples of care quality improvement through Telehealth (from the literature)

Aim for quality care with examples of care quality improvement thru Telehealth	
Safe care	– Reduction in mortality related to severe sepsis [17] – Increase in prescription accuracy [18, 19] – Improved prescription adherence [17] – Minimizing exposure of clinical staff to infected patients [20] – Reducing contagion and enhance the continuum of care [21, 22]
Effective care	– Improvement of compliance with clinical practice guidelines [23] – Improved care outcome [24] – Improved quality of life in patients chronic conditions [25] – Improve care service quality through patient engagement [17] – Direct improvement in care outcome [19]
Patient-centered	– Increased ease, and comfort for patients [26] – Better assess access to personalized care [27] – Increase satisfaction among patients with chronic disease [28]
Timely care	– Reducing wait time for care [29] – Improved school attendance thru timely diagnosis of minor illnesses [30]
Efficient care	– Reduce costs associated with hospital stays [18, 31] – Decreased emergency department utilization [3, 30] – Increase completeness of medical documentation [19] – Reduced hospital admissions [28] – Reduce patients insurance rates [29]
Equitable care	– Improving access to care for rural areas and underserved population [32] – Some challenges and opportunities for improvement through education [33], availability of supporting technology, and socio-economic status [34] – Potential reliance on others for children [30], people with disabilities and the elderly [34, 35]

[3, 30]. Finally, we have found mixed reports on the equity of care delivery. Some reports showed diverse outcomes of improving access to care for rural areas and underserved population [32], while bearing challenges through the need for education [33], availability of supporting technology and socio-economic status [34]. We also note studies that identified risks of inconsistent dependency on parents for children care and inequality of access [30], and accessibility for use in people with disabilities and the elderly [34, 35].

4 Discussion

4.1 Quality of Care Improvement Thru Telehealth

Providing Safe Care—Care is safe when the "*priority of care is for avoiding injuries to patients from the care they receive*" [9]. In the area of safety, the literature provides evidence of minimizing exposure of clinical staff to infected patients [20] and the reduction in mortality related to severe sepsis that otherwise would be a heightened risk in an in-person care setting [17]. However, the relevance of mortality rates in ICU telemedicine programs compared to the traditional onsite ICUs, have not been conclusive [19, 36]. On prescription accuracy, research reports an increase in appropriate antibiotic prescribing from 69 to 97% within six months with the use of telehealth services [19], sometimes due to a conservative approach of ordering antibiotics [18]. The use of tools such as reminders have improved prescription adherence, yet, studies have not found significant statistical relevance of guideline adherence by mode of communication, e.g. videoconference versus. telephone versus. webchat, etc. [17].

Quality through Effective Care—The aim of effectiveness points to "*providing evidence-based care for all who could benefit and refraining from providing services to those not likely to benefit*" [9]. Here also, the literature has connected telemedicine tools and automated reminder systems to the improvement of compliance with clinical practice guidelines and a betterment of the patient health outcome. Whilst clinical management was adherent to guidelines in 54.3% of the visits [23], prescription adherence through telemedicine visits was improved over urgent care visits [24] with an improved quality of life in patients with diabetes, blood pressure and high cholesterol levels [25]. Computer-assisted diagnosis and management in telemedicine was found to improve care service quality as it engages patients in their own health, where 92.9% of patients, during the telehealth consultation contributed to betterment of clinical management [17].

Patient-Centered Care—Patient-centered care is about "*providing care that is respectful of and responsive to individual patient preferences, needs, and values and ensuring that patient values guide all clinical decisions*" [9]. Technology platforms will soon become permanent gears within the patient homes. This facility will reduce costs associated with hospital stays, increased ease, and comfort for patients. On the other hand, by placing the technologies directly in patients' homes or at local clinics, care becomes more available [27] and personalized; in fact, 66% of consumers are willing to use telehealth for everything from prescription renewals to chronic disease management and behavioral health [28].

Timely Care—*By reducing waits and sometimes-harmful delays for both those, who receive and those who give care*, this aim for improvement of care is met [9]. Both patients and clinicians can benefit from improvements in timeliness with e-visit and telemedicine. They receive timely and immediate access to automated clinical information, diagnostic tests, and treatment results [9]. Patients have received useful immediate advice in 86% of cases [29]. Timely diagnosis of minor illnesses in children and adolescents, improved school attendance, and decreased emergency department utilization by 22% [30]. In Florida (Pediatric Associates in Florida), one research has found 75% reduction in patient wait times for urgent care conditions through its telehealth triage program, using virtual visits for low-acuity patients, the emergency departments wait times reduced from 2.5 h to 40 min [28].

Efficient Care—*Efficient care is about avoiding waste, in particular waste of equipment, supplies, ideas, and energy, as by reducing redundant laboratory tests, for instance* [9]. The use of telemedicine has caused visits of emergency department to decrease from 40 to 70% [3], almost eliminating inappropriate pediatric consultations in the first 14 months and increasing completeness of medical documentation from 45 to 85% within six months of use [19]. Studies reveal the good story about reduced hospital admissions by 35% among its home telehealth patient population [28]. As a direct improvement in care outcome, other studies report that the use of telemedicine has reduced hospitalizations by 50%, length of stay by 50%, and 30-day readmission rate by 75% [19]. Video visits combined with remote patient monitoring will enable healthcare organizations to better monitor patients. Additionally, telehealth programs can be cost saving for intermediate and high-risk patients over a 1- to 5-year window [31]. Costs are lower for e-visits [18], bringing the efficiency back into the health plan covering the patient [28] and then the patient's insurance rates [29].

Equitable Care (Equal Access)—Equitable care is about providing care with equal access. "*Care that does not vary in quality because of personal characteristics such as gender, ethnicity, geographic location, and socioeconomic status*". Telemedicine has taken care into hard to reach rural areas and underserved population [32]. Both the high-speed internet and mass spread of smartphones combined shall make it possible to implement telehealth consultations and quickly deploy video teleconsultations from a patient's home [37, 38]. Tele-audiology [39] and tele-dermatology [12] have reduced the number of patients required to attend face-to-face consultations. The adoption of telehealth as a recourse for some contagious conditions enhance the continuum of care, while preventing direct contact, promoting inclusion of all types of illnesses and improve patient outcome [21, 32]. Unfortunately, nearly half of the world population remains offline. Older adults with low socioeconomic status have limited access to internet-based services, a study found, especially in households of regions in Africa (71.8%), and Asia Pacific (51.6%) [34]. Poverty and the lack of education are the biggest barrier to the adoption of telemedicine in the developing world [33]. Equitable access also must address different age groups.

Children pose different challenges during examination in relation to the degree of cooperation from a child during the video conferencing and the need to rely on another person to elicit the physical signs to be able to make the proper diagnoses [30]. It is also essential to fund telemedicine infrastructure and ensure telemedicine technologies are compatible and easy to use for individuals with disabilities and older adults [34]. Older population experience barriers to telemedicine, namely, trust of technology, design, cognitive impairment, and physical limitations such as poor vision, hearing, or sensory impairment [35].

4.2 Managing Disruption

On the question of disruption, the second research objective, the scarce literature is vocal about the fact that telehealth utilization requires many adjustments. We have found works reviewing elements that may promote or impede adoption, depending on how they were addressed in the early stages of telehealth implementation. These factors are related to technology diffusion, lack of regulatory framework, relating adoption to type of practice, supply chain disruption and other organizational considerations. This section summarizes these factors with references from the literature findings (Table 3).

Elements of Technology Adoption—In the past, even prior to the pandemic, studies have attributed the slow adoption of telemedicine to technically challenged staff, resistance to change, patient demography and literacy [40, 41], high cost and reimbursement [42]. These are among the classical barriers to telehealth adoption, however, closer to the communities of practice, the slow uptake in Telehealth has been connected at the level of policy, reimbursement, organizational readiness, clinical are of focus, etc. [43]. Hence, practitioners and academia are collaborating to understand the essential components to successful implementation of a telehealth platform. Provider and staff training [34], patient education, an existing electronic medical record system, patient and provider investment in hardware, billing and coding integration, information technology support, audiovisual platforms, and patient and caregiver participation, etc. are some [21]. Others connect device interoperability [42], data integration, privacy, security of data handling to telehealth success [44] while enumerating clinical, administrative concerns [45], in addition to the socio-technical aspects of patient engagement and the patient-provider relationship [16].

Effectiveness of Telehealth Use and Adoption Seems to Vary by Practice—When compared with in-person sessions, for instance, attendance to group therapy sessions virtually was significantly lower by more than threefold. Common reasons cited for not attending virtual sessions were unavailability of technology, technological malfunction or poor digital literacy and the issues of maintaining conditions of privacy [46]. Whereas, chronic care patients have enjoyed convenience and cost savings from the comforts of their own home compared with an in-person visit [21].

Lack of Regulatory Framework—It is evident that the lack a regulatory framework to authorize, integrate, and reimburse telemedicine services, including in

Table 3 Examples of disruption from telehealth diffusion (from the literature)

Concepts	Examples
Elements of technology adoption	– Staff technology literacy, resistance to change, patient demography and literacy [40, 41] – High cost and reimbursement [42] – Provider and staff training [34] – Patient education, investment in hardware and technology, billing and coding integration, audiovisual platforms, and patient and caregiver participation [21] – Device interoperability [42] – Data integration, privacy, security of data handling [44] – Clinical, administrative concerns [45] – Patient engagement and the patient-provider relationship [16]
Effectiveness of use and adoption seems to vary by practice	– Group therapy sessions: Technological malfunction or poor digital literacy and the issues of maintaining conditions of privacy [46] – Care at home: Convenience and cost savings [21] – Hospitalization setting reduction of costs [18], resource utilization [30] and infection spread [17]
Lack of regulatory framework	– Policy, reimbursement [43] – Emergency and outbreak situations [37] – Informed consent, care coordination, privacy, and confidentiality, and resources for patient provider communication [47, 48]
Disruption in the supply chain	– Risk of fragmentation of current services and changes in the responsibilities of each actor in the supply chain of services [49]
Organizational considerations	– Organizational readiness [43] – Physician leadership traits, liability and the human factor [50] – Management of additional investments and resources [49] – Perceived value of technology and telehealth/telemedicine [51] – Models of practice and policies required [47]

emergency and outbreak situations has held back the implementation of Telehealth services, in some cases, notably France and Italy [37].

Disruption in the Supply Chain—Broader telehealth use and adoption may result in the emergence of new services corridors that disturb existing ones, introduce the risk of fragmentation of current services, which may lead to significant changes in the responsibilities of each actor in the supply chain of services [49].

Organizational Considerations—Integrating innovative technology into a business not only necessitates a large financial investment, but people partnership, policies, and technological aspects. The literature identifies key aspects of telehealth service delivery. Among these, physician leadership traits, reimbursement and licensure rules, liability and the human factor relate to organizational characteristics [50]. The disruption introduced by Telehealth could spawn several adjustments for organizations, such as additional investments and resources [49], authors reflect on factors of leadership, perceived value of telemedicine, and the organizational characteristics as key for the effectiveness of telehealth [51]. Pollard et al. [47] believed that the use of the telehealth model could enhance an organization's ability to evaluate adherence to protocols, standards, and professional behavior. They recommended establishing policies to safeguard both at the individual and organization level. These policies include informed consent, care coordination, privacy, and confidentiality, resources needed at home to optimize the treatment environment and troubleshooting technology, and direct-provider communication with the patient [48].

4.3 The Risk of Unintended Consequences and Gaps in the Literature

Telehealth technologies augment the efficiency and effectiveness of care by predominantly extending the boundary of competences of organization and the people to perform the tasks [52]. This phenomenon is supported by the socio-technical perspective [10], postulating that the technological aspects in the use of the technology place demands on the operators' perceptual, cognitive, or motor capabilities, and consequently, negative outcomes can be expected [53], sometimes beyond human factors and ergonomics [54].

Our search has identified valuable input for academia and practice, related to potential unintended consequences that must be considered, when implementing Telehealth. Such consequences can be factors that affect quality of care, improve or impede adoption, and therefore, need to be carefully assessed to enhance the governance of telehealth diffusion and reduce the risks. For illustration, we outline some unintended consequences found in the literature reviewed, serving to shape come best practice recommendations.

Risks of Unintended Consequences:

- *Impact of technology interruption on the care provided.*
- *Risks from data collection and manipulation practice.*
- *Ethical risks in practice including concerns of legal, privacy and confidentiality.*
- *Practitioner's frustration with technology and virtual care (risk of misdiagnosis).*
- *Information technology infrastructure and social challenges.*
- *Fit for use and usability during normal condition and crisis.*

The COVID-19 pandemic coupled with the rapid diffusion of telehealth services grant an unparalleled opportunity to examine related ethical, legal, privacy and confidentiality, information technology infrastructure and social challenges during a time of crisis in healthcare. Practitioners must address ethical concerns for collected health data such as traceability data, during and post pandemic [55]. Further, the diffusion of Telehealth warrants a focus on data collection and manipulation practices. Missing, incorrect, imprecise, and irrelevant data will affect the clinical decisions and in turn jeopardize the quality of care [56]. A quality improvement system shall be established to ensure that services are being provided within best practice guidelines. Guidelines may target education and training, review of clinical records and the ability to intervene in real time with all stakeholders in the system and monitor the quality of the services in telehealth [44, 47, 57, 58].

The literature stipulates that, the rapid diffusion of telehealth services grant an unparalleled opportunity to examine related ethical, legal, privacy and confidentiality, information technology infrastructure and social challenges in healthcare during a time of crisis. Maeder et al. [45] outlined that broadly clinical, administrative concerns, technical issues, legal/ethical concerns, and several other unintended consequences in the delivery of telehealth exist along with challenges affecting its adoption. Nevertheless, the governance of quality of the care provided virtually shall be ensured by monitoring compliance to standardized treatment protocols, data collection procedures, and professional behavior. DeJong et al. [59] elaborated that uniform transparency about care and referral protocols would be helpful. Creating a consumer-dominated regulator, which could compile information on e-visit websites' performance, may improve outcomes [59]. Future literature should focus on guidance for best practice on ethical data manipulation that may involve user engagement, full disclosure and feedback on justifiable use of information in order to maintain quality care in the ever-extending digital health ecosystem [55].

Moreover, physicians might perceive the absence of the physical contact with the patient leads to inadequate evaluation, missing a diagnosis, inappropriate treatment due to the lack of the tactile examination component, which may delay effective treatment [46, 49]. The delay in patient treatment may lead to higher care expenditures due to potentially preventable conditions. Further, the practice of virtual administration of care may expose health care professionals to "zoom fatigue" which reflects the tiredness and burnout with over utilizing of virtual platforms of communication [60].

Other examples of unintended consequences can range from ethical risks in practice to concerns of misdiagnosis and practitioner's frustration. The literature reviewed does not provide specific guidance for the safeguards needed in telehealth technologies to reduce such risks. To some degree, cases of abuse and maltreatment are detected when receiving care in person at healthcare organizations. When implementing telemedicine, organizations shall be aware of how to detect such cases (child abuse and other types of abuse) and enforce all the applicable reporting laws [47].

5 Contribution and Further Research Prospects

Telehealth can encourage personalized encounters and assist healthcare providers by increasing their ability to develop improved relationships with patients, which may lead to better patient compliance and thus enhance patient outcomes. Leveraging telehealth may produce a higher level of access and new ways for patients and providers to participate in the care system resulting in increased satisfaction for both patients and providers. Telemedicine while evolving and changing the current landscape of healthcare, it can in a way take us back to a time when home visits were a part of normal practice; however, it is now conducted virtually [58].

We recommend that future research and evaluation studies consider how risks and factors of potential unintended consequences inform telehealth projects, from their planning until their scaling-up [49]. For example, when evaluating the literature, there was lack of evidence in the context of the potential impact of technology interruption on the care provided. The literature did not completely address whether any adverse events took place while providing care virtually and more importantly, how an interruption in the virtual service affected the outcome. Poor connectivity issues, frequent interruptions in the telemedicine calls, login issues, and inadequate quality of image are some of the major technology related drawbacks to easing adoption, with an eminent risk of missed diagnosis [30], hampering the delivery of quality care. Therefore, access to telemedicine software shall be escorted with simple guidelines on its proper use and what to do in case an interruption happens.

Telehealth technologies contribute to equitable and patient centered by paving the way to address other pivotal challenges such as access to rural and underserved areas, availability of technological infrastructure, different people needs, data security, and regulatory framework in order to better help in the deployment of the global telehealth. The implementation of telehealth will help deliver the services and this is measured through the six aims of quality where it shall be as safe, effective, timely and effective, patient centered and responsive to a regular visit. This will help in bridging the gap between the provider and the patient, shorten the distances and expedite care.

Bridging the gap through care at a distance must account for the tradeoff of unintended consequences. Socio-technical theory depicts the harmonic synchronization between the technological aspects and social aspects to gain a successful implementation of a telehealth system [61]. When telehealth technologies are used, decision-making shall incorporate what services to retain or expand and how to measure success, ensure financing, and engage patients and staff [62]. Some noteworthy inquiries about the implementation of telehealth are value, effectiveness, privacy, security, connectivity, reimbursement, and availability issues that may arise from the adoption of telehealth [62]. When scoping to the future, healthcare organizations shall assess the organizational readiness, put the policies in places, and provide education and continuous support, check financial reimbursements, consider technology breakdowns, elaborate laws of physician provisioned services within these new boundaries, and most importantly, consider privacy and confidentiality.

6 Conclusion

From our review, we can infer that, telehealth is proclaimed to improve accessibility, especially in underserved areas, to meet patient needs [34]. Hence, telehealth may ameliorate the convenience for patients whilst lessening the health services cost and expanding opportunities for clinicians. As we look forward, virtual care will persist to build the needed foundation to provide safe and effective care with the right clinician, at the right time, and at the convenience of the patient.

Our scoping study was quite informative and good guidance for research and for practice in telehealth diffusion. Our work underscores the need for attention to how such technology diffusion impacts quality measures in care delivery and outcome. The provision of health care services through telehealth technologies has revealed a reassuring effect in the lives of patients. It has the potential to offer safe, timely and effective interaction with the healthcare provider at the convenience of the patient (according to his or her time schedule, saving travel time for those in rural areas). Hence, the delivery of quality care is possible through innovation in telehealth.

In conclusion, our investigation has provided adequate evidence to support the research objective. Yet, we beg to ask the following question: will telehealth remain a support system for well-defined needs or will it expand from specific applications to the mainstream of care delivery? How will the implementation of telehealth with the constantly evolving supportive technology empower healthcare system resilience? We are positive that these questions will prove as good contexts for further research and discovery.

References

1. Flores, A.P.D.C., Lazaro, S.A., Molina-Bastos, C.G., Guattini, V.L.D.O., Umpierre, R.N., Gonçalves, M.R., Carrard, V.C.: Teledentistry in the diagnosis of oral lesions: a systematic review of the literature. JAMIA **27**(7), 1166–1172 (2020)
2. Turer, R.W., Jones, I., Rosenbloom, S.T., Slovis, C., Ward, M.J.: Electronic personal protective equipment: a strategy to protect emergency department providers in the age of COVID-19. JAMIA **27**(6), 967–971 (2020)
3. Wosik, J., Fudim, M., Cameron, B., Gellad, Z.F., Cho, A., Phinney, D., Tcheng, J.: Telehealth transformation: COVID-19 and the rise of virtual care. JAMIA. **27**(6), 957–962 (2020)
4. Vilendrer, S., Patel, B., Chadwick, W., Hwa, M., Asch, S., Pageler, N., Sharp, C.: Rapid deployment of inpatient telemedicine in response to COVID-19 across three health systems. JAMIA. **27**(7), 1102–1109 (2020)
5. Li, G., Fan, G., Chen, Y., Deng, Z.: What patients “see” doctors in online fever clinics during COVID-19 in Wuhan? JAMIA **27**(7), 1067–1071 (2020)
6. Ramsetty, A., Adams, C.: Impact of the digital divide in the age of COVID-19. JAMIA **27**(7), 1147–1148 (2020)
7. Badr, N.G., Carrubbo, L., Ruberto, M.: Responding to COVID-19: potential hospital-at-home solutions to re-configure the healthcare service ecosystem (2021)
8. Mann, D.M., Chen, J., Chunara, R., Testa, P.A., Nov, O.: COVID-19 transforms health care through telemedicine: evidence from the field. JAMIA **27**(7), 1132–1135 (2020)

9. Baker, A.: Book: crossing the quality chasm: a new health system for the 21st century. BMJ **323**(7322), 1192 (2001)
10. Bostrom, R.P., Heinen, J.S.: MIS problems and failures: a socio-technical perspective. Part I: The causes. MIS Quarterly **1**(3), 17 (1977)
11. Levac, D., Colquhoun, H., O'Brien, K.K.: Scoping studies: advancing the methodology. Implement. Sci. **5**(1), 1–9 (2010)
12. Snoswell, C., Smith, A.C., Scuffham, P.A., Whitty, J.A.: Economic evaluation strategies in telehealth: obtaining a more holistic valuation of telehealth interventions. J. Telemed. Telecare **23**(9), 792–796 (2016)
13. Slonim, A.D., Pollack, M.M.: Integrating the institute of medicine's six quality aims into pediatric critical care: relevance and applications. Pediatr. Crit. Care Med. **6**(3), 264–269 (2005)
14. Ekeland, A.G., Bowes, A., Flottorp, S.: Effectiveness of telemedicine: a systematic review of reviews. Int. J. Med. Inform. **79**(11), 736–771 (2010)
15. Fisk, M., Livingstone, A., Pit, S.W.: Telehealth in the context of COVID-19: changing perspectives in Australia, the United Kingdom, and the United States. J. Med. Internet Res. **22**(6), e19264 (2020)
16. Tuckson, R.V., Edmunds, M., Hodgkins, M.L.: Telehealth. N. Engl. J. Med. **377**(16), 1585–1592 (2017)
17. Steinman, M., Morbeck, R.A., Pires, P.V., Abreu Filho, C.A.C., Andrade, A.H.V., Terra, J.C.C., Teixeira Junior, J.C., Kanamura, A.H.: Impact of telemedicine in hospital culture and its consequences on quality of care and safety. Einstein (São Paulo) **13**(4), 580–586 (2015)
18. Mehrotra, A., Paone, S., Martich, G.D., Albert, S.M., Shevchik, G.J.: A comparison of care at e-visits and physician office visits for sinusitis and urinary tract infection. JAMA Intern. Med. **173**(1), 72 (2013)
19. Kahn, J.M., Rak, K.J., Kuza, C.C., Ashcraft, L.E., Barnato, A.E., Fleck, J.C., Hershey, T.B., Hravnak, M., Angus, D.C.: Determinants of intensive care unit telemedicine effectiveness. An ethnographic study. Am. J. Respir. Crit.Al Care Med. **199**(8), 970–979 (2019)
20. Bains, J., Greenwald, P.W., Mulcare, M.R., Leyden, D., Kim, J., Shemesh, A.J., Sharma, R.: Utilizing telemedicine in a novel approach to COVID-19 management and patient experience in the emergency department. Telemed. E-Health. **27**(3), 254–260 (2021)
21. Smith, W.R., Atala, A.J., Terlecki, R.P., Kelly, E.E., Matthews, C.A.: Implementation guide for rapid integration of an outpatient telemedicine program during the COVID-19 pandemic. J. Am. Coll. Surg. **231**(2), 216-222.e2 (2020)
22. Monaghesh, E., Hajizadeh, A.: The role of telehealth during COVID-19 outbreak: a systematic review based on current evidence. BMC Public Health. **20**(1) (2020)
23. Schoenfeld, A.J., Davies, J.M., Marafino, B.J., Dean, M., DeJong, C., Bardach, N.S., Kazi, D.S., Boscardin, W.J., Lin, G.A., Duseja, R., Mei, Y.J., Mehrotra, A., Dudley, R.A.: Variation in quality of urgent health care provided during commercial virtual visits. JAMA Intern. Med. **176**(5), 635 (2016)
24. Halpren-Ruder, D., Chang, A.M., Hollander, J.E., Shah, A.: Quality assurance in telehealth: adherence to evidence-based indicators. Telemed. E-Health **25**(7), 599–603 (2019)
25. Flodgren, G., Rachas, A., Farmer, A.J., Inzitari, M., Shepperd, S.: Interactive telemedicine: effects on professional practice and health care outcomes. Published, Cochrane Database of Systematic Reviews (2015)
26. Donelan, K., Barreto, E.A., Sossong, S., Michael, C., Estrada, J.J., Cohen, A.B., Schwamm, L.H.: Patient and clinician experiences with telehealth for patient follow-up care. Am. J. Manag. Care. **25**(1), 40–44 (2019)
27. Lavin, B., Dormond, C., Scantlebury, M.H., Frouin, P.Y., Brodie, M.J.: Bridging the healthcare gap: building the case for epilepsy virtual clinics in the current healthcare environment. Epilepsy Behav. **111**, 107262 (2020)
28. Wyman, O.: Digital health's impact on the quadruple aim. Oliver Wyman. https://health.oliverwyman.com/2020/02/digital-health-and-its-impact-on-the-quadruple-aim.html (2020)
29. Liddy, C., Keely, E.: Using the quadruple aim framework to measure impact of heath technology implementation: a case study of eConsult. J. Am. Board Fam. Med. **31**(3), 445–455 (2018)

30. Gattu, R., Teshome, G., Lichenstein, R.: Telemedicine applications for the pediatric emergency medicine. Pediatr. Emerg. Care **32**(2), 123–130 (2016)
31. Liu, S.X., Xiang, R., Lagor, C., Liu, N., Sullivan, K.: Economic modeling of heart failure Telehealth programs: when do they become cost saving? Int. J. Telemed. Appl. **2016**, 1–9 (2016)
32. Qureshi, I., Raza, H., Whitty, M., Naqvi, Z.: Telemedicine implementation and benefits for quality and patient safety in Pakistan. Knowl. Manag. & E-Learn.: Int. J., 367–377 (2015)
33. Ashfaq, A., Memon, S.F., Zehra, A., Barry, S., Jawed, H., Akhtar, M., Kirmani, W., Malik, F., Khawaja, A.W., Barry, H., Saiyid, H., Farooqui, N., Khalid, S., Abbasi, K., Siddiqi, R.: Knowledge and attitude regarding telemedicine among doctors in Karachi. Published, Cureus (2020)
34. Zhai, Y.A.: Call for addressing barriers to telemedicine: health disparities during the COVID-19 pandemic. Psychother. Psychosom. **90**(1), 64–66 (2020)
35. Tan, L.F., Ho Wen Teng, V., Seetharaman, S.K., Yip, A.W.: Facilitating telehealth for older adults during the COVID-19 pandemic and beyond: strategies from a Singapore geriatric center. Geriatr. & Gerontol. Int. **20**(10), 993–995 (2020)
36. Barbash, I.J., Sackrowitz, R.E., Gajic, O., Dempsey, T.M., Bell, S., Millerman, K., Weir, D.C., Caples, S.M.: Rapidly deploying critical care telemedicine across states and health systems during the covid-19 pandemic. Nejm Catal. Innov. Care Deliv. (2020). https://doi.org/10.1056/CAT.20.0301
37. Ohannessian, R., Duong, T.A., Odone, A.: Global telemedicine implementation and integration within health systems to fight the covid-19 pandemic: a call to action. JMIR Public Health Surveill. **6**(2), e18810 (2020)
38. Knight, P., Bonney, A., Teuss, G., Guppy, M., Lafferre, D., Mullan, J., Barnett, S.: Positive clinical outcomes are synergistic with positive educational outcomes when using telehealth consulting in general practice: a mixed-methods study. J. Med. Internet Res. **18**(2), e31 (2016)
39. Singh, G., Pichora-Fuller, M.K., Malkowski, M., Boretzki, M., Launer, S.: A survey of the attitudes of practitioners toward teleaudiology. Int. J. Audiol. **53**(12), 850–860 (2014)
40. Trettel, A., Eissing, L., Augustin, M.: Telemedicine in dermatology: findings and experiences worldwide—a systematic literature review. J. Eur. Acad. Derm.Logy Venereol. **32**(2), 215–224 (2018)
41. Scott Kruse, C., Karem, P., Shifflett, K., Vegi, L., Ravi, K., Brooks, M.: Evaluating barriers to adopting telemedicine worldwide: a systematic review. J. Telemed. Telecare **24**(1), 4–12 (2018)
42. Nittas, V., von Wyl, V.: COVID-19 and telehealth: a window of opportunity and its challenges. Published, Swiss Medical Weekly (2020)
43. Chowdhury, A., Hafeez-Baig, A., Gururajan, R., Chakraborty, S.: Conceptual framework for telehealth adoption in Indian healthcare. In: 24th Annual Conference of the Asia Pacific Decision Sciences Institute: Full papers. Asia-Pacific Decision Sciences Institute (APDSI) (2019)
44. Larburu, N., Bults, R., van Sinderen, M., Hermens, H.: Quality-of-data management for telemedicine systems. Procedia Comput. Sci. **63**, 451–458 (2015)
45. Maeder, A., Mars, M., Hartvigsen, G., Basu, A., Abbott, P., Gogia, S.B.: Unintended consequences of tele health and their possible solutions. Yearb. Med. Inform. **25**(01), 41–46 (2016)
46. McKiever, M.E., Cleary, E.M., Schmauder, T., Talley, A., Hinely, K.A., Costantine, M.M., Rood, K.M.: Unintended consequences of the transition to telehealth for pregnancies complicated by opioid use disorder during the coronavirus disease 2019 pandemic. Am. J. Obstet. Gynecol. (2020)
47. Pollard, J.S., Karimi, K.A., Ficcaglia, M.B.: Ethical considerations in the design and implementation of a telehealth service delivery model. Behav. Anal.: Res. Pract. **17**(4), 298–311 (2017)
48. Pirtle, C.J., Payne, K.L., Drolet, B.C.: Telehealth: legal and ethical considerations for success. Telehealth Med. Today. **4**(2019)

49. Alami, H., Gagnon, M.P., Fortin, J.P.: Some multidimensional unintended consequences of telehealth utilization: a multi-project evaluation synthesis. Int. J. Health Policy Manag. **8**(6), 337 (2019)
50. Jimenez, G., Spinazze, P., Matchar, D., Koh Choon Huat, G., van der Kleij, R.M., Chavannes, N.H., Car, J.: Digital health competencies for primary healthcare professionals: a scoping review. Int. J. Med. Inform. **143** (2020)
51. Chen, J., Sun, D., Yang, W., Liu, M., Zhang, S., Peng, J., Ren, C.: Clinical and economic outcomes of telemedicine programs in the intensive care unit: a systematic review and meta-analysis. J. Intensive Care Med. **33**(7), 383–393 (2017)
52. Krings, B.J., Weinberger, N.: Assistant without master? Some conceptual implications of assistive robotics in health care. Technologies **6**(1), 13 (2018)
53. Read, G.J., Salmon, P.M., Lenné, M.G., Stanton, N.A.: Designing sociotechnical systems with cognitive work analysis: putting theory back into practice. Ergonomics **58**(5), 822–851 (2015)
54. Carayon, P.: Sociotechnical systems approach to healthcare quality and patient safety. Work (Reading, Mass.) **41**(0 1), 3850 (2012)
55. Badr, N., Drăgoicea, M., Walletzký, L., Carrubbo, L., Toli, A.M.: Modelling for ethical concerns for traceability in time of pandemic "Do no Harm" or "Better Safe than Sorry!". In: Proceedings of the 54th Hawaii International Conference on System Sciences, p. 1779 (2021)
56. Badr, N.G.: Guidelines for health IT addressing the quality of data in EHR information systems. In: Healthinf, pp. 169–181 (2019)
57. Kaplan, B.: Revisiting health information technology ethical, legal, and social issues and evaluation: telehealth/telemedicine and COVID-19. SSRN Electron. J. Published (2020)
58. Chuo, J., Macy, M.L., Lorch, S.A.: Strategies for evaluating telehealth. Pediatrics **146**(5), e20201781 (2020)
59. DeJong, C., Santa, J., Dudley, R.A.: Websites that offer care over the internet. JAMA **311**(13), 1287 (2014)
60. Sugarman, D.E., Horvitz, L.E., Greenfield, S.F., Busch, A.B.: Clinicians' perceptions of rapid scale-up of telehealth services in outpatient mental health treatment. Telemed. E-Health (2021)
61. Mosavi, N., Santos, M.: Implementation considerations for the applied business intelligence in healthcare (2021)
62. Haque, S.N.: Telehealth beyond COVID-19. Psychiatr. Serv. **72**(1), 100–103 (2021)

Mapping the Literature of Digital Transformation in the Context of Non-profit Organisations

Michele Cipriano and Stefano Za

Abstract Digital Transformation (DT) is a recurring theme in literature with regard to different business sectors. Among several aspects, scholars investigate organisational, technological, strategical or more distinctive traits concerning DT initiatives, such as motivation, implication or policy. However, only a few of them discuss DT initiatives focusing on the non-profit sector and the non-profit organisations (NPOs) in particular, which is the main aim of this work. This research takes over as a further step into a project intended to investigate DT initiatives in the context of NPOs. Specifically, this study comes after the development of a taxonomy identified by a systematic overview of the literature discussing DT in NPOs, afterwards used in classifying selected articles. This contribution seeks to apply some exploratory multivariate techniques performing a cluster analysis on the classification formerly pursued. To this end, we adopt the multiple correspondence analysis (MCA) and the hierarchical clustering on principal component (HCPC) methods by using some R packages. The outcome of this paper is threefold: (i) to analyse the associations between the multiple categorical variables defined by the taxonomy, (ii) to identify clouds of articles with similar discussion traits, and (iii) to group articles into clusters of similar contributions. Hence, we firstly pre-process the indicator matrix as input for the MCA. Next, we identify the principal components to reduce dimensionality. Afterwards, we adopt the Euclidean distance to find similarity among articles and Ward distance for partitioning. As a result, nine clusters recognise some recurrent patterns which would describe DT initiatives in NPOs.

Keywords Digital transformation · Non-profit organisations · Multiple Correspondence Analysis (MCA) · Hierarchical Clustering on Principal Components (HCPC) · Cluster Analysis

---

M. Cipriano (✉) · S. Za
University "G. D'Annunzio" of Chieti-Pescara, Pescara, Italy
e-mail: michele.cipriano@unich.it

S. Za
e-mail: stefano.za@unich.it

S. Za et al. (eds.), *Sustainable Digital Transformation*, Lecture Notes in Information Systems and Organisation 59, https://doi.org/10.1007/978-3-031-15770-7_17

1 Introduction

Digital Transformation (DT) in organisations represents a broadly debated theme among scholars [1, 2]. In general, DT calls the attention of scholars and practitioners since it is one of the major processes affecting society and the economy within our digital age [3–5]. In this perspective, several studies discuss organisational, technological, strategical [6–9] or more distinctive traits concerning DT initiatives [10–12]. Moreover, it also appears that the debate is structured in relation to different organisational sizes and business sectors [13, 14].

However, focusing on industries and organisational forms, scholars seem to consider massively public and private sectors [15, 16], while the non-profit sector (NPS) still appears under-investigated, specifically what is related to non-profit organisations. The purpose of this paper is to contribute to this debate. This research takes over as a further step into a broader project intended to investigate DT initiatives in the context of NPOs. In particular, this study aims to perform a cluster analysis focusing on the outcomes of a previous contribution [17].

The mentioned project started approximately in March 2020, and it is still ongoing. The first step of the project is based on a systematic review of the literature discussing DT initiatives in the context of NPOs through the development of a taxonomy of dimensions and relative sets of values [17]. Afterwards, the same taxonomy has been used to classify a set of selected articles that have been collected in performing the literature review (ibid). One of the outcomes from this step is a classification assigning for every dimension defined in the taxonomy one single value to each article in the refined dataset (ibid). It is noteworthy that categorical values represent the taxonomy dimensions and related sets of values. Then, the purpose of this study is to advance the analysis of such classification by applying some exploratory multivariate techniques investigating these data.

By exploring literature, it reveals that scholars often apply such techniques for the same or similar purposes. In particular, some scholars seek to map the literature through the analysis of clusters, that allows them to explain a phenomenon identifying correlations or patterns between several contributions [18–21]. Other scholars opt for one of the methods based on the principal component analysis (PCA) as a dimensionality reduction factor technique. These methods are generally used to analyse surveys or questionnaires data set [22–25]. Particularly when one intends to summarise and visualise a data set containing observations described by multiple intercorrelated variables [26].

For this purpose, we adopt the multiple correspondence analysis (MCA) and the hierarchical clustering on principal component (HCPC) methods by using the functions MCA and HCPC from the R packages *factoMineR* and *factoExtra* [27]. Our aim is threefold: (i) to analyse the associations between the multiple categorical variables defined by the mentioned taxonomy [17], (ii) to identify clouds of articles with similar discussion traits, and (iii) to group articles into clusters of similar contributions profile.

To this end, we firstly run the MCA to reduce the dimensionality of the dataset with the aim to project the cloud of articles on some dimensions [28]. In particular, we take into account the Euclidian distances between them according to their frequencies. Thus, we estimate the right number of the axis needed to be interpreted in relation to the percentage of inertia explained by each MCA dimension [29]. Next, we develop maps on these axes to visually observe the distances between the categories of the qualitative variables and between the articles, seeking to analyse our qualitative variables and the association between two or more of them. Afterwards, we move forward on the clustering approach by using the factors obtained from the MCA. Then, we use the HCPC function applying the principles of the Euclidean distance to define the distances between articles and Ward's [30] agglomeration method to construct the hierarchical tree [31, 32]. So that, we construct the hierarchical tree, and we make a partition by cutting it. Finally, we evaluate the relationship between the clusters by comparing their proportions through a statistical test based on the hypergeometric distribution [33–35].

The following section reviews the relevant theoretical underpinnings. In the methodology section, we summarise the exploratory multivariate techniques adopted to develop the cluster analysis. Afterwards, we provide some results describing them in relation to the first two principal components (axes 1:2). In the last section, we outline the generated clusters considering the relevant categories and articles representing them. Discussion and conclusions close the paper.

2 Theoretical Background

Digital Transformation (DT) in organisations is a recurring theme in literature in relation to different organisational sizes as well as business sectors [13, 14]. Vial [5] presents DT as a process whose purpose is to improve an entity, such as a process or a business unit, or other organisational elements. According to Vial [5], this process usually triggers significant change to the properties of the involved entity by combining information, computing, communication and connectivity technology [5]. Among the different streams of research, some scholars investigate how the DT phenomena affect the organisational structure [7, 36–38], business processes, people and their interactions [9, 39–42]. Some others explore more distinctive traits of DT initiatives such as motivation, implication or policy [10–12]. Other scholars seek to develop DT strategies looking at the integration and consolidation of different strategical levels, essential for the organisational design of DT processes [9, 43, 44].

However, focusing on industries and organisational forms, although public and private sectors are largely taken into consideration by scholars [15, 16], the non-profit sector (NPS) seems still under-investigated [13]. This is particularly true for non-profit organisations (NPOs) since the way how they seek to reach their objectives often differ significantly from those of for-profit firms [45–48]. For this reason, NPOs should deserve further investigation.

By looking at the non-profit sector, it still appears a contested environment nowadays since scholars use distinct ideological, cultural, and political connotations in different countries [49–51]. Moreover, the proliferation of blurring concepts and puzzling entities involved in the non-profit activity makes unclear the boundaries among its supposed constituent and stakeholders [52–55]. Salamon & Sokolowski [56] provide a re-conceptualisation of the non-profit sector by taking into account NPOs, mutual and cooperatives, social enterprises, and human actions (as volunteering or unpaid participation in demonstrations and social movements). In addition, they also observe that non-profit organisations (NPOs)/institutions (NPIs) do not represent the whole but the "common core" of the non-profit sector [56].

According to Salamon & Sokolowsky [56], an NPO is recognised as an (a) Institution (or organisation that could be either formally or legally formed or not), (b) Private (institutionally separated and not controlled by government), (c) Self-governing (able to control its activities without the operational control by any other entity, private, or governmental), (d) Non-profit-distributing (a legal prohibition is placed on any organisation's constituents or other stakeholders from receiving any quota of the surplus generated by the organisation's activities), and (e) Without compulsion (any participation with the organisation have to be voluntary as a matter of free choice) [56]. Notably, this definition only applies to those organisations whose organisational features fulfil such five characteristics [57]. Considering that a large-scale set of organisations are acknowledged in-scope of the non-profit sector, it should be noticed that not the whole range of cooperatives, mutual and social enterprises or volunteer work are institutionally constituted as an NPO [56, 57].

Nowadays, additional factors seem also to have a considerable impact on NPOs. One of them is represented by the information and communication technologies (ICT). The proliferation of the network economy driven by ICT has enhanced information flows through interlinked networks of goods and agents [58, 59]. In this perspective, an interesting study is that one provided by Joo et al. [60]. These authors have recently focused on smartphone users' awareness of mHealth apps affiliations [60]. Their study remarks that people are less likely to trust a for-profit organisation than an NPO or governmental organisation supporting a mHealth app. It also outlines that more and more users usually take on the risk of sharing sensitive information, preferring usability, functionality, and visual appeal of apps much more than protecting their privacy and related information (ibid). NPOs (seen as organisations making people healthier and contributing to the overall social good) boast high credibility and trust in comparison to private (seen as profit-seeking organisations) and governmental organisations (seen as secure organisations and backed by research) [60, 61].

Whereas the digital age has seen information becoming increasingly relevant for the entire economy, also fostering several societal changes, it seems that its implications and new rules significantly affect the role, the behaviour and the social, as well as the economic forms of NPOs [62]. Precisely, NPOs should serve society taking into consideration the broad-scale changes fostered by the pervasiveness of digital technology, covering new roles requiring the exploitation of digital capabilities (ibid). As a result, private enterprises, public institutions, or NPOs rethink organising and performing economic and social activities most effectively [10]. Indeed, some NPOs exploit digital-based communication using digital platforms and social media to interact with their stakeholders [63, 64]. Some others serve susceptible social categories by publicly funded social services through public/non-profit service networks [65].

That being said, it seems that NPOs may foster DT initiatives as a transformative way to pursue their missions and to sustain their existence [66]. DT initiatives may serve for the resilience of such organisations by steadying the relationship with societies and individuals [63, 67]. Therefore, it could be necessary to further investigate DT processes in the context of NPOs. Hence, we adopt the NPOs definition reported by Salamon & Sokolowski [56] to avoid any contrasting delineation about the sector, its size, and its composition. The next section presents the research protocol of this study.

3 Research Methods

Among different approaches used to summarise measures of associations between variables and individuals for large datasets (often based on questionnaires), multiple correspondence analysis (MCA) serves to study the association between multiple qualitative variables [22]. This research intends to combine the MCA method with the cluster analysis technique in order to locate similar articles profiles in the same characteristic space. MCA supports the manipulation of a data table (often storing a survey dataset) in building point clouds of the rows and point clouds of the columns, as any principal component methods that rely on the geometrical approach [28, 29, 68, 69]. In this perspective, MCA yields the cloud points of individuals and the cloud point of categories taking into account its principal axes [29]. In particular, these MCA axes or principal components represent synthetic quantitative variables that summarise all the categorical variables [68, 70].

According to Husson et al. [34], this study uses MCA as a pre-processing technique to apply a clustering approach on principal components then [34]. We use the MCA and the HCPC functions in the R environment [26, 32] through the *factoMineR* and *factoExtra* packages [27, 31, 34, 71]. This way, the analysis would be in agreement with the research aim by providing a means of how the discussion on DT in NPOs is characterised between differing articles groups. In other words, we adopt MCA to investigate the principal components accounting for as much of the variability in the data summarising the greatest amount of information. Then, we use these MCA principal components, serving as a method for denoising, to perform partitional and hierarchical clustering [32, 34, 72]. Specifically, we develop a three-stage research protocol tailored to this contribution by adopting the methods mentioned above (see Fig. 1). In addition, we develop several analyses carrying a large number of results by applying these methods. However, not all of the outcomes are presented in

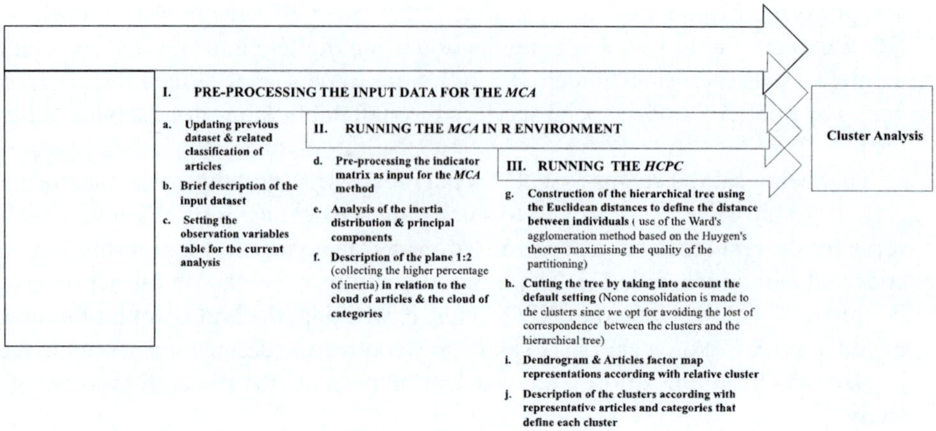

Fig. 1 Research protocol

this contribution which focuses on some preliminary investigation. For this reason, the corresponding authors are willing to provide any further results upon e-mail request. Next, the following paragraphs present each one of the three steps of the research protocol.

3.1 Description of Data & Classification Formerly Pursued

The data used in this paper consist of a classification of articles discussing DT in NPOs, that the present authors have performed in a previous study [17]. The classification has been pursued using a taxonomy based on five dimensions and related sets of values. Moreover, the dataset has been updated until this work started, last update in late April 2021. Among relevant outlets, we use the Scopus database to collect appropriate contributions since it is widely used by academics and practitioners in the field of social studies [73] and includes more sources than WoS (we retrieve 50% more contributions on Scopus than on WoS). The updated classification comprises 124 articles, which is arranged into an observation per variables table ($I \times D$), where the rows correspond to the articles (I) and the columns to the dimensions (D). The intersection between the *i-th* row and the *d-th* column in the table is the value assigned to the *ij* article and belonging to the *dj* dimension. The last column collects the ascending ordered ID of each article. In this study, such dimension is considered as a supplementary quantitative variable not relevant for calculations, while all the other dimensions are taken as active variables. By running the MCA on such dataset, we seek to identify the relationships between the various possible selected category for the variables, then the profile of similar groups of articles. Figure 2 provides some information describing the dataset (further information upon e-mail request).

Search Query	Main Ranked Field of Study (AJG*2021)	Journals	Articles
TITLE-ABS-KEY: "digit*" *AND* "no*profit" *DOCTYPE* "ar" AND *LIMIT-TO LANGUAGE* "English"	AJG*4*, Information Management	1	1
	AJG*3, Information Management	2	2
	AJG*2, Information Management	3	5
	AJG*4*, Marketing	1	1
	AJG*3, Marketing	2	2
	AJG*1, Marketing	3	5
	AJG*4, Organisational Studies	1	1
	AJG*3, Sector	1	6
	AJG*2, Sector	2	6
	AJG*1, Sector	3	5
	AJG*3, Accounting	1	1
	AJG*2, Social Sciences	1	1
	AJG*1, Psychology	1	1
	AJG*1, Public Sector and Health Care	1	1
	AJG*1, Strategy	1	1
	Others	102	115

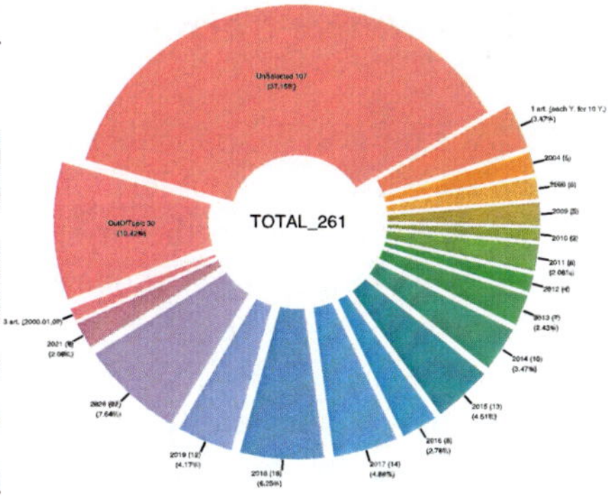

Fig. 2 Dataset summary

In addition, we also provide Table 1 showing the taxonomy dimensions and related set of values in relation to the proper code used in this study. Table 1 summarises the variables (taxonomy dimensions) and related categories (set of values of the taxonomy dimensions) used to build the indicator matrix. Notably, we present here the full name of each category in order to offer a more thorough comprehension. However, the outcomes of the analysis display a short-name tag facilitating their visualisation.

Table 1 Variables and related categories being used through the analytical methods

Variables	Categories
Organisational ambition	Analytics; Digital Device; Mobile; Platform & Ecosystem; Software Application; Social Media
Organisational scope	Crowdfunding; Crowdsourcing; Knowledge Sharing; Education; Community Development; Co-Production; Knowledge Management; Social Value Creation; Organisational Development
Organisational involvement	Non-profit Organisation Centred; Public Administration → Non-profit Organisation; Business & Non-profit Organisation ↔ Public Administration & Non-profit Organisation; Non-profit Organisation → Partnership; Public Administration & Non-profit Organisation → B2C; Hybrid Organisation
Organisational change	Digital Resource; Digital Process; Digital Interaction; Digital Organisational Change
Organisational operation	Individual; Business Unit; Whole Business; Amongst Inter-Organisational Business
Articles ID	[1:124]

3.2 Multiple Correspondence Analysis (MCA)

MCA is purposely applicable when one aims to analyse categorical data with more than two discrete variables. Greenacre and Blasius [69] start describing the MCA method in relation to the principal components analysis (PCA), and at the same time by looking at it as the one extending the correspondence analysis (CA). Indeed, CA is based on a crosstab or contingency table that limits the representation by only focusing on two qualitative variables [74, 75]. On the other hand, MCA allows obtaining maps where it is possible to visually observe the distances between the categories of multiple qualitative variables and between the observations [29].

According to Le Roux and Rouanet [28], this study follows on the more traditional application of MCA taking in input a table ($I \times Q$) where the rows correspond to the individuals (I) and the columns to the variables (referred as Q since they usually represent the answers of a questionnaire) [29]. In general, MCA is based on a distance measure technique analogous to the orthogonalization technique used in PCA [69]. Specifically, MCA transforms the association between categories of categorical variables into coordinates in a multidimensional space. To this end, MCA firstly codes the input data in the form of an indicator matrix. Such indicator matrix is based on a complete disjunctive table ($I \times K$) composed of dummy variables for each category [76]. In this particular study, the indicator matrix is constituted by I rows representing articles, and K columns that are the categories of the categorical variables Q. If the *Q-th* column of the original table has *Kq* categories, there would be *Kq* columns for this variable in the indicator matrix, each corresponding to one category of the *Q-th* variable. The record *yik* at the intersection of the *i-th* row and the *q-th* column is 1 if the *i-th* article takes category *q* of the *Q-th* variable, and 0 otherwise [68]. In short, each column reports 1 if the article took such category and a 0 if not; that is a "dummy" variable. In other words, MCA creates n binary columns for each variable with the limit to assign the value 1 to one of the columns only. Moreover, it is disjunctive because there is only one "1" in each block of columns, and all the rest are zeros, and complete since there has to be at least one "1".

However, this procedure generates additional artificial dimensions since several columns contribute to code one specific categorical variable. As a result, the total variance or inertia of the solution space is artificially inflated, and the first dimensions may be explained by an underestimated percentage of inertia [69, 77, 78]. In addition, there would be $I \times K$ sums of articles that have the *Ki* category so that each category has a sum value representing how many articles have been classified with it. Hence, the disjunctive matrix of dummy variables is denoted as Z of size $I \times K$ [77], considering that:

$$K = \sum_{q=1}^{Q} Kq \tag{1}$$

Therefore, the dimensionality of Z is given by the difference between categories and variables ($K - Q$), which also represents the total number of the MCA principal components [28]. Furthermore, Q represents the row margins of the disjunctive table, while the margins of columns are equal to $(Ik)_{k=1,...K}$, where Ik, in this study, indicates the number of articles taking the category K. Also, the grand total is equal to IQ (ibid).

It should be further noticed that all the articles have the same weight. For this study, there is no reason to attribute more meaning to some article over another. Consequently, the weight of each article is 1/I as the sum of the weights has to equal 1. In addition, since we work in the context of MCA, all categories, their coordinate values, their contributions as well as the quality of their representation are computed by adopting the chi-squared cosine measure (X^2), and the so-called "v-test" statistic [32, 69, 77, 78]. To measure the distance between two articles i and i', we consider the sum of the squares of the differences of the coordinates (chi-squared distance). Then, each square of the differences of the coordinates is weighted in relation to the weight of a category. The X^2 distance is defined by the equation:

$$\frac{I}{Q}\sum_{k=1}^{k}\frac{1}{Ik}(z_{ik}-z_{i'k})^2 \tag{2}$$

Moreover, these distances also identify a cloud of points that takes a centre of gravity G_N with coordinates c_k, k = 1, ..., K). While the total inertia is determined by:

$$\frac{1}{I}\sum_{i=1}^{I}d^2(\mathrm{I},\mathrm{G_N})=\frac{K-Q}{Q}=\frac{K}{Q}-1 \tag{3}$$

To measure the distance between two categories k and k', we take into consideration the cloud of the columns from the indicator matrix, which focus on the shape of a cloud of points formerly defined [32, 69, 77, 78]. The chi-squared distance for categories is:

$$\mathrm{d}^2(\mathrm{k},\ \mathrm{G_K})=\mathrm{I}\sum_{i=1}^{I}\left(\frac{Zik}{Ik}-\frac{1}{I}\right)^2=\frac{I}{Ik}-1 \tag{4}$$

The test statistic is based instead on the Gaussian distribution. Therefore, if a category shows a value approximately between −2 or above 2, it indicates that such category has a coordinate significantly different to 0. This value is useful for knowing which categories have large positive or negative values in each dimension. In other words, this is the so-called "eta2" value that represents the correlation ratio between each variable and each dimension. We use the eta2 values to draw and interpret the graph of the variables as a plot of the squared relationships. Another concept requiring particular attention is that concerning the eigenvalues (principal axes/components). This is so since each cloud is denoted by its principal axes l = 1, 2, ..., L [29]. According to Le Roux and Rouanet [29], an eigenvalue λl represents the variance of the projected cloud on the axis l. Such principal axes cross at the barycentre of a cloud. As a consequence, the first principal axis offers the best one-dimensional adaptation for the cloud. An eigenvalue can be calculated by the following formula:

$$\lambda\text{'}1 = \left(\frac{Q}{Q-1}\right)^2 (\lambda l - \bar{\lambda})^2 \tag{5}$$

where $\bar{\lambda}$ represents the means of eigenvalues [29, 78] which is defined as:

$$\bar{\lambda} = \frac{\left(\frac{K}{Q} - 1\right)}{(K - Q)} = \frac{1}{Q} \tag{6}$$

We use this value as a threshold measure in selecting the principal components needed to be interpreted in this contribution. Lastly, their sum is represented by the variance of the whole cloud; therefore, it is equal to K/Q −1, like the total inertia. The next section focuses on the last step of the research protocol.

3.3 Hierarchical Clustering on Principal Components (HCPC)

The last step of this research is based on the clustering approach [30, 35]. In line with the research aim, we perform a cluster analysis to identify similar profiles of articles into clusters. The general purpose is to collect articles similar to one another within the same cluster and dissimilar in others. Specifically, this study adopts Ward's agglomeration method [32]. We opt for Ward's [30] method in order to regroup articles by maximising the partitioning quality (ibid). Moreover, this is an agglomerative hierarchical clustering method that aptly complements the MCA approach. Indeed, Ward's [30] method is based on some measures that we already compute through the development of the MCA [34].

According to Blasius and Greenacre [35], this method takes into account an article i in a cluster q and a distance d, where $p(i)$ represents the weight associated with an article i. Then, we take $p(i) = 1/|q|$ if i belonging to q. In this perspective, we take into consideration q as the cluster and the cluster's centre, where q determines the centre by the following formula:

$$q = \frac{1}{|q|} \cdot \sum_{i \in q} i \tag{7}$$

Furthermore, we also look at an article i as a label or index among all the articles and the articles vector [35].

That being said, Ward's [30] method applies Huygen's [32] theorem in building homogeneous clusters since the growth of the within cluster-inertia is minimum at each step of the algorithm [30, 32, 79]. So that, the homogeneity of a cluster is dependent on the within inertia. Additionally, it also simplifies the decomposition of the total variance in between and within-group variance [30, 34, 35]. In other words, given the between-clusters variance B and the summed within-clusters variance W, the total inertia T is determined by the sum of both variances $(B + W)$ [35].

To this end, we perform the cluster analysis running the HCPC function in the R environment and using the MCA outputs [26, 32]. According to Husson et al. [34], the HCPC function relies on Ward's [30] criterion [33]. This function firstly computes the distance between articles using Euclidean distances. Secondly, it applies Ward's [30] agglomeration method to develop a hierarchical tree representing the sequence of nested partitions. Whereas the method firstly takes each article as a class, it finally generates a more general partition including all articles (in accordance with the desired pre-set level of partition). In addition, each branch of the hierarchical tree groups articles in relation to a shared set of properties [34, 35].

Furthermore, the articles in the hierarchical tree are arranged in relation to the significant MCA principal components [32, 34]. For this purpose, we select the principal components whose variance value is equal or greater than the mean value. In particular, since we opt for avoiding the loss of correspondence between the clusters and the hierarchical tree, no consolidation is made to the clusters. Therefore, we cut the tree at the corresponding level of the number of selected principal components. As a result, we develop a dendrogram illustrating the gain of within-cluster inertia when we partition Q clusters to Q-1 clusters. The outcome of this analysis follows next.

4 Results

This section offers some results carried out through the MCA and the HCPC analysis. Specifically, we focus on the interpretation of the plane depicting the first two axes for this contribution. Therefore, we seek to provide a thorough description of the involved articles, variable categories, and such two principal components. Although we develop the analysis in relation to more axes (in agreement with the descriptions in §3), in this paper, as a preliminary investigation, we consider and discuss the main two axes out of ten contributing to calculations. However, we are willing to provide further results upon e-mail request.

Notably, the results are based on interpretation rules postulated by some influential authors that contribute to developing these methods [68, 78, 80–84]. For example, suppose a group of articles is assigned to many categories, except one which is rare (appearing in the dataset with a limited frequency), and one of them takes over this rare category. In that case, the distance between the latter and the group is relatively large. On the other hand, when a rare category is shared between two articles, the distance is relatively small since they share a similarity anyway [22, 69, 77, 82, 85]. In general, there is no distance between articles taking the same set of categories, while there is a small distance between them if many categories are shared [26, 32]. As concern categories, there is a higher distance between articles as smaller is the frequencies of disagreement categories. In particular, when an article is assigned to infrequent (rare) categories, it is displayed far from the centre; therefore, it is close to the perimeter of the cloud. Lastly, variables including more categories contribute significantly to the variance of the cloud. However, the overall variance is also particularly susceptible to less frequent categories [29, 78].

That being said, the MCA function firstly constructs an indicator matrix composed of 124 articles and 30 dummy variables, including only one quantitative variable as illustrative (reporting the ID of the articles). Moreover, the analysis of the graphs does not detect any outliers. Afterwards, the investigation progresses on studying the inertia distribution to define the principal components (axes) that needed to be interpreted. The inertia of the first dimensions shows if there are strong relationships between variables and suggests the number of dimensions that should be studied. In our case, the first two dimensions express 19.44% of the total dataset inertia, which means that 19.44% of the articles or the variables cloud total variability is explained by this plane. This is a very small percentage, and the first plane represents a small part of the data variability. However, this value is greater than the reference value that equals 15.01%. The variability explained by this plane is thus significant since the reference value is the 0.95-quantile of the inertia percentages distribution obtained by simulating 2299 data tables of equivalent size based on a uniform distribution. Therefore, we remark that it is important also to interpret the dimensions greater or equal to the third one. To this end, an estimation of the right number of the axes to interpret suggests restricting the analysis to the description of the first ten axes. These axes present an amount of inertia more significant than those obtained by the 0.95-quantile of random distributions, which is 65.68% against 59.13%. Ergo, only these axes are carrying real information. Consequently, we re-run the MCA in order to set the execution of the following analysis standing to these axes. At this point, we describe plan 1:2 in relation to the pertinent cloud of articles and the cloud of categories belonging to it.

Figure 3 shows the three straightforward representations of the cloud origination for the combination of articles (left side), categories (right side) and joint display representing axes 1:2 (centre). Each point represents the coordinates for an article (displayed through its ID label) or for a category with regard to dimensions 1 and 2. Also, the points away from the origin show categories that deviate from the mean. By looking at the pictures in Fig. 3, it should be noted that dimension 1 (the x-axis) contrasts the two groups of articles to the right side of the distribution (1 & 3 quartiles) to that one to the left (2 quartile). All these articles make a higher contribution to the construction of the plane defined by axes 1:2. In particular, the groups composed by the articles (47, 118, 44, 43) and (63, 99, 42, 64, 77, 93) are characterised by a strongly positive coordinate on this axis. In contrast, a strongly negative coordinate represents the group including the articles (72, 55, 39, 41, 35, 81, 17, 73, 80, 87). In addition, the group of articles (63, 99, 42, 64, 77, 93) share a high frequency for the factors KnowShar, Platform, DigOrgChange, and WholeBus (factors are sorted from the most common). Conversely, this group of articles shares a low frequency for the factors CommDev, Social Media, DigInter, InterOrg and BusUnit (factors are sorted

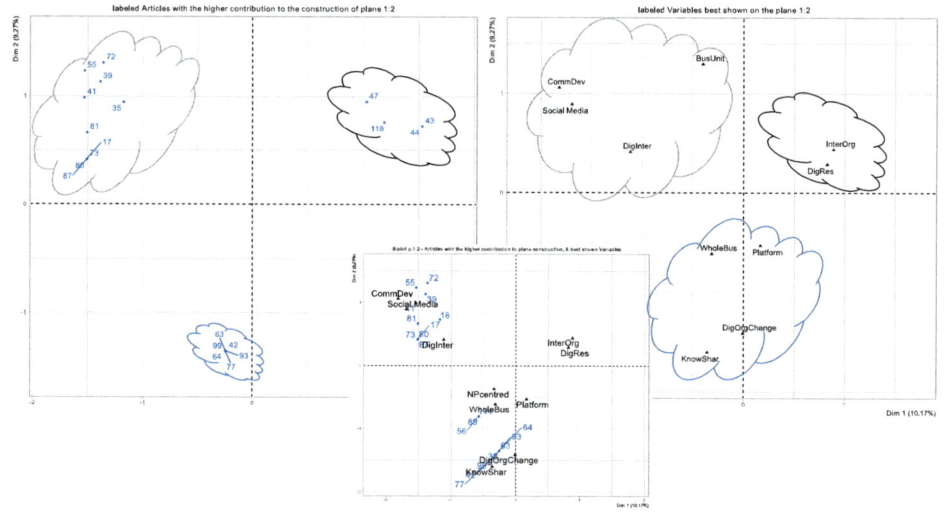

Fig. 3 Biplot of plane representing axes 1:2, Articles with the higher contribution to plane construction and best contributing categories

from the rarest). Furthermore, while the group of articles (47, 118, 44, 43) share a high frequency for the factors InterOrg, NP2Partner, Edu, DigRes, SoftApp (factors are sorted from the most common). In comparison, this group shares a low frequency for the factors NPcentred, WholeBus and DigInter (sorted from the rarest). Finally, the group of articles (72, 55, 39, 41, 35, 81, 17, 73, 80, 87) shares a high frequency for the factors DigInter, CommDev, Social Media, BusUnit (factors are sorted from the most common). In contrast, these articles share a low frequency for the factors KnowShar, Platform, DigOrgChange and DigRes (sorted from the rarest).

Focusing instead on dimension 2 (the y-axis), it opposes the two groups of articles to the top of the graph (1 & 2 quartiles) to that one to the bottom (3 quartile). So then, whereas a strongly positive coordinate characterises the two groups composed by the articles (72, 55, 39, 41, 35, 81, 17, 73, 80, 87) and (47, 118, 44, 43) on axis 2, the group including the articles (63, 99, 42, 64, 77, 93) is represented by a strongly negative coordinate on the same axis. Considering that the coordinates of the group of articles and that of the categories are the same for both the dimensions since both dimensions 1 and 2 construct this plane, we avoid repeating the same joint analysis among groups of articles and the categories characterising them (which would be the same).

Next, the dendrogram representing the hierarchical tree effortlessly shows the partition defining the clusters among several intuitive plots. For this study, the hierarchical tree takes the index of 10 to set the partition since the MCA highlights ten axes carrying real information. Afterwards, the software generated a partition of 9 clusters by cutting the tree taking such a setting. In addition, it also seems quite interesting to represent the generated clusters on the same plane of dimensions 1:2 used to interpret the MCA results. This way, one can easily visualise coloured articles on

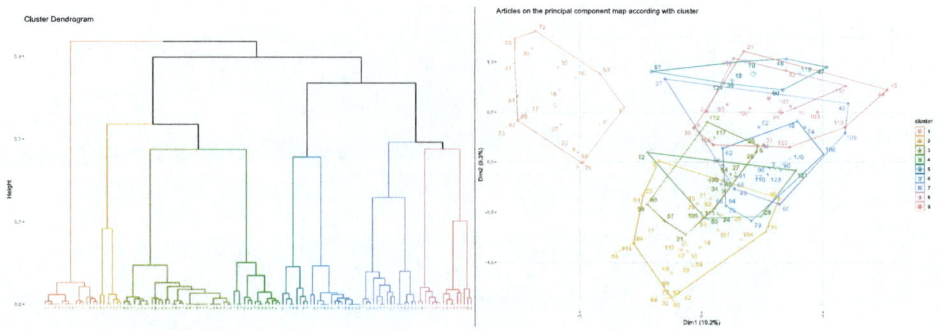

Fig. 4 Dendrogram and clusters on the factor map 1:2

the principal component map according to their clusters. The latter seems particularly useful for understanding the overlapping among clusters, possibly considering refining the partitioning. For example, by looking at this graph in Fig. 4, one can see that the clusters in this study are separated to a lesser extent one from another. Overall, it seems that only one cluster is distinct from the other, that is the cluster 1. In comparison, it also appears that clusters 2 and 9 opposing to cluster 1 show less overlapping among all the other clusters presenting large overlapping. This observation suggests that we could refine the partition as a further step. Figure 4 displays the two graphs discussed. The remainder of the paper covers the discussion section focusing on the description of the 9 clusters.

5 Discussion and Conclusion

This contribution seeks to apply some exploratory multivariate techniques performing a cluster analysis to a classification formerly pursued [17]. To this end, we run the MCA and the HCPC methods by using the corresponding function in the R environment. So that, we carefully set the data developing some pre-processing steps. Next, we firstly focus on the principal components contributing mainly to the construction of the selected axes. Specifically, we take into account the overall variances selecting the eigenvalues exceeding the threshold and carrying real information. Secondly, we analyse the distances between articles on the basis of these principal components. In particular, we present the cloud of articles in relation to the plane of axes 1:2, as well as the contributions of the categories. Furthermore, we also report the properties of these clouds with regard to the principal components, which contribute most to the construction of these two axes. Finally, we provide the biplot joint display (factor "map" of axes 1:2) by showing both the clouds of categories and articles as the geometric representations of interpoint distances [86]. Also, we briefly present the dendrogram of the hierarchical tree and the clusters plot on the factor map.

As a final stage of the systematic literature review underpinned in our broaden project, we close this contribution by describing the clusters in relation to their characteristics, also highlighting the model articles for each cluster. We provide a title and a short description presenting the proposal belonging to each cluster, allowing the reader to understand the different nuances that differentiate the content of the overlapping clusters. In short, these insights would identify some articles profiles concerning the discussion on DT in NPOs. Doing so, we summarise the clusters using the variables and the articles selecting only categories associated with a p-value less than 2% [32]. For this study, we avoid the description of the classes using the axes. Notably, we mainly use the "para" object for this description. It should be further noticed that the first article showed for each cluster represent the modal article for such class. In other words, this modal article is the one closest to the barycentre of each class [26, 32]. As a way of explanation, we also report only the first article concerning the "dist" object, which represents the distance of an article to the barycentre of the other classes (ibid). Then, the classification made on articles reveals 9 clusters, described following.

Cluster 1, "*connecting people*", is composed of articles such as 17, 73, 80, 87, 5. For class 1, the modal individual is 17, which is at a distance of 0.52 from the barycentre of class 1 articles. While article 55 is the one that is furthest from the barycentre of other classes. Moreover, this group is characterised by a high frequency for the factors CommDev, DigInter and Social Media (factors are sorted from the most common). In contrast, a low frequency is identified for the factors Platform, DigRes, DigProc, DigOrgChange, KnowMgt and KnowShar (factors are sorted from the rarest). The Cluster 1 profile seems to take on attributes particularly representative of DT phenomena in relation to the need for networking among people and organisations.

Cluster 2, "*innovating for sharing*", comprises articles such as 14, 67, 115, 11, 56. For class 2, the modal individual is 14, which is at a distance of 0.39 from the barycentre of class 2 articles. While article 84 is the one that is furthest from the barycentre of other classes. This group is typified by a high frequency for the factors KnowShar, DigOrgChange, WholeBus, Platform, OrgDev and NPcentred (from the most common). At the same time, a low frequency is determined for the factors InterOrg, Social Media, CommDev, BusUnit, DigProc, DigRes, KnowMgt and Ind (from the rarest). The Cluster 2 profile builds on some attributes particularly representative of DT phenomena in relation to the need to innovate an NPO firm/business for the purpose of knowledge sharing.

Cluster 3, "*creating value*", includes articles such as 111, 27, 59, 88, 30. For class 3, the modal individual is 111, which is at a distance of 0.43 from the barycentre of class 3 articles. While article 25 is the one that is furthest from the barycentre of other classes. Additionally, this group is categorised by a high frequency for the factors SocValCreat, DigRes and B&NPvsPA&NP (sorted from the most common). The Cluster 3 profile is based on attributes that are particularly representative of DT phenomena in relation to the need to create social value among people and organisations. Thus, we assign the name "creating value" to Cluster 3, also considering the characterising attributes concerning the collaborations among different businesses.

Cluster 4, "*innovating for fundraising*", is composed of articles such as 24, 50, 12, 34, 40. For class 4, the modal individual is 24, which is at a distance of 0.63 from the barycentre of class 4 articles. While article 28 is the one that is furthest from the barycentre of other classes. Moreover, this group is identified by a high frequency for the factors CrowFund and PA2NP (sorted from the most common). The Cluster 4 profile appears to take on some attributes particularly representative of DT phenomena in relation to the need to innovate an NPO in how it acts for fundraising. It is further noted that cluster 4 includes both articles assigned the value "PA2NP". This means that some discussion highlights the collaboration of a public administration in supporting an NPO for this specific purpose. However, we assign the label "innovating for fundraising" to Cluster 4, recognising the major attributes of such a profile.

Cluster 5, "*developing digital processes*", is made of articles such as 51, 48, 70, 36, 19. For class 5, the modal individual is 51, which is at a distance of 0.96 from the barycentre of class 5 articles. While article 70 is the one that is furthest from the barycentre of other classes. In addition, the articles of this group share a high frequency for the factors BusUnit, Analytics, PA&NPtoB2C, OrgDev and DigProc (sorted from the most common). In contrast, they share a low frequency for the factors Platform, NPcentred, WholeBus and DigInter (sorted from the rarest). The Cluster 5 profile builds on some attributes particularly representative of DT phenomena in relation to the need to innovate certain business processes. We notice that such initiatives mainly involve the collaboration of an NPO and a public administration, improving some services to civil benefit. For this reason, we assign the label "developing digital processes" to Cluster 5 since it seems to recognise the attributes exemplifying such a profile.

Cluster 6, "*innovating for knowledge*", is constituted of articles such as 95, 110, 120, 123, 58. For class 6, the modal individual is 95, which is at a distance of 0.36 from the barycentre of class 6 articles. While article 7 is the one that is furthest from the barycentre of other classes. Also, this group is characterised by a high frequency for the factors KnowMgt, DigProc, InterOrg, NPcentred and Platform (from the most common). In comparison, such articles share a low frequency for the factors DigInter and PA&NPtoB2C (from the rarest). The Cluster 6 profile is based on attributes that are particularly representative of DT phenomena in relation to the need to innovate an NPO firm/business for the purpose of knowledge management. Specifically, it seems that an NPO is involved in such initiatives to reach and improve this aim at an inter-organisational level.

Cluster 7, "*sourcing for digital*", comprises articles such as 49, 68, 66, 37, 45. For class 7, the modal individual is 49, which is at a distance of 0.83 from the barycentre of class 7 articles. At the same time, article 74 is the one that is furthest from the barycentre of other classes. Additionally, this group is typified by a high frequency for the factors CrowSour and HybridOrg (sorted from the most common). In contrast, a low frequency is determined for the factor NPcentred only. The Cluster 7 profile seems to take on attributes that are particularly representative of DT phenomena in relation to the need of an NPO to source digital competencies or resources among people and organisations. Notably, Cluster 7 shows the highest percentage of overlapping, that is, with six other clusters. In particular, the Cluster 7 profile is strongly characterised by various attributes concerning the involvement, partnership, or collaboration among different businesses. Hence, we assign the label "sourcing for digital" to Cluster 7, highlighting the key characteristics of such a profile.

Cluster 8, "*co-producing for innovation*", comprises articles such as 16, 85, 96, 107, 2. For class 8, the modal individual is 16, which is at a distance of 0.48 from the barycentre of class 8 articles. While article 100 is the one that is furthest from the barycentre of other classes. Furthermore, the articles of this group are categorised by a high frequency for the factors CoProd, InterOrg and PA&NPtoB2C (sorted from the most common). At the same time, they share a low frequency for the factors WholeBus and NPcentred (from the rarest). The Cluster 8 profile builds on some attributes that recognise DT phenomena concerning the co-production activity to innovate some services for citizen benefit. Similarly to cluster 5 (whit which it is showed the largest overlapping), we notice that such initiatives mainly involve the collaboration of an NPO and several businesses to improve or innovate infrastructures and related services for community benefit. We assign the label "co-producing for innovation" to Cluster 8 since it seems to represent congruously the attributes exemplifying such a profile.

Lastly, cluster 9, "*innovating for education*", is composed of articles such as 103, 122, 102, 113, 4. For this latter class 9, the modal individual is 103, which is at a distance of 0.81 from the barycentre of class 9 articles. While article 43 is the one that is furthest from the barycentre of other classes. Moreover, this group is characterised by a high frequency for the factors Edu, Ind, NP2Partner and DigRes (factors are sorted from the most common). In contrast, a low frequency is identified in relation to only one factor, which is WholeBus (factor sorted from the rarest). The Cluster 9 profile is based on attributes that are particularly representative of DT phenomena in relation to the need to innovate some educational services. Specifically, it seems that an NPO is often centrally involved to improve educational purposes (for itself or civils), but it is also collaborating with any organisations partner in other cases. We assign the label "innovating for education" to Cluster 9, recognising the key attributes of such a profile.

In conclusion, this work presents some limitations. Firstly, since we adopt a default approach in performing some traditional applications of the MCA and HCPC methods, our results could appear not refined adequately in relation to our research aim. Indeed, the cluster factor map in Fig. 4 reveals that our clusters present a significant overlapping. For this reason, in a future step, we could perform a different partition of the clusters. Specifically, we could reduce the number of clusters limiting the level of overlapping among them in order to identify articles profile that are objectively qualifiable.

Secondly, a further limitation is represented by the dataset used in this analysis. In particular, the cluster analysis relies on the review of the literature [17] and does not account for direct empirical evidence. Ergo, contributions concerning empirical case studies could be investigated in order to refine further the clusters analysis as a future research step. To this end, we could firstly develop a multiple case study research to identify objective profiles concerning the discussion of DT in NPOs. Afterwards, we could compare the resulting profiles with those identified analysing the literature to obtain a final refined and unique set of profiles describing the DT phenomenon in the context of NPOs.

References

1. Dang, D., Vartiainen, T.: Digital strategy patterns in information systems research. 23rd Pacific Asia Conference on Information Systems. Secure ICT Platform 4th Industrial Revolution, PACIS 2019 (2019)
2. Markus, M.L., Rowe, F.: Guest editorial: theories of digital transformation: a progress report. J. Assoc. Inf. Syst. **22**, 273–280 (2021). https://doi.org/10.17705/1jais.00661
3. El-Telbany, O., Abdelghaffar, H., Amin, H.: Exploring the digital transformation gap: evidence from organizations in emerging economies. In: 24th Pacific Asia Conference on Information Systems (2020). https://aisel.aisnet.org/pacis2020
4. Parviainen, P., Tihinen, M., Kääriäinen, J., Teppola, S.: Tackling the digitalization challenge: how to benefit from digitalization in practice. Int. J. Inf. Syst. Proj. Manag. **5**, 63–77 (2017). https://doi.org/10.12821/ijispm050104
5. Vial, G.: Understanding digital transformation: a review and a research agenda. J. Strateg. Inf. Syst. **28**, 118–144 (2019). https://doi.org/10.1016/j.jsis.2019.01.003
6. Bharadwaj, A., El Sawy, O.A., Pavlou, P.A., Venkatraman, N.: Digital business strategy: toward a next generation of insights. MIS Q. **37**, 471–482 (2013). https://doi.org/10.25300/MISQ/2013/37:2.3
7. Matt, C., Hess, T., Benlian, A.: Digital transformation strategies. Bus. Inf. Syst. Eng. **57**, 339–343 (2015). https://doi.org/10.1007/s12599-015-0401-5
8. Wiesböck, F., Hess, T.: Digital innovations embedding in organizations. Electron. Mark. **30**, 75–86 (2020). https://doi.org/10.1007/s12525-019-00364-9
9. Hess, T., Matt, C., Benlian, A., Wiesböck, F.: Options for formulating a digital transformation strategy. MIS Q. Exec. **15**, 123–139 (2016). https://doi.org/10.1108/10878571211209314
10. OECD: Vectors of Digital Transformation. OECD Digit. Econ. Pap., 1–38 (2019). https://doi.org/10.1787/20716826
11. Legner, C., Eymann, T., Hess, T., Matt, C., Bo, T., Urbach, N., Drews, P., Ma, A., Ahlemann, F.: Digitalisation: opportunity and challenge for the business and information systems engineering community. Bus. Inf. Syst. Eng. **59**, 301–308 (2017). https://doi.org/10.1007/s12599-017-0484-2
12. Muehlburger, M., Rueckel, D., Koch, S.: A framework of factors enabling digital transformation. 25th American Conference on Information Systems (2019)
13. Westerman, G., Calméjane, C., Bonnet, D., Ferraris, P., McAfee, A.: Digital transformation: a roadmap for billion-dollar organizations (2011)
14. Depaoli, P., Za, S., Scornavacca, E.: A model for digital development of SMEs: an interaction-based approach. J. Small Bus. Enterp. Dev. **27**, 1049–1068 (2020). https://doi.org/10.1108/JSBED-06-2020-0219
15. Hofmann, S., Sæbø, Ø., Braccini, A.M., Za, S.: The public sector's roles in the sharing economy and the implications for public values. Gov. Inf. Q. **36**, 101399 (2019). https://doi.org/10.1016/j.giq.2019.101399
16. Liere-Netheler, K., Packmohr, S., Vogelsang, K.: Drivers of digital transformation in manufacturing. In: Proceedings of the 51st Hawaii International Conference on System Sciences, pp. 3926–3935 (2018). https://doi.org/10.24251/HICSS.2018.493
17. Cipriano, M., Za, S.: Exploring the discourse on digital transformation in the domain of non-profit organisations. In: Ceci, F., Prencipe, A., Spagnoletti, P. (eds.) Exploring innovation in

a digital world. Lecture notes in information systems and organisation, vol. 51, pp. 198–231. Springer, Cham (2021). https://doi.org/10.1007/978-3-030-87842-9_15
18. Za, S., Spagnoletti, P., Winter, R., Mettler, T.: Exploring foundations for using simulations in IS research. Commun. Assoc. Inf. Syst. **42**, 268–300 (2018). https://doi.org/10.17705/1CAIS.04210
19. Vlačić, B., Corbo, L., Costa e Silva, S., Dabić, M.: The evolving role of artificial intelligence in marketing: a review and research agenda. J. Bus. Res. **128**, 187–203 (2021). https://doi.org/10.1016/j.jbusres.2021.01.055
20. Obradović, T., Vlačić, B., Dabić, M.: Open innovation in the manufacturing industry: a review and research agenda. Technovation **102**, 102221 (2021). https://doi.org/10.1016/j.technovation.2021.102221
21. López-Duarte, C., González-Loureiro, M., Vidal-Suárez, M.M., González-Díaz, B.: International strategic alliances and national culture: mapping the field and developing a research agenda. J. World Bus. **51**, 511–524 (2016). https://doi.org/10.1016/j.jwb.2016.05.001
22. Jorg, B., Michael, G.: Visualization of categorical data. Elsevier (1998). https://doi.org/10.1016/B978-0-12-299045-8.X5000-1
23. Tenenhaus, M., Young, F.W.: An analysis and synthesis of multiple correspondence analysis, optimal scaling, dual scaling, homogeneity analysis and other methods for quantifying categorical multivariate data. Psychometrika **50**, 91–119 (1985). https://doi.org/10.1007/BF02294151
24. Greenacre, M.: Correspondence analysis of multivariate categorical data by weighted least-squares. Biometrika **75**, 457–467 (1988). https://doi.org/10.1093/biomet/75.3.457
25. Greenacre, M.J.: Clustering the rows and columns of a contingency table. J. Classif. **5**, 39–51 (1988). https://doi.org/10.1007/BF01901670
26. Kassambara, A.: Practical guide to principal component methods in R (2017)
27. Husson, A.F., Josse, J., Le, S., Mazet, J., Husson, M.F.: Package 'FactoMineR' (2020)
28. Greenacre, M.J.: Correspondence analysis in practice. Chapman & Hall/CRC, Boca Raton, Florid (2017)
29. Le Roux, B., Rouanet, H.: Geometric data analysis from correspondence analysis to structured data analysis. Kluwer Academic Publishers (2004)
30. Ward, J.H.: Hierarchical grouping to optimize an objective function. J. Am. Stat. Assoc. **58**, 236 (1963). https://doi.org/10.2307/2282967
31. Team, R.D.C.: R: a language and environment for statistical computing. http://www.r-project.org (2008)
32. Husson, F., Lê, S.: Jérôme Pagès: exploratory multivariate analysis by example using R. CRC Press (2017). https://doi.org/10.1111/j.1751-5823.2011.00159_19.x
33. Le, S., Worch, T.: Analyzing sensory data with R. Chapman & Hall/CRC (2018)
34. Husson, F., Josse, J., Pagès, J.: Principal component methods—hierarchical clustering—partitional clustering: why would we need to choose for visualizing data. Appl. Math. Dep. (2010)
35. Blasius, J., Greenacre, M.: Visualization and verbalization of data. Chapman and Hall/CRC (2014). https://doi.org/10.1201/b16741
36. Bharadwaj, A., El Sawy, O.A., Pavlou, P.A., Venkatraman, N.: Digital business strategy: toward a next generation of insights. MIS Q. **37**, 471–482 (2013)
37. Demirkan, H., Spohrer, J.C., Welser, J.J.: Digital innovation and strategic transformation. IT Prof. **18**, 14–18 (2016). https://doi.org/10.1109/MITP.2016.115
38. Resca, A., Za, S., Spagnoletti, P.: Digital platforms as sources for organizational and strategic transformation: a case study of the midblue project. J. Theor. Appl. Electron. Commer. Res. **8** (2013). https://doi.org/10.4067/S0718-18762013000200006
39. Li, L., Su, F., Zhang, W., Mao, J.Y.: Digital transformation by SME entrepreneurs: a capability perspective. Inf. Syst. J. **28**, 1129–1157 (2017). https://doi.org/10.1111/isj.12153
40. Kane, G.C., Palmer, D., Phillips, A.N., Kiron, D., Buckley, N.: Achiving digital maturity. MIT Sloan Manag. Rev. **32** (2017)

41. Carillo, K., Scornavacca, E., Za, S.: The role of media dependency in predicting continuance intention to use ubiquitous media systems. Inf. Manag. **54**, 317–335 (2017). https://doi.org/10.1016/j.im.2016.09.002
42. Piccinini, E., Gregory, R.W., Kolbe, L.M.: Changes in the producer—consumer relationship towards digital transformation. In: 12th International Conference on Wirtschaftsinformatik, pp. 1634–1648 (2015)
43. Wiesböck, F., Li, L., Matt, C., Hess, T., Richter, A.: How management in the German insurance industry can handle digital transformation (2017). https://doi.org/10.7892/BORIS.105693
44. Chanias, S., Hess, T.: Understanding digital transformation strategy formation: insights from Europe's automotive industry. In: 20th Pacific Asia Conference on Information Systems (2016). http://aisel.aisnet.org/pacis2016/296
45. Bekkers, R., Wiepking, P.: A literature review of empirical studies of philanthropy: eight mechanisms that drive charitable giving. Nonprofit Volunt. Sect. Q. **40**, 924–973 (2011). https://doi.org/10.1177/0899764010380927
46. Steinberg, R., Powell, W.: The nonprofit sector, a research handbook. Yale University Press, London (2006)
47. Hansmann, H.B.: Reforming nonprofit corporation law. HeinOnline (1981)
48. Bois, C.D., Jegers, M., Schepers, C., Pepermans, R.: Objectives of non-profit organisations: a literature review. 4th Work. Challenges Manag. Third Sect. (2003)
49. Mirabella, R.M., Gemelli, G., Malcolm, M.-J., Berger, G.: Nonprofit and philanthropic studies: International overview of the field in Africa, Canada, Latin America, Asia, the Pacific, and Europe. Nonprofit Volunt. Sect. Q. **36**, 110S-135S (2007). https://doi.org/10.1177/0899764007305052
50. Herman, R.D.: Methodological issues in studying the effectiveness of nongovernmental and nonprofit organizations. Nonprofit Volunt. Sect. Q. **19**, 293–306 (1990). https://doi.org/10.1177/089976409001900309
51. Maier, F., Meyer, M., Steinbereithner, M.: Nonprofit organizations becoming business-like: a systematic review. Nonprofit Volunt. Sect. Q. **45**, 64–86 (2016). https://doi.org/10.1177/0899764014561796
52. Salamon, L.M., Anheier, H.K.: Defining the nonprofit sector a cross-national analysis. Manchester University Press, Manchester (1997)
53. Defourny, J., Pestoff, V.: Towards a European conceptualization of the third sector. In: Advances in public interest accounting, pp. 25–87 (2014). https://doi.org/10.1108/S1041-706020140000017001
54. Taylor, R.: Moving beyond empirical theory. In: Third sector research, pp. 1–9. Springer New York, New York, NY (2010). https://doi.org/10.1007/978-1-4419-5707-8_1
55. Corry, O.: Defining and theorizing the third sector. In: Third sector research, pp. 11–20. Springer New York, New York, NY (2010). https://doi.org/10.1007/978-1-4419-5707-8_2
56. Salamon, L.M., Sokolowski, S.W.: Beyond nonprofits: re-conceptualizing the third sector. Volunt. Int. J. Volunt. Nonprofit Organ. **27**, 1515–1545 (2016). https://doi.org/10.1007/s11266-016-9726-z
57. Knutsen, W.: The non-profit sector is dead, long live the non-profit sector! Volunt. Int. J. Volunt. Nonprofit Organ. **27**, 1562–1584 (2016). https://doi.org/10.1007/s11266-016-9696-1
58. Te'eni, D., Young, D.R.: The changing role of nonprofits in the network economy. Nonprofit Volunt. Sect. Q. **32**, 397–414 (2003). https://doi.org/10.1177/0899764003254900
59. Te'eni, D.: A cognitive-affective model of organizational communication for designing IT. MISQ. **25**, 251 (2001). https://doi.org/10.2307/3250931
60. Joo, E., Kononova, A., Kanthawala, S., Peng, W., Cotten, S.: Smartphone users' persuasion knowledge in the context of consumer mHealth apps: qualitative study. JMIR mHealth uHealth. **9**, e16518 (2021). https://doi.org/10.2196/16518
61. Fledderus, J.: Building trust through public service co-production. Int. J. Public Sect. Manag. **28**, 550–565 (2015). https://doi.org/10.1108/IJPSM-06-2015-0118
62. McNutt, J., Guo, C., Goldkind, L., An, S.: Technology in nonprofit organizations and voluntary action. Volunt. Rev. **3**, 1–63 (2018). https://doi.org/10.1163/24054933-12340020

63. Guo, C., Saxton, G.D.: Tweeting social change. Nonprofit Volunt. Sect. Q. **43**, 57–79 (2014). https://doi.org/10.1177/0899764012471585
64. Nah, S., Saxton, G.D.: Modeling the adoption and use of social media by nonprofit organizations. New Media Soc. **15**, 294–313 (2013). https://doi.org/10.1177/1461444812452411
65. Van Puyvelde, S., Raeymaeckers, P.: The governance of public–nonprofit service networks: four propositions. Nonprofit Volunt. Sect. Q. **49**, 931–950 (2020). https://doi.org/10.1177/0899764020913113
66. Svensson, P.G., Mahoney, T.Q., Hambrick, M.E.: What does innovation mean to nonprofit practitioners? International insights from development and peace-building nonprofits. Nonprofit Volunt. Sect. Q. **49**, 380–398 (2020). https://doi.org/10.1177/0899764019872009
67. Seo, H., Vu, H.T.: Transnational nonprofits' social media use: a survey of communications professionals and an analysis of organizational characteristics. Nonprofit Volunt. Sect. Q. **49**, 849–870 (2020). https://doi.org/10.1177/0899764020908340
68. Johs, H.: Multiple correspondence analysis for the social sciences. Routledge, Abingdon, Oxon; New York, NY: Routledge, 2018 (2018). https://doi.org/10.4324/9781315516257
69. Greenacre, M., Blasius, J.: Multiple correspondence analysis and related methods. Chapman & Hall/CRC, Londin (2007). https://doi.org/10.1007/s11336-006-1579-x
70. Greenacre, M.: Correspondence analysis. In: International encyclopedia of the social & behavioral sciences, pp. 1–5. Elsevier (2015). https://doi.org/10.1016/B978-0-08-097086-8.42005-2
71. Kostov, B., Bécue-Bertaut, M., Husson, F.: Multiple factor analysis for contingency tables in the FactoMineR Package. R J. 5, **29** (2013). https://doi.org/10.32614/RJ-2013-003
72. Le Dien, S., Pagès, J.: Hierarchical multiple factor analysis: application to the comparison of sensory profiles. Food Qual. Prefer. **14**, 397–403 (2003). https://doi.org/10.1016/S0950-3293(03)00027-2
73. Donthu, N., Kumar, S., Pattnaik, D.: Forty-five years of journal of business research: a bibliometric analysis. J. Bus. Res. **109**, 1–14 (2020). https://doi.org/10.1016/j.jbusres.2019.10.039
74. Banet, T.A., Lebart, L.: Local and partial principal component analysis (PCA) and correspondence analysis (CA). In: Compstat 1984, pp. 113–118. Physica-Verlag HD, Heidelberg (1984). https://doi.org/10.1007/978-3-642-51883-6_14
75. Kroonenberg, P.M., Greenacre, M.J.: Correspondence analysis. In: Encyclopedia of statistical sciences. John Wiley & Sons, Inc., Hoboken, NJ, USA (2004). https://doi.org/10.1002/0471667196.ess6018
76. Beaudouin, V.: Statistical analysis of textual data: Benzécri and the French school of data analysis. Glottometrics. **33**, 56–72 (2016)
77. Husson, F., Josse, J.: Multiple correspondence analysis. In: Multiple correspondence analysis for the social sciences, pp. 31–55. Routledge, Abingdon, Oxon; New York, NY: Routledge, 2018 (2018). https://doi.org/10.4324/9781315516257-3
78. Le Roux, B., Rouanet, H.: Multiple correspondence analysis. SAGE Publications, Inc (2009). https://doi.org/10.1177/007542429602400208
79. Wishart, D.: 256. Note: an algorithm for hierarchical classifications. Biometrics. **25**, 165 (1969). https://doi.org/10.2307/2528688
80. Chavent, M., Kuentz-Simonet, V., Saracco, J.: Orthogonal rotation in PCAMIX. Adv. Data Anal. Classif. **6**, 131–146 (2012). https://doi.org/10.1007/s11634-012-0105-3
81. Maupin, P., Apparicio, P., Lepage, R., Solaiman, B.: Multiple correspondence analysis for highly heterogeneous data fusion. An example in urban quality of life assessment. In: Proceedings of the Third International Conference on Information Fusion, vol. 2, p. WED5/26-WED5/33. IEEE (2000). https://doi.org/10.1109/IFIC.2000.859867
82. Nenadic, O., Greenacre, M.: Computation of multiple correspondence analysis, with code in R. SSRN Electron. J., 25–27 (2005). https://doi.org/10.2139/ssrn.847698
83. Husson, F., Josse, J., Saporta, G.: Jan de Leeuw and the French school of data analysis. J. Stat. Softw. **73**, 1–18 (2016). https://doi.org/10.18637/jss.v073.i06

84. Fithian, W., Josse, J.: Multiple correspondence analysis and the multilogit bilinear model. J. Multivar. Anal. **157**, 87–102 (2017). https://doi.org/10.1016/j.jmva.2017.02.009
85. Chateau, F., Lebart, L.: Assessing sample variability in the visualization techniques related to principal component analysis: bootstrap and alternative simulation methods. In: COMPSTAT, pp. 205–210. Physica-Verlag HD, Heidelberg (1996). https://doi.org/10.1007/978-3-642-46992-3_21
86. Greenacre, M.J.: Biplots in correspondence analysis. J. Appl. Stat. **20**, 251–269 (1993). https://doi.org/10.1080/02664769300000021

What is Governance of Blockchains? A Comparison of Theoretical and Empirical Findings on a Taxonomy-Level

Koen Smit, Sam Leewis, Robin de Jong, and John van Meerten

Abstract Blockchain is an emerging technology with the potential to disrupt and enable collaboration in ecosystem structures that are difficult if not impossible to achieve otherwise. An important aspect of collaboration in blockchain ecosystems is governance. Proper governance also ensures sustainable growth of a blockchain solution. The current body of knowledge features a growing number of contributions on this topic. This is promising as it allows for a meta-view of what entails governance, which has been done with some lenses, usually with an empirical one. This study focuses on comparing the empirical approach with the theoretical approach by looking at existing dimensions and characteristics that define blockchain governance, using an SLR. This resulted in identifying 11/18 dimensions and 18/42 underlying characteristics that were not identified in literature, 3 new and 14/18 overlapping dimensions and 26/42 underlying characteristics. The newly identified dimensions include (1) Incentives, (2) Trust, and (3) Smart Contracts. Future research should focus to extend on the blockchain governance taxonomies so that they can be operationalized. This helps better understanding of what entails blockchain governance from a conceptual level but will also aid blockchain professionals to design their blockchain governance in a sustainable way, taking into account all stakeholders.

Keywords Blockchain · Governance · Taxonomy · Comparison

K. Smit · S. Leewis (✉) · R. de Jong · J. van Meerten
HU University of Applied Sciences Utrecht, Utrecht, The Netherlands
e-mail: sam.leewis@hu.nl

K. Smit
e-mail: koen.smit@hu.nl

R. de Jong
e-mail: robin.dejong@hu.nl

J. van Meerten
e-mail: john.vanmeerten@hu.nl

S. Za et al. (eds.), *Sustainable Digital Transformation*, Lecture Notes in Information Systems and Organisation 59, https://doi.org/10.1007/978-3-031-15770-7_18

1 Introduction

Blockchain solutions are based on the reliable, correct, and secure distributed recording of transactions within and between organizations and individuals. Blockchain as a technology claims to offer disruptive opportunities [1]. An increase in popularity of blockchain technology and solutions can be observed in the recent years [2, 3]. One of the reasons for this is the lack of a centralized party responsible for the processing of transactions [4]. Because of this, trust, as an important factor in all kinds of transactions, is moved from the central party towards the technology and 'blockchain' code itself [5]. Because of this shift, the aspect of governance has become increasingly more important, as decentralized governance could be more difficult to achieve [6, 7].

Despite the initial research conducted since 2012 contributing to a solid foundation of the understanding of blockchain technology, researchers have mostly neglected the connection between this technology and organizational implementation, where proper governance plays an important role [8]. In the context of blockchain, governance is one of the fundamental aspects of blockchain design. Blockchain governance is defined as "*the means of achieving the direction, control, and coordination of stakeholders within the context of a given blockchain project to which they jointly contribute*" [9]. A governance system that encourages the ability to adapt and evolve to change is essential in a blockchain which aims to be successful long-term [10, 11]. Thus, in order to ensure the long-term sustainability of these organizations, it is necessary to incorporate, on top of the technical framework, a specific governance structure that enables people to discuss and coordinate as to how the technology should evolve [12]. Different types and perspectives of governance exist, which include IT governance and open-source software governance (OSS). Both IT and OSS governance are often referred to in Blockchain literature as both Bitcoin and Ethereum are open source projects [13]. There seems to be a logical overlap regarding the phenomenon of 'governance' between available body of knowledge on IT and OSS governance and blockchain governance, which will be further detailed in the next section. However, in the context of this research, the following definition of governance in general is adhered to: "*all processes of governing, undertaken by whether governments, markets, or networks, whether over families, tribes, formal or informal organizations, or territories, and whether through laws, norms, power, or language.*" [14].

In case everyone involved in a blockchain project agreed on what should be done and how, governance of blockchain solutions would not be a problem. Nonetheless, as in most human endeavors, the interests of various stakeholders are not perfectly aligned, which could create conflicts between these parties. These conflicts must be resolved and prevented to ensure optimal usage of the blockchain technology and solutions, as these are usually highly dependent on a decentralized approach featuring multiple types of stakeholders working together [15]. Blockchain solutions featuring a decentralized community where competitors participate on the same blockchain (e.g. Tradefinance by banks such as Barclays, Santander and BPN Paribas [16] are only possible because trust is shifted from a central party towards the technology itself as mentioned earlier.

The importance of governance is steadily recognized by the blockchain scientific community and as such, an increasing number of contributions with a focus on the governance of blockchain are added to the body of knowledge. While this is a good sign for the development of the maturity of the blockchain discipline and body of knowledge, to the knowledge of the authors, little work seems to be conducted to provide a clear overview on what constitutes the phenomena of blockchain with the goal to taxonomize it to support organizations with determining the quality of their governance of a blockchain solution. There are, however, some relevant contributions that should be mentioned and can be very valuable in pursuit of further operationalizing the governance phenomena for blockchain solutions. For example, the work of Werner et al., focuses on a governance taxonomy based on a document study including whitepapers of blockchain solutions. Another contribution comes from [9] and is based on a graduation project with a focus on the construction of a framework for the analysis and comparison of blockchain solutions regarding their governance situation. Based on the research gap identified, we aim to answer the following research question in this paper: '*What constitutes the phenomena of governance for blockchain solutions from a theoretical view compared to existing empirical governance taxonomies?*' To answer the research question, a purposeful and viable taxonomy, according to Nickerson et al., [17] is developed. The taxonomy aims to structure the research field of governance dimensions and mechanisms in the context of blockchain solutions. By doing so, it enhances transparency in this comparably young field, which lacks theoretical insights [18, 19]. The paper aims to compile all relevant dimensions, mechanisms, and characteristics of governance of blockchain.

The remainder of this paper is structured as follows. In the second section, this paper delves deeper into the background and related literature on what encompasses the phenomenon of governance in the context of blockchain technology as well as how a taxonomy could enrich the understanding of this aspect. In the third section, the type of research and associated research methods utilized in this study are discussed. In the fourth section, the data collection for this study is explained in detail. In the fifth section, the method of data analysis is described. In the sixth section, the results of this study are presented, comprising of a proposed taxonomy for the governance of blockchain technology, based on a theoretical as well as a practical foundation. In the seventh section, this study is discussed from a critical point of view, by providing limitations that could have implications for the generalizability and validity of the proposed taxonomy. In the eighth section, the conclusions are elaborated upon, accompanied with flanking comments on the application of the proposed taxonomy. In the ninth section, explicit directions for future research for further development, validation and generalization of the taxonomy are presented.

2 Background and Related Work

The primary purpose of a blockchain is to distribute ledgers to record transactions. As described in the previous section, on a technical level, blockchain transactions are often studied and much is known about its workings. However, this is not the case with regards to the governance of said blockchain solutions. A way to add to the current body of knowledge of blockchain governance is to perform a meta-level analysis regarding existing governance taxonomies.

2.1 Existing Governance Models

Previous studies show that there is a variation in utilized descriptors for blockchain governance aspects and perspectives. In the study conducted by van der Pelt et al., [9] a taxonomy has been developed that addresses dimensions and layers of blockchain governance. Furthermore, with regards to a study conducted to evaluate the taxonomy for governance mechanisms of blockchain-based platforms [20], we see that a taxonomy has been created based on dimensions and characteristics. This study indicates to have used the methods from the study published by Hein et al., [21]. However, this study notes that a taxonomy consists of dimensions and mechanisms, and also places them on a different level compared to the work of Werner et al., [20]. To create an overview of the diversity of blockchain governance models and utilized descriptors, the theory of developing taxonomies from Nickerson et al., [17] is used. This approach is grounded on a theoretical and empirical level and focuses specifically on the information systems domain, which makes it suitable to apply in this study. The approach of Nickerson et al., [17] indicates that when developing a taxonomy, dimensions (overarching key themes), as well as its characteristics (objects within a dimension with similar properties) need to be identified. For example, according to this definition, a dimension within the context of blockchain governance would be 'Corporate Structure' and a characteristic of this dimension would be either a 'Flat Structure' or 'Hierarchical Structure'. By using this alignment, the existing taxonomies can be evaluated against each other as shown in Table 1.

As can be observed from Table 1, not all models meet the taxonomy development criteria of Nickerson et al., [17]. One could notice that there is a great variety of wording when looking at the aspects of a governance taxonomy or model. This is also reflected in the previously mentioned differences between the contributions of Werner et al., [20] and Hein et al., [21]. When comparing the contributions in Table 1, it appears that there is also no agreement within the body of knowledge on blockchain governance with regards to what entails governance, in terms of its dimensions and characteristics. A substantial number of contributions are based on existent models, for example, IT governance [29] and open-source software governance (OSS governance) [9]. Based on these observations, one could argue that the maturity of the body of knowledge of blockchain governance is low.

Table 1 Overview of various blockchain governance models

Author(s)	Paper title	Dimensions	Characteristics
BRON [22]	Design Choices for Data Governance in Platform Ecosystems—A Contingency Model	Yes	No
BRON [23]	Blockchain Governance: An Overview and Prediction of Optimal Strategies using Nash Equilibrium	No	Yes
BRON [15]	Governance in the Blockchain Economy: A Framework and Research Agenda	Yes	Yes[a]
BRON [24]	The environment needs crypto governance	Yes[a]	No
BRON [25]	A Cross-Sectional Overview of Cryptoasset Governance and Implications for Investors	Yes	No
BRON [26]	Blockchain business networks Understanding the value proposal within centralized and decentralized governance structures	Yes[a]	No
BRON [27]	Governance challenges of blockchain and decentralized autonomous organizations	No	No
BRON [21]	Multiple-Case Analysis on Governance Mechanisms of Multi-Sided Platforms	Yes[a]	No
BRON [9]	Defining Blockchain Governance: A Framework for Analysis and Comparison	Yes	No
BRON [28]	Crowd work platform governance toward organizational value creation	Yes[a]	No
BRON [20]	Towards a taxonomy for governance mechanisms of blockchain-based platforms	Yes	Yes

[a] An indication that other descriptors have been used but it is the researchers' interpretation that the wording means the same

However, as stated earlier in this section, we aim to add to the maturity of existing taxonomies on blockchain governance by adding the viewpoint of the body of knowledge in a systematic way as most existing blockchain taxonomies are based on empirical data, secondary data or a combination. Based on this, we selected one core taxonomy to build further upon, being the work of Werner et al., [20], which is referred to as the Taxonomy of Platform Governance for Blockchain-based Platforms (hereafter: PGBP taxonomy). This choice is based on two criteria; (1) being very recent and (2) being based on empirical data.

3 Research Method

This research aims to create a taxonomy, which could support organizations with determining the quality of the designed or implemented governance of a blockchain solution. In order to achieve this, a blockchain governance taxonomy will be created.

This blockchain governance taxonomy will further identify the essence of what governance in the blockchain actually entails. The taxonomy is developed by identifying a set of dimensions, each dimension consisting of a set of characteristics, which further describe the dimensions of governance in a blockchain solution. A useful and valuable taxonomy is characterized by a set of five objective and subjective features [17, 30]: *concise, robust, comprehensive, extensible, and explanatory*. These features are taken into account in this study.

In this study, we follow the definition of a taxonomy of Nickerson et al., [17]: A taxonomy T is a set of n dimensions D_i, $(i = 1, \ldots, n)$ each consisting of K_i $(K_i \geq 2)$ mutually exclusive and collectively exhaustive characteristics $C_{ij}(j = 1, \ldots, K_i)$ such that each object under consideration has one and only one C_{ij} for each D_i. Stated in full:

$$T = \{D_i, i = 1, \ldots, n | D_i = \left\{C_{ij}, j = 1, \ldots, K_i; K_i \geq 2\right\}\} \tag{1}$$

To adhere to the features of a valuable taxonomy, we build upon the PGBP taxonomy [20]. Because of the predominant empirical focus of the selected taxonomy and to further adhere to the features of a valuable taxonomy, a Systematic Literature Review (SLR) [31] is conducted to review the body of knowledge of blockchain governance in order to extend the existing taxonomy with existing literature. By using this approach, we aim to strengthen the available knowledge on blockchain governance. Using a similar research approach, as used to build the PGBP and similar taxonomies, increases the probability that saturation occurs quickly and important findings are omitted unintentionally. Additionally, meta-studies solely using information collected online (e.g., from project websites or whitepapers) regarding blockchain projects are limited in a sense that these are often lacking important in-depth information about governance strategies or mechanisms applied.

The synthesis of the SLR will revolve around the coded contributions identified as relevant in the context of the research question. These will add to the existing taxonomies. In this phase, several interesting situations could arise: a new dimension or characterization is identified, which is not present in the currently available taxonomies. Additionally, dimensions or characteristics could be present in current taxonomies that are not identified by the SLR. The way each situation is analyzed and processed into the resulting taxonomy is described in the following section. The SLR approach allows this study to produce a clear and comprehensive overview of available evidence in the current body of knowledge regarding blockchain governance in relation to the PGBP taxonomy that we selected. This overview can be used to target knowledge gaps with regards to governance of blockchain solutions and helps in improving future work in the topic area.

4 Data Collection and Analysis

The data for this study is collected over a period of fourteen months, between July 2019 to September 2020, through a SLR. This is followed by the coding of the results from the SLR.

4.1 Systematic Literature Review (SLR)

The SLR started in July 2019 and was completed in September 2020, which includes the coding process. In total, four sets of search queries were used in the SLR, being: (1) Blockchain AND Governance, (2) Blockchain AND "Decision Rights", (3) Blockchain AND Governance AND "Decision Making", and (4) Blockchain AND Governance AND "Decision Rights". In addition to the concept of Blockchain Governance in general, we added decision rights and decision making to the search queries as both encompass an important aspect of Blockchain Governance [32–35]. The SLR resulted in the inclusion of 66 scientific contributions in total, see the SLR results per SLR activity in Fig. 1. The process of paper reviews for suitability was conducted by two researchers and validated by two other researchers, improving the validity and reliability of the search and identification process [36, 37]. When the primary researchers responsible for the identification of papers did not agree to include or omit a paper for the corresponding stage in the SLR, the paper was also considered by the two additional researchers.

4.2 Coding and Analysis

After the identification process was completed all 66 papers were coded using thematic coding, as shown in Table 2 This was conducted by two researchers and verified by two other researchers until all papers were coded and the quality of the coding was saturated. The coding sessions took place over a period of six weeks in four different rounds. The thematic coding during those sessions was based on the dimensions and characteristics presented by in the taxonomy of Werner et al., [20]. During these rounds, the researchers coded statements from the papers in relation to the dimensions and characteristics, however, the analysis also focused on whether

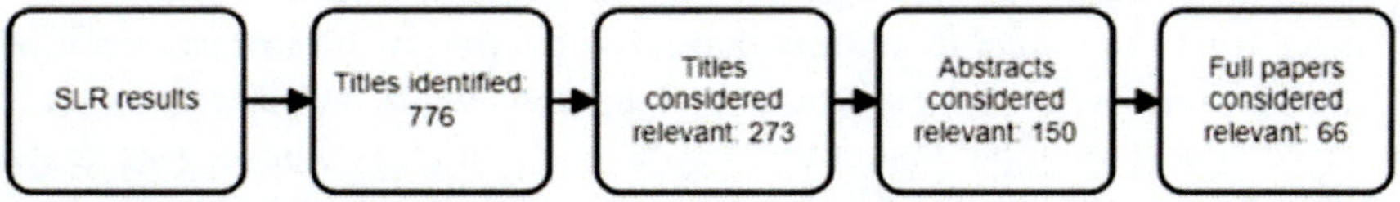

Fig. 1 SLR results scheme

Table 2 Example coding notation

Dimension	Characteristic	Code
Mining	Mining	"Each node collects the new transactions into a block, then works on finding a difficult "proof-of-work" for its block, which is called the "mining" process." [38]
	Pre-mining	"A tactic by developers launching Proof of Work cryptocurrencies to mine some quantity of the cryptocurrency for private benefit prior to public release." [25]
	Non-minable	*Not identified in the analyzed body of knowledge*
Decision rights	Company-based	"Hierarchy construction: Structure the decision hierarchy with the goal of the decision on the top, then the set of the criteria in the intermediate levels, and the set of Alternatives in the lowest level." [39]
	Community-based	"In decentralized digital platforms, decision rights are dispersed, and platform layers are loosely coupled, what we termed as agnostic platform." [40]

dimensions and characteristics were mentioned that seemed to be outside of the scope of the taxonomy of Werner et al., [20]. Such occurrences were also discussed with all four researchers and consensus was sought whether the snippet was indeed unique, representing a dimension or characteristic that is not mentioned in the taxonomy of Werner et al., [20], or that it should be coded to existing dimensions or characteristics.

5 Results

In this section, the dimensions and characteristics identified from the coding process are matched against the related existing dimensions identified by Werner et al., [20]. Furthermore, dimensions or characteristics are added if no dimensions or characteristics exist concerning the coded topic. Several coding's are shown as a representation of the dimension under which they are coded. As presented in Fig. 2, the existing taxonomy is expanded, and existing dimensions are validated by the results from the SLR.

The schematic overview of the taxonomy in relation to the results of our analysis presented in Fig. 2 features three key areas with regards to the results of the analysis. Firstly, the dimensions and characteristics from the PGBP taxonomy that are not represented in our results are indicated in red. Secondly, the dimensions and characteristics from the PGBP taxonomy that show overlap with our results are indicated in green. Thirdly, the dimensions and characteristics from our results that are not represented in the PGBP taxonomy are indicated in blue. Due to space constraints, the first two categories are not discussed in detail, but their coding's are available upon request.

Dimension	Sub-dimension	Characteristics					
Governance Structure	Funding	Private	2	Public	8		
	Decision rights	Company-based	7	Community-based	8		
	Corporate structure	Flat structure	1	Hierarchical	6		
	Centralization	Centralized	6	Semi centralized	1	Decentralized	16
Resources	Boundary Resources	Software	0	Data	0		
	Code transparency	Public	4	Private	0		
Accessibility & control	Openness	Public	6	Private	0		
	Sanctions	Existent	2	Non-existent	0		
	Consensus	Distributed	26	Delegated	7	Adapted	0
	Mining	Minable	7	Pre-mining	1	Non-minable	0
	Incentives	On-chain	7				
Trust & perceived risk	Verification	Permissionless	3	Permissioned	2		
	Bug-Bounty-Program	Existent	0	Non-existent	0		
	Trust	On-chain	12	Off-chain	**4**		
Dependencies	Codebase	New	1	Adapted	1	Altered	1
	Type of token	Utility	10	Asset	11		
	Smart contracts	On-chain	8				
Pricing	Pricing	Fix	0	Variable	1	Free	0
	Price stability	Existent	0	Non-existent	0		
External relationships	External relationships	Internal	0	External	0		
	Services	On-chain	8	Off-chain	3		

Fig. 2 Overview of the study's findings

5.1 Results not Represented by the PGBP Taxonomy

In total, three sub-dimensions with four underlying characteristics were identified. The PGBP taxonomy lacked the dimensions and characteristics explicitly focused on the topics of incentives, trust, and smart contracts, see Fig. 2. With regards to these topics, 31 coding's were identified in total.

Accessibility and Control—Incentives

Accessibility and control mechanisms in a general sense are an important aspect of blockchain governance, which can be derived from the number of dimensions and characteristics in Fig. 2. In total, seven coding's addressed incentives, which were classified as a sub-dimension of the accessibility and control dimension. However, only on-chain incentives were identified. For example, one coding defined the goal of incentives as: "*A system with aligned incentives allows agents to freely choose their own behaviors, but uses incentives to make them inclined to choose actions that coincide with goals of the system's design*" [15].

Trust and Perceived Risk—Trust

Blockchain solutions are organized and maintained by multiple stakeholders in an ecosystem, which requires trust in each other and the technology itself. This results in that trust is a topic that was identified most of all three topics described in this section. In terms of characteristics, both on-chain (12) and off-chain (4) codings were identified, which differs from the other two topics. For example, concerning on-chain trust, the following was coded: "*Trust is the keyword. Participants are no longer required to trust a single organization for the contents of the shared ledger, but they trust a blockchain business ecosystem instead, where no single party has the power to make unauthorized changes to recorded transactions*" [41]. The results also show that, although a lot of trust is moved towards the technology, off-chain trust is still an important aspect to take into account when collaborating in a blockchain ecosystem. For example, the following was stated about collaboration: "*Inter-organizational collaboration requires a consensus among collaborating parties, which proved to be a challenging task, inhibited by inter alia lack of trust amongst collaborators, own interest, or inter-firm rivalry*" [42], while the notion of going back from on-chain to off-chain trust for certain ecosystem activities is also mentioned, for example: "*Finally, economic incentives dictate that it is in everyone's best interest to maintain trust in the system. Reducing trust. Now that we've had a breaking change, those previously referencing the protocol must now go outside the blockchain and somehow figure out what the "right" new version is to use*" [43].

Dependencies—Smart Contracts

Many relevant contributions discussed the aspect of smart-contracts and some also did so in the context of blockchain governance. In total, eight coding's addressed smart contracts, which were classified as a sub-dimension of the dependencies dimension. The coding's are limited to the on-chain characteristic, which seems logical given the fact that smart contracts are designed to function on-chain only to add to the functional power of, and increase trust in, the blockchain ecosystem. An example how smart contracts are defined as an important dimension is: "*These smart contracts enabled the 2016 DAO to implement fairly sophisticated governance and exit rules autonomously on the blockchain*" [44].

6 Conclusion

To formulate this study, we revisit the research question stated earlier: '*What constitutes the phenomena of governance for blockchain solutions from a theoretical view compared to existing empirical governance taxonomies?*' To provide an answer to this question, four researchers identified 66 papers from the body of knowledge using an SLR, which were then thematically analyzed using the existing PGBP taxonomy from Werner et al., [20]. Based on this, three sub-dimensions were added to the PGBP taxonomy. Although differences were identified in this study between the conceptual and empirical knowledge on dimensions and characteristics making up blockchain governance, we conclude that the empirical approach of the PGBP taxonomy is solid, and relatively few additions are presented. Important to note is the difference of focus identified in comparing both perspectives, where scientific literature on a conceptual level often remains abstract, empirical studies are more detailed.

7 Discussion

The current state of the taxonomy presented in this paper is subject to several limitations. Taking into account the methodological process of constructing a taxonomy [17], more work has to be done with regards to satisfying the ending conditions (1) conciseness, (2) robustness, (3) comprehensiveness, (4) extendibility, and (5) explanatory. With regards to conciseness, the taxonomy currently includes 7 dimensions with 21 characteristics. For reference, Miller's [45] work on cognitive load is adhered too, stating that the number of dimensions should fall between five and nine. This makes it that the end condition of conciseness is not yet satisfied. Furthermore, while we argue that the end condition robustness is adequately satisfied from a theoretical level because of the saturation during data analysis, empirical robustness is not achieved in this study. From a theoretical level, the current taxonomy enables a sufficient means to differentiate dimensions and objects of interest. With regards to the comprehensiveness end condition, we argue that all dimensions are included from a conceptual level, but we hypothesize that both the comprehensiveness and robustness could be affected when the current taxonomy is covered during an empirical iteration of validation. This is acceptable as this was not the goal of this study. As far as the authors are aware, every dimension is conceptually unique and not repeated, while every characteristic of a dimension is unique as well. Next, the extendibility end condition is satisfied as we focused on a conceptual development approach in this first iteration of the taxonomy and we allowed for changes to the taxonomy when an empirical iteration complements the dimensions, but more importantly [46], the objects that we refer to as governance mechanisms in the taxonomy. We explicitly did not present the current taxonomy as set in stone on a conceptual and theoretical level, but especially not on an empirical level as the latter is focus of a follow-up study. Lastly, the explanatory end condition seems to be satisfied as this paper provides explanations of the nature of the dimensions and characteristics without describing every possible detail about the objects under study. Again, we argue that, on a conceptual level, this end condition is satisfied. However, the explanatory end condition could firmly benefit from empirical validation as people utilizing the taxonomy can value the usefulness of explanations for dimensions and characteristics best. Of course, we must also note that these end conditions could somewhat be interpreted as subjective, because whether someone using the taxonomy values its contents as concise and sufficiently explained largely depends on their background and experience with the subject. Though we still argue that the end conditions provide sufficient fundament for the construction of a taxonomy for the governance of blockchain solutions.

Apart from the methodological limitations regarding the construction of the taxonomy as described earlier, this study is subject to several other limitations. One could argue that the current taxonomy is affected by the population of coders involved in the data analysis. To mitigate this, the four coders independently coded the dimensions and characteristics of the taxonomy. Based on this coding process, 4 iterations were conducted in which consensus was sought when individual coding deviated. Furthermore, the current taxonomy is constructed by taking into account 66 contributions concerning governance of blockchain. While we believe that this collection of contributions is selected in a controlled and reliable manner, it could be the case that not all dimensions and characteristics are identified because of this selection. This is mainly attributable to the observed usage of synonyms in the research domain of blockchain and in particular that of governance of blockchain solutions [9, 47]. Another phenomenon influencing the current taxonomy is the amount of data originating from public versus private blockchain projects. While it is possible to engage with consortia that employ private blockchains, they seem to be less transparent about their (internal) governance structure taking into account the details made available via the web (i.e., via email inquiry or whitepapers). This is further strengthened that a larger number of contributions identified focused on governance of blockchains based on public blockchain solutions.

Lastly, while we argue that the use of a SLR is appropriate to theoretically review the body of knowledge on governance of blockchain solutions, the approach is also limited in certain ways. The first one being that the approach is time-consuming while also representing a snapshot of the body of knowledge at a given time(frame). Another limitation is the challenge to conclude the findings as well as the redundancy of information gathered causing saturation. The latter limitations are greatly mitigated as this study utilized an existing taxonomy to evaluate against, thus clearly presenting the differences between the different approaches used to construct a proper taxonomy in this field.

8 Future Research

The limitations detailed provide the objectives for future research directions. Firstly, future research could focus on further increasing the conciseness of the taxonomy, because the current taxonomy includes many dimensions and characteristics, which in turn decrease its acceptance due to a high cognitive load. On the other hand, one could argue that a higher conciseness potentially leads to lower robustness, but especially lower comprehensiveness or completeness as these ending conditions represent typical trade-offs. We argue that, based on future research, an optimum between these ending conditions with the goal to further strengthen its validity as well as its potential acceptance by blockchain practitioners.

Further research could also focus on the inclusion of governance subject matter experts and case studies to identify possible problems with regards to the robustness ending condition of the taxonomy. This refers to the ability to differentiate between dimensions and characteristics, which can be further valued by subject-matter experts. Case studies could be utilized to identify whether its governance mechanisms fit the current taxonomy. The same holds for the comprehensiveness ending condition, which focuses on the completeness of the taxonomy. Subject-matter experts could help identify missing dimensions and characteristics as well as to help validate how to operationalize the characteristics, for example, the types of incentives to stimulate community contributions to the codebase. Moreover, case study research can be applied with regards to completeness to see whether unique dimensions or characteristics are identified that are not included in the current taxonomy. This approach is specifically interesting to pursue with regards to the characteristics and governance mechanisms per characteristic as these are often defined by practitioners and are harder to identify from a conceptual level, see also [48].

An additional direction for future research would be to focus on validation by other researchers with the goal to further expand or reduce the current taxonomy so that it improves on the ending condition expendability. Furthermore, validation by other researchers could also improve on the ending condition explanatory, where more empirical approaches should be applied. It is important to utilize future research to establish with potential users of the taxonomy, being blockchain consortium stakeholders such as developers, legal experts, data, and project managers, to which extend all dimensions and characteristics are interpreted correctly. Furthermore, it is important that these stakeholders understand the location hierarchy of the dimensions, characteristics, and possible governance mechanisms. Lastly, with regards to pursuing the inclusion of empirical approaches in future research, one interesting direction would be to identify the perceived usefulness by potential users. This could be iteratively achieved by applying research methods and techniques such as semi-structured interviews, focus groups, delphi (study) rounds, and experiments (see for example [49] with research- and practice-oriented blockchain experts.

Besides the methodological face validity of the taxonomy presented in this paper, we also want to point out at some future research directions with regards to the internal validity. The current taxonomy is based on a rigorous coding process involving multiple coders and iterations to reach consensus about the dimensions, characteristics, and possible mechanisms. However, the internal validity could suffer from a smaller group of researchers defining an artefact such as the taxonomy presented in this paper. Future research should therefore aim to mitigate translation validity issues as much as possible. This could be mitigated also by including more research- and practice-oriented blockchain practitioners, which is in line with the mentioned directions earlier in this section. A last direction for future research is to ensure that the next iteration(s) of the taxonomy is based on dimensions, characteristics, and possible mechanisms from both private and public blockchain solutions. While the research teams believe that both types are included in the analyzed contributions that led to the current taxonomy, more certainty is required. This could further increase the usefulness of the proposed taxonomy, where blockchain practitioners are enabled to, based on the contingency factor public versus private blockchain solution, overview only the relevant dimensions, characteristics, and possible mechanisms. For example, permission levels as part of private blockchain solutions (permissioned), where this is not relevant for public blockchain solutions (permissionless).

References

1. Lemieux, V.L.: Trusting records: is Blockchain technology the answer? Rec. Manag. J. **26**, 110–139 (2016). https://doi.org/10.1108/RMJ-12-2015-0042
2. Gaggioli, A.: Blockchain technology: living in a decentralized everything. Cyberpsychology, Behav. Soc. Netw. **21**, 65–66 (2018). https://doi.org/10.1089/cyber.2017.29097.csi
3. Nofer, M., Gomber, P., Hinz, O., Schiereck, D.: Blockchain. Bus. Inf. Syst. Eng. **59**, 183–187 (2017). https://doi.org/10.1007/s12599-017-0467-3
4. Tama, B.A., Kweka, B.J., Park, Y., Rhee, K.-H.: A critical review of blockchain and its current applications. In: 2017 International Conference on Electrical Engineering and Computer Science (ICECOS), pp. 109–113. IEEE (2017). https://doi.org/10.1109/ICECOS.2017.8167115
5. United Nations. Department of Economic and Social Affairs: World economic and social survey 2018: reflecting on seventy years of development policy analysis. United Nations Publications (2018)
6. Bannink, D., Ossewaarde, R.: Decentralization: new modes of governance and administrative responsibility. Adm. Soc. **44**, 595–624 (2012). https://doi.org/10.1177/0095399711419096
7. Atzori, M.: Blockchain technology and decentralized governance: is the state still necessary? SSRN Electron. J. (2016). https://doi.org/10.2139/ssrn.2709713
8. Tasca, P., Tessone, C.J.: A taxonomy of Blockchain technologies: principles of identification and classification. Ledger. **4** (2018). https://doi.org/10.5195/ledger.2019.140
9. van Pelt, R., Jansen, S., Baars, D., Overbeek, S.: Defining Blockchain governance: a framework for analysis and comparison. Inf. Syst. Manag. **38**, 21–41 (2021). https://doi.org/10.1080/10580530.2020.1720046
10. ListedReserve: Blockchain Governance—ListedReserve—Medium

11. Curran, B.: What is Blockchain governance? Complete beginner's guide
12. De Filippi, P., Loveluck, B.: The invisible politics of Bitcoin: governance crisis of a decentralised infrastructure. Internet Policy Rev. **5** (2016). https://doi.org/10.14763/2016.3.427
13. Beck, R., Becker, C., Lindman, J., Rossi, M.: Report from Dagstuhl seminar 17132—opportunities and risks of Blockchain technologies. DAGSTUHL REPORTS. **7** (2017). https://doi.org/10.4230/DagRep.7.3.99
14. Bevir, M.: Governance: a very short introduction. Oxford University Press (2012)
15. Beck, R., Müller-Bloch, C., King, J.L.: Governance in the Blockchain economy: a framework and research agenda. J. Assoc. Inf. Syst., 1020–1034 (2018). https://doi.org/10.17705/1jais.00518
16. Zīle, K., Strazdiņa, R.: Blockchain use cases and their feasibility. Appl. Comput. Syst. **23**, 12–20 (2018). https://doi.org/10.2478/acss-2018-0002
17. Nickerson, R.C., Varshney, U., Muntermann, J.: A method for taxonomy development and its application in information systems. Eur. J. Inf. Syst. **22**, 336–359 (2013). https://doi.org/10.1057/ejis.2012.26
18. Filippi, P.D., Wright, P.A.: Blockchain and the law: the rule of code. Harvard University Press, Cambridge, MA, USA (2018)
19. Kang, J., Xiong, Z., Niyato, D., Ye, D., Kim, D.I., Zhao, J.: Toward secure Blockchain-enabled internet of vehicles: optimizing consensus management using reputation and contract theory. IEEE Trans. Veh. Technol. **68**, 2906–2920 (2019). https://doi.org/10.1109/TVT.2019.2894944
20. Werner, J., Frost, S., Zarnekow, R.: Towards a taxonomy for governance mechanisms of Blockchain-based platforms. Proc. Eur. Conf. Inf. Syst. **1** (2020)
21. Hein, A., Schreieck, M., Wiesche, M., Krcmar, H.: Multiple-case analysis on governance mechanism of multi-sided platforms. Multikonferenz Wirtschaftsinformatik, MKWI **2016**(3), 1613–1624 (2016)
22. Zhu, L.: Design choices for data governance in platform ecosystems: a contingency model, pp. 1–10
23. Khan, N., Ahmad, T., Patel, A., State, R.: Blockchain governance: an overview and prediction of optimal strategies using Nash equilibrium, pp. 1–18
24. Chapron, G.: The environment needs cryptogovernance. http://www.nature.com/news/the-environment-needs-cryptogovernance-1.22023 (2017). https://doi.org/10.1038/545403a
25. Carter, N.: A cross-sectional overview of Cryptoasset governance and implications for investors. Coinmetrics.Io (2016)
26. Carlson, H., Lejon, I.: Blockchain business networks—understanding the value proposal within centralized and decentralized governance structures (2019)
27. Rikken, O., Janssen, M., Kwee, Z.: Governance challenges of blockchain and decentralized autonomous organizations. Inf. Polity. **24**, 397–417 (2019). https://doi.org/10.3233/ip-190154
28. Shafiei Gol, E., Stein, M.K., Avital, M.: Crowdwork platform governance toward organizational value creation. J. Strateg. Inf. Syst. **28**, 175–195 (2019). https://doi.org/10.1016/j.jsis.2019.01.001
29. Vuuren, N.V.: A structured approach to the implementation of information technology (IT) governance principles to address application software project failure at a strategic and … (2019)
30. Bailey, K.D.: Typologies and taxonomies: an introduction to classification techniques. Sage Publications (1994)
31. Kitchenham, B., Pearl Brereton, O., Budgen, D., Turner, M., Bailey, J., Linkman, S.: Systematic literature reviews in software engineering—a systematic literature review. Inf. Softw. Technol. **51**, 7–15 (2009). https://doi.org/10.1016/j.infsof.2008.09.009
32. Constantinides, P., Henfridsson, O., Parker, G.G.: Introduction—platforms and infrastructures in the digital age. Inf. Syst. Res. **29**, 381–400 (2018). https://doi.org/10.1287/isre.2018.0794
33. Tiwana, A., Konsynski, B., Bush, A.A.: Research commentary—platform evolution: coevolution of platform architecture, governance, and environmental dynamics. Inf. Syst. Res. **21**, 675–687 (2010). https://doi.org/10.1287/isre.1100.0323

34. Tiwana, A.: Platform ecosystems: aligning architecture, governance, and strategy. Newnes (2013)
35. Wareham, J., Fox, P.B., Cano Giner, J.L.: Technology ecosystem governance. Organ. Sci. **25**, 1195–1215 (2014). https://doi.org/10.1287/orsc.2014.0895
36. Tinsley, H.E.A., Weiss, D.J.: Interrater reliability and agreement. In: Handbook of applied multivariate statistics and mathematical modeling, pp. 95–124. Elsevier (2000). https://doi.org/10.1016/b978-012691360-6/50005-7
37. Reis, H.T., Judd, C.M.: Handbook of research methods in social and personality psychology (2013). https://doi.org/10.1017/cbo9780511996481
38. Zou, J.: Accountability in cloud services, pp. 1–230 (2016)
39. Bouayad, H., Benabbou, L., Berrado, A.: An analytic hierarchy process based approach for information technology governance framework selection. ACM Int. Conf. Proceeding Ser. 2018 (2018). https://doi.org/10.1145/3289402.3289515
40. Kazan, E., Tan, C.-W., Lim, E.T.K.: Towards a framework of digital platform disruption: a comparative study of centralized & decentralized digital payment providers full research. Tan & Lim (2008)
41. Van Deventer, O., Berkers, F., Vos, M., Zandee, A., Vreuls, T., van Piggelen, L., Blom, A., Heeringa, B., Akdim, S., van Helvoort, P., van de Weem, L., van de Ruit, D.: Techruption consortium Blockchain—what it takes to run a blockchain together (2018). https://doi.org/10.18420/blockchain2018_06
42. Ziolkowski, R., Parangi, G., Miscione, G., Schwabe, G.: Examining gentle rivalry: decision-making in Blockchain systems. Presented at the (2019). https://doi.org/10.24251/HICSS.2019.550
43. Ehrsam, F.: Blockchain governance: programming our future (2021). https://www.fehrsam.xyz/blog/blockchain-governance-programming-our-future. Last Accessed 2021/05/26
44. Rodrigues, U.R.: Law and the blockchain. Iowa Law Rev. **104**, 679–729 (2019)
45. Miller, G.A.: The magical number seven, plus or minus two: some limits on our capacity for processing information. Psychol. Rev. **63**, 81–97 (1956). https://doi.org/10.1037/h0043158
46. Bowker, G.C., Star, S.L.: Classification and its consequences (1999)
47. Smit, K., Saïd, S., el Mansouri, J., van Meerten, J., Leewis, S.: Decision rights and governance within the Blockchain domain: a literature analysis. Proc. 24th Pacific Asia Conf. Inf. Syst. Inf. Syst. Futur. PACIS 2020 (2020)
48. Doty, D.H., Glick, W.H., Huber, G.P.: Fit, equifinality, and organizational effectiveness: a test of two configurational theories. Acad. Manag. J. **36**, 1196–1250 (1993). https://doi.org/10.5465/256810
49. Marshall, C., Rossman, G.B.: Designing qualitative research (2014)